Australia

DREAM TRIP

DARROCH DONALD
KATRINA O'BRIEN
ANDREW SWAFFER

C000175800

CONTENTS

THIS IS
AUSTRALIA

There are many island nations, but only one 'continent nation' – Australia – and this wide brown land is full of extremes and surprises. Its major cities frequently rank in the list of the world's most liveable and are comfortably some of the most frequented urban holiday destinations on the planet. But in truth, although home to over 80% of the nation's population, as well as sparkling ocean and harbour vistas and iconic architecture, they are not where you'll find Australia. For that you need to hit the road, discover the bush, head into the outback and – as the country's long-term custodians would say – go walkabout.

And once you're out there you'll be met by a sometimes bewildering array of opportunities. Unless you've years to spend you're not going to see it all, so it pays to plan your time carefully. For the same reason it also pays to plan your route just as carefully. And that's where we're hoping we can help. We, the authors of this book, have travelled these routes not just once but several

Wilsons Promontory, VIC

times, and over many years. We hope that in this volume we have managed to distil some of the awe, excitement and reverence that we've felt, so that we can guide you to some of those wondrous places and soul-enriching moments that we have been so privileged to experience.

Whether it's laying by some dying embers, wrapped up in a swag mesmerized by the desert stars, or snorkelling alongside a majestic, bus-sized whale shark, or trying to encompass the hundreds of generations that yawn between you and the artist who daubed that ancestral being or, stubby in hand, simply sitting on the verandah of an outback station taking in a golden evening sunset, we guarantee there'll be a true blue moment out there that will live with you forever.

So, whether you buy this guide or not, we do encourage you to find the time, blag the funds and take the Aussie roads less travelled. Who knows where they might take you?

Darroch Donald

Andrew Swaffer

Katrina O'Brien

Australia is vast; even larger in area than Western Europe and the equivalent of the contiguous United States.

Australia is the world's biggest island nation and about the same size as the USA, so careful planning is essential if you intend to venture beyond the obvious (and most iconic) 'must-sees' and get the most from what is, ultimately, a vast choice of destinations and memorable experiences.

If you have no more than three weeks for a visit, don't attempt to see too much of it, and certainly don't try to see all six states.

Where you choose to visit will primarily be determined by the time of year. Broadly speaking, the far north from October to April is extremely hot, humid and monsoonal so most visitors choose to enjoy the glorious summer weather in the cooler southern regions. A visit during May to September not only opens up the north,

but also allows an itinerary to range almost anywhere in the country.

As arrival will almost certainly be by air into Sydney or Melbourne, it's best to organize an itinerary accessible from these cities if you are on a shorter holiday. But if you have more time, venture further afield into the other states and use their capitals as gateways for the beginning and end of a longer tour.

All Australia has an efficient transport network linking its towns and cities, with only the island state of Tasmania that may require a ferry trip. The road systems and flight networks are excellent making travelling the considerable distances a straightforward experience. The only exception to this is an adventure 'outback' that needs very careful planning and equipment, least of which is a reliable 4WD. Affordable domestic flights, coach and rail link the major cities, but most visitors usually choose to get from A to B by campervan or car. Hiring a campervan for

→ DOING IT ALL

Eastern Circuit → Sydney → via coast → Brisbane → via coast → Townsville → offshoot to Cairns → Townsville → Tennant Creek → offshoot to Darwin and Kakadu circuit → Katherine → Tennant Creek → Alice Springs → Erldunda → Yulara (Uluru) → Erldunda → Adelaide → Grampians → Warrnambool → via coast → Melbourne → Canberra → Bathurst → Sydney.

Western Circuit → Perth → Kalbarri → Overlander → offshoot to Monkey Mia → Overlander → Exmouth → Tom Price → Karijini → Broome → via highway → Kununurra → Katherine → offshoot to Darwin and Kakadu circuit → Katherine → Alice Springs → Erldunda → Yulara (Uluru) → Adelaide → Port Augusta → via coast → Margaret River → via coast → Perth.

Visits measured in months rather than weeks open Australia up to the visitor and paint a much more accurate picture of the country

2

part, or all, of your journey is undoubtedly the best way to see Australia; you get to travel at your own leisurely pace and explore more out-of-the-way regions without being tied to a tour or a timetable. But with distances being so vast old master time can of course prove the greatest obstacle.

These suggested four itineraries each cover the highlights of Australia in a minimum of three weeks. But none are written in stone and they are far from exhaustible. Rather they are regional suggestions for travellers wishing to explore a certain part of the country, or for returning visitors to travel somewhere new. Trips can be easily extended by lingering a bit longer in a favourite place or by bolting on the requisite number of days for specific things they want to do, from a six-day hike on the Overland Track in Tasmania to driving a 4WD along the Gibb River Road in Western Australia.

3

1 Fitzroy Island, Great Barrier Reef 2 The Pinnacles, Western Australia 3 Emus

DREAM TRIP 1
SYDNEY → CAIRNS → ULURU

Best time to visit Broadly speaking, the peak season between Sydney and Brisbane is from mid-Dec to late Jan. Autumn to spring (Mar-Oct) is the peak season north of Rockhampton (Tropic of Capricorn), when dry, warm weather is the norm. The 'stinger season' Oct-May also presents its own dangers (jellyfish). Generally, accommodation and tourist sites in NSW and Queensland stay open year round, except in the far north in midsummer (Dec-Mar). The East Coast sees much higher rainfall than the average for Australia.

Sydney (page 35) is without doubt one of the most beautiful cities in the world and the main reasons for this are its harbour, Opera House and Harbour Bridge. The first thing you must do on arrival, even before you throw your bags on a bed and sleep off the jet lag, is get yourself down to Circular Quay, day or night, and let it blow you away. Sydney has a whole lot to offer visitors. With such remarkable and instantly recognizable icons, so many fascinating museums and art galleries, top-class restaurants and beaches, world-renowned festivals and cultural events, 24-hour entertainment and a whole host of exciting activities, the list just goes on and on. Allow at least three days to do Sydney justice. Inland from Sydney are the Blue Mountains (page 55) and vineyards of the Hunter Valley (page 62), where you could easily spend a weekend at a world-class B&B tasting wine.

Back on the coast north of Sydney New South Wales stretches to Tweed Heads and provides an endless chain of magnificent beaches

The first thing you must do on arrival, even before you throw your bags on a bed and sleep off the jet lag, is get yourself down to Circular Quay, day or night, and let it blow you away.

It's easy to see why the route from Sydney to Cairns is so popular: a 2685-km journey along some of the world's favourite coastline.

and scenic headlands. Heading north is a series of happening towns such as **Nelson Bay** (page 63), **Port Macquarie** (page 66) and – most famous of all – the surfing mecca of **Byron Bay** (page 73), each of which merit at least a night's stopover.

Although there is not much in it, of the two coastal sections Sydney to Brisbane and Brisbane to Cairns, the latter Queensland trip is the best. If pushed for time, you may like to consider doing one of these sections overland and then flying the other leg.

1 Sydney Opera House   2 Blue Mountains National Park   3 Byron Bay   4 Gold Coast   5 Hunter Valley

DREAM TRIP 1
SYDNEY → CAIRNS → ULURU

Heading north from New South Wales, you pass the forest of high rises strung along the Gold Coast (page 77), before experiencing the relaxing embrace of the state's capital, Brisbane (page 78), for at least a few days. Beyond 'Brizzie' the aptly named Sunshine Coast (page 84) tempts you with more magnificent beaches, before the peerless Fraser Island (page 88) – the world's largest sand island – only deepens your love affair with the Australian coastline.

Beyond Townsville (page 99), the capital of North Queensland, the tropical landscape becomes ever greener. Offshore, the Great Barrier Reef (page 110), an incredible world beneath the waves, draws visitors from the mainland like kids to a particularly well-stocked sweet shop. Exploring it could occupy anyone for months, never mind a week or two. However, an essential part of a trip here includes a reef island trip with snorkelling or a dive (you can do an introductory dive even if you are not certified). If you can tear yourself away from the Great Barrier Reef, the endlessly entertaining city of Cairns (page 105) is worth a night's stay, before taking a flight to the sacred rock of Uluru in Australia's Red Centre, for a complete contrast to the coast.

Further north of Cairns the Great Barrier Reef continues to amaze. The Atherton Tablelands (page 111), meanwhile, prove it's not all blistering heat and humidity.

The Great Barrier Reef draws visitors from the mainland like kids to a particularly well-stocked sweet shop.

1 Fraser Island **2** Duck billed platypus **3** Great Barrier Reef **4** Daintree National Park

→ GOING FURTHER

Beyond Cairns, make a thrilling 4WD trip north to
the tropical rainforests of **Daintree** and **Cape
Tribulation**. → page 118

Gulf of
Carpentaria

Coral Sea

Cooktown

9

Port Douglas

Atherton
Tablelands ✈ Cairns

7

Mission Beach

Dunk Island

8

*South
Pacific
Ocean*

NORTHERN
TERRITORY

Great Barrier Reef

6

QUEENSLAND *Capricorn Caves*

✈ Uluru **10**

5

Fraser Island

SOUTH AUSTRALIA

4 Brisbane

3 Byron Bay

NEW SOUTH WALES

2

Blue Mountains
National Park ♦ ✈ Sydney **1**

N

200 km
200 miles

1 Fraser Island 2 Annual Cockroach Races, Brisbane 3 Great Barrier Reef

→ WISH LIST

1 Explore Sydney Harbour, one of the world's great sights. 2 West of Sydney are the Blue Mountains, named after the colour of the sun-washed cloak of gum trees that liberally swathes the area. 3 Check out the waves in Byron Bay, New South Wales' surfing capital of cool. 4 Cheer for the fastest creepy-crawly at the annual Cockroach races on Australia Day in Brisbane. 5 Go on the 4WD adventure of a lifetime on Fraser Island. 6 Listen to classical music deep underground in the Capricorn Caves. 7 A rainforest walk around the Mission Beach and a day on Dunk Island. 8 Experience a tropical island fantasy on the Great Barrier Reef. 9 Get up at dawn in the Atherton Tablelands to catch a glimpse of a duck-billed platypus. 10 Visit the biggest rock in the world at Uluru.

Best time to visit First and foremost avoid summer. From Nov until Mar, 40 degree weeks, let alone days, are expected in the northwest and roads can be impassable in the far north because of the wet season (Kakadu National Park is usually pretty much inaccessible). For many visitors, the whale sharks are the big draw card when they migrate along the southwest coasts and June – mercifully in early winter – is the prime month.

Western Australia is big – very big – covering a third of the Australian continent (about the size of Western Europe). So be prepared for a long trip (over 5000 km and that's without the Dampier or Bungles side-trips). One stretch of this huge journey (the run-in to Broome) is nearly 300 km and is settlement-free and roadhouse-free the entire way (so check the tank before setting off!). But the huge, wide open spaces have a charm all their own (imagine a place the size of Western Europe with half a million inhabitants, excluding Perth). Human connections are richer and more valued – because they are so much rarer. Of all the journeys in this book, this one has the potential to be the most life-changing.

As with the other journeys in this book, time is the key. A fortnight would allow little more than a quarter (Perth-Exmouth, Exmouth-

The huge, wide open spaces have a charm all their own and human connections are richer and more valued. Of all the journeys in this book, this one has the potential to be the most life-changing.

1 The Pinnacles, Nambung National Park **2** Cottesloe beach **3** Cellar door, Margaret River winery

Broome, Broome-Kununurra, Kununurra-Darwin) of the trip. A month makes the entire route practical, though if you wanted to really take everything in it would feel like a rush – six weeks is about the shortest amount of time you would need to begin to properly appreciate the experience.

Try not to miss the beaches, such as Cottesloe, and their wonderful beach-front cafés.

Perth (page 121) is a green and spacious city, but the whole point of this journey is to get out of the metropolis. Try not to miss the beaches, such as Cottesloe (page 128), and their wonderful beachfront cafés, 'Freo' (page 129), Rottnest (page 131) and the Swan Valley wineries (page 132), but three days should be sufficient to take in the best the city has to offer. Then it's a full day's run-up to Kalbarri (page 139) – the first must-see stop – but that's if you don't stop, and few would want to miss the Pinnacles and they're not the only attractions on the way.

→ **GOING FURTHER**

Take a detour from Perth to the **Margaret River** region, renowned for its surfing and its wineries. → **page 136**

DREAM TRIP 2
PERTH → BROOME → DARWIN

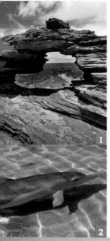

The gorges of Kalbarri National Park (page 140) should not be just seen through the 'window', but truly explored, and this is not the only reason to linger in this charming, if remote, seaside village. Two or three days can easily be spent here before embarking on the trip up to Shark Bay (page 142). Don't miss Hamelin (page 142) on the way; the significance of the stromatolites is quite humbling. Monkey Mia (page 143) is very touristy, but is still nevertheless most memorable. Make sure you take a couple of the boat trips and time spent on the beach outside of 'official' dolphin hours can be equally rewarding.

The wildlife gets even more impressive further north and a week could easily be spent snorkelling off the beaches of Coral Bay (page 145) and taking a boat trip to swim with whale sharks. Activities galore are touted at Coral Bay, but a simple snorkel over the reef can be the most awe-inspiring.

Another good day's drive will get you to the dramatic gorges of the Karijini (page 150). From this relatively unknown park it's a two-day drive to Broome (page 153) – perhaps a stay at Eighty Mile Beach (page 152) on the way – as well as the Dampier Peninsula (page 155)

The six weeks you might spend on the entire trip could easily be spent in this northern region of WA alone; you'll just want to keep on exploring.

1 Kalbarri 2 Monkey Mia 3 Cable Beach 4 Purnululu National Park 5 Gibb River Road

and the delights of the Kimberley. The six weeks you might spend on the entire trip could easily be spent in this northern region of WA alone; you'll just want to keep on exploring. The Gibb River Road (page 158) and Purnululu (the Bungles) (page 157) are once-in-a-lifetime experiences (both 4WD only) and several days could be rewardingly spent at El Questro (page 161), the 'private' national park. Most of the remaining leg is described in the Darwin to Adelaide journey, but we'll pause one last time at Kununurra (page 161), WA's lonely northeastern outpost. A good base for Eastern Kimberley, this small town has a lure all of its own.

Purnululu (the Bungle Bungles) is a once-in-a-lifetime experience.

→ GOING FURTHER

An alternative Derby-Kununurra route, the **Gibb River Road** is a challenging but rewarding 4WD track through remote parts of the Kimberley region.
→ **page 158**

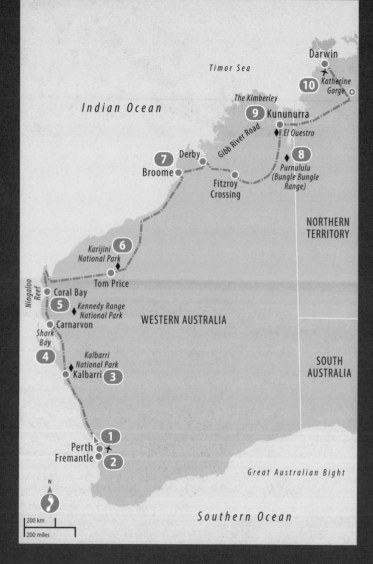

Timor Sea

Darwin

10 Katherine Gorge

Indian Ocean

The Kimberley

9 Kununurra

◆ El Questro

Gibb River Road

7 Derby

Broome

Fitzroy Crossing

◆ Purnululu (Bungle Bungle Range) **8**

NORTHERN TERRITORY

Karijini National Park **6**

Tom Price

Ningaloo Reef

Coral Bay

5 ◆ Kennedy Range National Park

Carnarvon

WESTERN AUSTRALIA

Shark Bay

4

Kalbarri National Park

◆ Kalbarri **3**

SOUTH AUSTRALIA

1

Perth

Fremantle

2

Great Australian Bight

N

200 km
200 miles

Southern Ocean

1 Karijini National Park **2** Swimming with sharks

1 Watch the spectacular sunset over the Indian Ocean from one of Perth's beaches. 2 In Fremantle stroll the cappuccino strip, eat fish and chips on the wharf then take a night tour of the prison. 3 Visit WA's prettiest seaside town, Kalbarri, and the spectacular inland gorges in its neighbouring national park. 4 Brilliant blue vistas hide a vast sea-grass plain, home to dolphins, dugongs, sharks and turtles in Shark Bay. 5 Snorkel over the Ningaloo Reef from the pristine beaches of Coral Bay, and swim with whale sharks. 6 Incredibly deep, tight gorges meet expansive views of red and gold ranges in the Karijini National Park. 7 Discover quasi-Asian architecture and the white-sand Cable beach in the laid-back town of Broome. 8 Go hiking in the Purnululu National Park (Bungle Bungle Range) and see its incomparable beehive-shaped domes. 9 Take a boat trip from the picturesque Kimberley town of Kununurra up the Ord River. 10 Canoe Katherine Gorge in the morning and in the late afternoon walk to Crocodile Rock for sunset.

DREAM TRIP 3
DARWIN → ULURU → ADELAIDE

Best time to visit North Australia has 2 seasons: wet and dry. It is uncomfortably humid in the wet season (Dec-May) and there may be monsoons and cyclones. Some accommodation and sights close in the far north at this time. In the centre and north, winter is the most popular time, with dry, warm weather the norm. Darwin, Katherine, Alice Springs and Uluru get busy May-Sep. In Southern Australia, Nov-Mar are the best months for hot, sunny weather, but avoid walking in the hill ranges then, as it's too hot.

The trip down the spine of Australia delves deeply into Australia's cultural and geological heritage and takes in some of the country's most iconic and awe-inspiring sights. At over 3000 km through mostly uninhabited desert it isn't for the faint-hearted, but will repay the effort many times over. To get the most out of this trip you will definitely need to avoid summer.

Three weeks just about allows the full journey as described below, but would allow very little relaxation and necessitates about 200 km of driving on average every day. If you can afford to stretch your trip to four weeks or longer then a little more quality time can be spent at some of the major attractions, such as Kakadu, the West MacDonnells and the Flinders Ranges.

Southwest of Darwin (page 167), Litchfield National Park (page 172) makes an interesting contrast to Kakadu (page 175) and scoring one of the isolated overnight camp spots can be an unexpected highlight of any NT trip.

At over 3000 km through mostly uninhabited desert this trip isn't for the faint-hearted, but will repay the effort many times over.

1 Kakadu National Park 2 Natural hot springs, Mataranka 3 Echidna (spiny anteater), Kangaroo Island 4 Daly Waters Pub, Daly Waters 5 Aboriginal rock art, Kakadu National Park

Katherine (page 180) is more than just a stopover town if you have the time and a pleasant day or two can be spent exploring the local sights. Just over 100 km south of Katherine is Mataranka (page 182). As well as surprisingly good facilities, the town is very close to Elsey National Park (page 182) with its palm-fringed hot springs. Between Mataranka and Tennant Creek (allow a day's drive) there's very little to detain most travellers, although it's well worth sparing at least an hour for refreshment at the pub in Daly Waters (page 183).

DREAM TRIP 3
DARWIN → ULURU → ADELAIDE

If you happen to have a spare afternoon at Tennant Creek (page 183) then check out Battery Hill or take a picnic out by Mary Ann Dam. The 500 km to Alice need only be broken by a look at the Devil's Marbles (page 184). You won't need long here to take in the best of this extraordinary rock formation, but make sure you don't miss it.

Alice Springs (page 186) can easily soak up several days of looking around but if you do have extra time, exploring and walking the gorges and trails of the West MacDonnell Ranges (page 189) can be more rewarding. Hermannsberg (page 191) is culturally fascinating.

At Marla, if you have a 4WD, you can choose the Oodnadatta Track (page 201) – a more interesting and direct route to the Flinders Ranges – or continue on to Coober Pedy (page 200). Heading south on the highway, the only place really worth pausing at before the Flinders is Woomera (page 203), with its Missile Park and Heritage Centre. Getting closer to civilization, although a day is sufficient to see Wilpena Pound (page 206), there really is a lot more to see in the Flinders Ranges (page 206) and several days can easily be spent exploring the area. Before you wend your way to the wine regions, there are some superb hill walks around Quorn (page 204).

1 Giant termite mound, Litchfield National Park 2 Devil's Marbles 3 Barossa Valley vineyard 4 Koalas in the wild 5 Coober Pedy 6 Oodnadatta Track

The trip isn't really complete without an excursion to Kangaroo Island where opportunities for wildlife spotting rank amongst the best in Australia.

The final run down to Adelaide also has some potential side-trips and stopovers. Mount Remarkable National Park (page 212) lives up to its name. If you like wine then two days would be a minimum in the Clare and Barossa valleys (page 213). Finally, once you've reached Adelaide (page 215), the trip isn't really complete without an excursion to Kangaroo Island (page 220). The opportunities for wildlife spotting rank amongst the best in Australia.

→ GOING FURTHER

Follow an ancient Aboriginal trading route, the unsealed **Oodnadatta Track**, across the Outback to Flinders Ranges. → page 201

→ ROUTE PLANNER

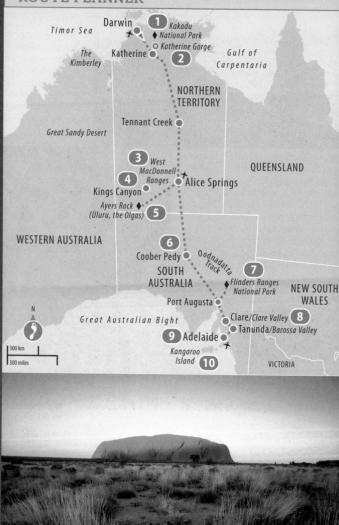

Timor Sea

Darwin ✈ **1**

Kakadu
♦ National Park
○ Katherine Gorge **2**

Katherine ○

The Kimberley

Gulf of
Carpentaria

NORTHERN
TERRITORY

Great Sandy Desert

Tennant Creek ●

3 West
MacDonnell
4 Ranges

QUEENSLAND

Kings Canyon ●

Ayers Rock ♦
(Uluru, the Olgas) **5**

✈ Alice Springs

WESTERN AUSTRALIA

6

Coober Pedy ●

Oodnadatta
Track

7

SOUTH
AUSTRALIA

♦ Flinders Ranges
National Park

NEW SOUTH
WALES

Port Augusta ●

Clare/Clare Valley **8**

Tanunda/Barossa Valley

Great Australian Bight

9 ● Adelaide ✈

Kangaroo
Island **10**

VICTORIA

N

300 km
300 miles

1

1 Uluru **2** Flinders Ranges

→ WISH LIST

1 Don't miss the ancient rock art and the perfectly picturesque Twin Falls in Kakadu National Park. **2** Take a boat cruise to see the spectacular Katherine Gorge or hike along one of the area's many walking trails for some superb views of waterfalls and waterholes. **3** Tour the gorges of the West MacDonnell Ranges, making a detour to see the Aboriginal Hermannsberg's Historic Precinct. **4** Walk around the rim of the Kings Canyon and stroll out later to watch the sun set on Carmichael Crag. **5** Watch the sunrise, then take a morning walk with an Anangu guide at Uluru. **6** Fossick for opals at the Outback mining town of Coober Pedy. **7** Walk up the ramparts of Wilpena Pound in the central Flinders Ranges, or even take a scenic flight over them. **8** Head to the Clare and Barossa Valleys for a wine tasting expedition. **9** Explore the grand old city of Adelaide, especially its excellent art gallery and museums **10** Take a trip over Kangaroo Island, explore the varied coastline and meet the koalas, seals and other prolific wildlife.

DREAM TRIP 4
MELBOURNE → TASMANIA → SYDNEY

Best time to visit The peak season between Melbourne and Sydney is similar to Sydney to Brisbane, from Dec to Jan, plus in winter (Jun-Sep) the mountainous areas of Victoria and Tasmania for skiing. Some coastal resorts and sights close during winter (May-Jul) in Victoria and Tasmania. The western coast of Victoria and the southwestern coast of Tasmania can get significant rainfall (over 1600 mm), spread over more than 160 days of the year.

A three-week trip will allow enough time to explore both Melbourne and Sydney as well as the more natural environments of the NSW coast and its plethora of national parks. Within this time frame you can also visit the unique and less classically Australian scenery of Tasmania.

Melbourne and Sydney will ideally require three to four days each with adjunct one or two day trips from both. The rest of the time can be allocated to Tasmania and/or the journey between the cities via the NSW coast or inland taking in the Snowy Mountains and perhaps the many attractions of the national capital, Canberra.

Make sure you allow enough days to explore the sights of Australia's 'second city', Melbourne (page 227), including its impressive museums and Eureka Tower Skydeck. For a day (or preferably an overnight) trip from Melbourne head out along the famous Great Ocean Road (page 241), one of the world's greatest coastal routes, or sample the vineyards and coastal scenery of the Mornington Peninsula (page 235).

1 Sun sets on the St Kilda foreshore, Melbourne, VIC 2 Eureka Tower, Melbourne 3 Dove Lake and Cradle Mountain, TAS 4 Wilsons Promontory

You can fly fairly cheaply from Melbourne to Hobart and hire a car, but if you have your own transport the ferry crossing from Port Melbourne is very much part of the experience. Using Hobart (page 245) as a base, see its attractions, including seeing sunrise from the summit of Mount Wellington (page 249). Heading southeast the Tasman Peninsula (page 250), including Port Arthur, is next. North of here is Freycinet National Park (page 251), one of Australia's best protected areas and a must-see, followed by Launceston (page 252) and its magnificent gorge, and Devonport (page 253). Head to the wilderness scenery of the West Coast (page 255) and Strahan (page 258) via the spectacularly rugged Cradle Mountain (page 254).

From Melbourne head out along the famous Great Ocean Road, one of the world's greatest coastal routes.

The trip from Melbourne to Sydney can tackled via the inland route through the Snowy Mountains (page 261) and the Australian capital of Canberra (page 264). Alternatively, take the coastal route via the Victorian East Coast and southern NSW coast, to take in Ben Boyd National Park (page 263).

The inland route is more convenient if you want more time in both cities and you can also overnight in Canberra and/or take a few days to explore the largest park in New South Wales, the Kosciuszko National Park (page 261), and the Snowy Mountains around Thredbo (page 264), one of the nation's few ski resorts.

Give yourself about a week to 10 days to fully immerse yourself in the coastal scenery and national parks along this route. Don't miss the sociable kangaroos at Murramurang National Park (page 267) just north of Batemans Bay (page 267). Ben Boyd, Jervis Bay (Booderee) (page 269) and Eurobodalla National Parks (page 267) are also well worth seeing.

→ GOING FURTHER

Take the wild, beautiful coast road from Bairnsdale to Batemans Bay, taking in the Ben Boyd and Croajingolong National Parks. → **page 262**

1 Tasmanian devil 2 Ben Boyd National Park 3 National Museum of Australia, Canberra 4 Kangaroo

3

4

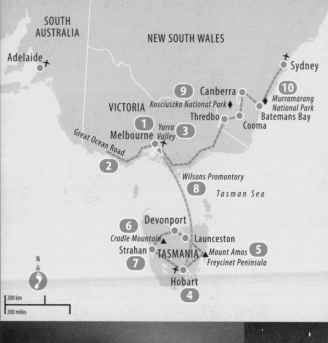

1 Freycinet National Park, Tasmania 2 Federation Square, Melbourne 3 Wombat 4 Twelve Apostles, Great Ocean Road

1 Take a stroll around Federation Square in Melbourne, visit Melbourne Museum and on a clear day, check out the view from Eureka Tower. **2** Don't miss where 12 Apostles become 11 along the Great Ocean Road. **3** Head up to Healesville Sanctuary and the Yarra Valley for a day's wildlife-spotting and wine tasting. **4** Visit the waterfront in Hobart, Tasmania, and then browse the stunning array of works at the Museum of Old and New Art (MONA). **5** Climb Mount Amos for the most striking views of the spectacular Freycinet Peninsula. **6** Try and climb Cradle Mountain on a clear day for magnificent views. **7** Make Strahan your base to see the vast harbour and its tributary rivers. **8** Explore the coastal walks and white sandy beaches of Wilsons Promontory. **9** Depending on the time of year, see winter snow or spring flowers in the Kosciuszko National Park. **10** Make friends with the tame kangaroos at Murramarang National Park.

4

Bondi Beach, NSW

DREAM TRIP 1:
Sydney→Cairns→Uluru 21 days

GOING FURTHER

33

DREAM TRIP 1
Sydney→Cairns→Uluru

Seasoned travellers often complain that the world's great cities can seem a trifle disappointing. But not so Sydney. That first sighting of its majestic harbour from Circular Quay, with the grand Opera House on one side and the mighty Harbour Bridge on the other, is one that always exceeds expectations.

The 900-km-long north coast of NSW has so many stunning natural features that, after a while, they all seem to merge into one golden memory of sun-drenched sands and crystal clear waters, with the constant soundtrack of rolling surf. From south to north, extended stops in Nelson Bay (Port Stephens), Port Macquarie, Coffs Harbour, and, of course, Byron Bay, are all recommended.

Heading north from NSW, you pass the forest of high-rise buildings strung along the infamous Gold Coast before emerging in the relaxing embrace of the state capital, Brisbane. Brisbane has enjoyed phenomenal growth in recent years and is one of the fastest developing regions in Australia. The reason for this revolves around its greatest assets: climate and lifestyle.

North of Noosa the coastal strip succumbs to the vast expanses of the Great Sandy Region, and offers a taste of something better: Fraser Island, the largest coastal sand island in the world and the biggest tourist attraction in Southern Queensland.

For many, the central and north coasts of Queensland are the highlight, with the sublime Whitsunday Islands. But it's not all about coral reef and tropical islands. Cairns is the region's tourist heart and gateway to the Great Barrier Reef. North of Cairns is the small, sophisticated resort of Port Douglas, a base for the wonderful Daintree National Park and the exhilarating route north to the wilds of Cape Tribulation. West of Cairns are the lush, green Atherton Tablelands. From Cairns you can take a flight to Uluru, the world's biggest and most mesmerising rock.

SYDNEY

Aussie writer and TV personality Clive James has described Sydney as looking 'like crushed diamonds', but even without such analogies the marriage of natural and man-made aesthetics cannot fail to impress. Over the last decade vast sums have been spent on inner-city rejuvenation, transportation and state-of-the-art venues to host high profile international sporting events like the 2000 Olympics and 2003 Rugby World Cup, both of which were resounding successes and only added to the city's global reputation. Yet even without such events, this is a city whose inhabitants know that their lifestyle is one of the best in the world and their metropolis one of the most impacting anywhere. It's hardly surprising then that Sydney also has a whole lot to offer tourists, from its fascinating museums and galleries and world-class restaurants and beaches to its renowned 24-hour entertainment.

→ARRIVING IN SYDNEY

GETTING THERE

Kingsford Smith Airport ① *9 km south of the city centre, www.sydneyairport.com*, has excellent facilities and its negotiation is straightforward. There is a **Tourism New South Wales** ① *T9667 9386*, information desk in the main arrivals concourse where help is at hand to organize transport and accommodation bookings, flight arrival information and airport facilities. There are ATMs, foreign exchange outlets, car hire, a post office and medical centre (open 0400-2300). The domestic terminal is a short distance west of the international terminal.

Public transport to the city centre is available within a short walk of the terminal building. The fastest and most convenient method is via the **Airport Link** rail service every 10-15 minutes. With only a few stops and taking less than 15 minutes to the CBD the $15.40 (child $10.30) one-way fare is exorbitant, but after a long journey the ease and convenience is undeniable. Taxis are available outside the terminal (south). A trip to the centre takes 30 minutes, $50. Various independent shuttle operators and courtesy accommodation shuttles also operate door-to-door from outside the terminal building, including **Kingsford Smith Transport** ① *T9666 9988, www.kst.com.au* , which runs every 20-30 minutes anywhere in the city ($14 one way and $23 return).

All interstate and NSW state destination trains arrive and depart from Sydney's **Central Railway Station** on Eddy Avenue, T131500. Countrylink ①*T132232, www.country link.info*, is the main interstate operator with a combination of coach and rail to all the main interstate and NSW destinations. They have a travel centre at Central Station (open 0630-2200), while Town Hall Station, Wynyard Station, Circular Quay and Bondi Junction all have on-the-spot **CityRail** information booths. The main **coach terminal** is in the Central Railway Station; Greyhound ① *T1300 473946, www.greyhound.com.au, daily 0730-1830*. Left luggage and showers are also available.

GETTING AROUND

Public transport in Sydney is generally efficient and convenient. The great hub of public transportation in the city centre revolves around Circular Quay at the base of the CBD. It is from there that most ferry (**Sydney Ferries**) and many suburban rail (**CityRail**) and bus

(**Sydney Buses**) services operate. The State Transit Authority (STA) owns and operates the principal suburban ferry and bus services. Other principal terminals are Wynyard on York Street for northbound bus and rail services, Town Hall on George Street and the Central Railway Station. For information about all public transport, T131500 (0600-2200), www.131500.com.au. Once in the city, ferry and rail route maps are available from information centres. The free leaflet *CBD Access Map Sydney*, available from the VICs or information booths, is a very useful map and guide for the disabled.

MOVING ON

The Blue Mountains (see page 55) are 1 hour 20 minutes (90 km) driving from Sydney. Although public transport to and around the Blue Mountains is good you are advised to take your own vehicle or hire one, allowing you to make the most of the numerous viewpoints and sights within the region. Trains are the best way to arrive independently, leaving Sydney's Central Station (Countrylink and CityLink platforms) on the hour daily, stopping at all major towns through the Blue Mountains, T132232. The journey to Katoomba takes about two hours and costs around $30 for a day return. Numerous coach companies and hostels offer day sightseeing tours from Sydney. Some may allow overnight stops. The VIC in Sydney, see below, can assist with the extensive choice and bookings. Most buses leave from Circular Quay; see Getting around above.

TOURIST INFORMATION

Beyond the visitor information booth at the airport international arrivals terminal, the first stop for any visitor should be the **Sydney Visitor Centre** ① *Level 1, corner Argyle St and Playfair St, the Rocks, T1800 067676, T9240 8788, www.therocks.com.au, daily 0930-1730*. The centre provides information, brochures, maps and reservations for hotels, tours, cruises, restaurants and other city-based activities. There is another **VIC** ① *Darling Harbour, Palm Grove between Cockle Bay Wharf and Harbourside, T1800 067676 , T9240 8788, www.sydneyvisitorcentre.com.au*. It offers similar services to the Rocks centre but has an emphasis on sights and activities within Darling Harbour itself. Neither centre issues public transport tickets. Manly, Parramatta, Homebush Bay and Bondi also have local information centres while small manned information booths are located on the corner of Pitt Street and Alfred Street, Circular Quay; opposite St Andrew's Cathedral near the Town Hall on George Street; and on Martin Place, near Elizabeth Street.

The main daily newspaper in Sydney is the excellent *Sydney Morning Herald*, which has comprehensive entertainment listings daily (see the pull-out *Metro* section on Friday) and regular city features. There are some excellent, free tourist brochures including the *Sydney Official Guide*, *This Week in Sydney*, *Where Magazine*, the very interesting suburb-oriented *Sydney Monthly* and, for the backpacker, *TNT* (NSW Edition), www.tntdownunder.com. For entertainment look out for *Drum Media*, www.drummedia.com.au, and *3-D World*, www.themusic.com.au. All these and others are available from the main VICs, city centre information booths or from cafés, newsagents and bookshops.

Sydney is without doubt one of the most beautiful cities in the world and the main reasons for this are its harbour, Opera House and Harbour Bridge. The first thing you must do on arrival, even before you throw your bags on a bed and sleep off the jet lag, is get yourself down to Circular Quay, day or night. Circular Quay also provides the main walkway from the historic and commercial Rocks area to the Opera House and the Botanical Gardens beyond. It's a great place to linger, take photographs or pause to enjoy the many bizarre street performers that come and go with the tides.

SYDNEY OPERA HOUSE
ⓘ *Information T9250 7777, bookings T9250 7111, www.sydneyoperahouse.com, lines open Mon-Sat 0900-2030 for the latest schedules, and for tours, see below.*

Even the fiercest critics of modern architecture cannot fail to be impressed by the magnificent Sydney Opera House. Built in 1973, it is the result of a revolutionary design by Danish architect, Jorn Utzon, and every day, since this bizarre edifice was created, people have flocked to admire it. At times the steps and concourse seem more like the nave of some futuristic cathedral than the outside of an arts venue, with hordes of worshippers gazing in reverential awe. With such adoration it was perhaps inevitable that the great Aussie icon would join the international A-list of man-made creations, being awarded World Heritage Site status in 2007. The Opera House is best viewed not only intimately

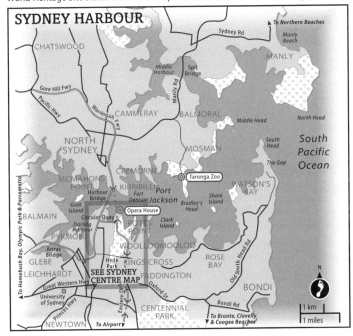

from close up, but also from afar. Some of the best spots are from Macquarie Point (end of the Domain on the western edge of Farm Cove) especially at dawn, and from the Park Hyatt Hotel on the eastern edge of Circular Quay. Also any ferry trip eastbound from Circular Quay will reveal the structure in many of its multi-faceted forms.

The Opera House has five performance venues ranging from the main, 2690-capacity Concert Hall to the small Playhouse Theatre. Combined, they host about 2500 performances annually – everything from Bach to Billy Connolly. The Opera House is the principal performance venue for Opera Australia, the Australian Ballet Company, the Sydney Dance Company, the Sydney Symphony Orchestra and the Sydney Theatre Company. There are two tours and three performance packages available. The **Sydney Opera House Tour** ① *every 30 mins, 1 hr, daily 0900-1700, $35, children and concessions $25*, provides an insider's view of selected theatres and foyers. The **Backstage Tour** ① *T9250 7777, 2 hrs, daily 0700, $155*, as the name suggests, takes you behind the scenes and includes breakfast in the staff restaurant. Other performance packages combine a range of performance, dining and tour options.

FROM THE OPERA HOUSE TO THE ROCKS

At the eastern edge of the quay, the **Opera Quays** façade provides many tempting, if expensive, cafés and restaurants as well as an art gallery and a cinema. After dark and on a warm summer's evening this surely has to be one of the best places on the planet for a convivial beer or G&T. Look out for the **Writers Walk**, a series of plaques on the main concourse with quotes from famous Australian writers.

The **Justice and Police Museum** ① *corner of Albert St and Phillip St, T9252 1144, www.hht.nsw.gov.au, daily 0930-1700, $10, children $5*, housed in the former 1856 Water Police Court, features a magistrates' court and former police cells, as well as a gallery and historical displays showcasing the antics and fate of some of Sydney's most notorious criminals. Nearby, facing the quay, is the former 1840 **Customs House** which now houses a major public library, several exhibition spaces, café-bars and on the top floor the long established and popular **Café Sydney**; see box, page 53. The ground floor – or city lounge as it is dubbed – comes complete with a newspaper and magazine salon, TV wall, internet access, information desk and a giant model of the Sydney CBD embedded beneath a glass floor.

At the southwestern corner of Circular Quay it is hard to miss the rather grand art deco **Museum of Contemporary Art** ① *T9245 2400, www.mca.com.au, Mon-Wed 1000-1700, Thur 1000-2100, free with a small charge for some visiting exhibitions, tours Mon-Fri 1100 and 1300, Sat-Sun 1100, 1300 and 1500*. Opened in 1991, it maintains a collection of some of Australia's best contemporary works, together with works by renowned international artists like Warhol and Hockney. The museum also hosts national and international exhibitions regularly.

A little further towards the Harbour Bridge is the rather incongruous **Cadman's Cottage**, overlooking the futuristic Overseas Passenger Terminal. Built in 1816, it is the oldest surviving residence in Sydney and was originally the former base for Governor Macquarie's boat crew. The cottage is named after the coxswain of the boat crew, John Cadman, who was transported to Australia for stealing a horse. The cottage is now the base for the **Sydney Harbour National Park Information Centre** ① *110 George St, T1300 361967, T9253 0888, www.nationalparks.nsw.gov.au, Mon-Fri 0930-1630, Sat-Sun 1000-1630, free*, which is the main booking office and departure point for a number of harbour and island tours.

THE ROCKS

Below the Bradfield Highway, which now carries a constant flow of traffic across the Harbour Bridge, is the historic Rocks village. It was the first site settled by European convicts and troops as early as 1788 and, despite being given a major facelift in recent decades (and losing its erstwhile reputation as the haunt of prostitutes, drunks and criminals), still retains much of its original architectural charm. Old and new is married in an eclectic array of shops, galleries, arcades, cafés and some mighty fine pubs and restaurants.

By far the best way to see the Rocks properly is to join one of the official **Rocks Walking Tours**, which give an entertaining and informative insight into the past and present. **Rocks Market**, held every weekend, is perhaps the most popular in Sydney. It features a fine array of authentic arts, crafts, bric-a-brac and souvenirs. For live entertainment head for the **Rocks Square** where you'll find jazz, classical or contemporary music every day from midday for two hours. The **Rocks Discovery Museum** ① *Kendal Lane, T9240 8680 www.rocksdiscoverymuseum.com.au, daily 1000- 1700, free (Discovery Dig $5)*, houses various highly interactive historical exhibits specific to the Rocks. During school holiday periods the 45-minute Discovery Dig offers kids the chance to dress up as junior archaeologists and dig up objects in fake (rubber) soil with an expert on hand to unravel the stories behind their finds. To escape the crowds, head up Argyle Street, and the steps to Cumberland Street, taking a quick peek at the historic row of cottages at **Susannah Place**, 58-64 Gloucester Street, west side, below the popular Australian hotel and pub, before walking through the pedestrian walkway to **Observatory Park**. This offers some fine views of the bridge and is home to the **Sydney Observatory** ① *T9921 3485, www.sydneyobservatory.com.au, exhibition daily 1000-1700, free, space theatre daily Mon-Fri 1430 and 1330, Sat-Sun 1100, 1200, 1430 and 1530, $8, children $6, evening tour $18, children $12, concessions $14*, which is Australia's oldest (book ahead). There is a quality exhibition here covering early aboriginal and European astronomy, as well as a 3D space theatre and telescope tours during the day and evening tours offering a chance to view the heavens. From Observatory Park it is a short walk further along Argyle Street to enjoy a small libation and a bite to eat at the **Lord Nelson**, Sydney's oldest pub, before walking north down Lower Fort Street to **Dawes Point Park** with its dramatic bridge perspectives.

THE HARBOUR BRIDGE

From near or far, above or below, day or night, the Harbour Bridge is impressive and imposing. The 'Coat Hanger', as it is often called, was opened in 1932, having taken nine years to build, and it remains one of the longest single-span bridges in the world. The deck supports eight lanes of traffic – accommodating around 150,000 vehicles a day – a railway line and a pedestrian walkway, and forms a crucial artery to the North Shore and beyond. For over six decades the best views from the bridge were accessed by foot from its 59-m-high deck, but now the **Bridge Climb** experience, which ascends the 134-m-high and 502-m-long span, has become one of the city's must-do activities. Not as thrilling, but far cheaper, are the views on offer from the top of the **Southeastern Pylon Lookout**, which can be accessed from the eastern walkway and Cumberland Street, the Rocks. The pylon also houses the **Harbour Bridge Exhibition** ① *T9240 1100, www.pylonlookout.com.au, 1000-1700, $15, children $6.50*. From below, the best views of the bridge can be enjoyed from Hickson Road and Dawes Point (south side) and Milson's Point (north side).

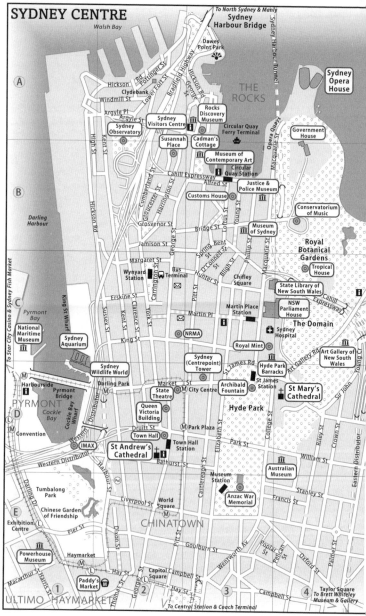

SYDNEY CENTRE

Walsh Bay

To North Sydney & Manly
Sydney Harbour Bridge

Sydney Harbour Tunnel

Dawes Point Park

THE ROCKS

Sydney Opera House

Hickson Rd
Clydebank
Windmill St
Argyle Pl
Argyle St
Sydney Observatory
Sydney Visitors Centre
Susannah Place
Cadman's Cottage
Rocks Discovery Museum
Circular Quay Ferry Terminal
Government House
Museum of Contemporary Art
Circular Quay Station
Cahill Expressway
Alfred St
Justice & Police Museum
Customs House
Conservatorium of Music
Grosvenor St
Bridge St
Museum of Sydney
Royal Botanical Gardens
Jamison St
Margaret St
Tropical House
Wynyard Station
Bus Terminal
Erskine St
Chifley Square
State Library of New South Wales
NSW Parliament House
Martin Place Station
Martin Pl
The Domain
King St
NRMA
Royal Mint
Sydney Hospital
Art Gallery of New South Wales
National Maritime Museum
Sydney Aquarium
Sydney Wildlife World
Darling Park
Sydney (Centrepoint) Tower
Hyde Park Barracks
St James Station
St Mary's Cathedral
Harbourside
Pyrmont Bridge
Market St
State Theatre
City Centre
Archibald Fountain
Queen Victoria Building
Hyde Park
Convention
Druitt St
Park Plaza
Town Hall
IMAX
St Andrew's Cathedral
Town Hall Station
Bathurst St
Australian Museum
Museum Station
Anzac War Memorial
Tumbalong Park
Chinese Garden of Friendship
World Square
Exhibition Centre
CHINATOWN
Powerhouse Museum
Haymarket
Paddy's Market
Capitol Square
Taylor Square
To Brett Whiteley Museum & Gallery
ULTIMO
HAYMARKET
To Central Station & Coach Terminal

Darling Harbour
Pyrmont Bay
To Star City Casino & Sydney Fish Market
PYRMONT
Cockle Bay

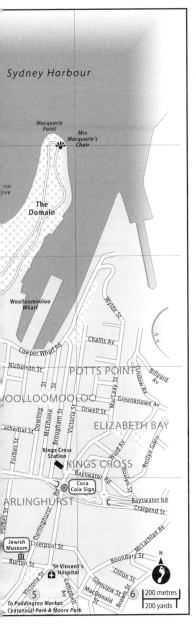

HARBOUR ISLANDS

Sydney Harbour is scattered with a number of interesting islands, most of which hold some historical significance. **Fort Denison**, just east of the Opera House, is the smallest, and by far the most notorious. Its proper name is Pinchgut Island – so called because it was originally used as an open-air jail and a place where inmates were abandoned for a week and supplied with nothing except bread and water. In 1796, the governor of NSW left a sobering warning to the new penal colony by displaying the body of executed murderer, Francis Morgan, from a gibbet on the island's highest point. The island was later converted to a fort in the 1850s (for fear of a Russian invasion during the Crimean War). There is a café and tours through Captain Cook Cruises, from $27, T9206 1111 or T9358 1999 . A little further east, off Darling Harbour, is **Clark Island**, a popular picnic retreat for those with their own transport (landing fee $6, must be pre-booked and pre-paid). East again, off Rose Bay, is **Shark Island**, so called due to its shape. Access is via Captain Cook Cruises leaving Circular Quay (Jetty 6) at the weekends (hourly from 0945-1645) $17 return, children $15, T9247 5033. West of the bridge is the largest of the harbour's islands, **Goat Island**, site of a former gunpowder station and barracks. For tours, contact NPWS, T9247 5033, from $24.

→CITY CENTRE

Many visitors find the city centre a chaotic place. It is cooler, owing to the high-rise blocks, but much noisier, disturbed by the collective din of corporate Sydney. Despite this, it is worth taking the plunge and joining the purposeful flood of humanity through its gargantuan corridors to discover some hidden gems.

MUSEUM OF SYDNEY

ⓘ *Corner of Phillip St and Bridge St, T9251 5988, www.hht.nsw.gov.au, 0930-1700, $10, children $5, family $20.*

The Museum of Sydney (MOS) was opened in 1995 and is a clever and imaginative mix of old and new. Built on the original site of Governor Phillip's 1788 residence and incorporating some of the archaeological remains discovered there, it contains uncluttered and well-presented displays that explore the history and stories surrounding the creation of the city, from the first indigenous settlers, through the European invasion and up to the modern day. Art is an important aspect of this museum and as well as dynamic and temporary exhibitions incorporating a city theme there are some permanent pieces, the most prominent being the intriguing *Edge of the Trees*, a sculptural installation. There is also a shop and café.

MACQUARIE STREET

Macquarie Street forms the eastern fringe of the CBD and is Sydney's most historic street and the site of many important and impressive buildings. Heading north to south, near the Opera House in its own expansive grounds is the **Government House** ⓘ *T9931 5222, Fri-Sun 1030-1500, guided tours only every ½ hr from 1030, grounds open daily 1000-1600, free,* a Gothic revival building completed in 1837. The interior contains many period furnishings and features, giving an insight into the lifestyle of the former NSW governors and their families. Further up Macquarie Street, facing the Botanical Gardens, is the **State Library of New South Wales** ⓘ *T9273 1414, www.sl.nsw.gov.au, Mon-Thu 0900-2200, Fri 0900-1700, Sat 1000-1700.* Its architecture speaks for itself, but housed within its walls are some very significant historical documents, including most of the diaries of the First Fleet. Also worth a look is the foyer floor of the **Mitchell Library** entrance, one of three Melocco Brothers' mosaic floor decorations in the city. The library hosts visiting exhibitions that are almost always worth visiting and offers an ongoing programme of films, workshops and seminars. There is a shop and café on site.

Next door, the original north wing of the 1816 Sydney Hospital, formerly known as the Rum Hospital, is now the **NSW Parliament House**. Free tours are offered when parliament is not in session, and when it is you can visit the public gallery. The south wing of the hospital gave way to the **Royal Mint** ⓘ *small museum display, Mon-Fri 0900-1700, free,* in 1854 during the gold rush. The **Hyde Park Barracks**, on the northern edge of Hyde Park, were commissioned in 1816 by Governor Macquarie to house male convicts, and later utilized as an orphanage and an asylum. The renovated buildings now house a modern museum displaying the history of the Barracks and the work of the architect Francis Greenway. Various themed tours are available, from $10, children $5.

CENTRAL BUSINESS DISTRICT (CBD)

Sydneysiders are very fond of the **Sydney (Centrepoint) Tower** ⓘ *100 Market St, T8223 3800, observation deck Sun-Fri 0900-2230, Sat 0900-2330, $25, children $15, family $65.* This slightly dated landmark, built in 1981, has a distinctive 2239-tonne golden turret. The view from one of Australia's highest buildings is mighty impressive. As well as enjoying the stunning vistas from the tower's observation deck, you can also experience a virtual 'Great Australian Expedition' tour or dine in one of two revolving restaurants. The more adventurous can even brave outdoors and experience **Skywalk**

① *day, dusk or night from $65, T9333 9222, www.skywalk.com.au*, a glass-floored platform. Given the high price of entry to the observation deck alone, make sure that you keep an eye on the weather forecast and pick a clear day.

While you are on Market Street it is worth taking a peek at the impressive interior of the 1929 **State Theatre** ① *49 Market St, T9373 6852, www.statetheatre.com.au*. Much of its charm is instantly on view in the entrance foyer, but the 20,000-piece glass chandelier and Wurlitzer organ housed in the auditorium steal the show. Just around the corner from the State Theatre, on George Street, taking up an entire city block, is the grand**Queen Victoria Building** ① *T9265 6800, www.qvb.com.au, Mon-Wed and Fri-Sat 0900-1800, Thu 0900-2100, Sun 1100-1700, tours available with pre-booking*. Built in 1898 to celebrate Queen Victoria's Golden Jubilee and to replace the original Sydney Markets, the QVB (as it is known) is a prime shopping venue, containing three floors of boutique outlets, but the spectacular interior is well worth a look in itself. At the northern end is the four-tonne **Great Australian Clock**, the world's largest hanging animated turret clock. It is a stunning creation that took four years to build at a cost of $1.5 million. When activated with a $4 donation (which goes to charity), the clock comes alive with moving scenes and figurines. At the southern end is the equally impressive **Royal Clock**, which includes the execution of King Charles I. There are also galleries, historical displays, restaurants and cafés.

Across the street from the QVB is the **Town Hall** ① *corner of George St and Druitt St, T9265 9819, 0900-1700, free, pre-booked tours T4285 5685*, built in 1888. It also has an impressive interior, the highlight of which is the 8000-pipe organ, reputed to be the largest in the world. Next door to the Town Hall is **St Andrew's Cathedral** ① *T9265 1661, free*, built between 1819 and 1868, with regular choir performances.

HYDE PARK AND AROUND

Hyde Park is a great place to escape the mania of the city and includes the historic grandeur of the 1932 Archibald Fountain and 1934 **Anzac War Memorial**. It's also great for people watching. At the northeastern edge of the park, on College Street, is **Saint Mary's Cathedral** ① *crypt 1000-1600*, which is well worth a look inside. It has an impressive and wonderfully peaceful interior, with the highlight being the Melocco Brothers' mosaic floor in the crypt. Further south along College Street is the **Australian Museum** ① *T9320 6000, www.austmus.gov.au, 0930-1700, $12, children $6, family $30 (exhibitions extra), Explorer bus, stop 13*, established in 1827, but doing a fine job of keeping pace with the cutting edge of technology, especially the modern Biodiversity and Indigenous Australians displays. Try to coincide your visit to the Indigenous Australians section with the live didgeridoo playing and informative lectures. Kids will love the Search and Discover section and Kidspace, a state-of-the-art mini museum for the under 5s.

ROYAL BOTANICAL GARDENS AND MACQUARIE POINT

The 30-ha **Botanical Gardens** ① *0700-sunset, free*, offer a wonderful sanctuary of peace and greenery only a short stroll east of the city centre. They boast a fine array of mainly native plants and trees, an intriguing pyramid-shaped **Tropical House** ① *1000-1600, small fee*, roses and succulent gardens, rare and threatened species and decorative ponds, as well as a resident colony of wild flying foxes (fruit bats). There is a visitor centre and shop located in the southeastern corner of the park. There you can pick up a self-guided tour leaflet or join a free organized tour at 1030 daily. A specialist Aboriginal tour, exploring the significance of the site to the Cadigal (the original Aboriginal inhabitants) and the first European settlers' desperate attempts to cultivate the site, is available on request. The **Botanical Gardens Restaurant** is one of the best places to observe the bats. You'll see lots of tropical ibis birds around the gardens – the descendants of a tiny group that escaped from Taronga Zoo.

From the Botanical Gardens it is a short stroll to Macquarie Point, which offers one of the best views of the Opera House and Harbour Bridge. Mrs Macquarie's Chair is the spot where the first governor's wife came to reflect upon the new settlement. One can only imagine what her reaction would be now.

THE DOMAIN AND THE ART GALLERY OF NEW SOUTH WALES

ⓘ *Art Gallery Rd, The Domain, T9225 1744, www.artgallery.nsw.gov.au, 1000-1700 and Wed 1700-2100, free (small charge for some visiting exhibitions), Explorer bus stop 12.*

Inside its grand façade, Australia's largest gallery houses the permanent works of many of the country's most revered contemporary artists as well as a collection of more familiar international names like Monet and Picasso. The Yiribana Gallery, in stark contrast, showcases a fine collection of Aboriginal and Torres Strait Islander works and is a major highlight. The Asian Gallery is also well worth a look. The main gallery features a dynamic programme of major visiting exhibitions, and there is a great bookshop and café. Be sure not to miss the quirky and monumental matchsticks installation by the late Brett Whiteley, one of the city's most celebrated artists, behind the main building. More of his work can be seen at the Brett Whiteley Museum in Surry Hills, see page 49. The Domain, the pleasant open park between the Art Gallery and Macquarie Place, was declared a public space in 1810. It is used as a free concert venue especially over Christmas and during the **Sydney Festival**.

→DARLING HARBOUR AND CHINATOWN

Created to celebrate Sydney's Bicentennial in 1988, revitalized Darling Harbour was delivered with much aplomb and has proved such a success that even the waves seem to show their appreciation. Day and night, ferries and catamarans bring hordes of visitors to marvel at its modern architecture and aquatic attractions or to revel in its casino and trendy waterside bars and restaurants. Framed against the backdrop of the CBD, it is intricately colourful, urban and angular. In contrast, the Chinese Garden of Friendship towards the southwestern fringe provides a little serenity before giving way to the old and chaotic enclave of Chinatown, the epicentre of Sydney's Asian community and the city's most notable living monument to its cosmopolitan populace.

SYDNEY AQUARIUM

ⓘ *Aquarium Pier, T8251 7800, www.sydneyaquarium.com.au, 0900-2200, $35, children $20, concessions $23, Explorer bus stop 21.*

This modern, well-presented aquarium has over 650 species, but it's not all about fish. On show is an imaginative array of habitats housing saltwater crocodiles, frogs, seals, penguins and platypuses. The highlight of the aquarium is the Great Barrier Reef Oceanarium: a huge tank that gives you an incredible insight into the world's largest living thing. Of course, many visit the aquarium to come face-to-face with some of Australia's deadliest sea creatures, without getting their feet, or indeed their underwear, wet.

SYDNEY WILDLIFE WORLD

ⓘ *T9333 9288, www.sydneywildlifeworld.com.au, 0900-2200, $35, children $20, (VIP guided tours available from $210 for two), Explorer bus stop 21.*

Established in 2006, this highly commercial attraction has 65 exhibits hosting 100 native Australian species and offers a more convenient and less time-consuming alternative to Taronga Zoo. Far more compact, it showcases nine impressive habitat exhibits, from the 'Flight Canyon' to the 'Nocturnal', housing all the usual suspects from the ubiquitous koala to the lesser-known and eminently appealing bilby. Although commercial profit is of course the primary goal here, cynics can rest assured that Sydney Wildlife World, in partnership with the Australian Wildlife Conservancy, has established the Sydney Wildlife World Conservation Foundation, through which funds will be raised to help safeguard Australia's threatened wildlife and ecosystems.

NATIONAL MARITIME MUSEUM

ⓘ *2 Murray St, T9298 3777, www.anmm.gov.au, 0930-1700, galleries and exhibitions $7, children and concessions $3.50; Big ticket (galleries and exhibitions, all vessels and Kids on Deck) $25 child and concessions $10. It is easily reached on foot across the Pyrmont Bridge, or by Monorail, LightRail or Explorer bus, stop No 19.*

The museum, designed to look like the sails of a ship, offers a fine mix of old and new. For many, its biggest attractions are without doubt the warship *HMAS Vampire* and the submarine *HMAS Onslow*, the centrepieces of a fleet of old vessels sitting outside on the harbour. Both can be thoroughly explored with the help of volunteer guides. The museum interior contains a range of displays exploring Australia's close links with all things nautical, from the early navigators and the First Fleet, to the ocean liners that brought many waves of immigrants. Don't miss the beautifully restored replica of the *Endeavour*, Captain Cook's famous ship of discovery, and the 1874 square-rigger, the *James Craig,* both of which are moored to the north of the museum at Wharf 7. Other museum attractions include a café, sailing lessons and a range of short cruises on historical vessels. Occasionally you can even take a multi-day voyage on board the *Endeavour* – but at a price!

SYDNEY FISH MARKET

ⓘ *T9004 1100, www.sydneyfishmarket.com.au, tours operate Mon, Thu and Fri from 0645, from $25, children $12 (book ahead on T9004 1143). Sydney Light Rail runs by, or catch bus 443 from Circular Quay or 501 from Town Hall, Explorer bus stop 19.*

For anyone interested in sea creatures, the spectacle of the Sydney Fish Market is recommended. Every morning from 0530, nearly 3000 crates of seafood are auctioned to a lively bunch of 200 buyers using a computerized clock system. The best way to see the action, and more importantly the incredible diversity of species, is to join a tour group, which will give you access to the auction floor. Normally the general public are confined to the viewing deck high above the floor. Also within the market complex are cafés, some excellent seafood eateries and a superb array of open markets where seafood can be bought at competitive prices.

POWERHOUSE MUSEUM

ⓘ *500 Harris St, Ultimo, T9217 0111, www.powerhousemuseum.com, 1000-1700, $12, children $6, concessions $5. Monorail, LightRail or Explorer bus stop No 15.*

With nearly 400,000 items collected over 120 years, the Powerhouse is the state's largest museum and half a day is barely enough to cover its floors. Housed in the former Ultimo Power Station, there is an impressive range of memorabilia, from aircraft to musical instruments, mainly with an emphasis on Australian innovation and achievement, and covering a wide range of general topics from science and technology to transportation, social history, fashion and design. There's a shop and café on site.

CHINATOWN

The Chinese have been an integral part of Sydney culture since the gold rush of the mid-1800s, though today Chinatown is also the focus of many other Asian cultures, including Vietnamese, Thai, Korean and Japanese. The district offers a lively diversion, with its heart being the Dixon Street pedestrian precinct, between the two pagoda gates facing Goulburn Street and Hay Street. Here, and in the surrounding streets, you will find a wealth of Asian shops and restaurants. At the northwestern corner of Chinatown is the **Chinese Garden of Friendship** ① *T9240 8500, www.chinesegarden.com.au, 0930-1700. $6, children $3, families $15,* which was gifted to NSW by its sister Chinese province, Guangdong, to celebrate the Australian Bicentenary in 1988. It contains all the usual beautiful craftsmanship, landscaping and aesthetics.

In stark contrast is **Paddy's Market** ① *corner of Hay St and Thomas St, 0900-1700*, one of Sydney's largest, oldest and liveliest markets, though somewhat tacky.

→CITY WEST

GLEBE

① *Bus from George St in the city (Nos 431 or 434).*

To the southwest of Darling Harbour, beyond Ultimo, and separated by the campus of **Sydney University** (Australia's oldest), are Glebe and Newtown. Glebe prides itself on having a New Age-village atmosphere, where a cosmopolitan, mainly student crowd sits in the laid-back cafés and browses old-style bookshops or bohemian fashion outlets. The **Saturday market** ① *Glebe Public School, Glebe Point Rd, T0419-291449, Sat 0930-1630,* provides an outlet for local crafts people to sell their work as well as bric-a-brac, clothes, etc.

NEWTOWN

① *Bus from Loftus St on Circular Quay, or George St (Nos 422, 423, 426, 428). The Newtown Railway Station is on the Inner West/Bankstown (to Liverpool) lines.*

South beyond the university is **King Street**, the hub of Newtown's idiosyncratic range of shops, cafés and restaurants. Here you can purchase anything from a black leather codpiece to an industrial-size brass Buddha, drool over the menus of a vast range of interesting eateries, or simply idle over a latte and watch a more alternative world go by. A few hours' exploration, Sunday brunch or an evening meal in Newtown's King Street is recommended. Don't miss **Gould's Book Arcade** at 32 King Street, www.goulds books.com.au.

LEICHHARDT

① *Bus Nos 436-438 or 440 from Circular Quay.*

Although receiving less attention than the eccentricities of Glebe and Newtown, Leichhardt is a pleasant suburb, famous for its Italian connections and subsequently its eateries and cafés. There are numerous places on Norton Street to enjoy a fine espresso, gelato or the full lasagne.

BALMAIN
ⓘ Bus from the QVB, Nos 441-444, or ferry from Circular Quay, Wharf 5.

Straddling Johnstons Bay and connecting Darling Harbour and Pyrmont with the peninsula suburb of Balmain is Sydney's second landmark bridge, the **Anzac Bridge**, opened in 1995. It is a modern and strangely attractive edifice, which makes an admirable attempt to compete with the mighty Harbour Bridge. The former working-class suburb of Balmain has undergone a quiet metamorphosis to become an area with some of the most sought after real estate in Sydney. The main drag of **Darling Street** now boasts an eclectic range of gift shops, modern cafés, restaurants and pubs, which provide a pleasant half-day escape from the city centre. Try the cosy **Sir William Wallace Hotel**, 31 Cameron Street, or the more traditional and historic 1857 **Dry Dock Hotel**, corner of Cameron and College streets. There's a popular Saturday market in the grounds of St Andrew's Church.

SYDNEY OLYMPIC PARK
ⓘ Centre, corner of Showground Rd and Murray Rose Av, near Olympic Park Railway Station, T9714 7888, www.sydneyolympicpark.com.au, 0900-1700, by train or RiverCat from Circular Quay (Wharf 5) to Homebush Bay Wharf.

Although the vast swathes of Sydney's Western Suburbs remain off the radar for the vast majority of tourists, there are a few major and minor sights worth a mention. Topping the list is the multi-million-dollar Sydney Olympic Park, about 14 km west of the centre, with its mighty stadium, the centrepiece of a vast array of architecturally stunning sports venues and public amenities. Tours of the venues by bus or bike are available; see the visitor centre at 1 Showground Road for details.

ANZ Stadium (formerly Stadium Australia) was the main focus of the games, being the venue for the opening and closing ceremonies, as well as track and field and soccer events. Although the Olympic flame has long been extinguished, it remains an important national venue for international and national Rugby Union, Rugby League, Aussie Rules football and soccer matches. Olympic Park was also the main venue for Catholic World Youth Day, and associated visit of Pope Benedict XVI in 2008, attracting well over 100,000 worshippers.

Next door is the state-of-the-art **Acer Arena**, which hosted basketball and gymnastics during the games and now offers a huge indoor arena for a range of public events from music concerts to Australia's largest agricultural show, the Royal Easter Show. Perhaps the most celebrated venue during the games was the **Aquatic Centre**, where the triumphant Aussie swimming team took on the world and won with the help of such stars as Ian Thorpe and Michael Klim. The complex still holds international swimming and diving events and is open to the public. The Olympic Park has many other state-of-the-art sports facilities and is surrounded by superb parkland. **Bicentennial Park** *ⓘ T9714 7524*, is a 100-ha mix of dry land and conservation wetland and a popular spot for walking, jogging, birdwatching or simply feeding the ducks.

PARRAMATTA AND AROUND
About 6 km further west from Homebush is Parramatta, often dubbed the city within the city, a culturally diverse centre that boasts some of the nation's most historic sites. After

the First Fleeters failed in their desperate attempts to grow crops in what is now the city centre, they penetrated the upper reaches of the Parramatta River and established a farming settlement, first known as Rose Hill before reverting to its original Aboriginal name. The oldest European site is **Elizabeth Farm** ① *70 Alice St, Rosehill, T9635 9488, 0930-1600, $8, children $4, family $17*, a 1793 colonial homestead built for John and Elizabeth Macarthur, pioneers in the Australian wool industry. The homestead contains a number of interesting displays and is surrounded by a recreated 1830s garden. Also of interest is the 1799 **Old Government House** ① *T9635 8149, Fri-Sun 0930-1600, $8*, in Parramatta Park. It is Australia's oldest public building and houses a fine collection of colonial furniture. **Experiment Farm Cottage** ① *9 Ruse St, T9635 5655, Tue-Fri 1030-1530, Sat-Sun 1130-1530, $7*, is the site of the colonial government's first land grant to former convict James Ruse in 1791. The cottage itself dates from 1834. The **Parramatta River**, which quietly glides past the city, is without doubt its most attractive natural feature and it offers a number of heritage walking trails. These and many other historical details are displayed at the **Parramatta Heritage and VIC** ① *346a Church St, T8839 3311, www.parracity.nsw.gov.au, daily 0900-1700*.

→CITY EAST

KINGS CROSS

① *By bus Sydney Explorer stop No 6 or regular bus services Nos 311, 323-325, 327, 333.*

Even before arriving in Sydney you will have probably heard of Kings Cross, the notorious hub of Sydney nightlife and the long-established focus of sex, drugs and rock and roll. Situated near the navy's Woolloomooloo docks, 'the Cross' (as it's often called) has been a favourite haunt of visiting sailors for years. The main drag, **Darlinghurst Road**, is the focus of the action, while Victoria Street is home to a rash of backpacker hostels. At the intersection of both, and the top of William Street, which connects the Cross with the city, is the huge Coca Cola sign, a popular meeting point. The best time to visit the Cross is in the early hours when the bars, the clubs and the ladies of the night are all in full swing. It is enormously popular with backpackers and Sydneysiders alike and can provide a great night out. It is also a great place to meet people, make contacts, find work and even buy a car.

Amid all the mania there are a number of notable and more sedate sights in and around Kings Cross. **Elizabeth Bay House** ① *7 Onslow Av, Elizabeth Bay, T9356 3022, www.hht.nsw.gov.au, Tue-Sun 1000-1630, $8, children $4, family $17*, is a revival-style estate built by popular architect John Verge for Colonial Secretary Alexander Macleay in 1845. The interior is restored and faithfully furnished in accordance with the times and the house has a great outlook across the harbour.

WOOLLOOMOOLOO

To the northwest of Kings Cross, through the quieter and more upmarket sanctuary of Potts Point, is the delightfully named suburb of Woolloomooloo. 'Woo' is the main east coast base for the Australian Navy and visiting sailors also weigh anchor here, heading straight for the Kings Cross souvenir shops. Other than the warships and a scattering of lively pubs, it is the **Woolloomooloo Wharf** and a pie cart that are the major attractions. The wharf has a rash of fine restaurants that are a popular dining alternative to the busy city centre. If the wharf restaurants are beyond your budget, nearby is one of Sydney's best cheap eateries. **Harry's Café de Wheels**, near the wharf entrance, is an institution, selling its own range of meat, mash, pea and gravy pies 24 hours a day (well, almost).

DARLINGHURST AND SURRY HILLS

The lively suburb of Darlinghurst fringes the city to the east, Kings Cross to the north and Surry Hills to the south. Both Darlinghurst and Surry Hills offer some great restaurants and cafés with Darlinghurst Road and Victoria Street, just south of Kings Cross, being the main focus. Here you will find some of Sydney's most popular eateries. The **Jewish Museum** ① *148 Darlinghurst Rd, T9360 7999, www.sydneyjewishmuseum.com.au, Sun-Thu 1000-1600, Fri 1000-1400, $10, children $7*, has displays featuring the Holocaust and the history of Judaism in Australia. To get to Darlinghurst, take bus No 311.

Surry Hills is a mainly residential district and does not have quite the pizzazz of Darlinghurst, but it is well known for its traditional Aussie pubs, which seem to dominate every street corner. One thing not to miss is the **Brett Whiteley Museum and Gallery** ① *2 Raper St, T9225 1881, Sat-Sun 1000-1600, free*. The museum is the former studio and home of the late Whiteley, one of Sydney's most popular contemporary artists. Both places can be reached on foot from the city via William Street, Liverpool Street or Oxford Street or by bus Nos 311-399.

PADDINGTON

① *By foot from southeast corner of Hyde Park via Oxford St, bus Nos 378-382.*
The big attraction in Paddington is **Oxford Street**, which stretches east from the city and southwest corner of Hyde Park to the northwest corner of Centennial Park and Bondi Junction. The city end of Oxford Street, surrounding Taylor Square, is one of the most happening areas of the city with a string of cheap eateries, cafés, restaurants, clubs and bars. It is also a major focus for the city's gay community. As Oxford Street heads west into Paddington proper it's lined with boutique clothes shops, art and bookshops, cafés and some good pubs. Many people coincide a visit to Oxford Street with the colourful **Paddington Market** ① *395 Oxford St, T9331 2923*, held every Saturday from 1000. Behind Oxford Street, heading north, are leafy suburbs lined with Victorian terrace houses, interspersed with commercial art galleries and old pubs, all of which are hallmarks of Paddington.

South of Oxford Street is the **Victoria Barracks**, a base for British and Australian Army battalions since 1848. It remains fully functional and visitors can see a flag-raising ceremony, and a marching band and join a guided tour on Thursdays at 1000.

Just to the south of the Barracks, in **Moore Park**, is the famous **Sydney Cricket Ground** (SCG) and, next door, the **Sydney Football Stadium** (SFS). The hallowed arena of the SCG is a veritable cathedral of cricket, considered by many as Australia's national sport. In winter the SCG is taken over by the Sydney Swans Australian Rules football team. The Sydney Football Stadium was, for many years, the focus of major national and international, Rugby Union, League and soccer matches but it now plays second fiddle to the mighty (and far less atmospheric) Telstra Stadium in Homebush. Tours of SCG and SFS are available to the public, Mon-Fri 1000, 1200 and 1400, Sat 1000, from $30, T1300 724737, www.sydneycricketground.com.au.

Fringing the two stadiums and Fox Studios Complex is **Centennial Park**, the city's largest green space. It provides a vast area for walking, cycling, horse riding, rollerblading and birdwatching. The Parklands Sports Centre also provides facilities for tennis, rollerhockey and basketball. In late summer there is a nightly outdoor **Moonlight Cinema** programme ① *www.moonlight.com.au*, which often showcases old classics.

WATSON'S BAY

① Ferry from Circular Quay, Wharves 2 and 4, or bus No 342 or 325.

Watson's Bay, on the leeward side of **South Head**, guarding the mouth of Sydney Harbour, provides an ideal city escape and is best reached by ferry from Circular Quay. As well as being home to one of Sydney's oldest and most famous seafood restaurants – Doyle's – it offers some quiet coves, attractive swimming beaches and peninsula walks. The best beaches are to be found at **Camp Cove** about 10 minutes' walk north of the ferry terminal. A little further north is **Lady Bay Beach**, which is very secluded and a popular naturist beach. The best walk in the area is the one- to two-hour jaunt to the 1858 **Hornby Lighthouse** and South Head itself, then south to the **HMAS Watson Naval Chapel** and the area known as **The Gap**. The area also boasts some interesting historical sites. Camp Cove was used by Governor Phillip as an overnight stop before reaching Port Jackson in the Inner Harbour. **Vaucluse House** ① *Wentworth Rd, T9388 7922, Fri-Sun 1000-1630, $8, children $4, family $17*, was built in 1827 and is a fine example of an early colonial estate. Many people spend a morning exploring Watson's Bay before enjoying a leisurely lunch at Doyle's, which sits just above the beach and ferry terminal on Marine Parade, or next door at the **Watson's Bay Hotel**, a more casual affair offering equally good views of the city skyline and a superb outdoor barbecue area (see box, page 53).

BONDI, BRONTE AND COOGEE BEACHES

① By car from the city, via Oxford St, by the Bondi and Bay Explorer, or buses Nos 321, 322, 365, 366 and 380. By rail go to Bondi Junction (Illawara Line) then take the bus (as above). For Coogee, bus Nos 372-374 and 314-315.

Bondi Beach is by far the most famous of Sydney's many ocean beaches. Its hugely inviting stretch of sand is a prime venue for surfing, swimming and sunbathing. Behind the beach, Bondi's bustling waterfront and village offers a tourist trap of cafés, restaurants, bars, surf and souvenir shops. For years Bondi has been a popular suburb for alternative lifestylers and visiting backpackers keen to avoid the central city. It is also the place to see or be seen by all self-respecting beautiful people. If you intend swimming at Bondi note that, like every Australian beach, it is subject to dangerous rips, so always swim between the yellow and red flags, clearly visible on the beach. Watchful lifeguards, also clad in yellow and red, are on hand. Bondi Beach is the focus of wild celebrations on Christmas Day with one huge beach party, usually culminating in a mass naked dash into the sea.

To the south of Bondi Beach and best reached by a popular coastal walkway is the small oceanside suburb of **Bronte**. This little enclave offers a smaller, quieter and equally attractive beach with a number of very popular cafés frequented especially at the weekend for brunch. A little further south is **Clovelly**, which has another sheltered beach good for kids and snorkelling. Many people finish their walk at **Coogee**, which has a fine beach and bustling waterfront. Although playing second fiddle to Bondi, it is popular with those keen to stay near the beach and outside the centre.

NORTH SYDNEY AND SURROUNDS

On the northern side of the Harbour Bridge a small stand of high-rise buildings with neon signs heralds the mainly commercial suburb of North Sydney. There is little here for the tourist to justify a special visit, but nearby, the suburb of **McMahons Point**, and more especially **Blues Point Reserve**, on the shores of Lavender Bay, offer fine city views. Another good vantage point is right below the bridge at **Milsons Point**. Kirribilli is a serene little suburb lying directly to the east of the bridge. **Admiralty House** and **Kirribilli House**, the Sydney residences of the governor general and the prime minister, sit overlooking the Opera House on Kirribilli Point. Both are closed to the public and are best seen from the water.

MOSMAN

ⓘ *By ferry from Circular Quay (Wharf 4) to Mosman Bay where buses run uphill to the commercial centre.*

Mosman has a very pleasant village feel and its well-heeled residents are rightly proud. Situated so close to the city centre, it has developed into one of the most exclusive and expensive areas of real estate in the city. However, don't let this put you off. Mosman, in unison with its equally comfy, neighbouring beachside suburb of **Balmoral**, are both great escapes by ferry from the city centre and offer some fine eateries, designer clothes shops, walks and beaches, plus one of Sydney's must-see attractions, **Taronga Zoo**.

TARONGA ZOO

ⓘ *T9969 2777, www.zoo.nsw.gov.au, 0900-1700, $44, children $22, concessions $32. Zoo Pass combo ticket (including ferry transfers and zoo), $51.50, children $26. Best reached by ferry from Circular Quay (Wharf 2), every 30 mins Mon-Fri from 0715-1845, Sat 0845-1845, Sun 0845-1745.*

First opened in 1881 in the grounds of Moore Park, south of Centennial Park, before being relocated to Bradley's Head, Mosman, in 1916, Taronga contains all the usual suspects of the zoological world. It also has the huge added attraction of perhaps the best location and views of any city zoo in the world. You will almost certainly need a full day to explore the various exhibits on offer and there are plenty of events staged throughout the day to keep both adults and children entertained. The best of these is the Free Flight Bird Show, which is staged twice daily in an open-air arena overlooking the city. If you are especially interested in wildlife it pays to check out the dynamic programme of specialist public tours on offer. The Night Zoo tour after hours is especially popular. Taronga is built on a hill and the general recommendation is to go up to the main entrance then work your way back down to the lower gate. Or for a small additional charge on entry you can take a scenic gondola ride to the main gate.

BALMORAL, MIDDLE HEAD AND BRADLEY'S HEAD

Balmoral Beach is one of the most popular and sheltered in the harbour. Here, more than anywhere else in the city, you can observe Sydneysiders enjoying something that is quintessentially Australian – the early morning, pre-work dip. Balmoral Beach overlooks **Middle Harbour**, whose waters infiltrate far into the suburbs of the North Shore. On **Middle Head**, which juts out into the harbour beyond Mosman, you will find one of Sydney's best and most secluded naturist beaches – **Cobblers Beach**. The atmosphere is friendly and the crowd truly cosmopolitan, though less extrovert visitors should probably

SYDNEY LISTINGS

WHERE TO STAY

Circular Quay and the Rocks

$$$ Lord Nelson Pub and Hotel, corner of Kent St and Argyle St, The Rocks, T9251 4044, www.lordnelson.com.au. This historic hotel has some very pleasant, new and affordable en suites above the pub. The added attraction here is the home-brewed beer, food and general ambience. The pub closes fairly early at night, so noise is not usually a factor.

$$$-$$ YHA The Rocks, 110 Cumberland St, T8272 0900, www.yha.com.au. Hugely popular given its location and its views right across Circular Quay to the Opera House and beyond. Many of the multishare and double/twin en suites have views and the rooftop deck is something many 5-star hotels in the area cannot match. It has all the regular, reliable YHA features and facilities. Limited (paid) parking near the hostel. Recommended.

City East

$$$$ L'Otel, 114 Darlinghurst Rd, Darlinghurst, T9360 6868, www.lotel.com.au. Classy, yet given its minimalist decor perhaps not everyone's cup of tea. Ultra hip and very much a place for the modern couple. Excellent personable service and a fine restaurant attached.

$$$$ Watson's Bay Hotel, T9337 5444, www.watsonsbayhotel.com.au. Set alongside the legendary seafood restaurant (see page 53) is this fabulous boutique hotel with 32 suites, each with its own breathtaking view from the balcony. Easily reached by ferry.

$$$$-$$$ Coogee Bay Boutique Hotel, 9 Vicar St, Coogee, T9665 0000, www.coogeebay hotel.com.au. Very pleasant, boutique-style rooms in addition to good, traditional pub-style options. Well-appointed, en suite, ocean views and good value. The hotel itself is a main social focus in Coogee both day and night.

City West

$$$$ Trickett's Luxury B&B, 270 Glebe Point Rd, T9552 1141, www.tricketts.com.au. A beautifully restored Victorian mansion, decorated with antiques and Persian rugs and offering spacious, well-appointed en suites.

City North

$$$ 101 Addison B&B, 101 Addison Rd, T9977 6216, www.bb-manly.com. For a fine B&B option in Manly try this historic 1-bedroom gem. Open fire, grand piano; say no more! Book well ahead.

$$$-$$ Glenferrie Lodge, 12A Carabella St, T1800 121011, T9955 1685, www.glenferrielodge.com. A vast, 70-room Victorian mansion with quality budget accommodation. The range of shared, single, twin, double, queen/king deluxe are above average with some having their own balconies. A good buffet breakfast is on offer as part of their B&B package. Wi-Fi.

avoid the peninsula on the eastern edge of the beach. Access is via a little-known track behind the softball pitch near the end of Military Road. You can also walk to the tip of Middle Head, where old wartime fortifications look out across North Head and the harbour entrance, or enjoy the walk to the tip of **Bradley's Head**, below the zoo, with its wonderful views of the city.

City Centre, Circular Quay and the Rocks

$$ Café Sydney, Level 5, Customs House, 31 Alfred St, T9251 8683. Daily for lunch, Mon-Sat for dinner. Set high above Circular Quay at the top of Customs House, this place offers superb views and alfresco dining. The food is traditional modern Australian with a good atmosphere and occasional live jazz.

$$ Forty One, Chifley Tower, 2 Chifley Square, T9221 2500, www.forty-one.com.au. Enjoys an international reputation for quality fine dining. Stunning views across the Botanical Gardens and harbour. Intimate yet relaxed atmosphere. Book well ahead.

City East

$$$ Doyle's on the Beach, 11 Marine Pde, Watsons Bay, T9337 2007, www.doyles.com.au. Daily lunch and dinner. Sydney's best-known restaurant for years. It has been in the same family for generations and has an unfaltering reputation for superb seafood, atmosphere and harbour/city views, which all combine to make it a one of the best dining experiences in the city, if not Australia. If you can, book well ahead and ask for a balcony seat. Sun afternoons are especially popular and you could combine the trip with a walk around the heads. Book well ahead.

City West

$$ Boathouse on Blackwattle Bay, Ferry Rd, T9518 9011, www.boathouse.net.au. Tue-Sun lunch and dinner. A quality upmarket (yet informal) seafood restaurant offering refreshingly different harbour views than those sought at Circular Quay and Darling Harbour. Here you can watch the lights of Anzac Bridge or the comings and goings of Sydney's fishing fleet while tucking into the freshest seafood.

$ Chinta Ria – The Temple of Love, Roof Terr, Cockle Bay Wharf, 201 Sussex St, T9264 3211, www.chintaria.com. Daily for lunch and dinner. With a name like that who can resist? Great aesthetics, buzzing atmosphere with quality Malaysian cuisine.

MANLY

ⓘ *By ferry from Circular Quay (Wharves 2 and 3), $7, children $3.50, 30 mins, or the JetCat, $9, child $6, 15 mins. Both leave daily on a regular basis.*

Manly is by far the most visited suburb on the North Shore and is practically a self-contained holiday resort, offering an oceanside sanctuary away from the manic city centre. The heart of the community sits on the neck of the **North Head** peninsula, which guards the entrance of Sydney Harbour. **Manly Beach** is very much the main attraction. At its southern end, an attractive oceanside walkway connects Manly Beach with two smaller, quieter alternatives, **Fairy Bower Beach** and **Shelly Beach**. As you might expect, Manly comes with all the tourist trappings, including an attractive, tree-lined waterfront, fringed with cafés, restaurants and shops and a wealth of accommodation options.

Connecting Manly Beach with the ferry terminal and **Manly Cove** (on the western or harbour side) is the **Corso**, a fairly tacky pedestrian precinct lined with cheap eateries, bars and souvenir shops. Its only saving grace is the market held at its eastern end every weekend. **Oceanworld** ⓘ *T8251 7877, www.oceanworld.com.au, 1000-1730, $20, children $12, concessions $14, regular tours available, 'Swim with the sharks' from $200, sharks fed on*

Mon, Wed and Fri at 1100, a long-established aquarium, although looking tired, is still worth a visit if you have kids or fancy a swim with the star attractions on the aquarium's unusual 'Swim with the sharks' tour. **Manly Art Gallery and Museum** ① *T9976 1420, Tue-Sun 1000-1700, free*, showcases an interesting permanent exhibition of historical items with the obvious emphasis on all things 'beach', while the gallery offers both permanent and temporary shows of contemporary art and photography. The 10-km **Manly Scenic Walkway** from Manly to Spit Bridge is an excellent scenic harbour walk, arguably the city's best. Meandering through bush and along beaches while gazing over the harbour, it's hard to believe that you are in the middle of Australia's biggest city. The walk starts from the end of West Esplanade, takes from three to four hours and is clearly signposted the whole way. Walk on a weekday if possible: Sundays can be very busy.

NORTH HEAD

The tip of North Head, to the south of Manly, is well worth a look, if only to soak up the views across the harbour and out to sea. The cityscape is especially stunning at dawn. Just follow Scenic Drive to the very end. The **Quarantine Station** ① *T9466 1500, www.q-station.com.au, tours Wed-Sat at 1500, Sun at 1000 and 1300, 2 hrs, from $25; Ghost Tours (can include lunch from $70 or dinner from $99) Wed-Sun 1930, 3 hrs, from $44; Family Tour Thu and Sun at 1800, 2 hrs, from $34, children $22, bookings recommended, bus No 135 from Manly wharf*, taking up a large portion of the peninsula, was used from 1832 to harbour ships known to be carrying diseases like smallpox, bubonic plague, cholera and Spanish influenza to protect the new colony from the spread of such nasties. The station closed in 1984 and is now administered by the NSW Parks and Wildlife Service. Luxury accommodation is available at the Quarantine Station and there is a good restaurant.

NORTHERN BEACHES

The coast north of Manly is indented by numerous bays and fine beaches that stretch 40 km to **Barrenjoey Head** at Broken Bay and the entrance to the Hawkesbury River harbour. Perhaps the most popular of these are **Narrabeen**, **Avalon** and **Whale Beach**, but there are many to choose from. Narrabeen has the added attraction of a large lake, used for sailing, canoeing and windsurfing, while Avalon and Whale Beach, further north, are smaller, quite picturesque and more sheltered. A day trip to the very tip of Barrenjoey Head is recommended and the area is complemented by **Palm Beach**, a popular weekend getaway with some fine restaurants. This is also where most of the day-to-day filming takes place for the popular Australian 'soapie' *Home and Away*. There are many water activities on offer in the area focused mainly on **Pittwater**, a large bay on the sheltered western side of the peninsula. Whether you come for a day trip or a weekend stay get hold of the free *Northern Beaches Visitors' Guide* from the Sydney VIC. The L90 bus from Wynyard goes via all the main northern beach suburbs to Palm Beach, every 30 minutes.

BLUE MOUNTAINS

The 'Blues', as they are affectionately known, form part of the Great Dividing Range, 70 km, or two hours, west of Sydney, and contain no less than five national parks covering a total area of 10,000 sq km. They are not really mountains at all, but a network of eroded river valleys, gorges, and bluffs, that have formed over millions of years. The result is a huge wonderland of natural features, from precipitous cliffs, to dramatic waterfalls and canyons, not to mention the most dramatic limestone caves on the continent. Once the home of the Daruk Aboriginals, the Blue Mountains were seen by the first Europeans merely as a highly inconvenient barrier to the interior and for almost a quarter of a century they remained that way, before finally being traversed in 1813 by explorers Blaxland, Wentworth and Lawson. To this day the impenetrable geography still limits transportation and essentially the same two convict-built roads and railway line completed over a century ago reach west through a string of settlements from Glenbrook to Lithgow on the other side. For decades the 'Blues' have been a favourite weekend or retirement destination for modern-day Sydney escapees, who welcome the distinctly cooler temperatures and the colourful seasons that the extra elevation creates. But superb scenery and climate aside, there are some excellent walking opportunities, as well as abseiling, canyoning and rock climbing. Given the region's popularity there are also a glut of good restaurants and a wide range of places to stay from showpiece backpackers to romantic hideaways.

→VISITING THE BLUE MOUNTAINS

GETTING AROUND

The route through the Blue Mountains is easily negotiable. From the west (Sydney) you take the M4 (toll), eventually crossing the Neapean River, before it forms the Great Western Highway at Glenbrook (65 km). Then you pass through Blaxland, Springwood, Faulconbridge and Woodford before arriving at Wentworth Falls. Here you reach the top of the main plateau at an average height of just above 1000 m. From Wentworth Falls the road then continues west through the northern edges of Leura and Katoomba, then north, through the heart of Blackheath and Mount Victoria. From Mount Victoria you then begin the descent to Lithgow (154 km). The rather peculiarly named Bells Line of Road provides another access point across the mountains from Windsor on the east to Mount Victoria on the Great Western Highway (77 km). Katoomba is the largest of the towns and has the best amenities.

MOVING ON

You can either go via Sydney and the coastal highway towards Newcastle to the Lower Hunter Valley, which is two hours (160 km) from the capital. Alternatively, you can head from the Bells Line of Road in the Blue Mountains towards Windsor and then head north along the inland scenic Route 69, which also brings you to the Upper Hunter Valley.

TOURIST INFORMATION

The main accredited VICs are in **Glenbrook**, **Katoomba** ⓘ *Echo Point, T1300 653408, www.visitbluemountains.com.au, daily 0900-1700,* **Lithgow** ⓘ *Great Western Highway, T6350 3230, www.tourism.lithgow.com, 0900-1700,* and **Oberon** (west, near the Jenolan Caves). The main NPWS office is at the **Heritage Centre** ⓘ *near Govetts Leap, Blackheath,*

T4787 8877, www.nationalparks.nsw.gov.au. If you are approaching from the east, stop at the Glenbrook VIC to begin with and stock up with the free visitor's guide and maps. All regional centres also offer a free accommodation bookings service. The NPWS stock a wide range of books covering the numerous walks within the national parks, as well as topographical maps.ngs you to the Upper Hunter Valley.

→THE NATIONAL PARKS

The Blue Mountains region contains five national parks which cover an area of 10,000 sq km, with half of that being considered 'wilderness area'. The largest, at an expansive 4876 sq km (and the second largest in the state after Kosciuszko National Park) is **Wollemi National Park**, to the north of the Bells Line of Road. It incorporates the state's most extensive officially recognized wilderness area and is very rugged and inaccessible. As well as its complex geology, topography, Aboriginal art sites and botanical features, it is also home to a rich variety of birds. Of all the parks in the region it is the one for the well-prepared modern-day explorer. There are basic NPWS campsites at Wheeny Creek, Colo Meroo, Dun's Swamp and Newnes. The main access is from Putty Road, 100 km northwest of Sydney or via Rylstone.

The most famous and accessible park is the 2470-sq-km **Blue Mountains National Park**, straddling the Great Western Highway and a string of mountain villages and towns, from Glenbrook in the east to Lithgow in the west. Only recently expanded in the 1980s, it contains natural features that range from deep canyons and forested valleys to pinnacles and waterfalls, as well as an abundance of flora and fauna. Although now receiving over one million visitors a year, much of the park remains extremely inaccessible, with over 500 sq km considered official wilderness area. Sadly, the Blue Mountains, like so many national parks in NSW, has suffered in recent years from the temporary impact of widespread bush fires. There are basic NPWS campsites at Euroka Clearing near Glenbrook, Ingar near Wentworth Falls and Perry's Lookdown near Blackheath. You can also camp anywhere within 500 m from roads and facilities. Access is from many points east and west off the Great Western Highway, or from the Bells Line of Road 70 km west of Sydney.

To the southeast of Kanangra-Boyd and the Blue Mountains National Parks is the 860-sq-km **Nattai National Park**. It touches the region's largest body of water, Lake Burragorang, and contains the region's largest populations of eastern grey kangaroos as well as many rare plants and animals. NPWS camping near the lake. Access is 110 km south of Sydney between Warragamba Dam and Wombeyan Caves Road.

GLENBROOK TO WENTWORTH FALLS
Proud of its European roots and its railway heritage, the pretty village of Glenbrook, just beyond the Nepean River, acts as the unofficial gateway to the Blue Mountains. Along with Katoomba this is the main tourism administration and information centre for the Blue Mountains. **NPWS Conservation Hut** ① *Fletcher St (off Falls Rd), T4757 3827*, can provide walks information and has a small shop and café. **Glenbrook VIC** ① *off the Great Western Highway, T1300 653408, www.visitbluemountains.com.au, daily 0900-1700*.

Fringing the village, south of the highway, is the southern section of the Blue Mountains National Park and access to numerous attractions, including the **Red Hands Cave**, a fine example of Aboriginal rock art. The distinctive hand stencils made on the cave wall are thought to be over 1600 years old. You can reach the cave either by road or by foot (8 km return) from the Glenbrook Creek causeway, just beyond the park entrance. There are also shorter walks to the **Jellybean Pool** and the **Euroka Clearing**, a basic NPWS campsite and the ideal spot to see grey kangaroos, especially early or late in the day. To reach the park gate ($7 per day, walkers free), take Ross Road behind the VIC onto Burfitt Parade and then follow Bruce Road. The lookouts at **The Bluff**, at the end of Brook Road (slightly further east off Burfitt, then Grey), are also worth a look. North of the highway in Glenbrook you can also follow signs to the **Lennox Bridge**, the oldest in Australia, built by convicts in 1833.

Beyond Blaxland and Springwood is the small settlement of **Faulconbridge**, home to the **Norman Lindsay Gallery and Museum** ⓘ *T4751 1067, www.norman lindsay.com.au, $12, children $6*. Lindsay (1879-1969) is just one of many noted artists who found the Blue Mountains conducive to their creativity and his studio remains very much the way he left it. For most, it is the stunning lookouts across **Wentworth Falls** and the **Jamieson Valley** that offer the first memorable introduction to the dramatic scenery of the Blue Mountains – assuming the weather is clear, of course. The car park is the starting point for some superb walking tracks, the best of which is the four-hour **Wentworth Pass Walk** that crosses the top of the falls and then descends precariously down to the valley floor. Then, if that were not enough, the track skirts the cliff base, through rainforest, before climbing back up via the dramatic **Valley of the Waters** gorge to the **Conservation Hut** (see above). From there it's an easy walk back to the car park. Another excellent walk is the five-hour **National Pass Walk** that follows a cutting halfway up the cliff, carved out in the 1890s. Both walks involve steep sections around cliff edges and laddered sections, but if you have a head for heights either one is highly recommended. Give yourself plenty of time and make sure you get maps from the Conservation Hut before you set out.

For something less demanding, try the **Den Fenella Track**, which will take you to some good lookouts, then you can return or preferably keep going (west) to the Conservation Hut along the **Overcliff Track**. Better still, is the magical **Undercliff Track** to **Princes Rock Lookout**.

LEURA

Although the pretty village of Leura plays second fiddle to Katoomba, the two essentially merge into one. Possessing a distinct air of elegance, the residents of Leura are proud of their village and in particular their gardens. **Everglades Gardens** ⓘ *37 Everglades Av, T4784 1938, www.evergladesgardens.org.au, 1000-1700, $10, concessions $8, children $4*, provide the best horticultural showpiece and have done since the early 1930s. **Leuralla and NSW Toy and Railway Museum** ⓘ *36 Olympian Pde, T4784 1169, www.toyandrailway museum.com.au, 1000-1700, $10, children $2*, is well worth a look, for kids and parents alike. There are several walks and lookouts around the cliff fringes in Leura with the best being the short 500-m walk to the aptly named **Sublime Lookout**, offering arguably the best view of the Jamieson Valley and Mount Solitary. Follow signs from Gladstone Road, west of the Mall.

KATOOMBA

Considered the capital of the Blue Mountains, the erstwhile mining town of Katoomba offers an interesting mix of old and new and a truly cosmopolitan ambience. As well as the wealth of amenities and activities based in the town, many come here simply to see the classic picture-postcard view of the Blue Mountains from the famous **Three Sisters lookout**. The steady stream of tourist traffic flows down Katoomba's main drag towards **Echo Point** to enjoy this view. It is little wonder the place is so popular. Built precariously 170 m above the valley floor, the lookout seems to defy gravity. Dawn and sunset are the best times to visit. From the lookout it is possible to walk around to the stacks and descend the taxing **Giant Stairway Walk** (30 minutes) to the valley floor. From there you join the **Federal Pass Track**, back through the forest below the cliffs to the **Katoomba Cascades** and **Orphan Rock** (a lone pillar that became separated from the nearby cliff over many centuries of erosion). From Orphan Rock it is a short walk to a choice of exits: the hard option, on foot, up the 1000-step Furbers Steps, or for the less adventurous, the Scenic Railway, see below. Give yourself three hours.

Katoomba presents many other excellent walking options, including the **Narrow Neck Plateau** (variable times) and the **Ruined Castle** (12 km, seven hours). The latter starts from the base of the Scenic Railway and can be made as part of an extended overnight trip to the summit of Mount Solitary. It's recommended, but go prepared. The **Grand Canyon** walk (5 km, four hours) from Neates Glen, Evans Lookout Road, Blackheath, is also a cracker.

West of Echo Point the junction of Cliff Drive and Violet Street will deliver you to the highly commercial **Scenic World** ① *T4782 0200, www.scenicworld.com.au, 0900-1700, Railway Skyway and Cableway $28, Skyway $16*, with its unusual scenic transportations. The

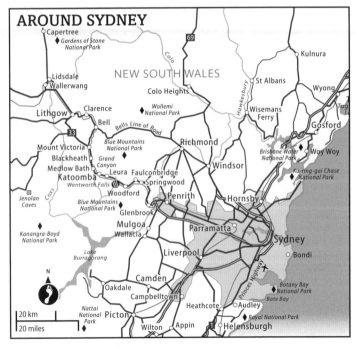

Scenic Railway option takes you on an exhilarating descent to the valley floor; on what is reputed to be the world's steepest 'inclined funicular railway'. At the bottom you can then take a boardwalk through the forest to see an old coal mine with an audiovisual display and bronze sculpture. In contrast, the **Scenic Skyway** provides a more sedate bird's-eye view of the valley floor and the surrounding cliffs. The last, and most recent, of the trio, is the **Scenic Cableway** that takes you on a 545-m ride into – or out of – the World Heritage-listed rainforest of the Jamison Valley. Once at the bottom, you can take the Scenic Walkway to the base of the Scenic Railway. In all, there are just under 3 km of elevated boardwalk, 380 m of which is accessible by wheelchair. If you survive that there is also a cinema showing a Blue Mountains documentary on demand and a revolving restaurant.

MEDLOW BATH, BLACKHEATH AND MEGALONG VALLEY

From Katoomba the Great Western Highway heads north through the pretty villages of Medlow Bath, Blackheath and Mount Victoria. Although not as commercial as their bustling neighbour, all provide excellent accommodation, restaurants and are fringed both north and south by equally stunning views and excellent walks. To the east is the easily accessible **Megalong Valley**, particularly well known for its horse trekking, with **Grose Valley** to the west. **Evans** and **Govetts Leap Lookouts**, east of Blackheath, provide the best easily accessible viewpoints, but there are also some lesser-known spots well worth a visit.

In **Medlow Bath** is the historic **Hydro Majestic Hotel**, built in 1903 and the longest building in Australia at the time. Though a hotel in its own right, its original function was as a sanatorium, offering all manner of health therapies, from the sublime – mud baths and spas – to the ridiculous – strict abstinence from alcohol. At the time the rarefied air in the Blue Mountains was hailed as a cure-all for city ills and people flocked to the Hydro. Today, although the mud baths (and thankfully the prohibition) have gone, the hotel still provides fine accommodation and a great spot for afternoon tea.

Blackheath is a sleepy little village with a lovely atmosphere, enhanced in autumn when the trees take on their golden hues. There are two lookouts well worth visiting. The first, **Evans Lookout**, is accessed east along Evans Lookout Road and provides the first of many viewpoints across the huge and dramatic expanse of the Grose Valley. One of the best walks in the region, which we recommend, the **Grand Canyon Trail**, departs from Neates Glen, off Evans Lookout Road (5 km, five hours). From there you descend through the rainforest and follow Greaves Creek through moss-covered rock tunnels and overhangs, before climbing back up to Evans Lookout. The other lookout, **Govetts Leap**, is a stunner and has the added attraction of the **Bridal Veil Falls**, the highest (but not necessarily the most dramatic), in the Blue Mountains. Just before the lookout car park is the **NPWS Heritage Centre** ⓘ *T4787 8877, www.npws.nsw.gov.au, 0900-1630*, which is worth a visit and can provide walking information, maps, guide and gifts. **Fairfax Heritage Track**, built to accommodate wheelchairs, links the centre with the lookout. From Govetts Leap you can walk either north to reach Pulpit Rock or south to Evans Lookout via the falls.

Although Govetts and Evans are both stunning, three other superb lookouts await your viewing pleasure and can be accessed from Blackheath. These are often missed, but no less spectacular. The first, **Pulpit Rock**, can be reached by foot from Govetts (2.5 km, 1½ hrs) or better still, by 2WD via (unsealed) Hat Hill Road. The lookout, which sits on the summit of a rock pinnacle, is accessed from the car park by a short 500-m walk. From the same car park then continue north to **Anvil Rock**, being sure not to miss the other short track to the bizarre geology of the wind-eroded cave. Perry Lookdown is 1 km before Anvil Rock and a path from there descends into the valley to connect with some demanding walking trails. Also well worth a visit is the aptly named **Hanging Rock**, which will, on first sight, take your breath away. Watch your footing and do not attempt to climb to the point, as tempting as it may be. It is also a favourite abseiling spot. Like all the other lookouts on the southern fringe of the Grose Valley, sunrise is by far the best time to visit. The rock can be reached along a rough, unsealed track (Ridgewell Road), on the right, just beyond Blackheath heading north. It is best suited to 4WD but if you don't have your own transport most local 4WD tours go there.

Megalong Valley, accessed on Megalong Valley Road, west of Blackheath town centre, provides a pleasant scenic drive and is one of the most accessible and most developed of the wilderness Blue Mountains valleys. **Megalong Australian Heritage Centre** ① *T4787 9116, www.megalong.cc, 0800-1730*, offers a whole range of activities from horse trekking and 4WD adventures, to livestock shows.

LITHGOW

Lithgow marks the western boundary of the Blue Mountains and was founded in 1827 by explorer Hamilton Hume. An industrial town and Australia's first producer of steel, its main tourist attraction is the remarkable Zig Zag Railway (see below), 10 km east in Clarence, as well as a scattering of historical buildings. The town also acts as the gateway to the Jenolan Caves and Kanangra-Boyd National Park to the south and the wilderness Wollemi National Park, to the north. Wollemi is one of the largest and the most inaccessible wilderness areas in NSW, a fact that was highlighted in no uncertain terms in 1994 with the discovery of the Wollemi Pine, a species that once flourished over sixty million years ago. The exact location of the small stand of trees is kept secret.

In **Clarence**, 10 km east of Lithgow, you will find the **Zig Zag Railway** ① *T6355 2955, www.zigzagrailway.com.au*, a masterpiece of engineering originally built between 1866 and 1869. Operated commercially up until 1910 as a supply route to Sydney, lovingly restored steam trains occasionally make the nostalgic 8-km (1½ hours) journey from Clarence to Bottom Points (near CityRail's Zig Zag Station). Phone for the latest schedules.

JENOLAN CAVES

① *T1300 763311, T6359 3911, www.jenolancaves.org.au, the main caves can only be visited by guided tour, daily from 1000-2000. Cave combo tickets from $30-$40. Caving adventure tours are also an option, costing from $80-$200.*

The Jenolan Caves, on the northern fringe of the Kanangra-Boyd National Park, south of Lithgow, comprise nine major (and 300 in total) limestone caves considered to be amongst the most spectacular in the southern hemisphere. After over 160 years of exploration and development – since their discovery in 1838 by pastoralist James Whalan – the main caves are now well geared up for your viewing pleasure with a network of paths and electric lighting to guide the way and to highlight the bizarre subterranean features. As well as guided cave tours, some other caves have been set aside for adventure caving, and above ground, there is a network of pleasant bush trails. If you are short of time the **Lucas Cave** and **Temple of Baal Cave** are generally recommended. The **Chiefly Cave** is the most historic and along with the **Imperial Cave** it has partial

BLUE MOUNTAINS LISTINGS

WHERE TO STAY

Leura has many excellent historic B&Bs and self-contained cottages and Katoomba has plenty of choice. Wentworth also has plenty of good B&Bs.

If you prefer something a bit quieter, the villages north of Katoomba – Medlow Bath, Blackheath and Mount Victoria – all provide some excellent accommodation.

There are plenty of places to stay in and around Jenolan. Prices are higher at weekends and you are advised to book ahead at any time of year, especially winter.

$$$$-$$$ Glenella Guesthouse, 56 Govetts Leap Rd, Medlow Bath, T4787 8352, www.glenellabluemountainshotel.com.au. Well known and surprisingly affordable, historic guesthouse, with a reputable restaurant attached, plus all the comforts including sauna, open fires and cable TV.
$$-$ No14 Budget Accommodation, 14 Lovel St, Katoomba, T4782 7104, www.no14.com.au. Another fine alternative, providing a peaceful, relaxed atmosphere in a old former guesthouse with double, twin, single and family rooms. Polished floors and an open fire add to the atmosphere.

wheelchair access. The **River Cave** is said to be one of the most demanding. On your arrival at the caves you immediately encounter the **Grand Arch**, a 60-m wide, 24-m high cavern that was once used for camping and even live entertainment to the flicker of firelight. Nearby, the historic and congenial **Caves House** has been welcoming visitors since 1898.

BELLS LINE OF ROAD

Bells Line of Road is named after Archibald Bell, who discovered the 'second' route through the Blue Mountains to Lithgow from Sydney, in 1823, at the age of 19. Starting just west of Richmond in the east, then climbing the plateau to fringe the northern rim of the Grose Valley, it provides a quieter, more sedate, scenic trip across the Great Divide. Just beyond the village of Bilpin, west of Richmond, the huge basalt outcrop of Mount Tomah (1000 m) begins to dominate the scene and supports the 28-ha cool-climate annexe of the **Sydney Botanical Gardens (Mount Tomah)** ① *T4567 3000, 1000-1600, Free*. Opened in 1987, the garden's rich volcanic soils nurture over 10,000 species, including a huge quantity of tree ferns and rhododendrons. Although the gardens are well worth visiting in their own right, it is the views, the short walks and the restaurant that make it extra special. Just beyond Mount Tomah (right) is the **Walls Lookout**, with its expansive views across the Grose Valley. It requires a one-hour return walk from the Pierces Pass Track car park but the effort is well worth it. Back on the Bells Line of Road and just a few kilometres further west is the junction (north, 8 km) to the pretty village of **Mount Wilson** which is famous for its English-style open gardens. These include **Linfield Park** and **Nooroo**. Also of interest is the **Cathedral of Ferns** at the northern end of the village. The **Wynnes** and **Du Faurs Lookouts** can also be reached from Mount Wilson and are signposted, east and west of the village centre.

SYDNEY TO BYRON BAY

With the lure of Byron Bay to the north, few take the time to explore the coast and national parks between Sydney and Port Macquarie. But to do so is to miss out on some of the best coastal scenery in the state. Myall Lakes National Park offers a superb diversion, and a couple of days exploring the beaches and lakes is highly recommended. Just inland are the vineyards of Hunter Valley, a name synonymous with fine wines and world-class vineyards, a little piece of Australia that conjures up images of mist-covered valleys and rolling hills, clothed in a patchwork of grape-laden vines. To the north are the high and secluded river valleys of the Barrington Tops National Park, an area renowned for its unpredictable climate and diverse wildlife, while back on the coast is Nelson Bay, an ideal stopover on the route north and gateway to the beautiful Tomaree Peninsula.

Port Macquarie itself is often unfairly overlooked. The fast-developing coastal town of South West Rocks near Smoky Cape and the sublime coastal Hat Head National Park are relaxing places to explore. It's well worth diverting inland, especially to the Dorrigo and Mount Warning national parks, which offer some superb views and bush walks.

→HUNTER VALLEY

This is really two distinct regions, the Lower Hunter Valley and Upper Hunter Valley, with the vast majority of the vineyards (over 80) in the lower region. The Hunter River and the New England Highway bisect both. The Lower Hunter Valley encompasses the area from Newcastle through Maitland to Singleton, with Cessnock to the south considered the 'capital' of the Lower Hunter Valley's vineyards, which are concentrated in a few square kilometres to the northwest. Though the region's true heritage lies below the ground, in the form of coal, it is vineyards that dominate the economy these days, producing mainly Shiraz, Semillons and Chardonnays. They range from large-scale producers and internationally recognized labels to low-key boutiques. Despite the sheer number, the emphasis in the Hunter Valley is definitely on quality rather than quantity. Though the vineyards are all comprehensively signposted around Cessnock, you are strongly advised to pick up the free detailed maps from the VIC.

For many, their first introduction to the great wine growing region is the drab and disappointing former mining town of **Cessnock**. Head north and west, however, and things improve as you reach the vineyard communities of **Pokolbin**, **Broke** and **Rothbury**.

With so many vineyards, choosing which to visit can be tough. There are many tours on offer, but for those with little prior knowledge it is advisable to mix some of the large, long-established wineries and labels with the smaller boutique affairs. Although many of the biggest names are well worth a visit, you will find a more, relaxed and personalized service at the smaller establishments. Also be aware that almost every vineyard has received some award or another and this doesn't necessarily mean one is better. The following are recommended and often considered the must-sees but it is not a comprehensive list.

Of the large long-established vineyards (over a century old), **Tyrells**, www.tyrrells.com.au, **Draytons**, www.draytonswines.com.au and **Tullochs**, www.tulloch.com.au. (all in Pokolbin) are recommended, providing fine wine and insight into the actual winemaking process. Tyrells also has especially nice aesthetics. **Lindemans**, www.lindemans.com, **McGuigans**, www.mcguiganwines.com.au (which is again in Pokolbin), and **Wyndhams**, www.wyndham estate.com (Branxton), are three of the largest and most well-known labels in the region,

ON THE ROAD

Hunter Valley wine tours

By far the best way to truly experience the area's delights, is to splash out on three days of relaxation, vineyard tours, fine dining and one of its dozens of cosy B&Bs. However, for the vast majority a day tour taking in about five wineries with numerous tastings and the purchase of one or two bottles of their favourite vintage to take home for special occasions, will sadly have to suffice.

As you can imagine there is a healthy crop of tour operators awaiting your custom, with a whole host of options and modes of transport, from the conventional coaches and mini-vans to horse-drawn carriages and bikes. Besides offering entertainment and insight they also prevent you from ending up behind bars with a drunk driving conviction. The vast majority of smaller operators will pick you up from your hotel. Many can supply lunch or dining options.

Local operators include **Vineyard Shuttle Service**, T4998 7779, www.vineyard shuttle.com.au, is a local mini-van firm offering both flexibility and good value, from $27. **Rover Coaches**, T4990 1699, www.rovercoaches.com.au, both offer exhaustive, conventional day tours from Sydney and Newcastle with a typical price (including lunch) from about $120.

Hunter Valley Wine Tours, T9498 8888, and **Oz Trails**, T9387 8390, both offer smaller personalized mini-van tours from Sydney and also visit the Hawkesbury River and Lake Macquarie regions. These cost from $100.

offering fine vintages and a broad range of facilities. McGuigans and Wyndhams also offer guided tours. Of the smaller boutique wineries, **Oakvale**, www.oakvalewines.com.au, **Tamburlaine**, www.tamburlaine.com.au, and **Pepper Tree** – with its classy restaurant and former convent guesthouse added attractions – are also recommended. All are located in Pokolbin. Then, for a fine view as well as vintage, head for the **Audrey Wilkinson Vineyard**, DeBeyers Road, Pokolbin, www.audreywilkinson.com.au, or **De Luliis**, Lot 21, Broke Road, www.dewine.com.au, with its lookout tower. The VICs have details.

→NELSON BAY AND AROUND

Nelson Bay is the recognized capital of an area known as **Port Stephens**, a name loosely used to describe both the natural harbour (Port Stephens) and the string of foreshore communities that fringe its southern arm. Nelson Bay is fast developing into a prime New South Wales coastal holiday destination and provides an ideal first base or stopover from Sydney. Other than the stunningly beautiful views from Tomaree National Park and from Tomaree Heads across the harbour to Tea Gardens and Hawks Nest, there are an ever-increasing number of activities on offer in the area, from dolphin watching to camel rides.

Even if you do nothing else around the Nelson Bay area except laze about on its pretty beaches, do climb to the summit of **Tomaree Head**, at the far east end of Shoal Bay, which is particularly spectacular at sunrise or sunset. The views that reward the 30-minute strenuous ascent are truly memorable.

The best beaches in the area are to be found fringing the national park, east and south of Nelson Bay. To the east, **Shoal Bay** is closest to all amenities while farther east still, within the national park boundary, **Zenith Beach**, **Wreck Beach** and **Box Beach** all provide great surfing, solitude and scenery. Two kilometres south of Shoal Bay the glorious beach that fringes **Fingal Bay** connects Point Stephens with the mainland. You can access the headland and its fine walking tracks at low tide. South of Fingal Bay, though not connected to it by road, **One Mile Beach** is a regional gem while **Samurai Beach**, just north of that, is the local naturist beach. West of One Mile Beach **Boat Harbour** gives way to **Anna Bay** which forms the northern terminus of **Stockton Beach**, stretching for over 30 km all the way down to Newcastle. It's well worth a visit simply to see the endless sweep of dunes. If you have 4WD you can 'let rip' but a permit must be obtained from the Council (or the VIC).

There is a healthy suburban population of **koalas** in the region and the best places to see them are the fringes of Tomaree National Park or wooded areas of the Tilligerry Peninsula (via Lemon Tree Passage Road, off Nelson Bay Road, 30 km south of Nelson Bay). There are guided walks.

→MYALL LAKES NATIONAL PARK

Myall Lakes National Park, or Great Lakes as it is known, combines beautiful coastal scenery with a patchwork of inland lakes, waterways and forest to create one of the best-loved eco-playgrounds in NSW. Just four hours north of Sydney, the only drawback is its inevitable popularity during holidays and weekends. However, given the sheer scale of the area (21,367 ha), of which half is water, there is always somewhere to escape the crowds. The main settlements fringing the national park are Tea Gardens and Hawks Nest on the northeastern shores of Port Stephens, Bulahdelah on the Pacific Highway to the northwest and the popular surf spots of Bluey's Beach and Pacific Palms to the north. If you have at least two days to spend here, the route below, from Tea Gardens in the south to Pacific Palms in the north, or vice versa, is recommended. A day fee per vehicle of $7 applies to the park.

TEA GARDENS AND HAWKS NEST

The little-known but fast-developing coastal settlements of Tea Gardens and Hawks Nest, on the northeastern shores of Port Stephens, serve not only as excellent holiday destinations in themselves but as the main southern gateway to the Myall Lakes National Park. Straddling the Myall River and surrounded by beautiful beaches, headlands, coastal wetlands and forest, these twin towns offer a wealth of activities from surfing to koala spotting, though most people come here simply to escape the crowds, relax and enjoy the beautiful scenery and laid-back atmosphere.

The place to be is **Bennetts** (Ocean Beach) at the southeastern end of Hawks Nest. From there you can access the **Yaccaba Walk** (3 km return) to the summit of the Yaccaba Headland, affording some memorable views across the mouth of Port Stephens and the numerous offshore islands. To reach Bennetts Beach, cross the bridge from Tea Gardens on Kingfisher Avenue, turn right on Mungo Brush Road, then left to the end of Booner Street. The bridge connecting the two towns is often called 'The Singing Bridge' because of its tendency to 'sing' in strong winds.

Another excellent but far more demanding walk is the **Mungo Track** that follows the Myall River through coastal forest to the **Mungo Brush Campsite** (15 km one way). It starts on the left, off Mungo Brush Road, 600 m past the national park boundary. The detailed booklet, *Walkers' Guide to The Mungo Track*, breaks the entire walk into sections with additional alternatives and is available from the VIC Tea Gardens, NPWS or Hawks Nest Real Estate on Tuloa Avenue. Look out for koalas along the way, especially late in the day. Dolphin-watching cruises, diving, golf, fishing charters and boat, sea kayak, canoe and surf ski hire are all readily available in the twin towns. Tea Gardens VIC has full listings.

HAWKS NEST TO BULAHDELAH

From Hawks Nest, Mungo Brush Road heads north, parallel with the Myall River, to meet the southern boundary of the Myall National Park (4.5 km). From there the road remains sealed and cuts through the littoral rainforest and coastal heath for 15 km to the Mungo Brush Campsite beside the Bombah Broadwater, the second largest of the Great Lakes.

Before reaching Mungo Brush consider stopping and walking the short distance east to the long swathe of deserted beach. **Dark Point**, about 5 km north of the southern boundary at Robinson's Crossing, is an interesting rocky outcrop and the only significant feature along this 44 km of beach between Hawks Nest and Seal Rocks. It is an interesting spot and the site of a midden (ancient refuse tip) used by the Worimi Aboriginal peoples for centuries before invading European cedar cutters displaced them. This particular example is thought to be at least 2000 years old. Lying tantalizingly offshore is **Broughton Island**, which is accessible by day trip from Nelson Bay.

From Mungo Brush the road skirts the northern shores of **Bombah Broadwater**, turning inland past increasingly thick stands of paperbark trees to reach the Bombah Point ferry crossing which – provided there is enough water – runs daily every half an hour from 0800 to 1800. There is a small fee. **Bombah Point** is dominated by the large yet unobtrusive EcoPoint Myall Shores Resort. On the same road, 10 km from Bulahdelah, are the **Bombah Point Eco Cottages**, see page 72

BULAHDELAH, SEAL ROCKS AND SANBAR

From Bombah Point 16 km of partly sealed roads takes you to the small community of **Bulahdelah** and the Pacific Highway. Bulahdelah has a helpful VIC and is the main venue for houseboat hire for the region. Four kilometres north of Bulahdelah, the Lakes Way – the main sealed access road through the Great Lakes region – heads east, eventually skirting Myall Lake, the largest of the lakes. Before reaching the lake, however, you may consider the short diversion 5 km north along **Stoney Creek Road**. Some 38 km into the southern fringe of the Bulahdelah State Forest, along Wang Wauk Forest Drive, is the **Grandis**, a towering 76-m flooded gum reputed to be the highest tree in NSW.

Back on the Lakes Way, between Myall Lake and Smiths Lake, Seal Rocks Road (unsealed) heads 11 km southeast to reach the coast and the pretty beachside settlement of **Seal Rocks**. The residents of this sublime little piece of wilderness know all too well that it is the jewel in the Myall and do not really want to advertise the fact. There is a superb beach and short rainforest and headland walks; the 2-km stroll to the **Sugarloaf Point Lighthouse** past the **Seal Rocks Blowhole** is well worth it. The views from the lighthouse (no public access to the interior) are excellent and Lighthouse Beach to the south is more than inviting. Seal Rocks lie just offshore and serve as a favourite regional dive site (they are home to numerous grey nurse sharks). Since 1875 there have been 20 shipwrecks, with the *SS Catterthun* being one of the nation's worst with the loss of 55 lives.

Back on the Lakes Way, just before **Smiths Lake**, look out for signs to the **Wallingat National Park**. If it is a fine day, an exploration (4WD and map required) of the forest is recommended, with the steep climb to **Whoota Whoota Lookout** providing fine views north over the lakes and coast.

Sandbar, 1 km past the turn off to Smiths Lake village, is also a sight for sore eyes. Here you'll find some excellent, quiet beaches (500-m walk), good birdwatching along the sandbar that holds the lake back from the sea and many lakeside activities based at the delightful caravan park.

PACIFIC PALMS AND BLUEY'S BEACH

Four kilometres north of Smiths Lake is the small community of **Pacific Palms** fringing the southern shores of Lake Wallis. Two kilometres east are the delightful little communities of **Bluey's Beach**, **Boomerang Beach** and **Elizabeth Beach**. While Pacific Palms boasts its lakeside charms and activities, Bluey's and its associates are something of a local surfing mecca. Bluey's Beach itself is idyllic and further north, beyond Boomerang Point, Boomerang Beach is only marginally less attractive. Further north, the rather unfortunately named Pimply Rock and Charlotte Head give way to **Elizabeth Beach**, which is an absolute stunner.

→PORT MACQUARIE

Officially declared as possessing the best year-round climate in Australia and blessed with a glut of superb beaches, engaging historic sites, wildlife-rich suburban nature reserves and water-based activities, the former penal colony of Port Macquarie is rightfully recognized as one of the best holiday destinations to be found anywhere in NSW. Due perhaps to more domestically oriented advertising, or simply the 6 km of road between the town and the Pacific Highway, it seems the vast majority of international travellers miss Port Macquarie completely as they charge northwards towards more high-profile destinations such as Byron Bay. But if you make the effort and short detour, you will not be disappointed.

Allman Hill on Stewart Street is home to the settlement's first cemetery (where the gravestones reveal the hardships and life expectancies). Nearby is Gaol Point Lookout, site of the first gaol, now offering pleasant views across the harbour and Town Beach. If you would like to quietly search the heavens, visit the **Observatory** ⓘ *Rotary Park on William St, www.pmobs.org.au, viewing nights Wed and Sun 1930 EST, 2015 DST, $8, children $7*. On the eastern side of Rotary Park is Town Beach, the most convenient for swimming with good surfing at the northern end. South of here, the **Maritime Museum** ⓘ *6 William St, T6583 1866, daily 1000-1600, $4, children $2*, is worth a look for a delve into the coast's history.

The 1869 **Courthouse** ⓘ *corner of Clarence St and Hay St, T6584 1818, Mon-Sat 1000-1500, $2*, served the community for over a century and has been refurbished faithfully. Across the road is the **Historical Museum** ⓘ *T6583 1108, Mon-Sat 0930-1630, $5*, housed in a former convict-built store (1835) and containing 14 rooms of historical artefacts.

St Thomas's Church ⓘ *corner of Hay St and William St, T6584 1033, Tue-Fri 0930-1200 and 1400-1600, donation welcome*, is the fifth oldest Anglican Church still in use in

Australia, built by convict labour in the late 1820s. Its most interesting feature actually lies buried beneath one of the pews, in the form of one Captain Rolland – the port's former gaol supervisor – who died from sunstroke. He was buried inside to avoid his body being dug up by vengeful convicts.

A healthy suburban population of koalas lives in the area's nature reserves and parks and numerous roadside signs are testament to this. In town, one of the best places to spot a wild koala is in Sea Acres Nature Reserve (see below), but if you have no joy there is always the **Koala Hospital** ⓘ *Lord St, T6584 1522, www.koalahospital.org.au, daily, donation welcome*, in the Macquarie Nature Reserve. Although you cannot see any sick marsupials, some of the pre-released critters are usually on display. Feeding takes place daily at 1500 and 1630. There's also the **Billabong Koala and Wildlife Centre** ⓘ *61 Billabong Drive, 10 km from the town centre, T6585 1060, www.billabongkoala.com.au, 0900-1700. $23, children $13*, which not only provides copious koala patting (1030, 1330 and 1530) but also the usual array of Australian natives such as wallabies, wombats and rainbow lorikeets in 2.5ha of landscaped gardens, with a café, barbecue and picnic areas. Step back in time with a visit to **Timbertown Wauchope** ⓘ *Oxley Highway, west of Wauchope, T6586 1940, www.timbertown.com.au, about 20 mins' drive west of Port Macquarie, daily 0930-1600, $20, children $16, family $65*, where you can ride the steam train, watch the bullock team display, observe the timber craftsmen at work and smell the coals of the blacksmith's fire.

The beaches that fringe the western suburbs of the town from the Hastings River mouth south to Tacking Point and beyond are simply superb, offering excellent swimming, fishing, surfing, walks and views. Whale-watching tours operate from June to November; prices start from around $50 per person. For further details, contact **Greater Port Macquarie VIC** ⓘ *T1300 303155*. North of the town, the great swathe of **North Beach**, stretching 15 km to Point Plomer, fringed by the diverse coastal habitats of Limeburners Creek Nature Reserve, provides almost total solitude. South, beyond Green Mound, Oxley Beach and Rocky Beach are less accessible. Beyond those, Flynn's Beach and Nobby's Beach are two other favourite spots with great views and good swimming as well as fossicking and snorkelling on the extensive rock platforms.

South of Nobby Head the coastal fringe gives way to Shelly Beach and the 72-ha coastal **Sea Acres Nature Reserve** ⓘ *T6582 3355, 0900-1630, $6, children $3, under 7s free, family $15*, one of the best places in town to spot wild koalas (particularly in the late afternoon). This sublime piece of rainforest is preserved with a 1.3 km boardwalk providing the ideal viewpoint. The boardwalk starts and finishes at the Rainforest Centre, which itself houses an interesting range of displays, a café and shop. Guided tours are available and recommended. Then it is on to Miners Beach, reached by coastal paths from the same car park. This is a favourite spot for naturists. At the terminus of Lighthouse Road is Tacking Point, named by Matthew Flinders in 1802, and the pocket-sized Tacking Point Lighthouse built in 1879. From there you are afforded great views south along Lighthouse Beach towards Bonny Hills and North Brother Hill.

→SOUTH WEST ROCKS AND HAT HEAD

South West Rocks is the best-kept secret on the NSW north coast. It has everything that Byron Bay has, except the footprints. Long swathes of golden sand, great fishing and swimming, a cliff-top lighthouse, stunning views and a superb local national park – Hat

Head – combine to make South West Rocks the ideal place to get away from it all for a few days. Here, you can watch dolphins surfing rather than people. South West Rocks is best reached and explored using your own transport.

PLACES IN SOUTH WEST ROCKS

South West Rocks sits at the southern bank of the Macleay River mouth and the western end of Trail Bay, where the colourful, wave-eroded rocks that earned the village its name form the perfect playground for swimmers and snorkellers. At the eastern end of Trial Bay the charming settlement of **Arakoon** fringes the Arakoon State Recreation Area and Laggers Point, site of the pink granite monolith of **Trial Bay Gaol** ① *T6566 6168, www.trialbaygaol.com, 0900-1700, $8*, built in 1886 and now housing a small museum that offers an insight into the torrid existence of its former inmates. Trial Bay was named after *The Trial*, a vessel that was stolen by former convicts and wrecked in the bay in 1816. Several other vessels with more conventional crews were wrecked in Trial Bay in the 1970s. A few rusting remnants still reach out from their sandy graves. At the terminus of Wilson Street, at the western end of Arakoon, is **Little Bay**, with its sublime, people-free beach. The car park also provides access to the **Graves Monument walking track** (2 km return) which provides memorable views back across Trial Bay and the Trial Bay Gaol. **Gap Beach**, accessed a little further south, is another fine spot, especially for the more adventurous surfer. South of Arakoon (3 km), Lighthouse Road provides access to the northern fringe of the **Hat HeadNational Park**, **Smoky Beach** and the **Smoky Cape Lighthouse**. The 1891 lighthouse is one of the tallest and oldest in NSW and provides stunning views south to Crescent Head and north down to the beckoning solitude of North Smoky Beach.

South of South West Rocks, accessed via Hat Head Village Road and Kinchela, the small village and headland of **Hat Head** sits in the heart of the national park separating the long swathes of Smoky Beach north and Killick Beach to the south. The village has a caravan park, limited amenities and walking access to Hat Hill, Korogoro Point, Connor's Beach and the Hungry Hill Rest Area.

→BELLINGEN AND DORRIGO NATIONAL PARK

Away from the coast, sitting neatly on the banks of the Bellinger River in the heart of the Bellinger Valley, is the pleasant country village of Bellingen, renowned for its artistic and alternative community, its markets, music festivals and laid-back ambience. Simple relaxation or country walks are the name of the game for travellers here, before they continue further inland to explore the superb national parks of Dorrigo (see page 69), and Oxley and New England, or resume the relentless journey northwards up the coast. The village has its own nickname used affectionately by the locals – Bello.

BELLINGEN

Bellingen's peaceful tree-lined streets are lined with some obvious heritage buildings, many of which are protected by the National Trust. The small **Bellingen Museum** ① *Civic Sq, 33 Hyde St, T6655 0382, Mon and Wed-Fri 1000-1400, $3*, contains a low-key collection of photos and artefacts from the mid-1800s. The **Old Butter Factory** ① *Doepel Lane, 0930 to 1700*, on the western approach to the village, and the unmistakable **Yellow Shed** ⓘ *2 Hyde St, 0930 to 1700*, are the two main arts and crafts outlets in the village, selling everything from opals to wind chimes. The Old Butter Factory also has a café and offers a range of relaxation and healing therapies including iridology, massage and a flotation tank. The colourful **Bellingen craft and produce market** is considered one of the best in the region and is held in the local park on the third Saturday of the month. The village also hosts a top quality **Jazz Festival** ⓘ *www.bellingenjazzfestival.com.au*, in mid-August, and the equally popular **Global Carnival** ⓘ *www.globalcarnival.com*, which is an entertaining celebration of world music held in the first week in October.

Nature lovers should take a look at the large (and smelly) flying fox (fruit bat) colony on **Bellingen Island** (which is now no longer an island) beside the river, within easy walking distance of the village. The best place to see the bats is from the Bellingen Caravan Park on Dowle Street (cross the Bridge off Hyde, on to Hammond then turn right into Dowle), while the best time is around dusk when they depart to find food. But even during the day it is an impressive sight indeed as they hang like a thousand fuzzy Christmas decorations from almost every tree.

DORRIGO AND DORRIGO NATIONAL PARK

Provided the weather is kind and the clouds do not blind you, you are in for a scenic treat here. Even the **Dorrigo National Park Rainforest Visitors Centre** ⓘ *T6657 2309, 0900-1700*, has amazing views. Sitting right at the edge of the escarpment, the view across the forested slopes and across the Bellinger Valley towards the coast is even better from the slightly shaky 100-m **Skywalk** that projects like a jetty out across the rainforest canopy. From its end you can survey the glorious scene and listen to the strange and distant calls of elusive rainforest birds. You may also see the odd python curled up in a branch or right next to the handrail. The visitors centre itself has some good interpretative displays and a small café. The main office and shop can provide the necessary detail on the excellent rainforest walks (ranging from 400 m to 5 km) that begin from the centre and descend in to the very different world beneath the forest canopy.

From the Rainforest Centre it is then a short, scenic 10-km drive along the edge of the escarpment to the **Never Never Picnic Area**, which is a fine network of rainforest walks, including the 5.5-km **Rosewood Creek Track** to **Cedar Falls**, the 4.8-km **CasuarinaFalls Track** and the 6.4-km **Blackbutt (escarpment edge) Track**. Before heading into Dorrigo township itself, it is worth taking the short 2-km drive to **Griffith's Lookout** for its memorable views across the Bellinger Valley. The road to the lookout is signposted about 1 km south of Dome Road off the Waterfall Way. Just north of Dorrigo (1.5 km), the **Dangar Falls** may prove a disappointment after long dry periods but after rain can become a thunderous torrent of floodwaters.

→COFFS HARBOUR

Roughly halfway between Sydney and Brisbane and the only spot on the NSW coast where the Great Dividing Range meets the sea, Coffs Harbour is a favourite domestic holiday resort and the main commercial centre for the northern NSW coast. Surrounded by rolling hills draped in lush banana plantations and pretty beaches, it's a fine spot to kick back for a couple of days.

The main activities in town are centred around the attractive marina where regular fishing, whale- and dolphin-watching cruises are on offer, together with highly popular diving and snorkelling trips to the outlying Solitary Islands. The island group and surrounding coast is gazetted as a marine park and considered to have one of the largest marine biodiversities in NSW.

Other principal attractions include Muttonbird Island, guarding the entrance to the harbour and offering sanctuary to thousands of burrowing seabirds and, in complete contrast, the kitsch Big Banana complex on the northern edge of the town. Often overlooked is the fast developing, but still pleasant, beachside community of Sawtell, which is worth the trip.

PLACES IN COFFS HARBOUR

The rather unsightly and uninspiring main drag, **Grafton Street**, has seen something of an improvement recently, with the creation of the Palms Centre Arcade and redevelopment of the Mall and Park Avenue, which, combined, form the hub of the town centre. From the end of the Mall, **High Street** heads 3 km southeast to the **harbour**, which is hemmed in by the town's three main beaches: **Park Beach**, which straddles Coffs Creek to the north, **Jetty Beach** beside the harbour and **Boambee Beach** to the south. Park Beach is the most popular and is regularly patrolled in summer. Jetty Beach is considered the safest. The view from **Beacon HillLookout**, at the end of Camperdown Street, off High Street, offers fine 360-degree views across the harbour, the coast, and the green rolling hills of the Great Dividing Range to the west. There are also numerous other, excellent beaches, stretching 20 km north all the way to Woolgoolga.

Linked to the mainland by the marina's 500-m sea wall is **Muttonbird Island Nature Reserve**, which offers more than just a pleasant walk and some memorable views back towards the town. From October to April Muttonbird Island and others in the Solitary Island group are home to thousands of breeding wedge-tailed shearwaters (muttonbirds) that nest in a warren of burrows across the entire island. The birds are best viewed just after dusk, when they return in number to feed their mates or chicks hiding deep within the burrows. Although the birds were once easily harvested for food, they are now, thankfully, fully protected. For obvious reasons, do not stray from the main pathway. Also keep a lookout for humpback whales which are often spotted just offshore from June to September.

The **Solitary Islands** offer some fine dive sites with such evocative names as Grey Nurse Gutters and Manta Arch, a wealth of marine life (90 species of coral and 280 species of fish) and the densest colonies of anemones and anemone fish (clown fish) in the world. For more details contact the VIC, see above. Coffs Harbour is one of the cheapest places on the NSW coast to get certified for diving.

It's incredible that by building an oversized banana next to the main highway, you attract people like bees to honey. Coffs' famous icon and monument of marketing genius, the **Big Banana** ① T6652 4355, www.bigbanana.com, 0900-1600, located just north of the town on the Pacific Highway, fronts a banana plantation that has 'grown' over the years and now hosts a new 'World of Bananas' attraction. As you can imagine it showcases just about all you need to know about bananas, plus a number of long-established activities, from a lookout (free) to toboggan rides, snow-tubing, ice skating and the obligatory café and shop selling lots of souvenir banana-meets-koala kitsch. It is, however, perhaps entertainment enough to sit in the café and watch people posing for photos in front of the Big Banana. This in itself will without doubt prove the age-old suspicion that human beings are indeed really weird.

Sawtell, a seaside village 6 km south of Coffs Harbour, is blessed with some fine beaches and a pleasant laid-back atmosphere that has quietly attracted domestic holidaymakers for years. Now the secret is well and truly out; like most of the East Coast's beachside communities the influx of city 'sea changers' may well prove its very demise. Other than the obvious attractions of the beach, the **Cooinda Aboriginal Art Gallery** ① *Shop 1/4, First Av, T6658 7901, www.cooinda-gallery.com.au*, relocated from Coffs Harbour, is well worth a look. It showcases some excellent examples of the unique and spiritually loaded 'dot-style'.

→COFFS HARBOUR TO BYRON BAY

YAMBA, ANGOURIE AND YURAYGIR NATIONAL PARK (NORTH)

The coastal fishing town of **Yamba**, 13 km east of the Pacific Highway (exit just before the Clarence River bridge) and on the southern bank of the Clarence River mouth, is famed for its prawn industry and its fine surf beaches. The Yamba-Iluka ferry shuttles back and forth daily, providing access to some sublime beaches and bluffs, a stunning rainforest reserve and the wilderness of Bundjalung National Park.

ILUKA AND BUNDJALUNG NATIONAL PARK

If you can give yourself at least two to three days to explore the Iluka area, you won't regret it. Other than the superb coastline contained within the southern sector of the Bundjalung National Park and one of the best campsites on the northern NSW coast at **Woody Head**, the big attraction at the sleepy fishing village of **Iluka** is the World Heritage Rainforest Walk through the **Iluka Nature Reserve**. The 136-ha reserve contains the largest remaining stand of littoral rainforest in NSW – a rich forest habitat unique to the coastal environment and supporting a huge number of species such as the charmingly named lily pilly tree and noisy pitta bird.

Iluka Beach is another fine quiet spot reached via Beach Road (head west from the end of Iluka Road). Further north, just beyond Iluka Bluff, **Bluff Beach** and **Frazer's Reef** are popular for swimming and fishing.

Two kilometres north of Iluka and Woody Head, the 18,000-ha wilderness of **Bundjalung National Park** with its 38 km of beaches, littoral rainforest, heathlands, unusual rock formations, lagoons, creeks and swamps is an eco-explorer's paradise. Sadly, access from the south is by 4WD only or on foot.

LENNOX HEAD

The small, beachside settlement of Lennox Head is world famous for the long surf breaks that form at the terminus of Seven Mile Beach and Lennox Point. Just south of the village the eponymous head offers excellent views north to Cape Byron and is considered a prime spot for hang-gliding and dolphin and whale spotting. The **Lennox Reef**, below the head, known as 'The Moat', is also good for snorkelling. At the northern end of the village **Lake Ainsworth** is a fine venue for freshwater swimming, canoeing and windsurfing.

SYDNEY TO BYRON BAY LISTINGS

Hunter Valley
$$$$ Peppers Guest House,
EkertsRd, Pokolbin, T4993 8999,
www.peppers.com.au. 48 de luxe rooms,
suites and a private homestead. All
beautifully appointed and with a tariff to
match. The homestead has all the usual
extras, including pool, spa and the
obligatory open fire. The in-house Chez Pok
Restaurant is widely regarded as one of the
best in the area.

Myall Lakes National Park
$$$$ Bombah Point Eco Cottages, 10 km
from Bulahdelah on the same road as Eco
Point Myall Shores Resort, Bombah Point,
T4997 4401, www.bombah.com.au. Consists
of 6 very classy, self-contained, modern
eco-friendly cottages in a peaceful setting.
Very popular, so book ahead.

South West Rocks and Hat Head
$$$$ Smoky Cape Lighthouse B&B,
T6566 6301, www.smokycape
lighthouse.com. The most unusual
accommodation in the area has to be these
former keepers' quarters. A totally
refurbished interior provides self-contained
or B&B options, modern facilities, 4-poster
and stunning views south across the

national park. 2-night stay minimum. Book
well in advance.
$$$ Horseshoe Bay Beach Park,
Livingstone St, T6566 6370,
www.horseshoebaypark.com.au. Overlooks
the river, ocean and the sheltered
Horseshoe Bay Beach and is within metres
of the town centre. Busy and beautifully
placed, this motor park offers cabins, onsite
vans and powered sites (some en suite).
Hugely popular with locals so book well
in advance.

Coffs Harbour
There is a rash of motels and resorts located
along the Pacific Highway on the north and
south approaches and along the waterfront
on Ocean Parade. There are plenty of motor
parks in the area with the best located north
or south of the town. The hostels are lively
places – very activity- and party-oriented.
$$$$ Friday Creek Retreat, 267 Friday
Creek Rd, Upper Orara, 17 km west of town,
T6653 8221, www.fridaycreek.com. Sheer
luxury, as well as complete peace and quiet
in a country setting is offered here. There are
9 superb fully self-contained cottages with
spas, open fires, hammocks and great views,
free bike hire, complimentary breakfast and
dinner by arrangement.

BYRON BAY

Anything goes in Byron Bay. This town would love to have its own passport control to prevent entry to anyone who is remotely conservative or thinks surfing is something you do in front of a computer. Only three decades ago 'Byron' was little more than a sleepy, attractive coastal enclave. Few strayed off the main highway heading north except a few alternative lifestylers who found it an ideal escape and the land prices wonderfully cheap. But news spread and its popularity exploded. It lacks the glitz of the Gold Coast and the conformity of many other coastal resorts, but there is little doubt it is perilously close to being a love-it-or-hate-it experience. Despite all this, however, it remains a beautiful place (no high-rise hotels here) and boasts a wonderfully cosmopolitan mix of humanity. Few leave disappointed.

ARRIVING IN BYRON BAY

Getting around You can enjoy all the offerings of Byron Bay on foot, or, to cover more ground, hire a bike. There are local bus services for getting around town and also to sights around Byron Bay such as Ballina and Lennox Head.

Tourist information Byron Bay VIC ① *80 Jonson St, T6680 8558, www.visitbyron bay.com, 0900-1700.*

PLACES IN BYRON BAY

The main attractions in Byron, beyond its hugely popular social and creative scene, are of course the surrounding beaches and the stunning Cape Byron Headland Reserve. There are over 37 km of beaches, including seven world-class surf beaches stretching from Belongil Beach in the west to Broken Head in the south. Byron also hosts an array of organized activities to lure you from your beach-based relaxation. Surfing is the most popular pastime.

Only metres from the town centre, **Main Beach** is the main focus of activity. It is patrolled and safest for families or surfing beginners. West of Main Beach, **Belongil Beach** stretches about 1 km to the mouth of Belongil Creek. About 500 m beyond that (accessed via Bayshore Drive), there is a designated naturist beach. East of the town centre, Main Beach merges with **Clark's Beach**, which is no less appealing and generally much quieter. Beyond Clark's Beach and the headland called **The Pass** – a favourite surf spot – **Watego's** and **Little Watego's Beaches** fringe the northern side of Cape Byron, providing more surf breaks and some dramatic coastal scenery. South of Cape Byron, **Tallow Beach** stretches about 9 km to Broken Head and is a great spot to escape the crowds (but note that it is unpatrolled). Several walks also access other more remote headland beaches within the very pretty **Broken Head Nature Reserve**. In the heart of Byron Bay itself, 2.5 km from the shore, is the small and clearly visible rocky outcrop known as **Julian Rocks Marine Reserve**. It is listed as one of Australia's top 10 dive sites, with over 400 species of fish, including sharks and manta ray, and turtles and dolphins often joining the party. If you are not a certified diver, a snorkelling trip to the rocks is recommended.

Crowning the **Cape Byron Headland** is the **Byron Bay Lighthouse** ① *T6685 5955, 0800-1930 (1730 in winter), 30 mins' walk from the town, 40-min tours available.* Built in 1901 it sits only metres away from Australia's easternmost point. As well as the dramatic coastal views east over Byron Bay and south down Tallow Beach to Broken Head, the headland provides some excellent walking opportunities, with the track down from the lighthouse to Little Watego's Beach being the most popular. Humpback whales can often been seen offshore during their annual migrations in midwinter and early summer, while dolphins and the occasional manta ray can be seen in the clear waters below the cliffs year round.

The town has a number of galleries worth seeing including the works of local photographer John Derrey, at **Byron Images** ⓘ *on the corner of Lawson St and Jonson St, www.johnderrey.com*. The VIC has full gallery listings.

NIGHTCAP NATIONAL PARK AND WHIAN WHIAN STATE FOREST

The World Heritage 8145-ha Nightcap National Park is located on the southern rim of the Mount Warning caldera and adjacent is the Whian Whian State Forest Park. Combined, they offer a wealth of volcanic features including massifs, pinnacles and cliffs eroded by spectacular waterfalls and draped in lush rainforest. Some unique wildlife also resides in the park, including the red-legged pademelon (a kind of wallaby), the Fleay's barred frog and the appealingly named wompoo fruit dove.

The main physical features of the park are **Mount Nardi** (800 m), 12 km east of Nimbin; **Terania Creek** and the **Protestors Falls**, 14 km north of the Channon; and **Whian Whian State Forest** and 100-m **Minyon Falls**, 23 km southwest of Mullumbimby. The 30-km Whian Whian Scenic Drive (unsealed), which can be accessed beyond the Minyon Falls, traverses the forest park and takes visitors through varied rainforest vegetation and scenery including the memorable **Peates Mountain Lookout**.

Popular long walking tracks include the moderate-to-hard 7.5-km **Minyon Loop**, which starts from the Minyon Falls Picnic Area and takes in the base of the falls and the escarpment edge, and the moderate-to-hard 16-km **Historic Nightcap Track**, which follows the former

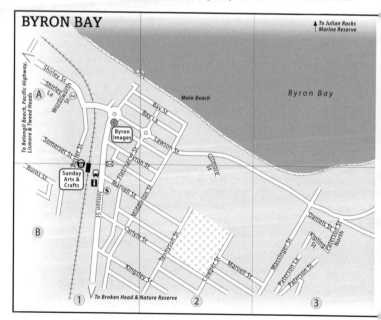

pioneer trails that once connected Lismore and Mullumbimby. Other shorter and easier possibilities are the 3-km **Mount Matheson Loop** and 4-km **Pholis Gap walks**, which both start from Mount Nardi, and the 1.5-km **Big Scrub Loop**, which starts from the Gibbergunyah Range Road in Whian Whian State Forest. It is said to contain some of the best remnant rainforest in the region. Protestors Falls, which were named after a successful six-week protest to prevent logging in the late 1970s, are reached on a 1.5-km return track from the Terania Creek Picnic Area.

The Mount Nardi section of the park is accessed via Newton Drive, which is off Tuntable Falls Road west out of Nimbin. The Terania Creek and Protestors Falls are reached via Terania Creek Road north out of the Channon, and the Minyon Falls and Whian Whian State Forest are reached via Dunoon or Goonengerry southwest of Mullumbimby.

MURWILLUMBAH

The pleasant sugar cane town of Murwillumbah sits on the banks of the Tweed River, at the eastern edge of the Mount Warning caldera, and serves as a gateway to the Rainbow Region. Most people who visit the town gather what information they need from the World Heritage Rainforest Centre (see below) and then 'head for the hills'; however, if you can spare an hour or so, the small **Tweed Regional Art Gallery** ① *Mistral Rd, T6670 2790, Wed-Sun 1000-1700*, is worth a look. As well as its permanent collection of Australian and international art, it features some fine works by local artists and also hosts the lucrative Doug Moran National Portrait Prize. Murwillumbah VIC shares its

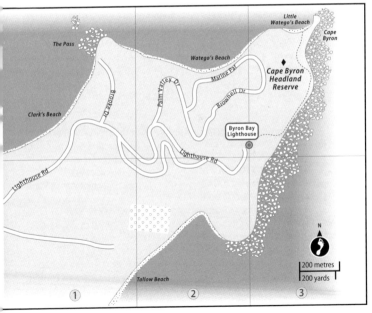

BYRON BAY LISTINGS
Where to stay

There is certainly plenty of choice in Byron, with the emphasis on backpacker hostels and upmarket boutique hotels, B&Bs and guesthouses. There are over a dozen very competitive backpackers in town, all having to maintain good standards. Mostly the choice comes down to availability – book well ahead for all accommodation but particularly the backpackers. If the options below don't suffice, the VIC has an excellent accommodation booking service. See www.byron-bay.com and www.byronbayaccom.net.

$$$$ Rae's on Wategos, overlooking Wategos's Beach, T6685 5366, www.raes.com.au. This sits firmly at the top of this price category and is the most luxurious hotel in Byron. It was voted in *Condé Naste Traveller* magazine (and others) as being in the top 50 worldwide. Although location has a lot to do with that accolade, the place itself is superb and cannot be faulted. Its in-house award-winning restaurant called Fish Café is also excellent and open to non-guests.

$$$$-$$$ Byron Beach Resort, 25 Childe St (Kendal St, off Shirley St), T6685 7868, www.byronbeachresort.com.au. East of the town centre, in contrast to the Arts Factory this option offers a wide range of modern, well-appointed options, from dorms and private double/twins with shared facilities, to luxury motel-style rooms with spas, or two-bedroom self-contained cottages. Quiet setting across the road from the beach. Onsite café, Sunday BBQs and Bistro next door. Other facilities include Foxtel, Wi-Fi bike, body/surf board hire and courtesy bus.

$$$-$ Arts Factory, Skinners Shoot Rd (via Burns St, off Shirley St), T6685 7709, www.artsfactory.com.au. This place takes some beating for the quintessential 'alternative' Byron experience. It offers a wide range of 'funky' accommodation, from the Love Shack and Island Retreats, to the Gypsy Bus, tepees and campsites. Excellent amenities, pool, sauna, internet, café (plus vegetarian restaurant nearby), bike hire, tours desk and unusual arts, relaxation, yoga or music-based activities including didgeridoo making and drumming. The Byron Lounge Cinema and Buddha Gardens Day Spa are also within the village. It may not be everybody's cup of herbal tea, but for an experience it is recommended.

office with the NPWS and the **World Heritage Rainforest Centre** ① *corner of Tweed Valley Way and Alma St, T6672 1340, www.destinationtweed.com, open till 1600.*

MOUNT WARNING NATIONAL PARK

The 1157-m peak of Mount Warning is all that remains of the magma chamber and vent that formed the vast caldera that shaped much of the Northern Rivers region. Other than its stunning scenery and rich flora and fauna, the great appeal of Mount Warning is the pilgrimage to the summit to see the first rays of sunlight to hit the Australian mainland. The moderate to hard 4.4-km ascent starts from the Breakfast Creek Picnic Area, 17 km southwest of Murwillumbah at the terminus of Mount Warning Road. To reach the summit for sunrise set off about 2½ hours beforehand. Murwillumbah, see above, serves as an overnight stop for those undertaking the dawn ascent. For the less energetic, Lyrebird Track crosses Breakfast Creek before winding 200 m through palm forest to a rainforest platform. Access to Mount Warning is via Mount Warning Road, 11 km south of Murwillumbah on the main Kyogle Road.

GOLD COAST

Heading north from NSW, you pass the forest of high-rise buildings strung along the infamous Gold Coast, which is located just before the state capital, Brisbane. With almost five million visitors a year the 'Coast with the Most' is Australia's most popular domestic holiday destination. It is a concrete jungle and a womb of artificiality, but for lovers of the laid-back beach lifestyle, socialites seeking a hectic nightlife, theme park and thrill ride junkies and shopaholics, it can promise more than just a surfers' paradise. For those of you itching to scratch the mighty Gold Coast from your travelling agenda at the mere prospect of such a place, think again. Even for the greatest cynic, the worst (or the best) of the Gold Coast can prove utterly infectious and lead to a thoroughly enjoyable experience. Turning your back on the coast, only an hour away is one of the Gold Coast's greatest assets and the 'Green behind the Gold', in the form of the Springbrook and Lamington National Parks, two of Queensland's best, and perfect retreats.

SPRINGBROOK NATIONAL PARK

This 2954-ha park, 29 km south from Mudgeeraba on the Pacific Highway, is the most accessible for the coast and sits on the northern rim of what was once a huge volcano centred on Mount Warning (see also page 76). The park is split into three sections: **Springbrook Plateau**, **Natural Bridge** and the **Cougals**.

Springbrook offers a rich subtropical rainforest habitat of ancient trees and gorges, interspersed with creeks, waterfalls and an extensive system of walking tracks. In addition, the park is well known for its many spectacular views including **Canyon**, **Wunburra**, **Goomoolahara** and the aptly named **Best of All**. Other attractions include the **Natural Arch** (1-km walk), a cavernous rock archway that spans **Cave Creek**, and the 190-m **Purling Brook Falls** (4-km walk). Natural Arch also plays host to a colony of glow worms.

LAMINGTON NATIONAL PARK

The 20,500-ha Lamington National Park sits on the border of Queensland and New South Wales and comprises densely forested valleys, peaks straddling the **McPherson Range** and an ancient volcanic area known as the **Scenic Rim**, about 60 km inland from the Gold Coast. The park is essentially split into two sections: the **Binna Burra** to the east and the **Green Mountains** (O'Reilly's) to the west. Combined, they offer a wealth of superb natural features and a rich biodiversity that can be experienced on over 100 km of walking tracks. The Green Mountains were first settled in 1911 by the O'Reilly family, who established a number of small dairy farms before consolidating their assets in 1915 with the opening of their now internationally famous guesthouse (see page 82). Other than the sense of escape and surrounding beauty, its most popular draw is the treetop canopy walkway: an ideal way to see the rainforest habitat. There are also some excellent walking tracks offering spectacular views and numerous waterfalls. Guided tours are available, along with a broad range of places to stay. The Green Mountains (O'Reilly's) section is accessed from Canungra.

The most accessible section is Binna Burra, 35 km south west of Nerang on the Pacific Highway. From Brisbane you can travel south via Nerang or via Mount Tamborine and Canungra. If you don't have your own transport, there are numerous tour operators. Like the Green Mountains, Binna Burra offers a wealth of excellent rainforest walking opportunities and plays host to another historic guesthouse. Guided tours are available from the lodge and there is a QPWS centre and campsite.

BRISBANE AND MORETON BAY

Brisbane has come an awfully long way since its days as a penal settlement, enjoying phenomenal growth in recent years and along with the Gold Coast is the fastest developing region in Australia. The reason for this is very simple and revolves almost entirely around its greatest assets: climate and lifestyle.

A lot of money was pumped into the city for its Expo 88 and Brissie has never looked back. South Bank, especially, represents the very essence of modern-day Brisbane with numerous cultural attractions and even its own inner-city beach. Australia's only true tropical city also enjoys a near-perfect climate. Wherever you go, alfresco restaurants, cafés and outdoor activities dominate. Nearby, the sand islands of Moreton Bay offer a wonderful opportunity to enjoy some peace and quiet.

ARRIVING IN BRISBANE

Getting around There is an efficient transport system with the river playing a large part in navigating the city. The main centre is within walking distance. The city tours are a great way to get around and see the sights, especially if you're short of time.

Tourist information Brisbane **VIC** ① *Queen Street Mall, Albert St and Edward St, T3006 6290, www.visitbrisbane.com.au, Mon-Thu 0900-1730, Fri 0900-1900, Sat 0900-1700, Sun 0930-1630,* offers free city maps and assists with tours and accommodation. **QPWS main office** ① *3rd floor, 400 George St, T1300 130372, Mon-Fri 0830-1630.*

→PLACES IN BRISBANE

CENTRAL BRISBANE

A number of historic buildings stand out amidst the glistening high-rise blocks. At the top end of Albert Street is **City Hall** ① *T3403 8888, 0800-1700 guided tours available, lift free, Mon-Fri 1000-1500,* with its 92-m Italian renaissance clock tower. Built in 1930, it became known as the 'Million Pound Town Hall' due to its huge and controversial construction cost. The ride in the old lift to the top for the views is a highlight but the interior of the building is also worth a look. On the ground floor is the **Museum of Brisbane (MoB)** ① *daily 0900-1700, free,* which showcases the various aspects of contemporary social history and culture with a heavy emphasis on local writers and artists. Around the corner on George Street and the riverbank is the grand 19th-century façade of the former **Treasury Building**, now a casino.

To the east beside the Botanical Gardens (note there are two in the city, see page 79 for the Botanical Gardens-Mount-Coot-tha) is the 1868 French Renaissance-style **Parliament House** ① *T3406 7562, www.parliament.qld.gov.au, Mon-Fri 1030-1430, free,* which was commissioned when Queensland was declared a separate colony in 1859. Visitors can join tours conducted by parliamentary attendants. Nearby is the **Old Government House** ① *2 George St, T3864 8005, www.ogh.qut.edu.au, 1000-1600, free,* which was built in 1862 as the official residence of the state's governors. In the last few years, the building has undergone a $15 million refurbishment. Displays tell the story of the house and there is a gallery exhibiting the works of the Australian artist William Robinson.

Further north, beyond the modern architecture and chic restaurants of Waterfront Place, Eagle Street Pier and the Riverside Centre, is **Customs House** ⓘ *399 Queens St, T3365 8999, www.customshouse.com.au, Mon-Fri 0900-1700, tours available on concert days*. Built in 1889, it resembles a miniature version of St Paul's Cathedral in London. Directly opposite the Customs House is the city's best-known and most-photographed sight – the **Story Bridge**. It was built between 1935 and 1940 and due to the lack of bedrock has some of the deepest (42 m) foundations of any bridge in the world. Recently Brisbane has emulated Sydney's highly successful Harbour Bridge Bridge climb experience and, although far less dramatic, the Story Bridge Adventure Climb still offers great views and may appeal. The dawn or dusk trip is recommended (see page 83).

Overlooking the high-rise blocks on the southern bank of the Brisbane River is the remarkable 17-ha 'oasis in the city' that is known as the **South Bank** ⓘ *visitor centre on the ground floor of South Bank House, on the corner of Ernest St and Stanley St Plaza, T3867 2051, www.visitsouthbank.com.au, daily 0900-1700*. Built primarily as the showpiece for Expo 88, the 1-km stretch of parkland remains a fascinating and functional recreational space and includes riverside walks, shops, restaurants and a swimming lagoon with its very own beach. This area is also the venue for the colourful **South Bank Lifestyle Markets** ⓘ *every Fri night, Sat and Sun*.

At the northwestern end of the park, straddling Melbourne Street, is the **Queensland Cultural Centre**, encompassing the State Library, Queensland Museum, Queensland Art Gallery, Gallery of Modern Art and Queensland Performing Arts Complex. **Queensland Art Gallery** ⓘ *T3840 7303, www.qag.qld.gov.au, Mon-Fri 1000-1700, Sat-Sun 0900-1700, free, tours available daily*, is Brisbane's premier cultural attraction, featuring a huge and diverse collection of Aboriginal, European, Asian and contemporary Australian art. Early works include paintings by John Russell and Rupert Bunny, two of the nation's most noted expat artists, as well as more familiar international names such as Rubens, Degas, Picasso and Van Dyck. The **Gallery of Modern Art** ⓘ *T3840 7303, www.qag.qld.gov.au, Mon-Fri 1000-1700, Sat-Sun 0900-1700, free, tours available daily*, is Australia's largest dedicated to the genre and includes the first Australian Cinémathèque, purpose-built to showcase the art of film. Another interesting feature is the drawing room, should you be feeling artistically inclined post-muse.

Next to the art gallery is the **Queensland Museum** ⓘ *T3840 7555, www.qm.qld.gov.au, 0930-1700, free*, which is noted for its prehistoric and natural history displays. The museum also has entertaining and educational interactive exhibits, guaranteed to keep little Einsteins amused for hours. On the opposite side of Melbourne Street is the **Queensland Performing Arts Complex**, which houses several theatres and concert venues. At the southeastern end of the South Bank you can find the **Queensland Maritime Museum** ⓘ *T3844 5361, www.maritimemuseum.com.au, 0930-1630, $8, children $3.50*, with all the usual relics from anchors to lifebuoys. Most of the larger vessels, including the Second World War warship *The Diamantina*, sit forlornly in the adjacent dry dock. All this is best viewed from the futuristic **Goodwill Bridge**, built in celebration of the 2001 Goodwill Games.

BRISBANE SUBURBS

West of the city, reached via Milton Road, is the **Botanical Gardens-Mount-Coot-tha** ⓘ *T3403 2535, 0830-1730, free, tours Mon-Sat 1100 and 1300 or pick up a free self-guided leaflet,*

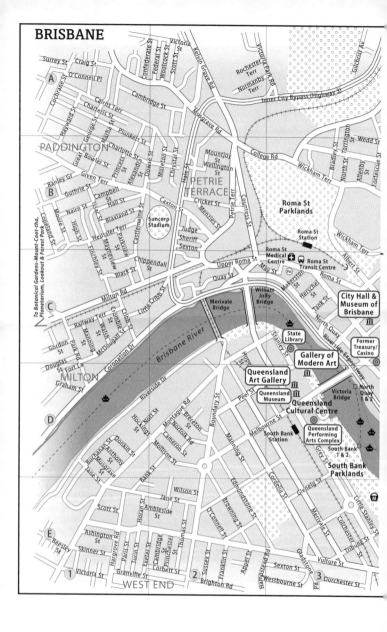

BRISBANE

A
Surrey St · Craig St
O'Connell Pl
Cochrane St
Confederate St
Federal St
Woolcock St
Scott St
Victoria St
Kelvin Grove Rd
Rochester Terr
Normanby Terr
Inner City Bypass (Highway)
Victoria Park Rd
Gilchrist Av

Cairns Terr
Charteris St
Cambridge St
Mugrave Rd
Torrington St
Wedd St
Hayward St
George St
Manra St
Plunkett St
Charlotte St
Mountjoy St
Wellington St
College Rd
Wickham Terr
Bradley St
North St
Allenby St
Fortescue St

PADDINGTON
Great Bowler St
Princess St
Alexandra St
Dowie St
Moreton St
Chrystal St

B
Ranley Gr · Given Terr
Guthrie St
Campbell St
Hall St
Blaxland St
Castlemaine St
Caxton St
Cricket St
Petrie Terr
PETRIE TERRACE
Countess St
Menzies St
Roma St Parklands
Wickham Terr

Nairn St
Isaac St
Heussler Terr
Mayneview St
Parkview St
Finchley St
Black St
Chippendall St
Suncorp Stadium
Judge St
Sheriff St
Sexton St
Upper Roma St
Roma St Station
Albert St

High St
Moore St
Railway Terr
Coombe St
Clubb St
Little Cribb St
Milton Rd
Quay St
May St
Roma St Medical Centre
Roma St Transit Centre
Roma St
Makerston St
Herschel St
Tank St
Roma St
North Quay
City Hall & Museum of Brisbane

C
Gordon St
Park Rd
Manning St
Walsh St
McDougall St
Coronation Dr
Merivale Bridge
William Jolly Bridge
Brisbane River
Riverside Expressway
Former Treasury/Casino

Douglas St
St Fort La
MILTON
Graham St
Riverside Dr
Stanley St
State Library
Gallery of Modern Art
Victoria Bridge
North Quay 1 & 2

D
Hockings St
Nott St
Montague Rd
Brereton St
Boundary St
Hope St
Queensland Art Gallery
Peel St
Queensland Museum
Queensland Cultural Centre
North Quay

Buchanan St
Anthony St
Donkin St
Musgrave St
Cameron St
Mollison St
Manning St
Melbourne St
South Bank Station
Queensland Performing Arts Complex
South Bank 1 & 2

Jane St
Bank St
Wilson St
Cordelia St
Edmonstone St
South Bank Parklands

E
Scott St
Horan St
Ambleside St
Jane St
Browning St
O'Connell St
Glenelg St
Grey St
Melville St
Colchester St
Tribune St
Little Stanley St

Beasley St
Ashington St
Skinner St
Hargrove Rd
Turin St
Cambridge St
Exeter St
Prince St
Thomas St
Corbett St
Granville St
Sussex St
Franklin St
Abbot St
Hampstead Rd
Sexton St
Westbourne St
Gladstone Rd
Vulture St
Dorchester St

1
Victoria St
2
Brighton Rd
3

WEST END

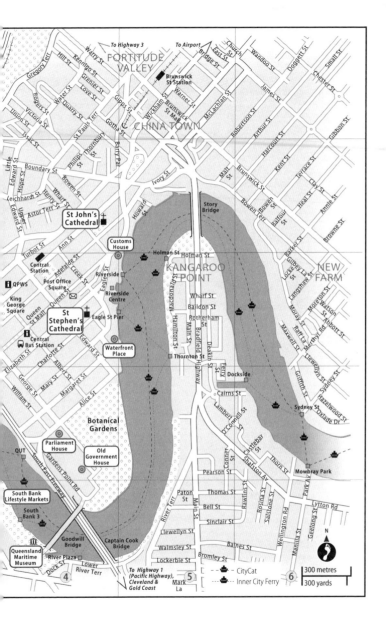

To Highway 3
To Airport
FORTITUDE VALLEY
Brunswick St Station
CHINA TOWN

Warry St
Kennigo St
Grenier St
Love St
Gipps St
Wickham St
Brunswick St
Warner St
Bridge St
East St
Church St
Wandoo St
Doggett St
Small St
Chester St
James St
McLachlan St
Robertson St
Arthur St
Harcourt St
Kent St
Terrace St
Clay St
Heal St
Annie St
Browne St
Gibbon St

Gregory Terr
Hill St
Roger St
Water St
Quarry St
Victoria St
Union St
Isaac St
Edward St
Little
Hope St
Boundary St
Bowen St
Leichhardt St
Astor Terr
Upper
Edward St
Henry St
Wharf St
St Pauls Terr
Gotha St
Thornbury St
Philips St
Barry Pde
Ivory St

St John's Cathedral

Customs House
Holman St
Holman St
KANGAROO POINT
Story Bridge
Baker St
Gilbey La
Locke St
Langshaw St
New Farm
Bowen Terr
Bowen Bowen
Balfour St

Central Station
Turbot St
Adelaide St
Ann St
Post Office Square
QPWS
King George Square
Queen St
Post Office Square

Riverside
Eagle St
Riverside Centre
Eagle St Pier
St Stephen's Cathedral
Queen St Mall

Central Bus Station
Elizabeth St
Charlotte St
Albert St
George St
Mary St
William St
Alice St
Margaret St

Waterfront Place
Wharf St
Baldon St
Rotherham St
Thornton St
Macrossan St
Hamilton St
Main St
Deakin St
Bradfield Highway

Ferry St
Dockside
Cairns St
Lambert St
Sydney St
Oxlade Dr
Hazelwood St
Griffith St
Llewellyn St
Sydney St
Merthyl Rd
Abbott St
Moray St
Watson St
Moreton St

Botanical Gardens
Parliament House
QUT
Old Government House
Gardens Point Rd
South-East Freeway

D'Connell St
Castlebar
Shafston Av
Thorn St
Mowbray Park
Connor St
Pearson St
Thomas St
Bell St
Sinclair St

South Bank Lifestyle Markets
South Bank 3
Goodwill Bridge
Queensland Maritime Museum
River Plaza
Lower River Terr
Dock St
Captain Cook Bridge
Paton St
River Terr
Main St
Llewellyn St
Walmsley St
Lockerbie St
Bromley St
Balnes St
Rosina St
Sailsone St
Wellington Rd
Manilla St
Geelong St
Park Rd
Lytton Rd

To Highway 1 (Pacific Highway), Cleveland & Gold Coast
Mark La
4
5
6

⚓ CityCat
⚓ Inner City Ferry

N

300 metres
300 yards

BRISBANE AND AROUND LISTINGS

Where to stay

Brisbane

$$$$-$$$ Il Mondo Boutique Hotel, 25 Rotherham St, T1300 665526, T3392 0111, www.ilmondo.com.au. Across the river on Kangaroo Point, this modern and chic hotel offers 1-3 bedroom suites and self-contained apartments, interesting aesthetics and relative peace from the centre. It is also within walking distance of all the action via a typical Brizzie ferry ride from the Holman St Wharf. In-house contemporary alfresco restaurant and a lap pool.

$$$$-$ Brisbane Northside Caravan Village, 763 Zillmere Rd (off Gympie Rd), on the northern approach, 12 km from the CBD, T1800 060797, T3263 4040, www.caravan village.com.au. This is the best motor park, offering a wide range of options from luxury cabins, en suite/standard powered and non-powered sites, pool, store, internet and an excellent camp kitchen.

Gold Coast

Accommodation agents include the **Gold Coast Accommodation Service**, Shop 1, 1 Beach Rd, Surfers, T5592 0067, www.goldcoastaccommodation service.com.au. The Gold Coast City Council operates a number of excellent facilities up and down the coast. Look out for their free *Gold Coast City Council Holiday Parks* brochure or visit www.goldcoasttouristparks.com.au.

$$-$ Trekkers, 22 White St, Southport, 2 km north of Surfers, T1800 100 004, T5591 5616, www.trekkersbackpackers.com.au. The best backpackers in the region. Small traditional suburban Queenslander, offering cosy, well-appointed rooms including en suite doubles with TV, good pool and garden. Great atmosphere, friendly, family-run business with the emphasis on looking after each guest rather than the turnover.

Hinterland and Islands

$$$$ O'Reilly's Rainforest Guesthouse, Lamington National Park Rd (via Canungra), Lamington National Park, T1800 88722, T5544 0644, www.oreillys.com.au. A range of room options from luxury suites to standard, pool, sauna, spa and restaurant. Package includes meals and some tours.

$$$$-$$ Tangalooma Wild Dolphin Resort, Moreton Island, T1300 652250, T3637 2000, www.tangalooma.com. A fine resort offering a wide range of beachside accommodation, from luxury self-contained apartments and standard rooms/units to new backpacker/budget beds, a restaurant, bistro/bar café, pools, an environmental centre, with dolphin feeding and watching, and many water sports and other activities.

Restaurants

Brisbane offers a vast choice. Outside the city centre and the Riverside (Eagle St) areas the suburbs of Fortitude Valley, New Farm (east), South Bank, the West End (south of the river) and Paddington (west) are well worth looking at. The main focuses for Brisbane's café scene are Brunswick St Mall in Fortitude Valley, South Bank parklands, West End (Boundary St) and Petrie Terrace/Paddington (Caxton and Given Terrace). Worth checking out are the stunning views from the **Summit Restaurant** at Mount Coot-tha; or a leisurely lunch or dinner cruise on a paddle steamer. And for something uniquely Brisbane, try the famed Moreton Bay Bug (a delicious and very weird-looking lobster).

Bushwacker Ecotours, T3720 9020 , www.bushwacker-ecotours.com.au. Day walking tours and overnight camping trips to Lamington and Moreton Island from $199.

Story Bridge Adventure Climb, 170 Main St, Kangaroo Point, Brisbane T1300 254627, T3514 6900, www.storybridgeadventure climb.com.au. This is emulating the success of the Sydney Bridge Climb and has, since 2005 added its own, er… edge! There are 3 adventure options both day and night including a photography tour, from $99-$130.

Tangalooma Wild Dolphin Resort, T1300 652250, www.tangalooma.com. Full day tour options to Moreton Island (from $45), with dolphin feeding/watching from $95.

considered Queensland's finest subtropical gardens, featuring over 20,000 specimens of 5000 species. Within the grounds is also a **Planetarium** and **Lakeside Restaurant** as well as picnic facilities, library and gift shop (0900-1700).

Set high above the gardens is the **Mount Coot-tha Lookout**, which offers superb views across the city and out across Moreton Bay to Moreton, North Stradbroke and Bribie Islands. Backing onto the lookout complex is the **Mount Coot-tha Forest Park** which consists of 1500 ha of open eucalyptus forest containing over 350 weird and wonderful native species, with a network of walking tracks. Catch bus No 471 from Ann Street or join a City Sights Tour.

Almost anywhere east of the Great Divide in Queensland, it seems you are never far away from a wildlife sanctuary and the opportunity to see (or cuddle) a koala. Brisbane is no different, hosting the **Lone Pine Koala Sanctuary** ① *Jesmond Rd, Fig Tree Pocket (southwest via Milton Rd and the western Freeway 5), T3378 1366, www.koala.net, 0830-1700, $33, children $22*, the oldest and the largest in the world. Having opened in 1927 and now housing around 130 of the famously adorable, yet utterly pea-brained tree dwellers, it offers a fine introduction, or reminder, of how unique Australia's wildlife really is. Also on display are the equally ubiquitous and marginally more bush-wise wombats, echidnas, kangaroos and the latest addition, 'Barak' the platypus. Bus No 430, from the 'koala platform' in the Myer Centre, Queen Street, will get you there, or hop aboard the Mirimar Boat Cruise on Cultural Centre Pontoon (located on the boardwalk outside the Queensland State Library) at 1000 (arrives 1120), which costs $65, children $38 (including admission) and returns at 1445, T0412 749426.

SUNSHINE AND FRASER COASTS

Just an hour north of Brisbane, the spellbinding volcanic peaks known as the Glass House Mountains herald your arrival at the aptly named Sunshine Coast. For those who can drag themselves away from the coast, the hinterland promises a wealth of more unusual attractions, while north of Noosa the coastal strip gives way to the Great Sandy Region, the largest coastal sand mass in the world, with Fraser Island, the largest coastal sand island in the world.

→NOOSA

To some the former surfing backwater of Noosa is now little more than an upmarket suburb of Brisbane. However, it does have one of the finest surf beaches in Queensland, a climate that is 'beautiful one day, perfect the next' and it is fringed with two unspoilt national parks. In the last three decades, the string of coastal communities known as 'Noosa' has metamorphosed into one of the most desirable holiday resorts and residential areas on the entire east coast with a corresponding population growth rate. Many Melbournians in have bought holiday properties here to escape the southern winter. But, if you can turn a blind eye to the pretentiousness of the place, it makes a worthwhile stop on your way north.

PLACES IN NOOSA
Noosa Heads is the main focus of activity with the main surf beach at **Laguna Bay** and the chic tourist shops, accommodation and restaurants along Hastings Street. To the south is **Noosa Junction**, with Sunshine Beach Road providing the main commercial shopping area. From **Noosa VIC** ⓘ *61 Hastings St, Noosa Heads, T1800 002624, T5430 5000, www.visitnoosa.com.au, 0900-1700*, get hold of the free *Noosa Guide* with a detailed road and locality maps.

To the west of Noosa Heads is the pretty 454-ha **Noosa National Park**, which offers an escape from all the sand and surf as well as some fine walks. The most popular of these is the 2.7-km **coastal track**, which starts beside the information office at the end of Park Road (T5447 3243) and takes in a number of idyllic bays and headlands, before delivering you at **Alexandria Bay**. From there you can return the way you came, explore the interior of the park, continue south to the very plush northern suburbs of **Sunshine Beach** or simply spend the day on the beach in relative isolation. Bear in mind that all the beaches that fringe the national park are unpatrolled and swimming is not recommended.

The Noosa River runs both west and south from Noosa Heads in a tangled mass of tributaries to join **Lake Weyba** (south) and **Lakes Cooroiba** and **Cootharaba** (west and north). **Gympie Terrace**, in Noosaville, runs along the southern bank of the river and is the focus for most river- and lake-based activities.

→COOLOOLA COAST

With access limited to 4WD only from Noosa from the south and a 76-km diversion from Gympie on the Bruce Highway from the north, the mainland – Cooloola Coast – section of the Great Sandy National Park, and its delightful, neighbouring coastal communities of Rainbow

Beach and Tin Can Bay, are all too often missed by travellers in their eagerness to reach Hervey Bay and Fraser Island. As well as the numerous and varied attractions and activities on offer within the 56,000-ha park – including huge sand blows, ancient coloured sands and weathered wrecks – Tin Can Bay offers an opportunity to feed wild dolphins. Rainbow Beach is an ideal rest stop off the beaten track, as well as providing southerly access to Fraser Island.

GREAT SANDY NATIONAL PARK

Along with Fraser Island, Great Sandy National Park forms the largest sand mass in the world. For millennia, sediments washed out from the river courses of the NSW coast have been steadily carried north and deposited in vast quantities. Over time the virtual desert has been colonized by vegetation that now forms vast tracts of mangrove and rainforest, which in turn provide a varied habitat for a rich variety of wildlife.

The most notable feature of the park is the magnificent multi-coloured sands that extend from Rainbow Beach to Double Island Point. Over 200 m high in places and eroded into ramparts of pillars and groves, with a palette of over 40 colours, from blood red to brilliant white, they glow in the rays of the rising sun. Carbon dating of the sands has revealed some deposits to be over 40,000 years old. It is little wonder that they are steeped in Aboriginal legend. According to the Kabi tribe, who frequented the area long before the Europeans, the mighty sands were formed and coloured by the Rainbow Spirit who was killed in his efforts to save a beautiful maiden. Other features of the park include the Carlo Sand Blow, just south of Rainbow Beach, a favourite haunt for hang gliders, and the wreck of the cargo ship *Cherry Venture*, which ran aground in 1973. The views from the lighthouse on Double Island – which is actually a headland, falsely named by Captain Cook in 1770 – will also prove memorable. All the features of the park can be explored by a network of 4WD and walking trails. At the southern end of the park (accessed from Noosa), the lakes Cootharaba and Cooroibah are popular for boating and canoeing.

RAINBOW BEACH AND TIN CAN BAY

Located at the northern edge of the park, the laid-back, yet fast developing, seaside village of Rainbow Beach provides an ideal base from which to explore the park and as a stepping-stone to Fraser Island. Inskip Point, 14 km north, serves as the southerly access point to the great island paradise. Tin Can Bay, west of Rainbow Beach on the banks of the Tin Can Bay Inlet, is a popular base for fishing and boating but by far its biggest attraction is the visiting wild dolphin called 'Mystique' who appears, religiously, for a free handout, usually early each morning around the Northern Point boat ramp.

→HERVEY BAY

The sprawling seaside town of Hervey Bay, the main gateway to Fraser Island, may lack 'kerb appeal', but more than makes up for this in the huge numbers of visitors who flood in to experience two mighty big attractions – Fraser Island and the migrating whales that use the sheltered waters of the bay as a temporary stopover. Considered by many to be the whale-watching capital of the world, Hervey Bay tries hard to stand on its own as a coastal resort and retirement destination, but – despite its sweep of golden sand – it fails. The concerted attempts to keep people on the mainland for anything more than a day seem futile and it has become one of Queensland's most depressing tourist transit centres.

Jutting out from the eastern Australian coast is the astounding 162,900-ha land mass known as Fraser Island, the biggest sand island in the world. Part of the Great Sandy National Park, which extends across to the mainland to the south, Fraser is now fully protected and was afforded World Heritage status in 1992. It is a very special place: a dynamic 800,000-year-old quirk of nature blessed with stunning beauty and a rich biodiversity. For the vast majority of visitors, the island may come as something of a surprise. Beyond a few sand blows and long, seemingly endless, stretches of beach, this is no Sahara. Blanketed in thick rainforest, pockmarked with numerous freshwater lakes and veined by numerous small streams, it surely confounds the preconceived notions of even the most experienced environmentalist. As well as its stunning beauty, sheer scale and rich wildlife, Fraser presents a great opportunity to try out a 4WD and also has one of the best resorts in the country. And despite the fact the island attracts over 300,000 visitors annually, it is still possible – only just – to find a little solitude.

VISITING FRASER ISLAND
Vehicle and passenger ferries depart daily for Fraser Island from both Hervey Bay and Rainbow Beach. For details and the latest schedules, contact Maryborough VIC, www.visitmaryborough.com.au, or see www.visitfrasercoast.com. By far the best way to experience Fraser Island is to stay for at least three days and hire your own 4WD.

EAST BEACH HIGHWAY (EURONG TO ORCHID BEACH)
Fringed by pounding surf on one side and bush on the other, barrelling up and down the 92-km natural highway of East Beach is an exhilarating experience in itself. The main access point for those arriving on the west coast is Eurong, where you can fuel up and head north for as far as the eye can see. Of course you will not be alone and at times the beach looks like a 4WD version of a bikers' meet on their way to a rock'n'roll gig.

There are a number of sights as you head north, the first of which is **Lake Wabby**, 4 km north of Eurong. Reached by foot – 4 km return on soft sand – Lake Wabby is one island lake that is at war with an encroaching sand blow, creating a bizarre landscape and the potential for lots of fun partaking in sand surfing and swimming. For a really stunning elevated view of the scene you can head inland for 7 km, on Cornwells Road, 2 km north of the beach car park. This in itself will test your 4WD skills. A walking track (5 km return) connects the lookout car park with the lake.

Next stop is **Eli Creek**, which offers a cool dip in crystal clear waters. Some 3 km beyond Eli Creek the rusting hulk of the *Maheno* – a trans-Tasman passenger liner that came to grief in 1935 – provides a welcome stop along the seemingly endless sandy highway. A further 2 km brings you to the unusual **Pinnacles** formation, an eroded bank of sand of varying gold and orange hues that looks like some bizarre sci-fi film set. Just south of the Pinnacles, the 43-km Northern Road circuit goes through ancient rainforest known as **Yidney Scrub**, taking in views of the huge **Knifeblade Sand Blow**, the pretty, small **Lake Allom** and **Boomerang Lakes**, which, at 130 m above sea level, are the highest dune lakes in the world.

Back on East Beach, the colourful sandbanks continue to the **Cathedral Beach Resort** and the **Dundubara** campsite, offering the fit and adventurous walker the chance to explore the turtle-infested **Lake Bowarrady** (16 km return). From Dundubara it is another 19 km to **Indian Head**. One of the very few genuine rocks on the island, the head offers a

FRASER ISLAND

Sandy Cape

A

Orchid
Beach ○
QPWS Ranger
Station
Waddy Point
Champagne Pools
Wathumba ○ Airstrip
Middle Head

Indian Head

*Hervey
Bay*

B

QPWS Ranger
Station
Lake
Bowarrady
Dundubara ○
Worolie Rd

Moon Point
Bullock Rd
Lake
Allom
Moon Pt
Boomerang
Lakes
Cathedral Beach ○

Northern Rd
Knifeblade
Sand Blow
The Pinnacles
Happy Valley Rd
Eli Creek
Maheno
Yidney Scrub

To Hervey Bay
Urangan ○

C

Passenger
Posan's Rd
Bogimbah Rd
Happy Valley ○

River
Heads ○
Kingfisher Bay
East Beach

*South Pacific
Ocean*

Smith Rd

Mary River Heads
Lake
McKenzie
QPWS Ranger
Station
Central Station
Lake
Wabby
Wanggoolba
Creek
Lake
Birrabeen
QPWS Ranger Station
Eurong ○

Lake
Benaroon
Lake
Boomanjin

Dillinghams Rd

Toby's Gap
Airstrip
Dilli Village ○

D

Hook Point
Inskip Point
To Rainbow Beach

N

5 km
5 miles

① ② ③

fine vantage point from which to view the odd shark and manta ray in the azure waters below (demonstrating why swimming in the sea is ill advised around Fraser). Just beyond Indian Head, at the start of Middle Head, the track turns inland providing access to **Orchid Beach** and **Champagne Pools**. Named for their clarity and wave action, they are perfect saltwater pools for swimming amongst brightly coloured tropical fish. Beyond the settlement of Orchid Beach and Waddy Point, travel with a 4WD becomes more difficult, with most hire companies banning further exploration north. But if you have your own vehicle, and enough experience, the northern peninsula can offer some welcome solitude and fine fishing spots all the way up to **Sandy Cape**, 31 km away.

THE LAKES

There are over 100 freshwater lakes on Fraser, forming part of a vast and complex natural water storage system. Surprisingly for a sand island, there is 20 times more water stored naturally here than is held back by the Wivenhoe Dam, which supplies the whole of Brisbane. The most popular and visually stunning lakes are scattered around the island's southern part. By far the most beautiful and frequented is **Lake McKenzie**, which can be accessed north of Central Station or via the Cornwells and Bennet roads from East Beach. With its white silica sands and crystal clear waters, it is quite simply foolish not to visit. Make sure to go either early in the day or late, to avoid the crowds. Also take sunglasses, sunscreen and insect repellent.

Further south, **Lakes Birrabeen** and **Benaroon** offer fine swimming and are quieter than McKenzie. Further south still is **Lake Boomanjin**, the largest 'perched' lake in the world, which means it ranks high on the humus podsol B Horizon with a large pH; ie it's very brown.

CENTRAL STATION

For those arriving on the west coast, Central Station provides the first glimpse of just how wooded Fraser Island really is. Shaded by towering bunya pine and satinay and thick with umbrella-like palms, this green heart of Fraser has its own unique biodiversity. In the 50-m canopies many of the island's 240 recorded species of birds reside, from brightly coloured lorikeets and honeyeaters to tiny fairy wrens. On the ground echidna and dingoes roam and beneath it there are earthworms as long as your arm! One of the most pleasant features of Central Station are the crystal clear waters and white sandy bed of **Wanggoolba Creek**, which is the main feature on the 450-m boardwalk.

SUNSHINE AND FRASER COAST LISTINGS

Where to stay

Noosa

Noosa is very much like a mini Gold Coast without the high-rise blocks, yet with the same massive range of 4-star resort complexes, self-contained holiday apartments and backpacker options. If you have a specific idea about what you want there are various agencies who can oblige including: **Accommodation Noosa**, T1800 072078, www.accomnoosa.com.au, and **Noosa Holidays**, T1800 629949, www.noosare.com.au.

$ Noosa River Caravan Park, 4 Russell St, Noosaville, T5449 7050, www.sunshinecoast holidayparks.com.au. This is the best motor park/camping option in the area. Hugely popular given its riverside location and views. Powered and non-powered sites, modern amenities and barbecue. Book at least 2 days in advance.

Hervey Bay

$$$-$ Colonial Backpackers Resort YHA, corner of Pulgul St and Boat Harbour Drive (820), T4125 1844, www.yha.com.au. Closest to the harbour, this excellent backpackers has a fine range of options from luxury villas and 1-2 bedroom cabins, to en suite doubles and dorms, a good bistro/bar, pool, spa, internet, bike hire and tours desk.

Fraser Island

$$$$Kingfisher Bay Resort, T1800 072555, T4120 3333, www.kingfisherbay.com.au. This multi-award-winning resort is one of the best resorts in Australia. More an eco-village than a resort, it is highly successful in combining unique and harmonious architecture with superb facilities and a wide variety of accommodation options (fully self-contained holiday villas, lodges and luxury hotel rooms) centred on a spacious central lodge with landscaped pools and gardens. Within the main lodge are 2 excellent, if pricey, restaurant/bars, with a separate bistro/pizzeria and shopping complex nearby. The resort also offers a wide range of activities and tours and hires out 4WD vehicles. There are regular daily ferry services from Urungan Boat Harbour. The resort also offers budget accommodation in its Wilderness Lodge but only through a multi-night stay option and in conjunction with its wide range of activities, tours and 4WD hire.

What to do

As you might expect, there are many tours on offer to Fraser from as far away as Brisbane and Noosa. To get the most from the island you really need at least 3 days, so a day tour should only be considered if you are hard pressed for time. If you want to explore the island in a short space of time try the excellent guided tour and accommodation packages on offer through the resorts, especially Kingfisher Bay, T1800 072555, www.kingfisherbay.com.au. Daily tours start at $169, children $99.

CAPRICORN COAST

Capricorn Coast begins north of Hervey Bay, where the great sand masses of the Fraser Coast give way to fields of sugar cane and, offshore, the start of the Great Barrier Reef. Near Bundaberg – or 'Bundy' – is Mon Repos, one of the world's most important and accessible mainland turtle rookeries. The once remote towns of 1770 and Agnes Water serve as gateway to the stunning southern reef island of Lady Musgrave, while even more beautiful Heron Island is accessed from the industrial port of Gladstone. East of Rockhampton, Queensland's 'beef capital', are the coastal resorts of Yeppoon and Emu Park, while just offshore Great Keppel Island offers many tourists their first taste of Queensland's many beautiful tropical island resorts.

→BUNDABERG AND SOUTHERN REEF

Little Bundaberg sits beside the Burnett River amidst a sea of sugar cane. The city relies far more on agriculture than tourism to sustain it and as a result is usually absent from most travel agendas. Many refer to the town as 'Bundy', though this affectionate nickname is most often used to describe its famous tipple, rum, which has been faithfully distilled in Bundaberg since 1883. Not surprisingly, the wonderfully sweet-smelling distillery is the biggest tourist attraction, while others nearby include the southern reef islands of Lady Musgrave and Elliot, both of which offer excellent diving, and the fascinating seasonal action at the Mon Repos Turtle Rookery.

BUNDABERG

Before filling the nostrils with the sweet smell of molasses and titillating the taste buds with the dark nectar at the distillery, it is perhaps worth taking a quick, and sober, look at one or two of the historical buildings dominating the city centre. Most prominent is the 30-m clock tower of **Post Office building**, on the corner of Bourbong Street and Barolin Street, which has been in continuous operation since 1890. A few doors down is the 1891 **Old National Australia Bank**, with its distinctive colonnades and spacious verandahs embellished with cast iron balustrades.

An equally popular retreat is the city's **Botanical Gardens Complex** ① *1 km north of the city centre, corner of Hinkler Av and Gin Gin Rd, T4152 0222, 0730-1700, $5, children $2, museums 1000-1600*. Added to the obvious botanical attractions and landscaped ponds and gardens are the **Fairymead House Sugar Museum**, which documents the history of the region's most important industry, and the modern **Hinkler Hall of Aviation** ① *T4130 4400, www.hinklerhallofaviation.com, $15, children $10, Mon-Sun 0900-1600*, which celebrates the life and times of courageous local pioneer aviator, Bert Hinkler. Born in Bundaberg in 1892, Hinkler was the first person to fly solo from Australia to England, in 1928. Sadly, after going on to break numerous other records, he then died trying to break the record for the return trip in 1933. There is also a working steam train that clatters round the gardens on Sundays.

Although a relatively small operation, the **Bundaberg Distillery** ① *Avenue St (4 km east of the city centre, head for the chimney stack), T4131 2999, www.bundabergrum.com.au, tours daily on the hour Mon-Fri 1000-500, Sat-Sun 1000-1400, from $22.50, children $6.75*, established in 1883, provides a fascinating insight into the distilling process. The one-hour tour begins with a short video celebrating the famous Bundy brand before you are taken to

ON THE ROAD

Coral Sea Islands

Lying 70 km east of the industrial town of Gladstone, just beyond the horizon, is one of the most beautiful of the picture-postcard Coral Sea Islands – Heron Island. As well as being a fairly accurate representation of most people's tropical fantasy, Heron is also considered one of the best dive sites on the reef. All this perfection comes at a price. Even getting there is an expensive business. Heron Island is 2 hours by launch or 30 minutes by helicopter. The resort launch leaves daily at 1100 from the Gladstone Marina on Bryan Jordan Drive in Gladstone and costs from $260 return. Contracted helicopters fly daily from Gladstone Airport for around $575 return. Contact the resort direct (below) or the VIC at the Marina in Gladstone, T4972 9000, www.gladstoneregion.info for bookings.

Accommodation is limited to the exclusive **$$ Heron Island Resort**, T1300 863248, www.heronisland.com. The resort offers luxury suites to beach houses, pool, an à la carte restaurant, bar, dive shop and a host of other activities.

view the various aspects of the manufacturing process. First stop is a huge 5-million-litre well of sweet-smelling molasses, which is gradually drawn through a maze of steel pipes, fermenters, condensers and distillers, before ending up in mighty vats within the maturing warehouses. With one vat alone being worth $5 million ($3 million of which goes to government tax) it is hardly surprising to hear the solid click of lock and key and to be mildly aware of being counted on the way out! Then, with a quickening pace, you are taken to an authentic bar to sample the various end products. Generous distillers they are too, allowing four shots, which is just enough to keep you below the legal driving limit.

MON REPOS TURTLE ROOKERY

ⓘ *Grange Rd, off Bundaberg Port Rd, T1300 130372, www.epa.qld.gov.au. Turtle viewing Oct-May, 1900-0600 (subject to activity), information centre open daily 24 hrs Oct-May and 0600-1800 Jun-Sep, $10.20, children $5.40.*

Supporting the largest concentration of nesting marine turtles on the eastern Australian mainland and one of the largest loggerhead turtle rookeries in the world, the Coral Coast beach, known as Mon Repos (pronounced 'Mon Repo'), is a place of ecological reverence. It can be found 12 km east of Bundaberg, near the coastal resort of Bargara. During the day Mon Repos looks just like any other idyllic Queensland beach and gives absolutely no indication of its conservation value. Yet at night, between mid-October and May, it takes on a very different aura. Hauling themselves from the waves, just beyond the tideline, with a determination only nature can display, the female turtles (often quite elderly) each dig a large pit in the sand and lay over 100 eggs before deftly filling it in and disappearing beneath the waves, as if they had never been there at all. To watch this happen, all in the space of about 20 minutes, is a truly magical experience. And it doesn't end there. Towards the end of the season, from January to March, the tiny hatchlings emerge from the nest and make their way as fast as they can, like tiny clockwork toys, towards the relative safety of the water. Watching this spectacle is moving and, strangely, hilarious, despite the knowledge that only one in 1000 of the hatchlings will survive to maturity and return to the same beach to breed. Of course, like any wildlife-watching attraction, there are no guarantees that turtles will show up on any given night, so you may need a lot of patience. While you wait at the Information Centre to be escorted in groups of about 20 to watch the turtles up close, you can view static displays, or better still, join in the staff's fascinating question-and-answer sessions, where you can learn all about the turtles' remarkable natural history, and sadly, the increasing threat that humans are posing to them. Best viewing times for nesting turtles are subject to night tides between November and February. Turtle hatchlings are best viewed from 1900 to 2400, January to March.

SOUTHERN REEF ISLANDS

Lady Musgrave Island, 83 km northeast of Bundaberg, is part of the Capricornia Cays National Park and the southernmost island of the Bunker Group. With a relatively small 14 ha of coral cay in comparison to a huge 1192-ha surrounding reef, it is generally considered one of the most beautiful and abundant in wildlife, both above and below the water. The cay itself offers safe haven to thousands of breeding seabirds and also serves as an important green turtle rookery between November and March. Then, between August and October, humpback whales are also commonly seen. With such a large expanse of reef, the island offers some excellent snorkeling and diving as well as providing a pleasant escape from the mainland.

Lady Elliot Island, about 20 km south of Lady Musgrave, is one of the southernmost coral cays on the Barrier Reef. It's larger than Musgrave and though the surrounding reef is smaller, it is very similar in terms of scenery and marine diversity. The island is also a popular diving venue with numerous wrecks lying just offshore (about $50 a dive).

→AGNES WATER, 1770 AND AROUND

With the dawning of the new millennium it was already obvious that both 1770 and Agnes would be changed from being fairly inaccessible, sleepy coastal neighbours into the next big thing on the southern Queensland coast. Sadly, this seems to have happened and they have fallen victim to the great East Coast property development phenomenon. As predicted, the money has moved in and the locals have moved out. Where wooded hillsides once created a soft green horizon, designer holiday homes owned by absentee landlords have appeared. Where once dunescapes created pockets of soporific seclusion, sterile and exclusive apartment resorts look set to dominate. Despite the decline, the two towns are still extremely picturesque and hemmed in by two fine national parks, Eurimbula and Deepwater. The Town of 1770 also acts as gateway to Lady Musgrave Island, an undeniable gem located 50 km offshore.

AGNES WATER AND THE TOWN OF 1770

Agnes Water has a beautiful 5-km beach right on its doorstep, which offers good swimming and excellent surfing. More remote beaches offering more solitude and great walking opportunities can be accessed within the national parks. The small **museum** ⓘ *Springs Rd, Sat-Sun 1000-1200, Wed 1300-1500, $2,* touches on Aboriginal settlement, Cook's visit and the subsequent visitations by explorers Flinders and King, as well as more recent maritime and European settlement history.

The Town (village) of 1770 nestles on the leeward side of Round Hill Head and along the bank of the Round Hill Inlet, 6 km north of Agnes, and is a popular spot for fishing and boating. It also serves as the main departure point for local national park and reef island tours and cruises.

DEEPWATER AND EURIMBULA NATIONAL PARKS

Deepwater National Park, 8 km south of Agnes, presents a mosaic of coastal vegetation including paperbark, banksias and heathland fringed with dunes and a sweeping beach studded with small rocky headlands. As well as fishing and walking, there are fine opportunities for birdwatching and it is often used as a nesting site by green turtles between January and April. The roads within the park are unsealed so 4WD is recommended.

To the northwest of Agnes is Eurimbula National Park. Indented by the Round Hill Inlet and Eurimbula Creek, it is an area covered in thick mangrove and freshwater paperbark swamps. It is less accessible than Deepwater and best explored by boat. Other than the interesting flora and fauna, highlights include the panoramic views of the park and coastline from the Ganoonga Noonga Lookout, which can be reached by vehicle 3 km from the park entrance, 10 km west of Agnes Water. Again a 4WD is recommended, especially in the wet season.

→ROCKHAMPTON AND AROUND

Straddling both the Tropic of Capricorn and picturesque Fitzroy River, Rockhampton – or 'Rocky' as it is affectionately known – is the dubbed the 'beef capital' of Australia. First settled by Scots pioneer Charles Archer in 1855 (yet strangely bestowed the Anglicized suffix 'Hampton', meaning 'a place near water'), the city enjoyed a brief gold rush in the late 1850s before the more sustainable bovine alternative finally sealed its economic fate. Although most visitors stay only very briefly, on their way to sample the coastal delights of Yeppoon and Great Keppel Island, Rocky has a truly diverse range of tourist attractions, from the historical and cultural to the ecological and even subterranean.

ARRIVING IN ROCKHAMPTON
Tourist information Capricorn Region VIC ①*Gladstone Rd, Rockhampton, T1800 676701, T4927 2055, www.capricorntourism.com.au, daily 0900-1700*, is in the Capricorn Spire, which marks the point of the Tropic of Capricorn (23.5° south), and caters for city and region. **Rockhampton VIC** ① *208 Quay St, T1800 805865, T4922 5625, www.rockhamptoninfo.com, Mon-Fri 0830-1630, Sat-Sun 0900-1600*, is housed in the grandiose 1902 Customs House.

CITY CENTRE
Established over 20 years ago, **Koorana Crocodile Farm** ① *Coowonga Rd, Emu Park, 33 km east of the city, T4934 4749, www.koorana.com.au, 1000-1500, $27, children $12, tours at 1030-1200 and 1300-1430, no public transport*, was the first private croc farm in Queensland and is home to some mighty large characters. Tours are available and there is an interesting video presentation that will avail you of many facts, the most memorable being that crocodile dung was once used for contraception (though quite how, thankfully, remains an enigma).

CAPRICORN COAST LISTINGS

Where to stay

$$$$-$$$ Beachshacks, 578 Captain Cook Drive, 1770, T4974 9463, www.1770beachshacks.com. Characterful, spacious, modern, fully self-contained bungalows with thatched roofs and decks overlooking the beach and next door to the local store and bottleshop.

$$$$-$$$ Coffee House Luxury Apartment Motel, corner of Williams St and Bolsover St, T4927 5722, www.coffeehouse.com.au. A tidy, modern establishment with well-appointed, fully self-contained apartments, executive and standard rooms. A fine in-house bistro that prides itself on its coffee.

$$$-$ Capricorn Caves Eco-Lodge and Caravan Park, Capricorn Caves, 23 km north of the city, T4934 2883, www.capricorncaves.com.au. Handy for visiting the caves.

What to do

1770 Environmental Tours, 1770 Marina, T4974 9422, www.1770larctours.com.au. An exciting and unique eco/history tour/cruise on board an amphibious vehicle (LARC), along the coast north of 1770 to Bustard Head and Pancake Creek. Book ahead.

1770 Great Barrier Reef Cruises, based at the Marina, 1770, T1800 631770, T4974 9077, www.1770reefcruises.com. Day trips and camping transfers to Lady Musgrave Island (51 km east of 1770), from $180, children $85 (plus $5 reef tax). The cruise, dubbed the 'See More Sea Less', allows a whole 6 hrs on the reef, including a stop on a floating pontoon that acts as an ideal base for snorkelling, diving and coral viewing. Departs daily at 0800. Lunch included and booking essential. A shuttle bus is available from Bundaberg. Camping transfers to the island cost a hefty $340.

CAPRICORN CAVES

ⓘ Olsen's Caves Rd, T4934 2883, www.capricorncaves.com.au, 0900-1600, standard tours $27, children $14; 3-hr caving from $75 (1300); abseiling, climbing wall and ropes courses from $35; 2-hr geological tour from $60. Accommodation packages also available.

This limestone cave system, 23 km north of Rockhampton, is well worth a visit. Privately owned and open to the public for over a century, the caves offer a memorable combination of subterranean sights and sounds and are home to an array of unusual wildlife. An entertaining guided tour takes you through numerous collapsed caverns, beautifully lit caves and narrow tunnels, to eventually reach a natural amphitheatre where stunning acoustics are demonstrated with classical music and then, utter silence. The venue is so special it is often used for weddings and Christmas carol concerts. During December and January, exiting visitors can witness a brilliant natural light spectacle created by the rays of the sun.

The cave system has been home to tens of thousands of bats and the odd harmless python for millennia, and although very few are seen, it adds that essential Indiana Jones edge. The more adventurous can go on an exhilarating two- to four-hour caving tour and come face to face with the bats and pythons while squeezing through the infamous 'Fat Man's Misery'. Also on offer is a new specialized cave geo tour revealing an ancient geological landscape and the marine fossils encrusted on the cave walls, evidence of the coral reef that existed 390 million years ago. An abseiling course, a climbing wall and a ropes course also feature.

WHITSUNDAY ISLANDS NATIONAL PARK

With over 70 sublime, sun-soaked islands, the Whitsundays are not only the largest offshore island chain on the east coast of Australia but the biggest tourist draw between Brisbane and Cairns. It is hardly surprising. Many of the islands are home to idyllic resorts, from the luxurious Hayman and Hamilton to the quieter, more affordable, South Molle, as well as a plethora of beautiful, pristine beaches. Here, for once, the term paradise is not merely tourist board hyperbole.

VISITING THE WHITSUNDAY ISLANDS

Getting there Proserpine Airport, 36 km west of Airlie Beach, on the mainland, and Hamilton Island Airport provide air access. Both are serviced by **Qantas**, T131313. **Lindeman** is the only other island with an airfield. For the latest local services from Mackay, Proserpine or Shute Harbour contact the VIC. **Air Whitsunday**, T4946 9111, www.airwhitsunday.com.au, offers fixed-wing and seaplane services to the islands. All local fixed-wing, helicopter and seaplane companies also offer scenic flights.

Shute Harbour, east of Airlie Beach, is the main departure point for scheduled ferry services that stop at most major island resorts. Ask at the VIC for the latest transfers and day packages.

Cruise Whitsundays, Abel Point Marina, Airlie Beach, T1800 426403/T4946 4662, www.cruisewhitsundays.com, offers an island resort transfer service to Hamilton, Daydream Island Resort and Spa, Long Island, and the Koala Adventure Resort on South Molle. Cruise Whitsundays also operates a connecting service from Whitsunday Coast Airport (Proserpine) through to Daydream and Long Islands. The average transfer cost is around $50. **Whitehaven Express**, T4946 6922, www.whitehavenxpress.com.au, runs a daily trip to Whitehaven Beach from Abel Point Marina (Cannonvale) at 0900, from $160, children $80. **Scamper Island Camping Connections**, T4946 6285, based at the ferry terminal, runs island transfers for campers by water taxi, from $65-160. Book ahead.

Tourist information Tourism Whitsunday ① *www.whitsundaytourism.com,* is the main tourist organization in the region but local agencies compete to provide information (and secure bookings). Shop around and start your search with www.whitsunday tourism.com. The **QPWS office** ① *corner of Shute Harbour Rd and Mandalay St, Airlie Beach, T137468, T4946 7022, www.derm.qld.gov.au, Mon-Fri 0900-1700, Sat 0900-1300,* is very helpful. Operators are always changing in the region so visit the VIC first to get the latest information, especially water transport logistics. The VIC has camping information and can issue permits. Note to obtain a permit you must have proof of return transportation.

SOUTH MOLLE ISLAND

South Molle (405 ha) is one of three little Molles (South, Mid and North) sitting about 8 km from Shute Harbour. Due to its close proximity to the mainland it is relatively cheap to reach, South Molle is popular with day trippers. With its varied habitats and hilly topography, the island has excellent walking and sublime views. The best of these is undoubtedly the 6-km **Spion Kop walk** that climbs through forest and over open grassland to some superb viewpoints across to the outer islands. The resort on the island is pleasant and casual.

LONG ISLAND

Aptly named Long Island is the closest island to the mainland and runs parallel with the uninhabited coastal fringes of the Conway National Park. A national park in its own right, much of its 800 ha of dense rainforest is inaccessible, save for a loose network of tracks that connect a number of pretty beaches near the major resorts at the northern end.

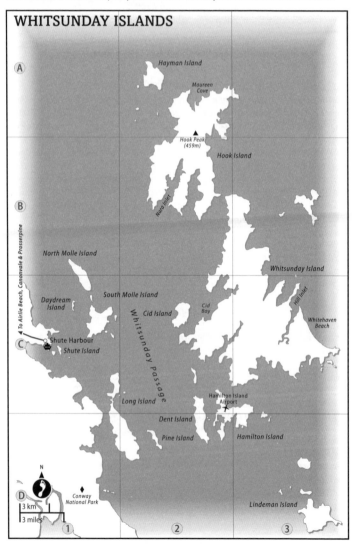

WHITSUNDAY ISLANDS

Hayman Island

Maureen Cove

Hook Peak (459m)

Hook Island

Nara Inlet

North Molle Island

Whitsunday Island

Daydream Island

South Molle Island

Cid Island

Cid Bay

Hill Inlet

Whitehaven Beach

Shute Harbour

Shute Island

Whitsunday passage

To Airlie Beach, Cannonvale & Prosserpine

Long Island

Hamilton Island Airport

Dent Island

Pine Island

Hamilton Island

N

Conway National Park

Lindeman Island

3 km
3 miles

DAYDREAM ISLAND

One of the smallest of the Whitsunday Islands – with a name almost as nauseating as the staff's shirts – Daydream is one of the closest islands to the mainland (just 5 km away) and the most accessible. As such its congenial, if compact, modern resort has become a popular holiday venue. On offer for guests are a host of activities including sail boarding, jet-skiing, parasailing, reef fishing, diving, snorkelling, tennis and even croquet. Don't expect too many walking tracks, other than the very short variety to the bar. Walking on little Daydream is like circling a small buffet table trying to decide what to choose. It is best just to sit back by the pool, shade your eyes from the staff's shirts and, well … daydream.

WHITSUNDAY ISLAND

At over 100 sq km, Whitsunday Island is the biggest in the group, boasting perhaps their biggest attraction – the 6-km white silica sands of **Whitehaven Beach**. Aerial views of this magnificent beach and the adjoining Hill Inlet repeatedly turn up in the pages of glossy magazines and on postcards as the epitome of the term 'tropical paradise'. Though best seen from the air, the beach is easily accessed by numerous day trips and island cruises, though in many ways this is its downfall. Thankfully uninhabited and without a resort, Whitsunday's only available accommodation comes in the form of eight QPWS campsites scattered around its numerous bays and inlets.

HOOK ISLAND

Hook is the second largest island in the group and the loftiest, with Hook Peak (459 m) being the highest point of all the islands. Like the others it is densely forested, its coastline punctuated with picturesque bays and inlets. The most northerly of these, **Maureen Cove**, has a fringing reef that offers excellent snorkelling. Lovely Nara Inlet, on the island's south coast, has caves that support evidence of early Ngalandji Aboriginal occupation. It is also a popular anchorage for visiting yachties.

LINDEMAN ISLAND

Lindeman Island, 20 sq km, is one of the most southerly of the Whitsunday group and the most visited of a cluster that make up the **Lindeman Island National Park**. It offers all the usual natural features of beautiful inlets and bays and has over 20 km of walking tracks that take you through rainforest and grassland to spectacular views from the island's highest peak, Mount Oldfield (7 km return, 212 m). The island has seven beaches, with Gap Beach providing the best snorkelling.

→AIRLIE BEACH

From a sleepy coastal settlement, Airlie Beach and its neighbouring communities of Cannonvale and Shute Harbour (known collectively as Whitsunday) have developed into the main gateway to the Whitsunday Islands. With over 74 islands, many idyllic resorts and a long list of beaches, including Whitehaven, which is often hailed as among the world's best, it comes as no surprise that little Airlie has seen more dollars spent in the name of tourism in recent years than almost anywhere else in the state. With all the offerings of the Whitsunday Islands lying in wait offshore, most people use Airlie simply as

WHITSUNDAY ISLANDS LISTINGS

Where to stay

$$$$ Paradise Bay, Long Island, T4946 9777, www.paradisebay.com.au. In almost perfect isolation on the island's western side, this is an architect's dream realized. It strives very successfully to create a relaxing eco-friendly retreat with a focus on the place rather than the amenities. Although basic and expensive, visitors very rarely leave disappointed. The accommodation is in comfortable en suite beachfront units. The hosts are very professional and friendly and there is a moody yet enchanting pet kangaroo. The lodge has its own yacht, which is part of an optional, and comprehensive, daily activities schedule. 3-night packages available.

$$$$-$$ Long Island Resort and Barefoot Lodge, Long Island, T1800 075125, T4946 9400, www.longisland resort.com.au. Offering its guests the perfect arrival point in Happy Bay, both atmosphere and amenities are casual but stylish. There are 2 options: the standard resort and the budget Barefoot Lodge that has access to resort facilities.

QPWS campsites Whitsunday Island
There are numerous QPWS campsites throughout the islands. The most popular include Whitehaven Beach, southern end. It can accommodate up to 60 and has toilets, but no water supply. For information and full listings call T13 74 68, www.derm.qld.gov.au.

What to do

Airlie Beach
With numerous dive shops, umpteen cruise operators, over 74 islands and almost as many vessels, the choice of water-based activities and trips is mind blowing. The 2 most popular trips are Whitehaven Beach and Fantasea's floating Reefworld pontoon, which offers the chance to dive, snorkel or view the reef from a semi-submersible or underwater observatory. Note that both options are also the most commercial and most crowded. The main ferry companies also offer island transfers and island day tripper specials with South Molle being a popular and good value choice. The outer reef offers the clearest water and most varied marine life. There are numerous options with all local dive shops and most of the larger cruise companies offering day or multi-day trips and courses.
Dive Australia, Sugarloaf Rd, T4946 1067, www.scubacentre.com.au. A range of 3-day liveaboard Open Water Courses from $649.

an overnight stop but the town itself can be a great place to party or just relax and watch the tourist world go by.

Right in the heart of town, and the focus for many, is the new and glorious **lagoon** development. In the absence of a proper beach (and the accompanying threat of marine stingers between October and May) it has to be said that the local authorities have created a fine (and safe) substitute. In anticipation of going out to the islands you can secure some good views of them in the **Conway National Park** between Airlie and Shute Harbour. There is a self-guided 6.5-km circuit walk through mangrove forest on the way to a lookout on the summit of Mount Rooper offering a slightly obscured view of Hamilton, Dent, Long and Henning Islands.

TOWNSVILLE TO CAIRNS

Considered the capital of Queensland's north coast and the second largest city in the state, Townsville attracts a considerable number of both domestic and international visitors drawn by its enviable tropical climate and the huge range of activities on offer, not to mention the considerable attraction of Magnetic Island lying offshore.

PLACES IN TOWNSVILLE

SS Yongala is a passenger ship that sank with all 121 crew – and a racehorse called Moonshine – during a cyclone in 1911. Located about 17 km off Cape Bowling Green, it is often touted as one of Australia's best dives, offering diverse habitats and a huge range of species, including enormous manta rays, colourful coral gardens and even the odd human bone. Since the wreck sits at a depth of 29 m and is subject to strong currents, the dive presents a challenge and requires an above average level of competency.

The long-established **Reef HQ Aquarium** ⓘ *2-68 Flinders St East, T4750 0800, www.reefhq.org.au, 0930-1700, $27, children $21,* is not on a par with Sydney Aquarium's remarkable Reef Exhibit, but it still provides an excellent introduction to the reef. The centrepiece is a huge 750,000-litre 'Predator Exhibit', complete with genuine wave action, a part replica of the famous (local) *Yongala* wreck, an 'interactive island' and myriad colourful

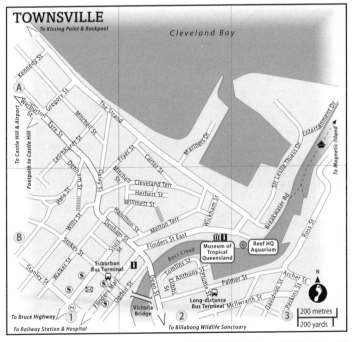

corals, fish and the obligatory sharks. Feeding takes place on most days at 1500, but equally interesting is the 'Danger Trail', a guided presentation (daily at 1300) that introduces some of the most deadly and dangerous creatures on the reef, such as the nasty box jellyfish. The star of the show, however, is the stonefish, which has to be the ugliest fish on the planet.

Next door to Reef HQ, the newly renovated **Museum of Tropical Queensland** ① *Flinders St East, T4726 0600, www.mtq.qm.qld.gov.au, 0930-1700, $15, children $9*, provides an impressive insight into the region's maritime history, with the story of HMS Pandora, the British 17th-century tall ship that is closely linked with that of the better known HMS Bounty. It was the *Pandora* that was dispatched by the British Admiralty in 1790 to bring the Bounty mutineers to justice, but her own voyage to the South Pacific proved no less notorious. After capturing 14 of the mutineers on the island of Tahiti and going in search of those who remained on the *Bounty*, the *Pandora* ran aground on the Barrier Reef, with the loss of 31 crew. The wreck was rediscovered near Cape York in 1977, resulting in a frenzy of archaeological interest, and the many exhibits and artifacts are on show in the museum today. There is an interactive science centre to keep the less nautically inclined suitably engaged. The café has fine views across the river.

Fringing the shoreline east of the city centre is **The Strand**, which is said by some to be the most attractive public waterfront development in Australia, providing an ideal spot to soak up the rays, take a stroll or break a leg on rollerblades. It is also designed to serve as protection against cyclones, but you won't find any signs advertising the fact. One of the most attractive features of the Strand is the collection of 50-year old Bunyan fig trees that look like columns of melted wax. At its westerly terminus – **Kissing Point** – there is a man-made rockpool, which provides safe swimming year round and complete protection from the infamous 'marine stingers'. There is also a popular fish and chip shop and seafood restaurant next to the pool, but unless you want an enforced hunger strike while you wait in line, it is best avoided.

As well as the enigmatic sugar shaker building, Townsville's skyline is dominated by **Castle Hill**, which glows orange in the rays of the rising sun. If you cannot drag yourself out of bed to see for yourself, then you can always make the climb to the summit by car or on foot and take in the memorable views, day or night. Access by car is at the end of Burk Street, off Warburton Street. The Goat Track to the summit is off Stanton Street, at the end of Gregory Street, also off Warburton.

Billabong Wildlife Sanctuary ① *17 km south of the city, next to the Bruce Highway, T4778 8344, www.billabongsanctuary.com.au, 0800-1700, $30, children $19*, is one of the best in Queensland. Fringing an authentic billabong (water hole or stagnant pool), it houses an extensive collection of natives, from the leggy cassowary to the sleepy wombat. There are many tame roos and emus lazing on paths around the park, as well as more dangerous individuals such as crocs and poisonous snakes. Various shows and talks throughout the day give you an opportunity to learn about the animals and, if you wish, to handle the more docile serpents and baby crocs. Don't miss the wonderfully smelly fruit bat colony next to the lake.

Magnetic Island is Townsville's biggest tourist attraction and the most easily accessible tropical island bolthole on the reef. Lying only 8 km offshore and baking in over 320 days of sunshine a year, 'Maggie' has always been a popular holiday spot, but its discreet permanent population also adds charm and an authenticity lacking in most of the resort-style islands. In fact, it is considered by many in the region as the most desirable suburb in Townsville. With its amenities concentrated in the eastern and northeastern fringes of the island, Maggie boasts a much larger area of wild and fairly inaccessible terrain giving an overall impression of wilderness and escape. With over half the island given over to national park, encompassing over 40 km of walking tracks, 20 picture-postcard bays and beaches, as well as a wealth of activities and some great budget accommodation, not to mention a resident population of koalas, the island certainly does earn its name in the number of visitors it attracts, though the real derivation is from Captain Cook (who else?) whose compass had a small fit as he passed by in 1770.

VISITING MAGNETIC ISLAND
There are regular ferry services from Townsville to Nelly Bay. The best way to explore the island is to hire a 4WD or moke. The four main villages spread along its eastern coastline are served by public transport. Tours are also available.

Tourist information VIC ① *Shop 1, Nelly Bay, T4758 1862, 0800-1630*, is a short walk from the ferry. It offers transportation, accommodation and activity bookings.

AROUND MAGNETIC ISLAND
With over 20 beaches to choose from there are plenty of places to set up camp and just relax. Although there is excellent swimming and some good snorkelling spots – most notably the left side of Arthur Bay – care must be taken during the stinger season from October to May, when you are advised to swim only in the netted areas at Picnic Bay and Horseshoe Bay. The most popular beaches are **Rocky Bay**, between Picnic Bay and Nelly Bay, and **Alma Bay**, just north of Arcadia, though the most secluded and most beautiful are **Arthur Bay**, **Florence Bay**, **Radical Bay** and **Balding Bay**, at the northeast corner of the island. All four are accessed via the unsealed Radical Bay Track, 8 km north of Picnic Bay (but note that all vehicle hire companies place restrictions on unsealed roads, so you may have to walk). Beyond these bays is **Horseshoe Bay**, the biggest on the island and a popular spot for swimming and water sports.

There are many excellent walking tracks on the island with the two most notable being the **Horseshoe Bay to Arthur Bay track** (3 km, two hours one way) and in the same vicinity, the **Forts Walk** (2 km, 1½ hours return). The Horseshoe Bay to Arthur Bay track can be tackled in either direction and takes in all the secluded bays and some low-lying bush. Many allow themselves extended stops at one of the beaches since it can be very difficult to drag yourself away. The Forts Walk starts at the Radical Bay turn-off and follows the ridge past some old gun emplacements to the old observation tower lookout. This track is also one of the best places to observe koalas. Late afternoon (when they are awake and feeding) is the best time to see them. Another short walk to **Hawking's Point lookout** above Picnic Bay is also worthwhile. It starts at the end of Picnic Street (600 m, 30 minutes). To visit the more remote areas on the south and west coast requires your own 4WD, a boat or a very long trek. The unsealed track west starts from Yule Street, Picnic Bay, beside the golf course. Sadly, the island's highest peak Mount Cook (497 m) is inaccessible. Magnetic Island is a superb and relatively cheap venue to learn to dive. There are also some excellent dive sites around the island, including the wreck of the *Yongala*.

→HINCHINBROOK ISLAND NATIONAL PARK

From the moment you first see it, Hinchinbrook Island casts its irresistible spell. Even from afar, the green rugged peaks possess a dramatic air of wilderness. Heading north from Townsville, the Bruce Highway passes Ingham before crossing the Herbert River. It then climbs to reach the breathtaking lookout across to Hinchinbrook, its mountainous outline and velvety green cloak of rainforest seemingly almost connected to the mainland by the huge expanse of impenetrable mangrove swamps and smaller islands.

AROUND THE ISLAND

At almost 40,000 ha, Hinchinbrook is the largest island national park in the world and, having changed little since white settlement in Australia, remains one of the most unspoilt. Crowned by the 1142 m peak of Mount Bowen, it is a wonderland of sheer cliffs, forested slopes and pristine beaches inhabited with some of the state's weirdest and most dangerous wildlife. And unlike many of its peers along the Queensland coast, Hinchinbrook presents more of a challenge than a relaxing excursion. Most who choose to visit the island do so for a day, but you can stay longer at one of two designated campsites or in the lap of luxury at its one and only (expensive) resort, **Hinchinbrook Island Wilderness Lodge & Resort**. For true explorers, though, there is only one mission – the famed **Thorsborne Trail**. This 32-km, 4-day (minimum) bushwalk, also known as the East Coast Trail, is one of the best in the country and takes in a wide range of habitats along the east coast, from Ramsay Bay in the north to George Point in the south. Given its obvious popularity, only 40 intrepid souls are allowed on the track at any one time and you must book, sometimes up to a year in advance. The best time to do it is from April to September, which avoids the very wet and the very dry, but the topography of Hinchinbrook can create inclement weather at any time. The track is not graded and in some areas is rough and hard to traverse and insect repellent is an absolute must. The QPWS centre provides detailed information on the track and issues the relevant camping permits. Its excellent broadsheet *Thorsborne Trail* is a fine start.

→MISSION BEACH AND DUNK ISLAND

Taking its name from a former Aboriginal mission established in the early 1900s, Mission Beach is the loose term given to an idyllic 14-km stretch of the Queensland coast from Bingil Bay in the north to the mouth of the Hull River to the south. The area is not only noted as the main tourist centre between Townsville and Cairns, but for the importance of its rainforest biodiversity, being home to many unique plants and animals. These include the umbrella-like licuala palm and the rare cassowary. There is plenty to see and do here, but it is as much a place to relax from the rigours of the road, as it is to explore its many natural delights. The superb offshore resort of Dunk Island is no exception.

MISSION BEACH

Wet Tropics Environmental Centre ① *next door to the VIC, 1000-1700*, offers a fine introduction to the rainforest ecology and habitats of the region. If you plan on doing any rainforest walks, this is the place to get directions and all the relevant details. The centre also acts as a nursery for rainforest plants, collected, by all accounts, from cassowary droppings! Also of note are the records kept of the great bird's all-too-frequent disagreements with local automobiles. Before leaving this area, take a look at the large tree just to the south of the VIC and Environmental Centre. It is the seasonal home to a large colony of metallic starlings and in spring (August) becomes a hive of activity when the birds return to their own extensive and exclusive piece of real estate, in the form of countless, beautifully woven nests.

The main tracts of accessible rainforest are to be found in the **Tam O'Shanter State Forest** that dominates the region and contains one of the largest tracts of coastal lowland rainforest in northern Queensland. There are a number of excellent walks on offer, but take plenty of insect repellent. The best and the most moderate of these is the **Licuala Walk**, accessed and signposted off the Tully-Mission Beach Road. It's a 1.2-km stroll under the canopy of the rare and beautiful licuala palms. On a hot day the torn lily pad-like leaves offer a cool and quiet sanctuary. There is also a special 350-m section designed for kids, where they can 'follow the cassowary footprints' to find a surprise at the end of the walk. If you are fit enough for a longer walk, the 7-km (two hours) **Licuala-Lacey Creek Track** also starts at the car park. This track cuts through the heart of the Tam O'Shanter Forest and links Licuala with Lacey Creek, taking in the upper Hull River, a giant fig and lots of mosquitoes on the way. At Lacey Creek there is another short rainforest walk (1.1 km, taking 45 minutes), accessed and signposted off the El-Arish-Mission Beach Road. Just north of Mission Beach and Clump Point is the 4-km (2 hours) **Bicton Hill Track**. It is a stiff, yet pleasant climb to the summit though views are rather disappointing once you get there. Yet another option is the historic, 8-km (4 hours' return) **Kennedy Track** (named after local explorer Edmund Kennedy), which heads from South Mission Beach to the mouth of the Hull River.

Other than the rainforest and Dunk Island, the big attractions in these parts are the beaches. There are over 65 to choose from, blending together into one 14-km long stretch of glorious, soft sand backed by coconut palms. While sunbathing here might be heavenly enough, you may also be tempted into the water to swim and to snorkel. But if your visit is between October to May, play it safe and stick within the netted areas off Mission and South Mission beaches, in order to avoid 'stingers'.

DUNK ISLAND

Once named (far more suitably) Coonanglebah by the Aboriginals, meaning 'The Island of Peace and Plenty', this island was renamed Dunk by Captain James Cook in 1770 after Lord Dunk, First Lord of the Admiralty. But whatever its official label, this 730-ha national and marine park, lying less than 5 km off Mission Beach, certainly offers plenty and is one of the most beautiful island parks north of the Whitsundays. Until February 2011 that is, when Cyclone Yasi (a Category 5) tore across the region. Indeed, the eye of the storm passed directly across this stretch of coastline and wiped out much of the human infrastructure on the island and the mainland.

TOWNSVILLE TO CAIRNS LISTINGS

Where to stay

Townsville

$$$-$ Walkabout Palms Caravan Park, 6 University Rd, Wulguru, T1800 633562, T4778 2480, www.walkaboutpalms.com.au. This 4-star park has good facilities and is connected to the 24-hr petrol station. Although not central to the city, which is 7 km away, it's in a good position for the transitory visitor as it's right on the main north-south highway.

$$ Yongala Lodge, off the Strand on Fryer St, T4772 4633, www.historicyongala.com.au. Named after the famous local shipwreck, offers a range of contemporary motel units from single to 2-bedroom, a pleasant Mediterranean/ international restaurant and is a pebble's throw from the waterfront.

Magnetic Island

$$-$ Bungalow Bay Koala Village (YHA), 40 Horseshoe Bay Rd, Horseshoe Bay, T1800 285577, T4778 5577, www.bungalowbay.com.au. Set in spacious grounds, offering everything from a/c chalets (some en suite) and en suite multi-share to camp and powered sites with camp kitchen. Regular, mass lorikeet feeding and resident koala in its own boutique wildlife park. Lively place with popular late night bar and bistro, pool, spa and internet but a little further away from the beach.

Mission Beach

$$$$-$$$ Sejala, 1 Pacific St, Mission Beach, T4088 6699, www.sejala.com.au. 5-star luxury in the form of a stunning beachfront villa with private pool or a choice of 3 arty (and cheaper) self-contained beach huts with shared plunge pool.

$$$-$$ Sanctuary Retreat, 72 Holt Rd, Bingil Bay, T1800 777012, T4088 6064, www.sanctuaryatmission .com. An interesting eco-retreat; wildlife enthusiasts will love it. The minimalist and secluded forest huts are in a setting designed to nurture and attract the local wildlife rather than scare it away. Restaurant, internet and pick-ups. Good value.

At the time of going to press reconstruction of the resort was still taking place and visitation still under review. However, if you do make it over – whether staying at the redeveloped resort or as day visitor – there is plenty to see or do. The vast majority come to relax big style, but if you can drag yourself away from the beautiful stretch of palm-fringed beach either side of the wharf in **Brammo Bay**, you can experience the island's rich wildlife or sample some of the many activities on offer. The island has 13 km of walking tracks and the reception in the main resort building can provide free maps and information. There are plenty of options, from the short 15-minute stroll to see **Banfield's Grave** at the eastern end of the resort complex, to a complete Island Circuit (9.2 km, three hours). The energetic may also like to attempt the stiff climb (5.6 km, three hours' return) to the summit of Mount Kootaloo (271 m), the island's highest peak.

CAIRNS AND THE GREAT BARRIER REEF

Far North Queensland offers more to see and do than any other region in Australia. The bustling tourist centre of Cairns is the gateway to the Great Barrier Reef and Wet Tropics Rainforest that, between them, offer a seemingly endless choice of activities, from world-class diving to wilderness outback tours. West of Cairns the lush, green plateau of the Atherton Tablelands is a cool retreat from the coast, while to the north, Cape Tribulation and Port Douglas are popular excursions. Few venture beyond Port Douglas but those adventurous souls who try will experience the very best that 4WD has to offer, and be exposed to some of Australia's true wilderness.

→CAIRNS

Wedged between rolling hills to the west, the ocean to the east and thick mangrove swamps to the north and south, Cairns is the second most important tourist destination in Australia, only after Sydney. With the phenomenal Great Barrier Reef on its doorstep, Cairns was always destined to become a major tourist hotspot, but the attractions don't end there. With the ancient rainforest of Daintree National Park just to the north, this is one of the very few places on earth where two such environmentally rich and diverse World Heritage listed national parks meet.

ARRIVING IN CAIRNS

Getting around   The centre of Cairns is compact and easily negotiable on foot. The waterfront with its new lagoon complex serves as the social focus of the city during the day along with the many hostels, hotels, shops and restaurants along the Esplanade and in the CBD. South of the CBD, the new Lagoon and Trinity Pier complex gives way to Trinity Inlet and Trinity Wharf, where the reef ferry and interstate coach terminals are based. Local bus operators serve the outskirts of the city. Bike hire is readily available. Buy maps from **Absells Map Shop**, Main Street Arcade off Lake Street (85), T4041 2699.

Moving on   From Cairns, carry on overland north of Cairns, all the way up to Cape York, over 1000 km away (see box, page 118). Cairns also has flights to many international destinations, see page 272, and Uluru, see page 196. Many hotels and hostels provide shuttle services to and from the airport, on the northern outskirts of the town, www.cairnsairport.com.au. **Coral Reef Coaches** ① *T4098 2800, www.coralreef coaches.com.au*, offers regular services to and from the city and throughout the region, from $20. **Cairns City Airporter (Australia Coach)** ① *T4087 2900*, runs services to the city and to/from Port Douglas, Cape Tribulation and Mission Beach. A taxi costs about $25, T131008.

Tourist information   The number of independent commission-based information centres and operators in Cairns is famously out of control. For objective information and advice on accommodation and activities, visit the accredited **Tourism Tropical North Queensland** ① *Gateway Discovery Centre, 51 the Esplanade, T1800 093300, T4051 3588, www.ttnq.org.au, 0830-1730*. The **QPWS office** ① *5B Sheridan St, T137468, www.derm.qld.gov.au, Mon-Fri 0830-1630*, has information on national parks and the Barrier Reef Islands, including camping permits. Also useful are www.wettropics.gov.au and www.greatbarrierreef.org.

PLACES IN CAIRNS

The majority of tourist activities in Cairns are of course focused on the Great Barrier Reef. The choice is vast and includes diving and snorkelling, cruising, sailing, kayaking and flightseeing. On land the choices are no less exciting with everything from bungee jumping to ballooning. See page 117 for details. The city itself also has many colourful attractions.

The **Lagoon Complex**, which overlooks the mudflats of Trinity Bay, is the city's biggest attraction and its new social hub. Cleverly designed and with shades of the popular Brisbane and Airlie Beach urban lagoons, it is now the place to see. A café is on site.

Cairns Regional Art Gallery ① *corner of Abbott St and Shields St, T4046 4800, www.cairnsregionalgallery.com.au, Mon-Sat 1000-1700, Sun 1300-1700, $5, free for children*, is housed in the former 1936 Public Curators Offices. Since 1995 the gallery has been an excellent showcase for mainly local and regional art as well as national visiting and loan exhibitions. The **KickArts Centre of Contemporary Arts** ① *96 Abbott St, T4050 9494, www.kickarts.org.au, Tue-Sat 1000-1700, café and bar from 1100-late, free*, intriguingly guarded on the outside by five man-sized jelly babies, is home to three resident arts companies and is never short of artistic programmes. Visiting international exhibitions also feature. Also worth a visit is the **Tanks Art Centre** ① *46 Collins Av, T4032 6600, www.tanksartscentre.com, Mon-Fri 1000-1600*, on the northern outskirts of the city. Three former diesel storage tanks are now used as a dynamic exhibition and performance space for the local arts community.

The **Rainforest Dome** ① *T4031 7250, www.cairnsdome.com.au, 0800-1800, $22, children $11*, housed in the glass rooftop dome of the **Reef Hotel Casino**, is a strange mix of hotel, casino and small zoo, but once you are inside the dome itself it soon proves a very enjoyable experience and a far better bet than $20 on the card tables downstairs. There are over 100 creatures, from the ubiquitous koalas to 'Goliath' the salty croc. For some divine inspiration head for **St Monica's Cathedral** ① *183 Abbott St, entry by donation*, to see the unique stained glass windows known as the 'Creation Design'. The huge and spectacularly colourful display even includes the Great Barrier Reef, complete with tropical fish. Leaflets are on hand to guide you through the design.

If you know very little about the reef and its myriad fascinating and colourful inhabitants, and especially if you are going snorkelling or are a first-time reef diver, you would greatly benefit from an appointment with **Reef Teach** ① *2nd floor, Mainstreet Arcade, between Lake St and Grafton St, T4031 7794, www.reefteach.com.au, Tue-Sat show at 1830, $18*. Created by the rather over-animated Irish marine biologist and diver Paddy Cowell and his equally enthusiastic staff, it offers an entertaining two-hour lecture on the basics of the reef's natural history, conservation and fish/coral identification.

SKYRAIL RAINFOREST CABLEWAY AND KURANDA SCENIC RAILWAY

Skyrail ① *T4038 5555, www.skyrail.com.au, daily 0815-1715, $45 one way ($89 return), children $23 ($34), price excludes Cairns transfers*. **Kuranda Scenic Railway** ① *T1800*

577245, T4036 9333, www.ksr.com.au, departs Cairns 0830 and 0930 (except Sat), departs Kuranda 1400 and 1530, $48 single ($72 return), children $24.

The award-winning Skyrail Rainforest Cableway, 15 minutes north of Cairns on the Captain Cook Highway, is highly recommended in both fine or wet weather and is perhaps best combined with a day tour package to Kuranda via the Kuranda Scenic Railway (see below). The once highly controversial Skyrail Gondola project was completed in 1995 and at 7.5 km is the longest cable-gondola ride in the world. It gives visitors the unique opportunity to glide quietly above the pristine rainforest canopy and through the heart of the World Heritage listed **Barron Gorge National Park**.

From the outset the mere prospect of such an intrusion into the ancient forest caused international uproar. Botanists and conservationists the world over were immediately up in arms and high-profile local demonstrations took place. But the fears and protestations proved groundless and now Skyrail is a highly impressive project that encompasses environmental sensitivity and education, with a dash of fun thrown in for good measure.

The journey includes two stops: one to take in the views and guided rainforest boardwalk from Red Peak Station (545 m) and another at Barron Falls Station where you can look around the entertaining Rainforest Interpretative Centre before strolling down to the lookouts across the **Barron River Gorge** and **Barron Falls**. The centre has displays and some clever computer software depicting the sights and sounds of the forest both day and night, while the short walkway to the falls lookout passes some rather unremarkable remains of the 1930s Barron Falls hydroelectric scheme construction camp. A word of warning here: prepare to be disappointed. Ignore the postcards or promotional images you see of thunderous, Niagara-like falls. They only look like that after persistent heavy rain and/or during the wet season. Sadly, for much of the year – from April to December – the falls are little more than a trickle. From the Barron Falls Station you then cross high above the Barron River before reaching civilization again at the pretty Kuranda Terminal. When crossing the rainforest you may be lucky enough to see the unmistakable Ulysses butterfly, which has now become a fitting mascot symbolic of the North Queensland rainforest.

The Kuranda Scenic Railway wriggles its way down the Barron Gorge to Cairns and provides an ideal way to reach the pretty village of Kuranda (see page 111). To add to the whole experience, you are transported in a historic locomotive, stopping at viewpoints along the way (which provides respite from the rambling commentary). Skyrail can be combined with the Kuranda Scenic Railway for around $102, children $51. Tickets available on the web, from travel agents, tour desks, hotels, motels, caravan parks and at the VIC.

TJAPUKAI

ⓘ T4042 9900, www.tjapukai.com.au, 0900-1700, day rates $36, children $18; night rates $99, children $50.

Tjapukai, pronounced 'Jaboguy', is an award-winning, multimillion dollar Aboriginal Cultural Park lauded as one of the best of its kind in Australia. It is the culmination of many years of quality performance by the local Tjapukai tribe. The 11-ha site, located next to the Skyrail terminal in Smithfield, offers an entertaining and educational insight into Aboriginal mythology, customs and history and, in particular, that of the Tjapukai. The complex is split into various dynamic theatres that explore dance, language, storytelling and history and there is also a mock-up camp where you can learn about traditional tools, food and hunting techniques.

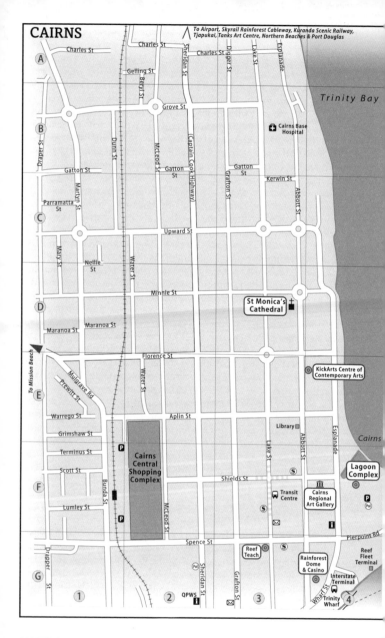

CAIRNS

To Airport, Skyrail Rainforest Cableway, Kuranda Scenic Railway, Tjapukai, Tanks Art Centre, Northern Beaches & Port Douglas

Charles St

Charles St

Charles St

Trinity Bay

Getting St

Grove St

Cairns Base Hospital

Gatton St

Gatton St

Gatton St

Kerwin St

Draper St

Dunn St

McLeod St

(Captain Cook Highway)

Grafton St

Abbott St

Parramatta St

Martyn St

Upward St

Mary St

Nellie St

Water St

Minnie St

St Monica's Cathedral

Maranoa St

Maranoa St

Florence St

KickArts Centre of Contemporary Arts

To Mission Beach

Mulgrave Rd

Prewitt St

Water St

Aplin St

Library

Cairns

Warrego St

Grimshaw St

Cairns Central Shopping Complex

P

Lake St

Abbott St

Esplanade

Lagoon Complex

Terminus St

Scott St

Bunda St

Shields St

Transit Centre

Cairns Regional Art Gallery

P (Pol)

Lumley St

P

McLeod St

Spence St

Reef Teach

Pierpoint Rd

Reef Fleet Terminal

Drapper St

Sheridan St

QPWS

Grafton St

Rainforest Dome & Casino

Interstate Terminal

Wharf St

Trinity Wharf

(1) (2) (3) (4)

A B C D E F G

For many, the highlight is the opportunity to learn how to throw a boomerang or to play a didgeridoo properly without asphyxiating. To make the most of the experience give yourself at least half a day. Tjapukai also offers a new 'Tjapukai by Night experience', which begins at 1930 with an interactive, traditional and dramatic *corroboree* ritual, which is followed by an impressive buffet of regional foods and an entertaining stage show. Transfers are readily available for an extra charge and there's a shop and quality restaurant.

OTHER EXCURSIONS

North of the airport the thick mangrove swamps give way to the more alluring northern beaches and the expensive oceanside resorts of **Trinity Beach** and **Palm Cove**. Both make an attractive base to stay outside the city or a fine venue in which to swing a golf club or to catch some rays. The VIC has listings.

Other than Trinity Beach and Palm Cove the most northerly of the beaches, **Ellis Beach** is recommended. The northern beaches are also home to the **Cairns Tropical Zoo** ① *Clifton Beach, 22 km, T4055 3669, www.cairnstropicalzoo.com, open 0830-1730, $33, children $17*, which houses crocs, snakes, wombats and a range of species unique to tropical North Queensland. It is very touchy-feely and there are various shows on offer with everybody's favourite – the 'Cuddle a Koala Photo Session' – taking place daily at 0930 and 1430, $16 extra.

Some 40 km north of Cairns, on the road to Port Douglas, is **Hartley's Crocodile Adventures** ① *T4055 3576, www.crocodile adventures.com, 0830-1700, $33, children $17*, which is one of the best wildlife attractions in the region. Long-term resident and near octogenarian croc 'Charlie', was, until his death in September 2000, the star exhibit. Despite his demise, the park has been greatly enhanced by a recent relocation and impressive renovations, and still hosts plenty of heavyweights (fed daily at 1100 and 1500). There are plenty of other animals in evidence, including the ubiquitous koala, wallabies and cassowaries. There's also a restaurant and shop. Just north of Hartley's Creek is the Rex Lookout from where you can get your first glimpse of Port Douglas and the forested peaks of the Daintree National Park and Cape Tribulation in the distance.

→NORTHERN GREAT BARRIER REEF ISLANDS

Cairns is the principal access point to the some of the top attractions of the Great Barrier Reef. The GBR is sometimes referred to as the largest single living entity on earth and is certainly the largest coral reef on the planet, stretching 2000 km from Cape York to the Tropic of Capricorn and up to 250 km at its widest point. Diving is the great attraction here, but if that's not your thing, then you should at least take a day cruise to one of the islands to sample the good life and go snorkelling. If you seek solitude there are a number of islands that can be visited independently and where camping is permitted, but you must arrange all transportation. Bookings and permits are essential. For information contact the QPWS Office in Cairns. For Lizard Island, see page 118.

GREEN ISLAND

Once you arrive in Cairns it won't take long before you see postcards of Green Island, a small outcrop of lush vegetation, fringed with white sand and surrounded by azure and green reefs. The island, named after Charles Green, the chief observer and astronomer on board Captain Cook's ship, *Endeavour*, is a textbook cay – formed by dead coral – and will fulfill most people's fantasy of a tropical island. Only 45 minutes (27 km) away by boat, and part of the inner reef, it is the closest island to Cairns and, at 15 ha, one of the smallest islands on the reef. It is home to an exclusive resort but is designed more the day tripper in mind, with concrete pathways leading to food outlets, bars, dive and souvenir shops, a pool and some well-trodden beaches.

Despite its size, you can still grab a snorkel and mask and find a quiet spot on the bleached white sand. The best place to snorkel is by the pier itself, where the fish love to congregate around the pylons. Here you may see what appears to be a large shark. It is, in fact, a shark ray or 'bucket mouth', a charming and friendly bottom feeder and totally harmless. Another fine set of dentures can be seen at **Marineland Melanesia** ⓘ *T4051 4032, 0930-1600, $15, children $7.50*, in the heart of the island, with its small collection of aquariums and marine artifacts, all presided over by Cassius, a crocodile with plenty of attitude. If you are unable to go diving or snorkelling, you can still experience the vast array of colourful fish and corals from a glass-bottom boat or a small underwater observatory ($6) both located by the pier. Although nothing remarkable, the latter was reputedly the first underwater observatory in the world.

There are a number of tour options for Green Island, giving you the opportunity to combine, diving and/or snorkelling to the outer islands with a few hours exploring the island. Or you may just want to pay the ferry fare and use the island's facilities, go snorkelling or laze on the beach. You can walk right round the island (1.5 km) in 20 minutes.

FITZROY ISLAND

Fitzroy, part of the inner reef, just 6 km off the mainland and 25 km south of Cairns, is a large 339-ha continental island surrounded by coral reef. It is mountainous and offers more of an escape than the others, with pleasant walking tracks through dense eucalyptus and tropical rainforests rich in wildlife. One of the most popular walks is a 4-km circuit to the island's highest point, 269 m, with its memorable views and modern lighthouse. A scattering of quiet beaches provide good snorkelling and diving. The best beach is **Nudey Beach** which is not, as the name suggests, a base for naturists. It can be reached in about 20 minutes from the island's resort. Fitzroy was used by the Gunghandji Aboriginal people as a fishing base for thousands of years and in the 1800s by itinerants harvesting bêche-de-mer, or sea cucumbers. It is named after Augustus Fitzroy, Duke of Grafton, who was the British prime minister when the *Endeavour* left England.

FRANKLAND ISLANDS

A further 20 km south of Fitzroy Island is the Frankland Group, a small cluster of continental islands of which 77 ha are designated a national park. The islands are covered in rainforest and fringed with white sand beaches and coral reef. They offer a wonderfully quiet retreat in comparison to the larger, busier islands. There are QPWS camping areas on Russell and High Islands. Permits and bookings can be obtained through the QPWS in Cairns.

→ATHERTON TABLELANDS

The Atherton Tablelands extend inland in a rough semi-circle from the Cairns coast to the small mining settlements of Mount Molloy in the north, Chillagoe in the west and Mount Garnet in the south: in total an area about the size of Ireland. At an average height of over 800 m, and subsequently the wettest region in Queensland, the Atherton Tablelands are most extraordinary: here, you'll find lush fields and plump cattle, tropical forests busting with birdsong, huge brimming lakes, high – and at times thunderous – waterfalls and even kangaroos that live in trees (see page 115). The further west you go the drier it gets until, at the edge of the Great Divide Range, the vast emptiness of the outback takes over. Given their inherent beauty, the Tablelands, especially the small and pretty settlements like Yungaburra, are the favourite retreat of Queensland's coastal dwellers, as well as tourists in search of peace and quiet, greenery and, above all, cooler temperatures.

KURANDA

The small, arty settlement of Kuranda has become the main tourist attraction in the Atherton Tablelands, thanks to its proximity to Cairns, a scenic railway and its markets. But while there's no doubting its appeal, particularly the spectacular means of access, Kuranda has, to a large extent, become a victim of its own popularity. The town was first put on the map in 1891 with the completion of the railway, providing a vital link between the Hodgkinson Gold Fields and the coast.

Kuranda's main attraction is its permanent markets: **Heritage Markets** ① *just off Veivers Drive, daily 0900-1500*, and the nearby **Original Markets** ① *Therwine St, daily 0900-1500*. Other stalls and permanent shops are also strung along the village's main drag, **Coondoo Street**. The emphasis is on souvenirs, with much of it being expensive and tacky, but there are some artists and craftspeople producing pieces that are both unusual and good quality, so shop around. In addition to the markets themselves, the **Australis Gallery** ① *26 Coondoo St*, is worth a look, showcasing some fine work by local artists.

Below the Heritage Markets is **Koala Gardens** ① *T4093 9953, www.koalagardens.com, 0900-1600, $17, children $9*, which offers the inevitable photo sessions for $16 on top of the admission price. Also next to the Heritage Markets is **Birdworld** ① *T4093 9188, www.birdworldkuranda.com, 0900-1600, $17, children $9*, which is a free-flight complex showcasing some of Australia's most colourful (and audible) avian species. There is much emphasis on the endangered cassowary, though the numerous parrots and lorikeets will provide the best photo opportunities.

Another wildlife attraction is the **Australian Butterfly Sanctuary** ① *8 Veivers Drive, T4093 7575, www.australianbutterflies.com, 1000-1600, $17, children $9*. It is reputedly the world's largest and houses about a dozen of the country's most brilliant and beautiful Lepidoptera in a huge free-flight enclosure, well landscaped like a rainforest complete with stream and waterfalls. A bright red or white hat is recommended.

To complete the tour of all things winged and wonderful you could also consider a visit to **Batreach** ① *T4093 8858, www.batreach.com.au, Tue-Fri and Sun 1030-1430, entry by donation*, an independent wild bat rescue and rehabilitation hospital at the far end of Barang Street. Here you will get close up and personal with a number of species, most notably, the huge flying fox – a sort of startled-looking dog on a hang-glider. Those who think bats are vicious creatures, invented by witches and horror movie makers, will have their ideas changed here. There is a large local colony of flying foxes in the **Jum Rum Creek Park**, off Thongon Street. Follow the noise – and the unmistakable musty smell.

The award-winning **Rainforestation Nature Park** ① *T4085 5008, www.rainforest. com.au, 0900-1600, attractions $42, children $21, transportation and tours extra*, is located a few kilometres east of Kuranda on the Kuranda Range Road. Set amidst a rainforest and orchard setting it offers yet another chance to experience aboriginal culture and mingle with captive native animals. There is also an exhilarating one-hour tour of the complex and rainforest in an amphibious army vehicle.

If you did not arrive in Kuranda via the Skyrail or railway and it is the wet season then take a look at the **Barron Falls**, which can be accessed via Barron Falls Road (Wrights Lookout) south of the town. In 'the Wet' the floodgates are opened above the falls and the results can be truly spectacular.

CHILLAGOE

Given its isolation, yet easy access, from Cairns, the former mining settlement of Chillagoe presents an ideal opportunity to experience the outback proper, without having to embark on a long and difficult 4WD journey from the coast. It's a fascinating little place, somewhat out of character with the rest of the Atherton Tablelands, and combines mining history with natural limestone caves and Aboriginal rock paintings. Chillagoe was a cattle station before the discovery of gold in the late 1880s dramatically transformed both the settlement and the landscape. The establishment of a rail link in 1900 led to a sharp increase of incomers and for the next 40 years the area produced almost 10 tonnes of gold and 185 tonnes of silver, as well many more tonnes of copper and lead. Those boom days are long gone and the population has declined dramatically, but the town retains a hint of its former importance in the sun-baked mining relics that remain.

The **Hub Interpretative Centre** ⓘ *Queen St, T4094 7111, www.chillagoehub.com.au, 0800-1700*, is the best source of local information and introduction to the settlement's mining history and can provide directions to the most obvious mining relics. **QPWS** ⓘ *on the corner of Cathedral St and Queen St*, offers guided tours of three of the local limestone caves. There are more caves and old copper mines about 10 km west of the town at **Mungana**, also the location of some Aboriginal rock paintings.

LAKE TINAROO AND DANBULLA FOREST

Barron River Tinaroo Dam was completed in 1958, creating a vast series of flooded valleys that now make up Lake Tinaroo and provide the region with essential irrigation. The lake itself has an astonishing 200 km of shoreline and is a popular spot for water sports, especially barramundi fishing. Indeed, some say the lake contains the biggest 'barra' in Australia. The Danbulla Forest that fringes its northern bank is bisected by 28 km of unsealed scenic road that winds its way from the dam slipway, at Tolga, to Boar Pocket Road, northeast of Yungaburra.

Other than the various campsites, viewpoints and walks on offer, highlights include **Lake Euramoo**, a picturesque double explosion crater lake, **Mobo Creek Crater**, something of a geological odyssey, and the unmissable **Cathedral Fig**. Signposted and reached by a 5-minute walk, this example of the strangler fig species is indeed a sight to behold. The tree – though it is hard to see it as such – is 500 years old, over 50 m tall and 40 m around the base and is worth visiting at dawn, when its many avian inhabitants are full of chatter. Several types of nocturnal possum also inhabit the tree and are best seen with a torch after dark.

From the Cathedral Fig you emerge from the forest onto Boar Pocket Road. The short diversion to the **Haynes Lookout**, left on Boar Pocket Road, heading from the forest towards Gillies Highway, is worthy of investigation. The track passes through beautiful woodland before emerging at the edge of the mountain and the memorable views across the **Mulgrave River Valley** and **Bellenden Ker Range**. When the winds are right hang-gliders often use the site. Check out the message written on the launch pad.

For more information on the Danbulla Forest scenic drive and self-registration campsites ($2), contact the **QPWS** ⓘ *83 Main St, Atherton, T4091 1844, or their Tinaroo Office, T4095 8459*. The area is best explored in your own vehicle or on a regional tour.

YUNGABURRA AND AROUND

While Kuranda may be the most visited and high profile town in the Atherton Tablelands, sleepy little Yungaburra is the main event. Formerly called Allumba, it has changed little in over a century and offers a wonderful combination of history, alternative lifestyle and a cool and tranquil retreat from the coast. As well as an impressive gathering of listed historical buildings, it has good places to stay, eat and shop and is surrounded by some of the best scenery in the Tablelands. Lakes Tinaroo, Barrine and Eacham, see below, are all within a short drive and provide the focal point for a number of walks, scenic drives and water-based activities. The most spectacular way to reach Yungaburra is via the Gillies Highway and Mulgrave River Valley just south of Cairns. From the valley floor the road climbs almost 800 m up to the top of the Gillies Range. There is currently no official visitor information centre in the village, but the locals are always glad to help. There is also a useful website, www.yungaburra.com. The local **QWPS** office ① *Lake Eacham, T4095 3768*, provides information about campsites and all things environmental.

Most of the listed historical buildings were built from local wood, between 1910 and 1920. Two of the finest examples are **St Mark's** and **St Patrick's churches**, on Eacham Road. Other fine examples are evident on Cedar Street, next to the Lake Eacham Hotel. Look out for the *Yungaburra Heritage Village* leaflet, available from the VICs in Cairns and Atherton, or from most local businesses. Just a few minutes southwest of the village, on Curtain Fig Tree Road, is the 800-year-old **Curtain Fig Tree**, another impressive and ancient example of the strangler species (*Yungaburra* is Aboriginal for fig tree).

Yungaburra is also one of the best, and most accessible, places in the country in which to see that surreal quirk of nature, the duck-billed platypus. **Peterson Creek**, which slides gently past the village, is home to several pairs. The best place to see them is from the bottom and north of Penda Street, at the end of Cedar Street, and the best time is around dawn or sometimes at dusk. Sit quietly beside the river and look for any activity in the grass that fringes the river or on its surface. They are generally well submerged but once spotted are fairly obvious. Provided you are quiet they will generally go about their business, since their eyesight is fairly poor.

A few kilometres east of the village are two volcanic lakes, **Lake Barrine** and **Lake Eacham**. Lake Barrine is the largest and has been a tourist attraction for over 80 years. It's fringed with rainforest and circled by a 6-km walking track. Two lofty and ancient kauri pines, amongst Australia's largest species, are located at the start of the track. The long-established **Lake Barrine Rainforest Cruise and Tea House** ① *T4095 3847, www.lakebarrine.com.au*, is nestled on the northern shore and offers 40-minute trips on the lake ($16, children $8). Just south of Lake Barrine and accessed off the Gillies Highway, or from the Malanda Road, is Lake Eacham. Once again it is surrounded by rainforest and a 3.5-km walking track and is a favourite spot for a picnic and a cool dip. The most southerly fingers of Lake Tinaroo can also be accessed northeast of the village via Barrine Road.

MALANDA AND MILLAA MILLAA

The little village of Malanda marks the start of the famous Tablelands waterfalls region. Malanda has its own set of falls but they are actually amongst the least impressive in the group and the village is more famous for milk than water. Dairying has always been the raison d'être in Malanda. The first herds of cattle were brought by foot from the north of NSW – a journey that took a gruelling 16 months. Today, there are over 190 farmers in the region producing enough milk to make lattes and shakes from here to Alice Springs. The main attraction, other than a cool dip in the swimming hole below the falls, is the neighbouring **Malanda Falls Environmental Centre and Visitors Information** ① *T4096 6957, www.malandafalls.com, 0930-1630*, which has some interesting displays on the geology, climate and natural history of the Tablelands.

A further 24 km south of Malanda is the sleepy agricultural service town of Millaa Millaa, which also has waterfalls and is surrounded by fields of black and white Friesian cattle. The **Millaa Millaa Falls** are the first of a trio – the others being the **Zillie Falls** and **Ellinjaa Falls** – which can be explored on a 16-km circuit accessed (and signposted) just east of the town on the **Palmerston Highway**, which links with the Bruce Highway just north of Innisfail. There are a few lesser-known waterfalls on the way and Crawford's

Lookout, on the left, with its dramatic view through the forest to the North Johnstone River – a favourite spot for rafting.

The **Millaa Millaa Lookout** (at 850 m) just to the west of Millaa Millaa on the recently upgraded East Evelyn Road, is said to offer the best view in North Queensland. On a clear day you can see 180 degrees from the Tablelands to the coast, interrupted only by the Bellenden Ker Range and the two highest peaks in Queensland, Mount Bartle Frere (1622 m) and Mount Bellenden Ker (1591 m). South of here are the impressive volcanic Undara Lava Tubes.

MOUNT HYPIPAMEE NATIONAL PARK

Mount Hypipamee National Park is a small pocket of dense rainforest with a volcanic crater lake, waterfalls and some very special wildlife. During the day the trees are alive with the sound of many exotic birds such as the tame Lewin's honeyeaters, but it is at night that it really comes into its own. Armed with a torch and a little patience (preferably after midnight) you can see several of the 13 species of possum that inhabit the forest, including the coppery brush tail, the green ringtail, and the squirrel glider who leaps and flies from branch to branch. If you are really lucky you may also encounter the park's most famous resident, the Lumholtz's tree kangaroo, one of only two species of kangaroo that live in trees.

The 95,000-year-old **Crater Lake** – which is, in fact, a long, water-filled volcanic pipe blasted through the granite – is a 10-minute walk from the car park. With its unimaginable depths, algae-covered surface and eerie echoes it is quite an unnerving spectacle, like some horrific natural dungeon. The park has picnic facilities but no camping.

CAIRNS AND GREAT BARRIER REEF LISTINGS
Where to stay

Cairns

There is plenty of choice and something to suit all budgets. Most of the major hotels and countless backpackers are in the heart of the city, especially along the Esplanade, while most motels are located on the main highways in and out of town. If you are willing to splash out, want access to a proper beach and wish to escape the city, ask at the VIC about the numerous apartment and resort options at Palm Beach and other northern beach resorts (about 20 mins north of the city). Prices fluctuate according to season, with some going through the roof at peak times (May-Sep). Prices are often reduced and special deals are offered through 'the Wet' (Jan-Mar). Despite the wealth of accommodation pre-booking is still advised.

There is plenty of choice of backpackers with over 30 establishments, almost all within easy reach of the city centre. Most people gravitate towards the Esplanade where a string of places sit, virtually side by side, but you are advised to look into other options too. Another small cluster of quieter hostels lies just west of the railway station. All offer the usual facilities and range of dorms, twins and doubles. Look for rooms with a/c or at least a powerful fan and windows that open, and check for approved fire safety regulations.

$$$$-$ Cairns Coconut Caravan Resort, on the Bruce Highway (about 6 km south, corner of Anderson Rd), T4054 6644, www.coconut.com.au. Offering sheer class and with all mod cons, this is one of the best facilitated in the country.

$$$ Cairns Reef and Rainforest B&B, 176 Sydney Close, Bayview Heights, T04-1777 1291, www.cairnsreefbnb.com.au. A good option if you want to escape the mainstream options. Located at the south west fringes of the city it offers Balinese style bungalows in a quiet bush setting. Hot tubs, a pool, sumptuous breakfasts and exceptional hosts.

$$ Gilligan's Backpackers Hotel and Resort, 57 Grafton St, T4041 6566, www.gilligansbackpackers.com.au. Pitched somewhere between a backpackers and modern 3-star hotel. There is no doubting its class or range of facilities. It has a large pool, internet café, chic bar with dance floor and big screen TV. Rooms vary from spacious doubles with TV and futon lounge to traditional dorms. Not the place to stay if you are looking for peace and solitude.

Reef Islands

$$$$ Lizard Island Resort, T1300 863248, T613 9426 7550, www.lizardisland.com.au. A spectacular island resort with accommodation in lodges and chalets. But the pick of the lot is the superb (and very expensive) Pavilion Suite, with its plunge pool and 4-poster daybed. The resort also boasts a 5-star restaurant and an exciting range of guest complimentary activities from windsurfing to guided nature walks.

What to do

Cairns

With hundreds of operators in the city vying (sometimes quite aggressively) for your tourist dollar, you are advised to seek unbiased information at the official and accredited VIC. Then shop around before choosing a specific activity, trip, or tour (or combination thereof) to suit your desires, your courage and your wallet. If you are looking to combine activities and save a few dollars try **Raging Thunder**, 52 Fearnley St, Portsmith, T4030 7990, www.ragingthunder.com.au.

Cruises

There are many companies offering half, full or multi-day cruise options that concentrate on sailing, diving or just plain relaxing, with various island stopovers, reef pontoon visits and all manner of water-based activities thrown in. In general, for a basic Inner Reef Island trip without extras, expect to pay anywhere between $85-150. For an Outer Reef Cruise with snorkelling, anything from $125-250. For an Outer Reef Cruise with introductory dive from $135-250 and for a luxury 3-day cruise with accommodation, meals and all activities included, about $500-1300.

Big-Cat Green Island Reef Cruises, Reef St Terminal, 1 Spence St, T4051 0444, www.greenisland.com.au; **Great Adventures**, Reef St Terminal, T4044 9944, www.great adventures.com.au; **Reef Magic**, T4031 1588, www.reefmagic cruises.com.au; **SunloverCruises**, T1800 810512, www.sunlover.com.au; and **Reef Encounters**, T4051 5777, www.reefencounter.com.au, are the main cruise operators in Cairns and like all the main operators are based at the new Reef Fleet Terminal on Spence St.

Diving

Cairns is an internationally renowned base for diving and there are dozens of dive shops, operators and schools. It is also an ideal place to learn, though certainly not the cheapest, costing from $345 for the most basic courses with no accommodation up to $490-1750 for an all-inclusive liveaboard course. Shop around and choose a reputable company with qualified instructors. The best diving is on the outer reef where the water is generally clearer and the fish species bigger. The following are just a sample and are not necessarily recommended above the many other operators. Almost all offer competitive rates and options for certified divers and snorkellers. Also see www.divingcairns.com.au.

GOING FURTHER

Far North

Port Douglas

Like Cairns, Port Douglas places great emphasis on reef and rainforest tours, with only a few attractions in the town itself pulling in the crowds. About 6 km from the centre of town, at the junction of Captain Cook Highway and Port Douglas Road, the **Rainforest Habitat Wildlife Sanctuary** ① *T4099 3235, www.rainforesthabitat.com.au, 0800-1730, $32, children $16*, is well worth a visit, offering a fine introduction to the region's rich biodiversity and natural habitats. Port Douglas is rather proud of its lovely **Four Mile Beach**, which attracts cosmopolitan crowds of topless backpackers and the more conservative resort clients.

Mossman Gorge and the Daintree Wilderness National Park

Built on the back of the sugar cane industry in the 1880s, **Mossman** sits on the banks of the Mossman River and has one of the world's most exotic tropical gardens at its back door in the form of the Daintree Wilderness National Park. Although the 80-year-old, fern-covered tall raintrees that form a cosy canopy on its northern fringe are a sight in themselves, it is the Mossman Gorge, some 5 km west of the town, that is its greatest attraction. Here, the Mossman River falls towards the town, fringed with rainforest and networked with a series of short walks. Many combine a walk with another big attraction – the cool swimming holes.

At the edge of the tiny, former timber town of **Daintree** is the biggest local attraction – the croc-infested **Daintree River**. Visitors can embark on a cruise on the river in search of these gargantuan saltwater crocodiles. There are several cruise operators to choose from. You can either pick up the cruise near the village itself or at various points south to the Daintree/Cape Tribulation ferry crossing, but most people arrive on pre-organized tours.

Cape Tribulation

Although Cape Tribulation is the name attributed to a small settlement and headland that forms the main focus of the region, the term itself is loosely used to describe a 40-km stretch of coastline within Daintree National Park and the start of the Bloomfield Track to Cooktown. It was Captain Cook who bestowed the name 'Tribulation', before his ship ran aground here in 1770. This and other names are indeed fitting for a place of such wild and, at times, inhospitable beauty. People come to this remote wilderness not only to witness a rainforest rich in flora and fauna, but also to experience nature in the raw. Beyond Cape Tribulation the road gradually degenerates to form the notorious, controversial blot on the landscape known as Bloomfield Track. From here you are entering real 'Tiger Country' and a 4WD is essential.

Cooktown

Like Cairns and Port Douglas, Cooktown has grown in stature as a popular tourist destination. There is plenty to see and do here, with the **James Cook Museum** ① *corner of Furneaux St and Helen St, T4069 5386, Apr-Jan 0930-1600 (reduced hours Feb-Mar), $8, children $3*, the undeniable highlight. housed in a former convent built in 1889 and touted as one of the most significant museums in Australia. **Lizard Island** is home to Australia's most northerly, and most exclusive, reef island resort (see page 116). The island lies 27 km off Cooktown and is almost 1000 ha, with the vast majority of that being national park.

DREAM TRIP 2:
Perth→Broome→Darwin 28 days

Perth and around, including the beaches 3 nights, page 121

Geraldton 1 night, page 137
4 hrs 45 mins (430 km) by car or 1 hr by plane from Perth

Kalbarri 2 nights, page 139
1 hr 50 mins (155 km) by car from Geraldton

Shark Bay 2 nights, page 142
4 hrs 45 mins (475 km) by car from Kalbarri

Carnarvon 2 nights, page 144
4 hrs 20 mins (330 km) by car from Shark Bay

Coral Bay 2 nights, page 145
1 hr 35 mins (140 km) by car from Carnarvon

Exmouth 2 nights, page 146
2 hrs 45 mins (150 km) by car from Coral Bay

Tom Price for Karijini National Park
2 nights, page 150
8 hrs 20 mins (570 km) by car from Exmouth

Pardoo Roadhouse for Eighty Mile Beach 1 night, page 152
7 hrs 30 mins (575 km) from Tom Price

Broome 2 nights, page 153
6 hrs 40 mins (600 km) by car or 1 hr by plane from Port Hedland

Derby 1 night, page 156
3 hrs (220 km) by car or 30 mins by plane from Broome

Halls Creek 1 night, page 157
6 hrs (547 km) by car from Derby

Purnululu National Park (Bungle Bungle Range) 2 nights, page 157
4-5 hrs (160 km) by car from Halls Creek

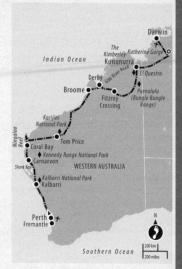

Kununurra 1 night, page 161
4 hrs 10 mins (305 km) from Purnululu National Park

Katherine 2 nights, page 180
6 hrs 20 mins (510 km) by car from Kununurra

Darwin 2 nights, page 167
4 hrs (310 km) by car from Katherine or 1 hr by plane from Kununurra

GOING FURTHER

Margaret River page 136
3 hrs (280 km) by car from Perth

Gibb River Road page 158
Starts at Derby, ends at Kununurra

DREAM TRIP 2
Perth→Broome→Darwin

Western Australia is big – very big – covering a third of the Australian continent (about the size of Western Europe). So be prepared for a long trip (over 5000 km and that's without the Dampier or Bungles side-trips). But the huge, wide open spaces have a charm all their own. Human connections are richer and more valued – because they are so much rarer. Of all the journeys in this book, this one has the potential to be the most life-changing.

Perth is a green and spacious city, with some great beaches including Cottesloe, but many promptly head for the southwest corner, where the warm Indian Ocean laps snowy surf beaches, with a hinterland of caves, forest and wine regions.

North of Perth the landscape becomes more arid. Stay in the charming, if remote, seaside village of Kalbarri while exploring the dramatic gorges of the national park. Shark Bay rears dolphins, dugongs and turtles, while further north the Ningaloo Reef attracts the mighty whale shark. Monkey Mia is very touristy, but still very memorable.

East of here, the raw red country of the Pilbara reaches its zenith in the magnificent narrow gorges of Karijini National Park. After Broome you'll reach the Dampier Peninsula and the delights of the Kimberley, with some of the most stunning yet little-visited range country in Australia. The Gibb River Road and Purnululu (the Bungles) are once-in-a-lifetime experiences and several days could be rewardingly spent at El Questro, the 'private' national park. Most of the remaining leg is described in the Darwin to Adelaide journey, but we'll pause one last time at Kununurra, WA's lonely northeastern outpost and a good base for Eastern Kimberley.

PERTH AND AROUND

One of the most isolated cities in the world, Perth is a green, clean and spacious city on the banks of the wide, blue Swan River. The city is about three times the size of Greater London (with an eighth of the population), contained by coastline to the west and the low Perth Hills of the Darling Range to the east. Although it is about the same age as Adelaide, there is little evidence of its past. History and culture are not major preoccupations of the 'sandgropers', although the city hosts an excellent international arts festival. It's a sparkling, modern place, reminiscent of American cities with its freeway, flyovers and dependence on the car.

Perth's best asset is an incredible climate. The sun simply never stops shining and each perfect sunny day is taken for granted. The endless expanse of blue sky and sea is a constant reflection in both the city's skyscrapers and residents' sunglasses. This makes for a city lived in the outdoors where the beaches, ocean, river and parks are the favourite haunts of the friendly, laid-back people of Perth.

The city centre is often criticized for being soulless by day and empty by night and it is true that it suffers from a lack of inner-city residents. The action in Perth is to be found out in the central and coastal suburbs, where you can watch the sun set into the Indian Ocean, see a film outdoors, go sailing on the river or stroll the café strips.

→ARRIVING IN PERTH

GETTING THERE

Perth Airport ① www.perthairport.net.au, a little over 10 km east of the city centre, has two terminals: domestic and international. With no direct link between the two, transfers are via the perimeter highways (shuttle $8, transfer vouchers for passengers flying with Qantas or OneWorld available at Qantas ticketing counter, T9365 9777). The **domestic terminal**, on Brearley Avenue, has a wide range of services including ATMs, **Travelex** foreign exchange, luggage lockers, cafés and all the major car hire firms. There are several transport options into Perth: a taxi costs around $30; the **Connect Airport Shuttle**, T1300 666 806, www.perthairportconnect.com.au, meets all flights ($15 one way, $25 return); the **Transperth** bus No 37 (bus stop opposite Qantas terminal, $3.70, 35 minutes) runs to the Esplanade Busport. Buses leave at least every 30 minutes (hourly after 1840) Monday-Friday 0600-2240; every 30-60 minutes on Saturday 0650-2240; and hourly on Sunday 0820-1820. The **international terminal**, Horrie Miller Drive, is slightly further out. Facilities are just as comprehensive and the **Thomas Cook** foreign exchange counters remain open before and after all flights. There is, however, no public bus route from this terminal, so it's either the shuttle ($18 one way, $30 return, details as above) or a taxi (about $35). There are also shuttles to Fremantle, T9457 7150, www.fremantleairport shuttle.com.au, and Scarborough, T0427 082652 (pre-booking required, $30-60).

Wellington Street Bus Station is the main terminal for interstate coaches and some independent state services. Greyhound ① *East Perth Terminal, T1300 473946, www.grey hound.com.au*, runs the interstate services to Adelaide, Darwin and beyond. TransWA ① *T1300 662205 and T9326 2600, www.transwa.wa.gov.au*, operates most coach and train services within the state from the East Perth Terminal. The **Railway Station** on Wellington Street services the five suburban lines, while most metropolitan buses terminate at the **Esplanade Busport**.

GETTING AROUND

Both Perth and Fremantle have free city centre buses known as CATs (Central Area Transit), T136213, circulating the city on three different routes every seven to five minutes during the day and less regularly at night. Transperth ① *T136213, www.transperth.wa. gov.au, Mon-Thu 0500-2430, Fri-Sat 0500-0200, Sun 0500-2400*, operates the city's buses, trains and ferries and has several information centres where you can pick up timetables and ask for help. These are located at the Esplanade Busport, the main Railway Station and Wellington Street Bus Station. Urban bus routes tend to radiate out from the city centre, and travelling between peripheral areas, though usually possible, can be a tortuous affair. It is far simpler to take the train, services run regularly.

City sightseeing ① *T9203 8882, www.citysightseeingperth.com.au, $27.50, children $10, concessions $22.50,* buses leave regularly throughout the day from major tourist sights in central Perth and operate a hop-on hop-off system. There is also the City Explorer ① *T9322 2006, www.perthtram.com.au, $30, children $12, concessions $25, sectional trips available for $8, children $4,* which offers a hop-on hop-off service by tram and open-top double-decker bus. The ticket is valid for two days and takes in Perth's major and historic attractions including Hay Street, Barrack Street Jetty, Kings Park, the Perth Mint and also stops at some of the major hotels.

As it's a fairly flat city Perth is ideal for cycling. Pick up detailed maps of cycle routes: *Bikewest Perth Bike Map Series* is good. Places to hrie bikes include About Bike Hire, Causeway car park, corner Plain Street and Riverside Drive, East Perth, T9221 2665, www.aboutbikehire.com.au, $36 for 24-hr rental and Cycle Centre, 282 Hay Street, opposite Perth Mint, T9325 1176, $25 a day. Ferries sail from Barrack Street Jetty over to South Perth.

ORIENTATION

The core of the city lines the banks of the Swan River from its mouth at Fremantle to the central business district (CBD), 19 km upstream, just north of an open basin known as Perth Water. Perth is contained by the coast to the west and the low 'Perth hills' of the Darling Ranges to the east, a corridor about 40 km wide. In the last 10 years the city has expanded rapidly along the sand dunes of the north coast to Joondalup and to the south almost as far as Rockingham. The northern suburbs, which are serviced by the freeway and the Joondalup train line, are a sea of new brick bungalows and modern shopping malls.

The city centre is a small grid, just north of the river, of about 2 km by 1 km. The river is bordered by a strip of green lawn throughout the entire city area, and there is a walking trail alongside the river on both north and south banks. However, although the CBD faces the river, it is cut off from it by busy roads and freeways so the foreshore is not quite the asset it could be.

TOURIST INFORMATION

The Perth Visitor Centre ① *Forrest Pl, T9483 1111 and T1300 361 351, www.western australia.net, Mon-Thu 0830-1800, Fri 0830-1900, Sat 0930-1630, Sun 1200-1630,* is the main VIC for the state. You can pick up free maps and brochures for Perth and Fremantle, and booklets on each state region. It acts as a travel agent and sells national park passes. There is an information kiosk at the junction of Forrest Place and the Murray Street Mall; it's run by volunteers and not aimed specifically at tourists but it's a good place to ask for directions or advice. Free walking tours of the city leave from the kiosk Monday-Saturday at 1100 and Sunday at 1200. The **Traveller's Club** ① *92-94 Barrack St, T9226 0660, www.travellersclub.com.au, Mon-Sat 0900-2000, Sun 1000-2000*, is a very useful contact point for backpackers. It offers help and information, has travellers' noticeboards, cheap internet and acts as a tour booking centre. Aside from the VIC, information on national parks can be obtained from the **Department of Environment and Conservation (DEC)** ① *T9334 0333*. DEC produces a small brochure on each park and excellent publications on walking, fauna and flora. It is also possible to visit the **DEC information centre** ① *17 Dick Perry Av, Kensington, Mon-Fri 0800-1700*, to collect brochures, but this is out of the way.

→PLACES IN PERTH

Perth (population: 1.7 million) is primarily an outdoor city, a place to soak up the perfect sunny climate by going to the beach, sailing on the Swan River or walking in Kings Park. The city has few grand public institutions and much of its early colonial architecture has been demolished to create a glossy modern city. The most impressive cultural sights are gathered together in the plaza called the Cultural Centre, just north of the railway line in Northbridge. The Art Gallery and the Western Australian Museum are both excellent and give a fine insight into the history and culture of the state. Kings Park, just west of the city centre, is the largest green space close to any state capital and is the city's most popular attraction. The park is regularly used by the locals for its views, peaceful walks and picnic spots, café and outdoor cinema. Swan Bells tower also has good city views, and can easily be combined with a visit to Perth Zoo, which is an unexpected oasis of bush and jungle set back from the river shore of South Perth.

The city centre is laid out in a grid just north of the river. Four main streets run east–west within this grid. St George's Terrace is the commercial district, full of skyscrapers and offices. Hay and Murray streets are the shopping and eating streets, while Wellington borders the railway line and is slightly seedier. Just north of the railway line is Northbridge. This is reached by a walkway from Forrest Place, over Wellington Street and the Perth train station to the Cultural Centre. Northbridge lies just to the west of the plaza, bordered by William Street. This whole area is undergoing regeneration, with a lot of building work and landscaping taking place around the Cultural Centre. The main shopping district is contained within the Hay and Murray Street Malls and the arcades running between the malls.

ART GALLERY OF WESTERN AUSTRALIA

① *Perth Cultural Centre, T9492 6600 and T9492 6644 (for bookings), www.artgallery.wa.gov.au, Wed-Mon 1000-1700, free; guided tours run most days, Blue CAT route, stop 7, walkway to Perth train station, car parking within the Perth Cultural Centre precinct.*

The gallery forms the southern point of the **Cultural Centre** triangle of public institutions. The main gallery was built in 1979 to house the **State Art Collection** and the clean lines of its featureless exterior walls conceal cool white hexagonal spaces inside. The ground floor is used for temporary exhibitions and this is where the state's most prestigious visiting exhibitions are shown. The central spiral staircase leads to the Aboriginal Art and Contemporary Art collections on the first floor. The gallery's collection of **Aboriginal Art** is one of the most extensive and impressive in Australia, encompassing bark paintings from Arnhem Land, dot paintings by Central Desert artists and works by WA artists such as

Jimmy Pike and Sally Morgan. The gallery has an excellent shop stocking fine craft work and a huge range of art books. The spacious, relaxed café opposite does good casual Mediterranean-style food (Monday-Friday 0800-1700, Saturday-Sunday 0900-1700).

PERTH INSTITUTE OF CONTEMPORARY ARTS (PICA)

ⓘ *Perth Cultural Centre, T9228 6300, www.pica.org.au, Tue-Sun 1100-1800, free entry, Blue CAT route, stop 7.*

Just down the steps from the Art Gallery is PICA, which showcases Australian and international visual, performance and cross-disciplinary art. The exhibitions change regularly and there are performances of contemporary dance and theatre to be enjoyed. PICA prides itself on nurturing new talent and challenging its visitors.

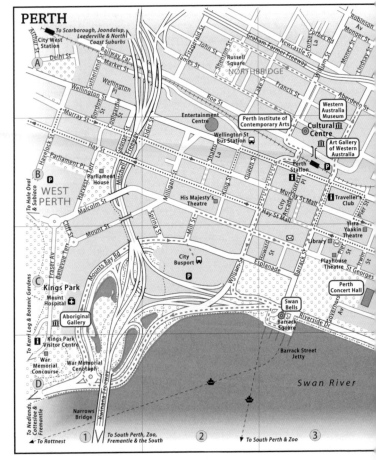

WESTERN AUSTRALIAN MUSEUM

ⓘ *Perth Cultural Centre, T9212 3700, www.museum.wa.gov.au, 0930-1700, free, Blue CAT route, stop 7.*

The natural science collection of the Western Australian Museum came together during the gold boom of the 1890s when the new settlers had the money to think up fine public facilities. The site held the combined functions of the state library, museum and art gallery until 1955 and sprawls over a large area containing many different architectural styles. The main entrance on James Street joins the Jubilee Building and Hackett Hall. The Jubilee Building was built in 1899 in Victorian Byzantine style, from Rottnest and Cottesloe sandstone. It houses the **Mammal Gallery**, which still displays specimens in their cedar and glass cases from 1903 and bird, butterfly and marine galleries. The

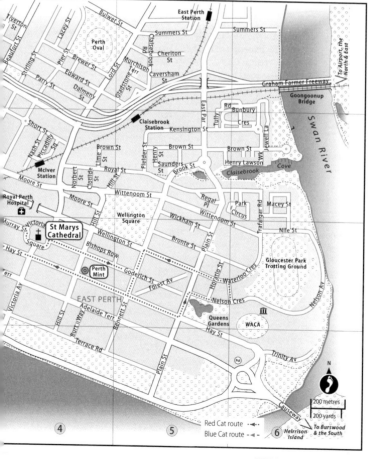

Red Cat route ·-◄·-
Blue Cat route -◄·-

Diamonds to Dinosaurs Gallery is here, which takes you on a journey through time from the origins of the universe to the evolution of life on Earth. Some of the fossils on display are incredible. The beautiful Hackett Hall was built to house the library in 1903 and still retains the original fittings, now a backdrop to the museum's best exhibition, *WA Land and People*. This is a contemporary look at Western Australia from its ancient geological beginnings to Aboriginal life, European invasion and the ways in which the land has both shaped and been shaped by its residents. The fascinating **Aboriginal Gallery** is in the Beaufort Street Gallery, the former art gallery. This is called Katta Djinoong, meaning 'see us and understand us' and goes a long way towards its aim. The exhibition examines the past and present of WA's different indigenous groups, and contemporary issues such as the 'stolen generation'. There is a museum shop and a café.

PERTH MINT
ⓘ *310 Hay St, T9421 7223, www.perthmint.com.au/visit, Mon-Fri 0900-1700, Sat-Sun 0900-1300, tours every hour Mon-Fri0930-1530, Sat-Sun 0930-1130, gold pours on the hour, entry and tours $15, children $5, concessions $13, Red CAT route, stop 11.*

During the 19th century London's Royal Mint established three branches in Australia. The last to be opened, just two years before Federation, was in Perth as a direct result of the gold-rushes that were then gripping the colony and stripping it of ready currency. Although it no longer produces day-to-day currency, the mint is still the major refiner of WA gold and buys and sells it at market prices. They also mint a wide range of commemorative medals and coins. Several display rooms are open to the public. Some have windows through to the production area, others contain some of WA's most historic and largest nuggets, and one contains a solid 400 oz gold bar, which you are allowed to handle. There are regular guided tours and some culminate in a live 'gold pour', quite a spectacular sight.

SWAN BELLS
ⓘ *Barrack Sq, T6210 0444, www.ringmybells.com.au, daily from 1000 (closing times vary seasonally), $11, children and concessions $8, the bells are rung Sat-Tue and Thu 1200-1300 and visitors can have a go Wed and Fri 1130-1230, Blue CAT route, stop 19.*

It is little known in England that the church bells of St Martin-in-the-Fields, the ones that ring in the new year at Trafalgar Square, are almost brand new and made from Western Australian metals. The original bells, cast in the 1700s from bell metal that was possibly first poured a thousand years ago and used to celebrate Captain Cook's home-coming, were found to be stressing the church tower, and it was decided to gift them to WA to commemorate Australia's bicentenary in 1988. The bell-chamber is easily accessed and walled with almost sound-proof doubled-glazed windows. These are now the only church bells in the world you can watch without being deafened.

KINGS PARK
ⓘ *T9480 3659, www.bgpa.wa.gov.au, 0930-1600, free, No 33 bus from St Georges Terr to Fraser Av or Blue CAT bus to stop 21 and walk up Jacob's Ladder.*

This huge playground for the city and central suburbs is just about everything you could want a park to be. A large area of natural bush, threaded through with unsigned bush walks, is bordered to the south and east by broad bands of carefully manicured lawns and gardens, these in turn encompassing the excellent **Botanic Gardens**. From many of these are tremendous views across to the city centre and Barrack Street jetty, particularly beautiful at sunset, and very popular with picnickers. The main visitor area is at the end of Fraser Avenue, opposite the **State War Memorial**, one of many memorials in the park as well as one of the best city-viewing spots. There's a **kiosk** ① *daily 0900-1700*, some superb tea-rooms and restaurants, the visitor centre and public toilets. Here you can pick up a map of the park, self-guided walking maps, and details of the various events and activities.

NORTHBRIDGE AND AROUND

Across the railway line from Perth CBD, and in the same area as the Cultural Centre, is Northbridge. Best known for its restaurants, bars and clubs, it is also home to a good cinema and some interesting small speciality boutiques. Perth's **Chinatown** can be found here and there are an astonishing variety of Asian restaurants and grocers, excellent for those who are self-catering. Northbridge has undergone urban regeneration in the last few years to make it a safer place to visit and to promote Perth as a 24-hour city. The **Northbridge Piazza**, at the corner of Lake Street and James Street, is a new community space where there is free Wi-Fi access, outdoor furniture and a big screen. Since its unveiling in 2009 the Piazza has played host to Perth's New Year celebrations, the **Summer Film Festival**, and has become a popular place for screening live sports.

CENTRAL SUBURBS

The suburbs north of the river and west of the city centre are some of the most attractive in the city. These suburbs all have their own character and most have eating and shopping strips that are more lively than the city centre. **Subiaco** is a stylish eating destination, although it is more expensive than Northbridge and too trendy for some. It now has a large, busy suburban commercial strip but it had spiritual beginnings far from its current celebration of materialism. Between Subiaco and the city centre, **West Perth** is mostly a professional suburb where architects, accountants and dentists have their offices. There are also lots of apartments and it makes a very convenient base close to Kings Park, Subiaco restaurants, the city and the freeway. Just north of Subiaco, **Leederville** is an alternative and funky suburb with some great cafés, a lively pub and an arthouse cinema with indoor and outdoor screens. The shops are all independent establishments selling books, clothing, homewares and music. **East Perth** is developing into a centre for accommodation and eating but is still fairly quiet and businesslike. It is also a convenient base, although parking can be difficult. **Claremont** has some great shopping and is the haunt of ladies who lunch.

Just across Perth Water, **South Perth** has the best city views and a lovely foreshore. This is a great place for sailing or waterskiing and there are hire outlets here during the summer. Several cafés and restaurants are located right on the riverbank, a pleasant place to spend a few hours. In South Perth, the incongruous **Old Mill** ① *T9367 5788, Tue-Fri 1000-1600, Sat-Sun 1300-1600, gold coin donation, by Narrows Bridge, catch a ferry to Mends St jetty, then walk towards the bridge (10 mins) or take bus No 108 or 109 from the Busport*, tucked under the freeway, is an unusual survivor from the early days of the Swan River Settlement in the 1830s. Although the windmill looks quaint, it is technically an industrial site and one of the oldest in the state. It was built in 1835 by William Shenton to grind wheat that fed the young colony. On a windy day the mill averaged 680 kg of flour a

day and its location by the river meant that the flour could easily be transported to the city. An exhibition in the whitewashed miller's cottage explains the history of the mill.
Perth Zoo ① *20 Labouchere Rd, T9474 0444, www.perthzoo.wa.gov.au, 0900-1700, $20, children under 15 $10, concessions $16-17, Transperth ferry from Barrack St jetty to Mends St jetty, then 5-min walk or catch bus No 30 or 31 from the Esplanade Bus Station,* covers just 19 ha in a block between the river and the freeway but manages to squeeze in 1300 animals in attractive natural settings. The three main habitats are the Australian Bushwalk, Asian Rainforest and African Savannah. The zoo participates in a native species breeding program, Western Shield, which aims to save the many local WA species close to extinction, releasing zoo-bred animals in to the wild.

PERTH BEACHES

The coastal suburbs are where you'll see Perth locals at their most relaxed. Surfwear is the customary attire and although you may not want to become familiar with a surfer's feet, you will because bare feet on the street or in shops are entirely unremarkable. Swimming is fine at all of the beaches, although there is often a steep shore break. As always in Australia, watch out for rips. If you want the reassurance of lifeguards, swim between the flags at Cottesloe, or Scarborough beaches. City Beach, Floreat and Trigg also often have lifeguards on duty at weekends in summer. Swanbourne is a nudist beach and Trigg is mostly for surfers but the rest are used by all. All west coast beaches are most pleasant in the morning before the sea breeze, known locally as the Fremantle Doctor for the relief it brings, kicks in from the south in the afternoon. Early evening is also lovely at the beach, when the sun melts into the Indian Ocean and there are often magnificent sunsets.

Cottesloe, 11 km from city centre, 7 km from Fremantle, is Perth's most attractive and lively beach suburb. The blindingly white beaches of Cottesloe and North Cottesloe slope into the clear, warm water of the Indian Ocean and there is usually a bit of a swell for bodysurfing. It's not glitzy and owes its contented, laid-back atmosphere to its happy locals who far outnumber visitors. One long, sweeping beach extends the 12 km from Cottesloe to Scarborough, incorporating a nudist section near the military base at Swanbourne. This whole stretch of coast is a favourite of surfers and windsurfers alike and swimming can be hazardous. Stick to the patrolled areas. Midway are two small developed enclaves, and these make two of the best spots on the Perth coast if you want to get away from the serious crowds. City Beach has an extensive grassy foreshore hard up against a very broad section of beautiful white-sand beach. Just a few hundred metres north, **Floreat Beach** is much more modest in scale, but with a superb children's playground and BBQs.

Where Cottesloe is an almost accidentally popular beach suburb, laid-back and effortless, the attractions of **Scarborough** are more carefully designed. The suburb is dominated by the Rendezvous Observation Tower, the only skyscraper on the entire city coastline. A kilometre or so north of Scarborough the long sweep of beach that has extended practically all the way from Port Beach finally starts to break into a series of smaller bays and coves. The sand at this breakpoint is called Trigg Beach, and it is one of the city's best surfing spots. A little further north Mettam's Pool is one of the few beaches on the Perth coast that favours swimmers and snorkellers over surfers, due to an offshore reef, close to the surface, that has created a sheltered 'pool'.

The beach suburbs of **Hillarys and Sorrento**, 25 km from centre, have put themselves well and truly on the map, particularly for families, by building Hillarys Boat Harbour. It's known for the shops, restaurants and activities on and around the mall-like Sorrento Quay, a pier which almost bisects the harbour and ensures a very well-protected beach.

→AROUND PERTH

The region around Perth presents a microcosm of the southern half of the state with some exceptional beaches, wildlife encounters, extensive bushland, a wine region and some of Western Australia's oldest European heritage. Much can be seen on day trips from Perth. A visit to Perth is incomplete without time spent in the small historic outpost of Fremantle, which is also the principal jumping-off point for Rottnest Island, the penal settlement-turned-holiday playground. The Swan Valley is Perth's very own wine region and a pleasant place for lunch in a vine-covered courtyard on a sunny day.

FREMANTLE

Ports are not usually known for their charm but Fremantle (population: 25,600), 20 km from Perth, is a fine exception. Founded at the same time as Perth, Fremantle has kept the 19th-century buildings that Perth has lost and retained its character and spirit. A strong community of immigrants and artists contribute to the port city's alternative soul. Freo, as the locals call it, is full of street performers, markets, galleries, pubs and restaurants as well as fishing boats and container ships. Many Southern Europeans have settled here and their simple Italian cafés have merged into the busy cappuccino strip of the olive-tree-lined South Terrace. Fishing Boat Harbour has become an alternative hub of eating and entertainment activity, and manages to mix some seriously good restaurants in with some of the country's biggest fish and chip shops. Fremantle's lively atmosphere draws people from all over Perth, particularly at weekends, and it makes an interesting base for travellers.

Arriving in Freemantle The private Fremantle Airport Shuttle ⓘ *T9457 7150, www.fremantleairportshuttle.com.au*, runs between Perth airport and Fremantle and offers a door-to-door service from terminal to hotel if booked in advance. Fares are $30 single, $40 for two, add $10 for each additional passenger for groups of up to four. They will soon be running a timetable service ($15 per person). A cheaper ($3.70, concessions $1.50), but much longer, option from the domestic terminal is to take the No 37 bus to the Esplanade Busport (see page 121) and change. A taxi will cost around $55. The main service between the Esplanade Busport and Fremantle is the 106, every 30 minutes daily 0845-2100, then 2115, 2215 and 2315; the journey takes about 45 minutes (single tickets $3.70, concessions $1.50). The train runs from Perth to Fremantle regularly throughout the day and the journey takes 30 minutes ($3.70, concessions $1.50).

The Travel Lounge ⓘ *16 Market St, T9335 1614, www.thetravellounge.com.au, Mon-Fri 0800- 2000, Sat-Sun 1000-1800*, acts as a general booking agent and net café and is also happy to provide information and advice to all travellers. The **VIC** ⓘ *Kings Sq, T9431 7878, www.fremantle.com.au, Mon-Fri 0900-1700, Sat 1000-1500, Sun 1130-1430*, is located in the town hall and is also runs a tours and accommodation booking service. Also try www.visitfremantle.com.au.

PLACES IN FREMANTLE

There are some interesting historic sights in Freo but it is also well worth having a walk around the well-preserved port precinct of the west end. Phillimore Street and Cliff Street, and the surrounding streets, contain some lovely Victorian buildings, such as the Customs House. If exploring Freo's sights on foot, there are plenty of refuelling café-stops.

Not actually round, the 12-sided 1831 **Round House** ① *between High St and Bathers Bay, T9336 6897, 1030-1530, gold coin donation, volunteer guides available if visitors want to know more*, was built on the commanding promontory of Arthur Head, and the precinct still affords good views over the boat harbour and across to offshore islands. As convicts did not reach the Swan River colony until 1850, Western Australia's oldest building need not necessarily be a gaol, but the fact remains that it is. Built as a prison for immigrant and native wrong-doers, it was too small to house the large number of British convicts and slowly became redundant, last being used as a lock-up in 1900.

The striking **Western Australian Maritime Museum** ① *Victoria Quay Rd, T9431 8444, www.museum.wa.gov.au/maritime, main museum Thu-Tue 0930-1700, $10, children $3, concessions $5; submarine tours Thu-Tue every 30 mins, 1000-1600 (1 hr), $8, children $3, concessions $5 (buy ticket at museum first, joint tickets available for $15, children $5, concessions $8); Shipwreck Galleries, Cliff St, 0930-1700, gold coin donation*, sits on the quay looking out towards the western horizon. The six themed galleries look at WA's past and future as a community on the edge of the Indian Ocean. With significant historic objects and boats that highlight the state's sporting and adventure heritage (such as *Australia II*, the yacht that wrestled the America's cup from the USA in 1983), the exhibitions tell many fascinating stories of human endeavour. Part of the museum, the *Oberon* class submarine **HMAS Ovens**, was commissioned in 1969 and saw active service for over 25 years. It is 90 m long and had a crew of over 60. Today it is in dry-dock and part of the WA Maritime Museum. The submarine is in very much the state it was when decommissioned in 1995, giving a rare glimpse into the strange lives of the submariners who crewed it. The fascinating and entertaining tours are conducted by volunteers, many of whom are former or serving submariners.

Housed in a complex of old dock buildings the original Maritime Museum is now called the **Shipwreck Galleries** and is primarily dedicated to the preservation and display of artefacts from the principal WA shipwrecks, mostly of the Dutch East India Company. Intermingled with the recoveries are charts, logs and journals from the period and the combination presents an interesting historical overview of European exploration of Australia's west coast.

Dating from 1852, **Fremantle Prison** ① *1 The Terrace, T9336 9200, www.fremantle prison.com.au, entry by tour only, every 30 mins 1000-1700 (1 hr), $18, children $9.50, concessions $15 (choose between Doing Time Tour and Great Escapes Tour or do both for $24, children $15.50, concessions $21), torchlight tours Wed and Fri evening, bookings required, $24, children $14, concessions $20, tunnels tours run regularly from 0900, bookings required, $59, children $39, concessions $49*, was built as a replacement for the Roundhouse when it became clear to the governors of the Swan River colony that a much bigger prison would be required. The building of Fremantle Prison was one of the first tasks to be undertaken by the first convict groups and took about five years to construct. In this time they built themselves a prodigious set of buildings in a huge walled enclosure, the main cell block dominating and brooding over an expansive parade ground. Such was the solidity of construction that the prison was still in use as recently as 1991.

Fremantle Arts Centre ① *1 Finnerty St, T9432 9555, www.fac.org.au, 1000-1700, free*, is an impressive but imposing Gothic limestone building dating back to the 1860s. It was built by the convicts to house those of their colleagues who had gone mad and were deemed a danger to fellow inmates and their jailers, but although still a part of the convict system it seems to have been built with considerably more flair than the stolid penitentiary just down the road. The building was converted to a museum and arts centre between 1965 and 1972, the museum closed in 2009. The magnificent wooden staircases and floors and spacious high-ceilinged rooms are ideal for its current purpose as an arts centre. The centre is run by a dynamic arts organization and is well worth a visit. It holds regular exhibitions of contemporary visual arts and crafts, runs arts courses and literary events, acts as a small but respected publisher and hosts free music in the courtyard every Sunday 1400-1600 (January-April). There is also a great craft shop, a small bookshop and a leafy courtyard café.

→ROTTNEST ISLAND

Rotto, as the locals call it, once a penal settlement, is now Perth's holiday playground. Just 20 km west of the city, it feels a long way from the metropolitan commotion. Generations of Perth families have come to frolic here every summer and it's a traditional place to celebrate the end of school, university or parental control. The entire coast is one long cordon of quite magical sandy bays and clear aquamarine water and so, understandably, come summer, many beaches get very busy. However, even at this time, you'll find almost deserted stretches towards the western and southern parts of the island. The offshore reefs are full of brightly coloured fish, exotic corals and limestone caves, and littered with wrecks. The island itself is 11 km long and 4 km wide and covered in low bushy scrub with some patches of eucalypt woodland. Much of this provides cover for the island's famous small wallaby, the quokka, after which the island was dubiously named. There are few permanent human residents as the island is carefully managed to preserve the environment and scarce water resources. The number of overnight visitors is kept to a sustainable level and cars are not allowed.

ARRIVING ON ROTTNEST ISLAND

There are two ways of getting to Rotto: by air (from Jandakot Airport) and ferry. The cheapest way is to take public transport to Fremantle and take a ferry from there. The island has a **VIC** ① *Thomson Bay Settlement, T9372 9732, Sat-Thu 0730-1700, Fri 0730-1930.* Also in Thomson Bay is a small shopping mall with a post office, ATM, takeaways, general store, bakery and clothes/gift shops. The general store stocks books and has a bottle shop. It also offers a free delivery service to the island's accommodation from 0800-1800. There is a similarly stocked store at Geordie Bay, where there's also a café serving light meals in peak season. Both open daily. The island has a nursing post, T9292 5030, a pharmacy (located at the **Wellness Centre**), police station, T131 444, and ranger's office, T9372 9788. See also www.rottnestisland.com.

PLACES ON ROTTNEST ISLAND

While **Thomson Bay Settlement** has the ferry terminal, is the main settlement and has most of the island's services, it is also something of an open-air museum, and the general layout is claimed to be Australia's oldest intact streetscape. Most interesting is the part of the Lodge known as the **Quod**, and the heritage precinct in front of it. Once one of the most feared places on the island, it was built in 1838 to house dozens of Aboriginal criminals in horrendous conditions. There were still prisoners on the island when it was converted into a tourist hostel in 1911. Most of the current double rooms were once two cells holding about 10 men. The **museum and library** ① *museum daily 1045-1530, gold coin donation; library 1400-1545, free*, just behind the general store in the mall, are the main repositories of the islands history. Museum displays include the early days as a prison for Aboriginal men, island shipwrecks, military use and its development as Perth's holiday isle.

Beaches are what Rottnest is all about for most visitors. There are over a dozen picture-postcard bays with white-sand beaches and usually clear, intensely blue water. Reefs lie just offshore from some beaches and many are enclosed by dramatic limestone headlands. The most sheltered are along the north shore and these also get the busiest, especially the **Basin**, the most picturesque bay on the island. The Basin has covered picnic tables and toilets, adding to its popularity. Other small bays a bit further from Thomson Bay include **Little Armstrong** on the north shore and **Little Salmon** on the south. The water can get choppy in the afternoons at the latter. **Longreach** and **Geordie** are long sweeping bays overlooked by accommodation and often crowded with boats. **Salmon Bay** in the south is of a similar scale, clear of boats and can be good for boogie boarding, though there are no facilities.

→SWAN VALLEY

The Swan Valley is Perth's wine region, just a 45-minute drive from the city. In truth it's half a valley, bordered to the east by the Darling Range, but running flat to the west all the way to the northern Perth suburbs. It was settled early in Perth's history and vines were being grown by 1836 at what is now Houghtons, the valley's best-known winery. All sorts of other fruit and vegetables are also grown here, and it seems that almost every other house has a sign outside advertising table grapes and rock melons. At the southern end of the valley is Guildford, an inland port established in 1829, but falling out of favour early in its history, which helped preserve many early Victorian buildings.

ARRIVING IN SWAN VALLEY
Getting there and around Trains leave from East Perth station to Guildford and Midland, but this isn't the ideal way to tour the valley. Ideally you need your own transport, or to take a tour. A taxi to or from Perth airport costs $30, double that from Perth.

Tourist information The main **VIC** ① *on the corner of Meadow and Swan Sts, T9379 9400, www.swanvalley.com.au, 0900-1600*, for the region is in Guildford. The helpful staff will advise visitors on a route depending on what they'd like to taste (ie only sparkling wines).

WINERIES
There are some 40 wineries in the region, ranging from one of the largest producers in the state to several one-person operations. Most offer wines in the $15-30 range. Cellar door

hours vary widely, and Monday to Tuesday is probably the worst time to visit as some of the smaller wineries keep these as their days off. Many have cafés or restaurants, most of which have outdoor vine-covered courtyards.

The following is only a small selection of the wineries operating in the Swan Valley, the route outlined below takes visitors on a circuit starting and finishing at the VIC. Travel north along West Swan Road to find **Sandalford** ① *3210 West Swan Rd, T9374 9374, www.sandalford.com, cellar door 1000-1700*, one of the two heavyweights in the valley offering an extensive range of wines. The 2005 Prendiville Reserve Cabernet Sauvignon is the specialty. Winery tours run from 1100-1500 and are rounded off with a full appreciation and tasting session ($22), and every Saturday (at 1100) you can become a winemaker for a day on a tour that includes an exclusive blending session and a set lunch ($125). Wines cost $14-90.

Little River ① *2 Forest Rd, T9296 4462, www.littleriverwinery.com, daily 1000-1700*, is signposted further up West Swan Road. Wines include the rare Viognier Marsanne and are priced $14-144. **Edgecombe Brothers** ① *Gnangara and West Swan Rds, T9296 4307, www.edgecombebrothers.com.au, daily 1000-1700*, is family-run and one of the most laid-back and welcoming wineries in the valley. Wines cost $18.50-68. The unpretentious shop sells an excellent range of home-produced jams, sauces and produce. The café serves breakfast, a simple light lunch using seasonal ingredients or cream tea. Try the famous Muscat ice cream. As the West Swan Road merges with the Great Northern Highway head south again and turn off onto Memorial Avenue. Here visitors will find **Mann** ① *105 Memorial Av, T9296 4348, Aug-Dec Wed-Sun 1000-1700*, a one-man operation continuing three generations of expertise in producing a smooth, dry Mithode Champenoise. A bargain at $20. Jack Mann has also produced an entirely new variety of grape, the Cygneblanc, though the wine is a little pricier at $30. Also on Memorial Avenue is **Upper Reach** ① *Memorial Av, T9296 0078, www.upperreach.com.au, daily 1100-1700*, a friendly winery that produces some of the valley's finest wines, particularly their Shiraz and Chardonnay. Wines cost $15-30. They also rent out a fully self- contained 2-bedroom cottage with indoor spa and views of the vineyard (**SSS-SS**). Note Saturday night is only available as part of a two-night booking.

PERTH AND AROUND LISTINGS

WHERE TO STAY

Central Perth

St George's and Adelaide Terraces are home to many of the big modern, glitzy hotels in Perth, all with superb balcony rooms overlooking the riverside parks and the river itself.

$$$$ The Duxton, 1 St George's Terr, T9261 8000, www.duxton.com. The closest to the city centre and its rooms and services are, by a whisker, the benchmark for the rest. Wi-Fi. The main restaurant is also good.

$$$ Sullivans, 166 Mounts Bay Rd, T9321 8022, www.sullivans.com.au. Just below Kings Park, this comfortable, modern hotel has 68 rooms (some with balcony and river views) and 2 apartments. Also pool, free bikes, free internet, parking, restaurant, café and 24-hr reception. Convenient location, free city bus (Blue CAT) at door.

$$-$ Perth City YHA, 300 Wellington St, T9287 3333. One of the few hostels in Perth CBD, the rooms are nothing special but the facilities are good. The communal spaces and bathrooms are large and clean, and there is even a gym. Cheap meals in the bar. Parking. It is next to the train line so it's noisy.

Northbridge and around

$$$$-$$ Northbridge Hotel, corner of Lake and Brisbane Sts, T9328 5254, www.hotelnorth bridge.com.au. Renovated old corner hotel with veranda. Luxurious hotel rooms (50) with spa and full facilities, bar and mid-range restaurant. Budget rooms in the old part of the hotel with shared facilities, TV, fridge.

$$-$ The Emperor's Crown, 85 Stirling St, T9227 1400, www.emperorscrown.com.au. Friendly hostel with dorms, twins, triples and en suite doubles. Away from the main hubbub of Northbridge but near the CAT bus stop. Pricey for a hostel and no breakfast included, but rooms are clean, communal spaces are large and bright and there is a café next door. Recommended.

$$-$ Underground, 268 Newcastle St, T9228 3755. Massive central hostel with dorms, pool, bar, well-equipped kitchen and spacious internet and guest area. Breakfast available. No BYO, fully licensed, free drink on arrival. 24-hr reception. Parking and internet available. Recommended.

East Perth

$$$$-$$$ Novotel Langley, 221 Adelaide Terr, T9221 1200, www.novotelperth langley.com.au. Opposite the **Sheraton**, does a commendable job at offering a similar experience at a slightly cheaper price. Parking.

$ Exclusive Backpackers, 156 Adelaide Terr, T9221 9991, www.exclusive backpackers.com. 25 good-quality rooms, particularly the doubles. Quiet communal areas are homely and characterful, kitchen basic. Internet and laundry facilities, reception closes at 2230.

RESTAURANTS

Central Perth

There are several food courts in the city that are cheap but can be messy and crowded. There is a good one upstairs in the City Arcade with an outdoor terrace overlooking Murray St Mall. Also try the Carillion Arcade.

$$$ Fraser's, Fraser Av, T9481 7100, www.frasersrestaurant.com.au. Breakfast on Sun from 0800, lunch daily from 1200, dinner daily from 1800. One of the city's best in terms of food, location and ambience. The view of the city is slightly obscured by trees, but it's still impressive and there are a few terrace tables to make the most of it. Cuisine is Modern Australian, predominantly seafood, with a few grills, and it's supported by an extensive, quality wine list. The attached **Botanical Café** (T9482 0122) is open daily 0700-2200, and offers slightly cheaper, good-quality food.

$ Annalakshmi, Jetty 4, Barrack St, T9221 3003, www.annalakshmi.com.au. Tue-Sun 1200-1400, Tue-Sun 1830-2100, closed Sat for lunch. Friendly Indian vegetarian buffet where all profits go to food and arts charities. There is no set price – you simply pay what you can afford. No alcohol allowed. Booking advised.

$ Arirang, 91 Barrack St, T9225 4855, www.arirang.com.au. Daily 1130-1500, Sun-Thu 1730-2130, Fri-Sat 1730-2200. Unusual Korean BBQ restaurant with a stylish, contemporary interior. Charcoals are brought to the table for you to cook your own meat in a central well. Good fun with a focus on the best fresh food and Korean culture.

Northbridge and around

$$$-$$ Brass Grill Restaurant, corner of William and James Sts, T9227 9596, www.thebrassmonkey.com.au. Tue-Sat 1800-late Fri for lunch 1200-1430. This brasserie on the balcony is one of the most pleasant places to dine in Northbridge. The Modern Australian menu changes regularly to reflect the use of fresh seasonal produce. Recommended.

$$$-$$ The Chimney, 171 James St, opposite Cinema Paradiso, T9328 6870. A friendly, stylish restaurant serving modern Australia and Italian meals. There is also a good wine list. Outdoor seating is available in the courtyard. Recommended.

$ Maya Masala, corner of Lake St and Francis St, T9328 5655. Daily 1130-late.

Wonderful Indian food in groovy, contemporary style. Specialities are dosa, thali, curries and tandoori but also particularly perfect Indian sweets. Prices are almost too good to be true. Licensed and BYO. Recommended.

Cottesloe

$$$-$$ Blue Duck, 151 Marine Parade, T9385 2499, www.blueduck.com.au. Daily 0630-2100. A long-standing Cottesloe favourite, the café hangs above the beach with mesmerizing views. Particularly good for breakfast, light lunches include wood-fired pizzas and pasta, more emphasis on fish and seafood for dinner. Takeaway fish and chips available 1200-2100. Recommended.

Scarborough to Sorrento

$$$-$$ Wild Fig Café, 33 West Coast Dr, Waterman's Beach, T9246 9222, www.wildfig.com.au. Daily 0630-late. Relaxed, people- and eco-friendly and the staff donate all tips and corkage to charity. It serves lots of tasty snacks and salads, juices and smoothies, and has live music Tue-Fri and Sun nights. Tue is curry and Wed vego night. Licensed and BYO. Also takeaway and free Wi-Fi. Recommended.

Hillarys and Sorrento

$$-$ Spinnakers, 95 Northside Dr, T9203 5266, www.spinnakerscafe.com.au. Sun-Tue 0800-1700, Wed-Sat 0800-2300. Ploughs its lone furrow on the 'opposite' side of the harbour to all the rest. Its great position is enhanced by friendly service, fresh simple meals and a bright decor. The few covered tables on the outside decking are the ones to go for. BYO only. It serves delicious banana pancakes and more for breakfast, coffee and terrific cakes until 1730. Recommended.

GOING FURTHER

MARGARET RIVER AND AROUND

The Margaret River area is famous for two things: wineries and surf. The region produces some of Australia's best premium wines and the surf is also exceptional. Contrary to many travellers' expectations, neither are in Margaret River itself, but it does make a convenient base for these attractions. Most wineries are north, almost as close to Dunsborough as Margaret River, and the beach is at the river mouth near the Prevelly.

MARGARET RIVER

There are some talented artists and craftspeople in the southwest region and visiting galleries is an enjoyable experience. Many studios are in the countryside but there are a few galleries in Margaret River that showcase regional work.

PREVELLY

Another coastal settlement spilling downhill among dense coastal tea tree, **Prevelly** is Margaret River's closest beach, 9 km away, and where the legendary international surf competition, **Margaret River Pro**, is held in April. **Surfers Point**, at the northern edge of Prevelly, is a powerful reef break and the surfers' car park there is a great place to watch the action. Around the corner is a perfect crescent of beach where the eucalypt green of Margaret River meets the aquamarine of the Indian ocean. At the southern end is **Gnarabup Beach** where a humble but picturesque café perches above the water.

WINERIES

The small but select number of wineries around Margaret River itself mostly lie along or just off Boodijup Road, the turn-off to which is just south of town. **Leeuwin Estate** ① *Stevens Rd, T9759 0000, www.leeuwinestate.com.au, cellar door 1000-1630, tours 1100, 1200 and 1500, restaurant open daily for lunch and Sat for dinner*, may not be the oldest winery in the region, but is the best known. Apart from a stylish restaurant, excellent wines and fascinating art gallery, the key feature is the gently sloping lawned amphitheatre. Wines cost $22-100. **Minot** ① *off Exmoor Drive, opposite the Eagles Heritage Centre, T9757 3579, www.minot wines.com.au*, 'cellar door' is simply a modest table outside the owners' bungalow home. They produce a light, refreshing Semillon Sauvignon Blanc, and a rich, velvety Cabernet that is well worth going out of the way for. Call ahead. **Redgate** ① *Boodijup Rd, T9757 6488, www.redgatewines.com.au, 1000-1700*, is nothing fancy but its range of reds and whites is well respected, and it welcomes picnickers. Wines cost $19-40. If you want a slightly different winery experience, head to **Swallows Welcome** ① *Wickham Rd (unsealed), T9757 6348, 1100-1700*, a few kilometres east of this core group, on the other side of the Bussell Highway. Here Tim Negus will offer you tastings of his wines and you can visit Patricia Negus' studio, her botanical paintings are fantastic. **Xanadu** ① *T9758 9520, www.xanaduwines.com, 1000-1700, tapas from 1000, meals 1200-1600 and on Sat 1700-2100*, is first on the right, after about 4 km. Everything about this place is smart and savvy, but casual. Wines cost $18-80. Recommended.

THE COASTAL ROUTE NORTH

This coastline got its name from the Batavia, a Dutch trading ship that was wrecked on the Houtman Abrolhos Islands in 1629, close to Geraldton. The Batavia is famous for the gruesome behaviour of its survivors, but it is only one of many shipwrecks on this coast. Strong westerly winds and an absence of safe, sheltered harbours meant ships were regularly smashed onto the reefs and rocks of this unforgiving coastline. Settlements such as Cervantes are crayfishing towns of little of interest except for the Pinnacles in the Nambung National Park. Geraldton is a large city where you can stock up on supplies and explore an excellent maritime museum focusing on the story of the Batavia. It is also good for watersports: the windsurfing is known worldwide and there is excellent diving and snorkelling both on a brand-new artificial reef and on the coral reefs of the Houtman Abrolhos Islands, 60 km offshore.

NAMBUNG NATIONAL PARK AND THE PINNACLES
ⓘ *The park entry fee is $11 per car.*
This national park protects an otherworldly forest of spiky rocks rising out of a yellow sandy desert. The Pinnacles are one of the most recognizable images of Western Australia and they are certainly a striking sight, one well worth making a detour for. Dutch sailors passing by in the 17th century marked them on their charts and likened them to the crumbling remains of an ancient city. The rock formations are surprisingly extensive, covering an area of several square kilometres, and there are thousands of them, taking varied forms from narrow towers 5 m high to modest stubs. The best time to see the park is in the soft light of early morning or at sunset, although sunset is quite busy with tour groups. A 4-km one-way loop road (sandy but hard packed and so suitable for 2WD) traverses the main area of formations and you can stop along the way and walk among them. The Interpretive Centre has information on the wildlife that lives in the Nambung National Park, details on how the Pinnacles were formed and the history of the area. There are two picnic spots by the beach on the way out, at **Kangaroo Point** and **Hangover Bay**.

→GERALDTON

Often dismissed as a large and uninteresting port city, Geraldton (population: 20,000) does have a fantastic sunny climate and strong, reliable westerlies which make it a mecca for windsurfers. It is also the base for dive and snorkel tours out to the Houtman Abrolhos Islands (see below). Geraldton has all the services of a large town; this will be the last place to find such services for many hundreds of kilometres when you head north. The **VIC** ⓘ *T9921 3999, www.geraldtontourist.com.au, Mon-Fri 0900-1700, Sat-Sun 1000- 1600*, is located in the Bill Sewell Complex, along with a simple café and a backpacker hostel.

The city has many interesting sights (many free, or requesting only a token fee) and some, notably the gallery and museum, are of a high standard. The waterfront area around the museum is being developed into a townhouse and marina complex and is likely to become an attractive part of the city. The **Old Geraldton Gaol Craft Centre** ⓘ *Chapman Rd, T9921 1614, Mon-Sat 1000-1530, entry by donation*, located just south of the Bill Sewell tourist complex, is a whitewashed old gaol built in 1858 and last used in 1986. There are 16 cells along a central corridor and several exercise yards. Information sheets along the corridor explain some of the history of the gaol including amusing correspondence between the gaoler and his boss. The gaol is rather run down but has been taken over by an army of craftspeople who look after it and sell their work from the cells. The **Western Australian Museum Geraldton** ⓘ *1 Museum Place, T9921 5080, www.museum. wa.gov.au, Thu-Tue 0930-1630, by donation*, is an impressive museum focusing on the maritime and so appropriately has been built next to the sea. A wall of glass overlooks the ocean and the floor of warm, polished timbers is evocative of a ship's deck. The Shipwreck Hall is the heart of the museum's collection. The dimly lit space contains relics from the wrecks of the *Batavia* and *Zuytdorp* and tells the stories of those ships and others of the Dutch East India company wrecked on the Midwest coast or the Abrolhos Islands in the 18th century. On a small rise overlooking the city, the **HMAS Sydney Memorial** ⓘ *Mt Scott, accessible from car park on Gummer Av*, is a beautiful landmark built in 2001 to remember the victims of the *HMAS Sydney* tragedy. This Australian naval ship was lost in 1941 when none of the 645 crew survived and, despite many extensive searches, the ship was not found until March 2007, 240 km west of Shark Bay at a depth of about 2500 m. **Geraldton Regional Art Gallery** ⓘ *24 Chapman Rd, T9964 7170, Tue-Sat 1000-1600, Sun and public holidays 1300-1600, free*, is housed in the former Town Hall, built in 1907, and features regular touring exhibitions and local contemporary art. **St Francis Xavier Cathedral** ⓘ *open daily, guided tours Mon, Wed and Fri 1000, $5*, is the town's Catholic cathedral, a splendid edifice in golden stone built between 1916 and 1938, and designed by the indefatigable Monsignor John Hawes. To some, the inside of the building, with its grey and orange stripes, will seem fairly psychedelic. At the **Fisherman's Harbour** during the crayfishing season it is possible to tour the **Live Lobster Factory** ⓘ *T9921 7084, Nov-Jun, Mon-Fri 0930, $10, children $5, closed shoes must be worn, 3 km from the town centre on West End's northern shore*, to find out more about this valuable industry.

HOUTMAN ABROLHOS ISLANDS

The Houtman Abrolhos Islands (commonly just called the Abrolhos) are a maze of low coral islands lying 60 km west of Geraldton. Essentially built-up reefs, they are uninhabited, except for a few crayfishermen in the short island season (March to June). Their low-lying nature and treacherous outlying reefs mean they are very difficult to spot and they are the final resting place of at least 19 vessels, including the ill-fated *Batavia*. Indeed the name Abrolhos is thought to be a corruption of the Portugese words for 'keep your eyes open'. The principal attraction for visitors, however, are the crystal-clear waters and huge diversity of sealife. As the recipient of the final gasp of the warm tropical currents that spill down Australia's west coast, the islands encompass the world's most southerly coral reefs but also have a rich variety of more temperate species, a mix quite fascinating to marine biologists. They are also home to sea lions, turtles and dozens of species of sea birds. Snorkelling and diving here is outstanding for coral gardens and many types of reef and pelagic fish. The islands can be reached either via air or sea, but air is the better option for a short trip as the views are wonderful and the sea crossing can be a bit rough.

NORTHAMPTON

This historic town on the Nokanena Brook, the first of Western Australia's mining towns, still has many fine old-stone buildings, but little is made of them. Northampton exists to service the surrounding wheat district and lies on the main highway north, 55 km from Geraldton and 105 km from Kalbarri. However, its passing trade has dropped off significantly since the coast road to Kalbarri was sealed in 2000 and there are few facilities for visitors. There is a fine Catholic church, **St Mary in Ara Coeli**, built in 1936 to a design by talented architect-priest Monsignor John Hawes. Its rough-hewn stone and restrained decoration is typical of Hawes' work, although he had originally planned a more Byzantine style. The Priest of Northampton, Father Irwin, insisted on a Gothic design and Hawes agreed but the whitewashed interior with its round arches and shutters retains a Mediterranean feel. The impressive two-storey building next door is the former **Sacred Heart Convent**, also designed by Hawes. The **VIC** ① *Old Police Station, Hampton Rd, T9934 1488, Mon-Fri 0900-1500, Sat 0900-1200,* has brochures for a heritage walk.

KALBARRI

The most picturesque coastal town in the state, 155 km from Geraldton and 250 km from Overlander roadhouse, Kalbarri sits at the mouth of the Murchison River where it winds through shoals of sand to the ocean. At the entrance a triangular rock rises above the surf and marks the difficult zigzag passage through the reef to the ocean. The reef protects the calm waters of the inlet, forming a safe harbour for the crayfishing fleet moored here and a tranquil place for swimming, sailing and fishing. A long grassy foreshore lines the riverbank and the town is laid out along the foreshore, facing the sparkling blue water of river and ocean.

Kalbarri Wildflower Centre ① *1 km north of town, behind the tourist info bay, T9937 1229, Jul-Nov, Wed-Mon 0900-1700, $5, children free, guided tours by appointment,* has a large number of the local wildflowers in a small area bordering the national park. A 2-km trail takes in hundreds of species, bursting into flower from July to October. **Kalbarri Oceanarium** ① *north end of Grey St by the marina, T9937 2027, www.kalbarri explorer.com.au/oceanarium.htm, Mon-Sat 1000-1600, $7, children $5,* is a modest-sized but well-stocked outfit with a dozen tanks featuring most of the species of fish and crustaceans that can be found in the sea off Kalbarri. It includes a tank of seahorses and a children's touch pool. **Rainbow Jungle** ① *3 km south on Red Bluff Rd, T9937 1248, www.rainbowjungle kalbarri.com, Mon-Sat 0900-1700, Sun 1000-1700, $13.50, concessions $11.50, children $5,* claims to be the foremost Australian parrot breeding centre and is certainly one of the more impressive aviaries in the country. Most of the many parrots fly around in large enclosures, well watered and visitors get to stroll amongst them. It's worth a visit even on a hot day. Opposite Rainbow Jungle is a parking bay for an ocean **beach**. Once on the sand it is about 4 km north to **Chinamans Rock** and beach at the mouth of the Murchison River, and 800 m south to **Jakes**, Kalbarri's well-known surf break. This is not recommended for beginners, though the bay just before it is great for boogie-boarding, as is **Red Bluff beach** 1 km further south. **Murchison House Station** ① *T9937 1998, www.murchisonhousestation.com.au, access to the station is via tour only (4 hrs, can be booked through the VIC), which leave most days Jul-Dec and include morning tea, also offers guided self-drive 4WD tours to the homestead,* is one of WA's most historic properties. The station has had a colourful history, witnessing the fatal crash of one of the three planes involved in WA's first commercial flight, and later as the home and playground of Prince Mukramm Jah, the eighth Nizam of Hyderabad. The original homestead and old woolshed are still standing and the area around the current homestead is littered with the prince's playthings, including several decrepit military vehicles and gigantic earth-movers. A visit is recommended. The **VIC** ① *70 Grey St, T9937 1104 or T1800 639468, www.kalbarriwa.info, 0900-1700,* is opposite the foreshore.

KALBARRI NATIONAL PARK

ⓘ *For information call the DEC ranger, T9937 1192, $11 per vehicle (inland gorges only). Note that there is no drinking water available in the park, so if walking in the summer months make sure you bring enough as it can get very hot in the gorges.*

The Murchison River meanders through deep gorges of spectacular red and white banded rock with the most striking formations and tight loops of riverbed enclosed within the park. In winter and spring, the park is also renowned for its beautiful display of wildflowers. On the route running east to the highway, you can see many blooms including banksias, grevilleas, kangaroo paws, the appropriately fluffy lambswool and brightly coloured featherflowers. The park also extends along the coast and contains high coastal cliffs, gorges and magical sheltered coves. Along the coast road, the heath is dominated by the waving stems of white plume grevillea, also called smelly socks for its less than pleasant locker-room fragrance. The dramatic gorges and cliffs, cut by the sea into rugged notches and rock platforms, are quite different from the inland gorges. This wealth of natural beauty in the park is complemented by a great range of tours, activities and services. There are many excellent lookouts over the gorges and a few walking tracks aimed at reasonably agile walkers.

South of the river mouth, the ocean beaches gradually rise to a long stretch of golden sandstone cliffs. This southern coastline is also part of the national park and there are a series of excellent lookouts and tracks down the rock platforms and beaches. **Red Bluff** is the imposing knoll that can be seen from the town beaches and is the first of the park lookouts, 5 km from town. There is an 800-m return walk to the top of the bluff from where you can see the whole coastline and this is also a great spot in calm weather for whale watching in winter. A loop walk from **Mushroom Rock** to **Rainbow Valley** takes one to 1½ hours and allows you to explore the rock platforms and the arid hillside. **Pot Alley Gorge** is a delightful narrow gorge with interesting rocks and a pretty beach – the ideal place for secluded swimming or sunbathing. **Eagle Gorge** also has a good sandy beach reached from a track by the lookout but less protected, and extensive rock platforms to explore (8 km from town). Towards the southern end the cliffs become higher and less accessible but more impressive. The last two lookouts, **Island Rock** and **Natural Bridge**, are both remnants left behind by the cliffs as they retreat before the waves, and are particularly beautiful at sunset.

There are three main points to access the inland gorges, all situated at scenic bends and loops in the river's course, and all via unsealed roads. Shortly after leaving town there is also a great lookout over Kalbarri called **Meanarra Hill**, reached by a short walk from the car park. After a further 11 km the first park turn-off is on the left. This leads to Nature's Window (26 km) and Z-Bend (25 km). **Nature's Window** is a rock arch that overlooks a tight bend in the river called **The Loop**. The walk around the Loop is excellent, following the ridge at first and then dropping down to the riverbed (8 km, three hours). At **Z-Bend** (a few kilometres drive away) there is a lookout over a right angle in the gorge and with some careful rock hopping you can get down to the river and explore. Take the unmarked but well-used track to the right of the lookout. This is also a lovely place for a swim as the river does not flow all year round and is often a series of calm shallow pools. You need to return to the main road and travel another 24 km to get to **Hawks Head** and **Ross Graham**. These are both good lookouts and there are easier tracks down to the river. It is possible for experienced walkers to tackle the 38 km (four days) from Ross Graham Lookout to The Loop or shorter two-day walks, but you must notify the ranger and plan carefully. There are picnic tables and toilets at all the car parks. Nature's Window and Z-Bend also have gas BBQs.

THE COASTAL ROUTE NORTH LISTINGS

WHERE TO STAY

Geraldton

$$$ Broadwater Mariner Resort, 298 Chapman Rd, a 5-min drive out of town, T9965 9100, www.broadwaters.com.au. Spacious self-contained accommodation, a large pool, communal BBQ areas and secure parking. There's an adjoining restaurant serving good meals.

$$-$ Foreshore Backpackers, 172 Marine Terr, T9921 3275, www.foreshorebackpackers. bigpondhosting.com. This homely 50-bed hostel in a spacious old house faces a small beach. There are sunny verandas, hammocks, dorms and single and double rooms, all with lovely old wooden furniture. Recommended.

Kalbarri

The bulk of accommodation here is located in complexes of self-contained units mostly located on the foreshore. Prices drop in low season.

$$$$-$$$ Kalbarri Edge Resort, 22 Porter St, T9937 0000, www.kalbarriedge.com.au. Self-contained accommodation, all with Wi-Fi, and some have washing machines and balconies. There is a pool, a gym and even giant chess. The restaurant serves Modern Australian fare with emphasis on seafood.

$$$-$ Pelican's Nest and Kalbarri Backpackers YHA, corner Mortimer and Wood Sts, T9937 1430, www.pelicansnest kalbarri.com.au. En suite motel and studio rooms with private balcony and chalets. Backpacker accommodation next door with pool, BBQ and internet. The hostel is large but friendly, has en suite dorms, free boogie board and snorkel hire. Bicycle hire $20 per day and cycle tours. Recommended.

WHAT TO DO

Geraldton

The clean waters off Geraldton can be excellent for diving, but winds and silt from the Chapman River also often ruin visibility. The best time is mid-Feb to mid-May. Geraldton calls itself, not unreasonably, Australia's windsurfing capital, and there are good wind conditions.

Batavia Coast Dive Academy, 153 Marine Terr, T9921 4229, www.bcda.com.au. Hires out scuba gear and run shore and boat dives. Also has snorkelling and Open Water courses.

Sail West, Point Moore, T9923 1000, www.sailwest.com.au. Hires out windsurfers and surfboards from next to the lighthouse.

Kalbarri and Kalbarri National Park

There are dozens of river, sea and bus tours available, plus a good many adventure activities. All can be booked via the VIC. Some can be very demanding in hot weather, check what is supplied and be well prepared with drinks and for the sun.

Kalbarri Adventure Tours, T9937 1677, www.kalbarritours.com.au. Runs more adventurous day trips into the inland gorges ($90), tours depart Mon, Wed, Fri and Sun. This is a great way to see what the national park has to offer if you have just a day to do so. They also offer hike-only-tours to the park's most famous and beautiful spots. Bring lunch. Recommended.

The Specialists, T9937 1050, www.the specialists.com.au. Tours include 6-8 hrs of fishing and a light BBQ lunch, $210, share line $270. They also run sunset and whale-watching (Jul-Dec) cruises, kite surfing tours and 3-day trips to the Abrolhos Islands.

THE GASCOYNE

The hot and arid Gascoyne region sits between two distinct hooks on the shoulder of the coastline – from Shark Bay in the south to the North West Cape in the north, and inland for a few hundred kilometres. In the waters off this region marine life is abundant; in the rest of the country, only the Great Barrier Reef can rival them. The sheltered waters of Shark Bay harbour dugongs and turtles as well as dolphins, which come in to shore to be fed by hand at Monkey Mia. Further north, a coral fringing reef – Ningaloo Reef – lines the coast for more than 250 km. When the coral spawns in March each year it attracts the world's largest fish, the whale shark, to feed on this caviar-like soup for several months. Snorkelling alongside them as they feed is one of the most thrilling experiences this great island nation can offer. On a wonderfully accessible level, at some points the reef comes so close to shore that you are able to snorkel among coral, fish, turtles and rays straight off the beach. Come in summer and you can watch the turtles laying and hatching. Inland, you can find the red dirt and open spaces of Outback country around the Kennedy Ranges or Mount Augustus.

→SHARK BAY

Shark Bay is formed by two long peninsulas lying parallel to the coast, like the prongs of a fork. The middle prong is the Peron Peninsula, and the western prong is formed by the Zuytdorp Cliffs and Dirk Hartog Island. These are the most westerly bits of land in Australia, forming an extraordinary sheltered marine environment in its countless small bays. The waters of Shark Bay are always a startling turquoise and as clear as a swimming pool thanks to its shallowness; the average depth of the bay is 10 m and much of it is no deeper than 1 m. It is most famous for its colony of dolphins, some of which come into shore at Monkey Mia, but there are also dugongs, turtles, rays and sharks living in these waters and all are easily seen on a boat trip or from the shore. The land is also a refuge for wildlife. Although its low arid scrub and red sand looks too harsh and barren for anything to survive, the Francois Peron National Park is the focus for a program to save endangered native species. The small town of Denham and the tourist facilities at Monkey Mia provide comfortable lodging for visitors but most of the Shark Bay region is a wilderness. Shark Bay was declared a World Heritage Area in 1991 for its rare stromatolites, extensive seagrass beds, endangered animals and natural beauty.

HAMELIN POOL

Hamelin Pool is a wide shallow estuary on the eastern side of Shark Bay, 35 km from the Overlander Roadhouse and 105 km from Denham. It elicits great scientific interest today because of the resident colonies of **stromatolites**. These boulder-like formations are the direct result of sediments becoming trapped by thin organic mats of cyanobacteria over thousands of years. In the 1880s this spot was chosen as the site of one of WA's **telegraph repeater stations** ① *T9942 5905, $5 per person, guided tours only*, because of its relative ease of provisioning by sea. The original station is now a modest museum, partly devoted to an explanation of the stromatolites and partly to preserve the heritage of the telegraph system. The shady compound is something of an oasis in the baking hot conditions, and the tearoom is a welcome place to grab a cold drink. **Shell Beach**, 50 km from Hamelin, is one of the most accessible examples of a beach entirely made up of tiny white shells, and it slopes gently into the bay for hundreds of metres. The shells are the bivalve cardiid cockle, a type of saline-tolerant cockle only found in Shark Bay. Deep under the beach the shells cement together when rainwater dissolves their calcium carbonate and the resulting coquina limestone has been readily utilized around Shark Bay as a building material.

→DENHAM

Denham (population: 1200) is a friendly town that services much of the tourist trade on its way to Monkey Mia, 30 km away on the eastern side of the Peron Peninsula. The main industry is fishing, replacing the one that brought Europeans, Malaysians and Chinese people here in the 1850s: pearling. Recently the industry has been revived and pearl farms have been established in the bay, producing fine black pearls. The town has a grassy foreshore, with BBQs and picnic tables, and has fuel and a supermarket. The **Shark Bay World Heritage Discovery Centre** ① *29 Knight Terr, www.sharkbayinterpretive centre.com.au, daily 0900-1800, $11, child $6, concessions $8,* is located in the VIC and the opening hours are the same. The Discovery Centre has some interesting displays and films, which inform about the history and wildlife of Shark Bay.

FRANCOIS PERON NATIONAL PARK
① *For more information contact DEC, 89 Knight Terr, Denham, T9948 1208. $11 car, camping $7 per person. Visitor centre daily 0800-1630.*
Named after a French naturalist who explored Shark Bay as part of Baudin's expedition on the *Geographe* and *Naturaliste* in 1801 and 1803, the Francois Peron covers the northern tip of the Peron Peninsula, from the Monkey Mia road north to Cape Peron, an area of 52,500 ha. A dramatic series of cliffs and bays, where red rocks merge into white sand and turquoise sea, encloses a dry and arid region with many salt-pans (birridas) dotting the low sandy plains. The park is home to malleefowl, bilbies, woylies, bandicoots, the Shark Bay mouse and many other species. This mostly nocturnal wildlife is not often seen but thorny devils are common and dolphins, dugongs and turtles may be spotted from the cliffs at Cape Peron. There is a **visitor centre** at the old station homestead that aims to educate visitors about Project Eden, and an outdoor hot tub fed by an artesian bore that visitors are welcome to use. The homestead is usually accessible by 2WD (10 km, unsealed) but the rest of this peaceful, remote place is only accessible by high-clearance 4WD (check with the DEC for up-to-date road and track information).

MONKEY MIA
① *For information contact DEC, Shark Bay, T9948 1208 or the Monkey Mia Reserve T9948 1366. Day pass $8, children $3, family $15 (valid for 24 hrs). Family holiday pass $30 (valid for 4 weeks).*
Dolphins have lived in Shark Bay for millennia but the current encounters with humans only began in the 1960s when fishermen began to hand feed dolphins. The dolphins were happy to accept a free feed and visited settlements regularly. Even though the place is incredibly remote, over 800 km from Perth and 330 km from Carnarvon, the pull of wild dolphins is irresistible and has made the area internationally famous. Interaction with the dolphins is carefully managed to keep them wild and minimize the impact of hundreds of visitors a day. One of the best things to do in Monkey Mia is to leave the beach and take a boat cruise and see the dolphins in their own environment, as well as many other incredible animals such as

dugongs and turtles. Despite the number of visitors, Monkey Mia itself is just a small low-key resort. The visitor centre overlooking the beach where the dolphins swim into shore has displays on the biology and behaviour of dolphins and shows videos on marine life.

Free spirits wanting to commune with nature may be a little disappointed with the Monkey Mia experience. This is how it works: the dolphins swim into a section of beach by the jetty that is closed to boats and swimmers. When the dolphins arrive people line up along the beach, perhaps for 100 m or more. You are not allowed to enter the water beyond your knees, and a DEC officer will stand in the water making sure that the dolphins are not disturbed. The dolphins are often only a few feet away and nuzzle the officers' calves while the officers chat about them. When the DEC officers decide to feed the dolphins everyone is asked to step out of the water and a few lucky souls are picked to come forward and give a dolphin a fish. Only mature female dolphins are fed and they get no more than a third of their daily requirements so they will not become dependent on handouts. Once the feeding is finished the dolphins usually swim away, but if they don't you can step back in the water to your knees again. Even in such crowded and controlled conditions it is wonderful to be so close to these wild dolphins. When they roll on their sides and look up at you can't help feeling that these creatures really are as curious about you as you are about them (or maybe they're just wondering where you're hiding the fish). To get the best out of the experience plan to spend the whole day at Monkey Mia or make it an overnight trip. The dolphins usually arrive about 0800 and after they have been fed the main crowds disappear. Dolphin feeding is allowed three times between 0800 and 1300 and there is a good chance that the dolphins will reappear and you'll have a more intimate encounter. Take an afternoon and sunset cruise and you can't fail to have an awesome day.

THE OVERLANDER TO CARNARVON
ⓘ *Distance: 200 km.*
The vegetation gets a little more sparse and scrubby but there is little else to enliven this featureless drive. One bright spot is the welcoming **Wooramel Roadhouse** (**$**, 75 km from the **Overlander**, T9942 5910), which pumps relatively cheap fuel, as well as breakfasts, snacks and burgers. It has an ATM, donger rooms with shared facilities and a caravan park with powered and unpowered sites. Meals and fuel are available 0700-1800. Just short of Carnarvon, the highway north is interrupted by a T-junction, the focus of a cluster of 24-hour roadhouses, fruit plantations and caravan parks. Turn left for the town centre, 5 km away, right for the Blowholes, Quobba, the Kennedy Range, and destinations further north.

→CARNARVON AND AROUND

Of many ports set up by settlers in the mid-1800s along the west coast, Carnarvon (population: 6900) is one of the few survivors and has consolidated its early prosperity by making the most of the water that flows in great volume down the Gascoyne River. Most of the time the mighty riverbed is exposed as a wide ribbon of sand but the Gascoyne flows deep underground all year round and it is tapped by local fruit growers for irrigation. Consequently, Carnarvon appears as something of an oasis among the dry, scrubby plains to the north and south, 480 km from Geraldton, 370 km from Exmouth and 360 km from Nanutarra Roadhouse. Vast plantations of banana and mango trees are mingled with colourful bougainvillea, poinciana trees and tall palms. Other than a couple of plantations with tours and tropical cafés, Carnarvon has few tourist pretensions, but does make a useful base for exploring the rugged coastline to the north, including the Blowholes, and the impressive Kennedy Range, 200 km inland. A lot of Australians and backpackers come to Carnarvon for work, as attested by the many caravan parks. For information contact **VIC** ① *corner of (the main) Robinson St and Camel Lane, T9941 1146, www.carnarvon.org.au, Oct- Apr Mon-Fri 0900-1700, Sat-Sun 0900-1200, May-Nov Mon-Fri 0900-1700, Sat 0900- 1400, Sun 0900-1200.*

KENNEDY RANGE NATIONAL PARK
① *For more information contact the DEC office in Carnarvon, T9941 3754; road conditions, T9943 0988 or T138138. Entry $11 per vehicle, camping fees $7 per person at Temple Gorge.* Just north of the main Carnarvon T-Junction is an unsealed right turn onto Gascoyne Junction Road. This becomes sealed for a fair way, before becoming unsealed again around about the turn-off for Rocky Pool, 38 km from the highway. This permanent waterhole in the Gascoyne River is a popular camping spot in winter and there is a toilet close by. **Gascoyne Junction** is a tiny, dusty community another 130 km on with a hotel and expensive but very handy fuel. Turn left at the crossroads for the Kennedy Range, straight on for Bidgemia Station.

The Kennedy Range forms a dramatic flame-coloured mesa, 75 km long, running north to south. The range is a long drive from anywhere on an unsealed road, but this park offers the chance to experience the outback, and perhaps a local station stay. Much of the range is inaccessible, but on the eastern side there are three narrow gorges that can be explored and a campsite right at the base of the 100-m cliffs. Each gorge is less than a kilometre apart and there are short walks along the creek beds. The Kennedy Range contains such interesting rocks that you'll wish you had a geologist with you. In fact, the sheer variety of the rock shapes and colours is so captivating that it is hard to remember to lift your head and look at the stunning cliffs above. The cliffs themselves are at their best at dawn when they can take on some seriously impressive yellow, orange and red hues. The campsite has a toilet but no other facilities. Take plenty of water. Roads are fine for 2WD except after heavy rain, when the roads will be closed.

CARNARVON TO CORAL BAY
Some 140 km of Carnarvon and 225 km south of Exmouth is the **Minilya Roadhouse** ① *T9942 5922, just over the bridge, 0600-2100, meals until 2030*, with air-conditioned bathrooms, a rare treat along this long stretch of road. Dedicated to quality, the roadhouse (**$$-$**) serves above-average cheap meals and takeaways, has comfortable donger rooms and lawned caravan sites. It also sells the last relatively cheap fuel if you're heading north.

→CORAL BAY

This pretty shallow bay is just a notch in a long coastline of white sand, dunes and desert but this is the most accessible spot on the northwest coast where the **Ningaloo coral reef** is within 50 m of the shore. The reef is full of colourful fish, clams, sea cucumbers, rays and even the odd turtle, though the coral itself is more notable for its intricate shapes and forms than any vibrancy of colour. All you need to do is grab a snorkel, mask and fins and wade in. There are also a variety of boat trips that take you further out onto the reef to snorkel or dive with manta rays, turtles and whale sharks, or spot humpback whales, dugongs and dolphins; near-Utopia for anyone who loves marine wildlife. The settlement itself is a small, relaxed beach resort where you can walk barefoot from your door to the beach in two minutes. Coral Bay is changing fast though and each year there are more operators, activities and visitors. There's no independent VIC; half a dozen local tour operators have set up booking offices that sell their own, and usually most of their competitors', tours. For free information on the Coral Bay environment and wildlife, call into the **Coastal Adventure Tours** office and internet café in the Coral Bay Shopping Centre. Facilities in Coral Bay are modest, but you will find a supermarket, newsagents, a few gift shops, including a good jewellery shop selling handmade pieces and a beauty spa. Fuel is available at the **Coral Bay Shopping Village**, near the People's Park Caravan Village.

→EXMOUTH AND AROUND

Exmouth (population: 2500) sits on the eastern side of the North West Cape, 150 km from Coral Bay, facing the calm waters of the Exmouth Gulf and separated by the low hills of Cape Range from the pristine beaches of the **Ningaloo Marine Park**. Despite the marine riches of the cape, the town doesn't have a coastal feel. It's a practical place that was built to service the local military bases and to withstand the seasonal cyclones. However, Exmouth's proximity to the **Ningaloo Reef** and its extraordinary wildlife make it a special place for eco-tourism. It is possible to swim with whale sharks, watch turtles laying and hatching, spot migrating humpback whales, snorkel over coral from the beach, and dive on almost untouched sites. The only drawback is the intense heat and aridity of the cape – most people visit in winter when temperatures drop to 25-30°C. Exmouth is well set up for travellers, with a good range of accommodation, tours and activities to make the most of what it has to offer. The helpful **VIC** ① *Murat St, T9949 1176, T1800 287328, www.exmouthwa.com.au, Nov-Mar Mon-Fri 0900-1630, Apr- Oct daily 0900-1630*, is on the main through road.

CAPE RANGE NATIONAL PARK

① *Milyering VIC, 13 km inside the northern park boundary and 50 km from Exmouth, T9949 2808, open 0900-1545.* $11 per vehicle, camping $7.
Cape Range National Park is an unforgiving, rocky strip of land on the western side of North West Cape, adjoining the Ningaloo Marine Park. The glittering turquoise sea fringing the park just seems to emphasize its aridity and kangaroos have to seek shade under bushes only knee high. However, this is the place to access the wonderful Ningaloo Reef and at places such as Turquoise Bay the reef is only metres from shore so you can snorkel off the beach among a dazzling parade of fish.

Turquoise Bay, a beautiful white swimming beach, is a further 10 km south. There are a few shade sails and a toilet here but no other facilities. About 15 km from Milyering is **Mandu Mandu Gorge**, where there is a 3-km (return) walk into the dry gorge. Right at the end of the sealed road is **Yardie Creek**, a short gorge with sheer red walls above the creek and a colony of black-footed rock wallabies. Yardie Creek has a picnic area, a one-hour boat cruise along the creek (check with the VIC for running times) and a short, rocky track (1.5 km return) along the northern side of the gorge. There are also two gorges that can be accessed from the eastern side of the cape, **Shothole Canyon** and **Charles Knife**. There are great views of the gulf from these rugged gorges but the roads are unsealed and very rough.

ON THE ROAD

Swimming with whale sharks

Imagine swimming with a shark the size of a bus, in water 1 km deep. You stand on the back of the boat all suited up in snorkel, fins and wetsuit and the Dive Master shouts 'go, go, go'. Adrenalin surges and suddenly you're looking at a mouth as big as a cave coming straight for you. Shock paralyses for a second as your mind screams to get out of the way!

Swimming with whale sharks may be one of the most memorable and exciting things you do in your lifetime. The whale shark is a plankton feeder that isn't the slightest bit interested in gobbling you into its wide gaping mouth but is alarmingly huge when you are only a few metres away. These rare, gentle beasts can reach 18 m but are more often seen at 4-12 m. Little is known about them except that they travel in a band around the equator and arrive to feed at the Ningaloo Reef after the coral spawning in March and April. The sharks swim just under the surface as sunlight sparkles on their blue-grey bodies and delicate pattern of white spots. When spotted by a boat, snorkellers jump in and accompany a shark, just like the fleet of remora fish that hang around its mouth and belly. Some sharks seem mildly curious about their new flapping friends but others seem about as bothered as an elephant by a gnat. However, the interaction has only occurred for about 15 years and it is not known what impact swimmers have.

Fishermen had seen a few on the Ningaloo Reef over the years but it wasn't until the late 1980s that marine biologists began to realize just how unusual but regular these sightings were. During the 1990s tours were developed to take visitors out to swim with the whale sharks and it has become big business in Exmouth. DEC has developed strict guidelines for swimming and boating around them and it is hoped that this will keep the whale sharks undisturbed. Of course these are wild creatures and sightings are not guaranteed (although you will generally get a second trip for free if you don't see any). Experiences can vary from hectic five-minute swims to magical 40-minute floats.

Turtles come ashore in the Cape Range National Park to breed and lay eggs and it is possible to have the rare experience of watching them doing so. Nesting turtles lumber onto the northern end of the cape (Hunters, Mauritius, Jacobsz and Jansz beaches) during November to February at night just before high tide and for two hours afterwards. Hatchlings emerge January-April between the hours 1700-2000 and scamper to the water's edge. Turtles must not be disturbed by noise, light or touching – it is very important to follow the CALM code of conduct for turtle watching (pick a copy up at their office in town) or the turtles may stop nesting here.

EXMOUTH TO NANUTARRA ROADHOUSE

ⓘ *Nanutarra Roadhouse is 280 km from Exmouth.*

If heading north there is a sealed short-cut connecting the Exmouth Road with the North West Coastal Highway. Halfway along this road is **Giralia** ⓘ *130 km from Exmouth, T9942 5937, www.giralia.net.au*, which is one of the best station stays in the region (**$$$-$$**). It has air-conditioned en suite B&B rooms located in the main homestead. Rates include a two-course dinner. Close to the main house, completely rebuilt following the devastation of Cyclone Vance in 1999, is a self-contained family cottage that sleeps up to five, budget accommodation in singles and doubles with shared bathrooms and a bush camp (**$**). There are basic kitchen facilities and guests can use the swimming pool. There are several 4WD tracks on the station, some leading to the tidal flats of Exmouth Gulf 30 km north, well known locally for excellent fly fishing. After the following junction with the main highway the slow greening of the landscape continues and the monotonous flat becomes punctuated with low hill ranges, the first signs of the Pilbara. The **Nanutarra Roadhouse** ① *T9943 0521*, is by the Ashburton River, which always has some decent-sized waterholes. The roadhouse (**$$-$**) has a few air-conditioned donger rooms, campsites and a café (meals 0630-2200). Fuel is available until 2400. Note that this roadhouse is known as the most expensive in WA so expect to pay significantly more per litre. It marks one of the north's major junctions, and from here it's 350 km to **Tom Price**.

THE GASCOYNE LISTINGS

WHERE TO STAY

Carnarvon

$$$-$ Plantation Caravan Park, 589 Robinson St next to the Caltex Petrol Station, T9941 8100 and T1800 261166, www.plantation-caravan-park.wa.big4.com.au. Located a bit outside town next to banana and mango plantations, this Big4 caravan park has grassy sites, en suite cabins, a pool and internet access. Friendly staff.

Coral Bay

Coral Bay is booked out weeks in advance for school and public holidays.
$$-$ Ningaloo Club, T9385 6655, www.ningalooclub.com. A large hostel set around a pool-filled central courtyard with a pleasant communal deck area. The kitchen is small but well equipped. Recommended.

Exmouth

$$$-$ Ningaloo Lighthouse Caravan Park, 17 km north of town on Yardie Creek Rd, T9949 1478, www.ningaloo lighthouse.com. Well-run shady park with grassy sites and smart self-contained chalets, some with wonderful sea views. Good facilities. Well-placed if planning to head in to the national park in the morning.
$$ Ningaloo Lodge, Lefroy St, T9949 4949 and T1800 880949, www.ningaloo lodge.com.au. Comfortable motel with twins and doubles, courtyard pool and communal kitchen, shaded outdoor BBQ area, dining, television and games rooms. Free Wi-Fi.

Cape Range National Park

$$$$ Sal Salis Ningaloo Reef, T9571 6399, www.salsalis.com.au. The only commercial accommodation within the park. Luxury en suite safari tents overlook the ocean and beach. All power is solar generated and each bathroom has a composting toilet, herb soaps and eco-shampoos. Price includes all meals, drinks and activities including park fees, guided kayaking, guided gorge walks and snorkelling.

WHAT TO DO

Coral Bay

There is a profusion of booking offices around town. The caravan on the beach hires out snorkelling gear ($7.50 half-day, $15 full-day). Unless you specifically want to see turtles, sharks or rays, then it is hard to beat simply snorkelling off the main beach (head out beyond the 5 knot sign just south of the main beach then drift back towards the moorings). Most boat operators offer a half-day snorkel. Fish feeding occurs at the main beach every day at 1530.

Exmouth

Diving on the Ningaloo can be exceptional, with hundreds of species of fish and coral. There are a number of operators in town. Half a dozen boats offer day trips to snorkel with whale sharks (see box, page 147) for around $350-400, and most offer a free follow-up trip if they fail to find one first time around.

Cape Range National Park

If you have your own transport you can snorkel from many beaches in the park where you can expect to see a great variety of fish and coral, although the coral is not very brightly coloured, and perhaps turtles, rays and reef sharks (harmless!). The best site is **Turquoise Bay** but take care as there is a very strong current and a break in the reef.

THE PILBARA

The Pilbara has iron in its ancient dark-red stone and its very soul. More than half of Australia's mineral wealth is mined and exported from the region and almost every town has been created by mining companies in the last few decades. Most of the Pilbara's population lives on the coast, but the most striking and distinctive landscapes are inland. It is a region of stark beauty, coloured red and gold. Stony, rounded ranges extend in every direction, sitting like pincushions across the landscape, covered as they are in spinifex grass and bleached to a mellow gold. This scenery is seen at its best in one of Australia's finest national parks, Karijini. Here, deep, narrow gorges have been carved into the Hamersley Range to create an oasis of rock pools and waterfalls, some reached only by nerve-jangling adventure routes.

TOM PRICE

Owned by Pilbara Iron, a subsidiary of one of the world's largest mining companies, Rio Tinto, Tom Price (population: 6500) is an attractive company town surrounded by the **Hamersley Ranges**. Brilliant green grass and palm trees have been cultivated, which makes a change from the film of red dust that coats most mining towns.

Day tours operate out of Tom Price to **Karijini National Park** and there are regular tours to the Rio Tinto open-cut mine. There are fantastic views of the area from **Mount Nameless**, actually called Jarndrunmunhna for countless years, accessible both by foot and 4WD from the road to the caravan park. The walking track from the caravan park to the summit (1128 m) takes about two to three hours return (and if you park here you'll avoid the very rough unsealed 2-km access road to the trail car park). Tom Price is the highest town in WA at 747 m above sea level so the ascent of Mount Nameless is not too arduous. The VIC ① *Central Rd, T9188 1112, www.tompricewa.com.au, Jun-Oct Mon-Fri 0830-1700, Sat-Sun 0830-1230, Nov-May Mon-Fri 0930-1530, Sat 0900-1200,* is very helpful and knowledgeable.

KARIJINI NATIONAL PARK

① *For more information contact the VIC, T9189 8121, Apr-Oct daily 0900-1600; Nov-Mar daily 1000-1400 or the DEC Pilbara T9182 2000. The park is generally open all year round, although most pleasant Apr-Sep. A tour is a good way to see Karijini, especially if you want some adventure, but choose carefully, checking that the age and activity level will suit you. Park fees $11 per person, camping $7 per person. Water available but must be treated.*

Northern and central Australia contain so many impressive red-walled gorges that some visitors get gorge fatigue, but Karijini's gorges are the dessert course you'll find you still have room for. The park contains extraordinarily deep and narrow gorges full of waterfalls, swimming pools and challenging walks, yet it is hardly known, even within Australia. The park sits within the heart of one of the world's most ancient landscapes, the **Hamersley Plateau**, where creeks have carved 100-m-deep chasms into layers of 2500-million-year-old sedimentary rock. You enter the park from the plateau and descend into the gorges, which means there are excellent lookouts. The most spectacular view can be seen from **Oxers Lookout**, where four gorges meet below the golden spinifex and crooked white snappy gum trees of the plateau.

Getting around Although this is the state's second largest park, all of the facilities and walks are found fairly close to each other in the northern section of the park, above Karijini

Drive. Head first for the innovative **visitor centre**. An interpretive display explains the history and geology of the park and the viewpoint of its Banyjima, Yinhawangka, and Kurrama traditional owners. The main roads into the park are sealed, others are unsealed and rocky (2WD but remote driving rules apply and punctures are common). Walking and swimming are the main activities but Karijini is also known for exciting adventure trails. As some gorges are just 1-2 m wide, or filled with water, you cannot walk between the gorge walls but have to clamber along the steep sides on narrow ledges of dark red ironstone, swimming through difficult sections. Follow the circular walk markers, as these designate the best route to take. The routes beyond Kermits Pool in **Hancock Gorge** and Handrail Pool in **Weano Gorge** should only be attempted with a guide. There are easy walks but you will not be able to see the best of this awesome park unless you are reasonably fit and agile.

Moving on   From Auski Roadhouse on the eastern fringe of Karijini National Park, head east and then north towards Nullagine and then Marble Bar. This route is along unsealed roads, but is a pretty alternative to heading north from Auski Roadhouse towards Port Hedland.

Places in the park   There are two main areas to visit in the park. **Dales Gorge** is 10 km east of the visitor centre, where you can walk up the gorge to a wide cascade, **Fortescue Falls**, and beyond the falls to **Fern Pool**, a lovely, large swimming hole (1 km). Return to the top of the gorge by the same path or walk down the centre of the gorge and turn left at the end to join the trail to **Circular Pool**, a lush rock bowl dripping with ferns. At the point where you turn, a steep path joins the car park to the pool (800 m) so you don't need to retrace your steps. There is also an easy rim trail overlooking Dales Gorge and Circular Pool (2 km).

The other main area is 29 km west of the visitor centre, at the junction of **Weano, Joffre, Hancock** and **Red gorges**. There are lookouts here, including **Oxer Lookout**, and trails into Joffre (3 km), Knox (2 km), Weano Gorge (1 km to Handrail Pool) and Hancock Gorge (1.5 km to Kermits Pool). These all involve some scrambling, but the latter two offer a taster of Karijini adventure that most people can manage without a guide. One of the prettiest gorges to visit is **Kalamina Gorge**. The turn-off is 19 km west of the visitor centre, and it is also one of the easiest to explore. A short, steep track leads to the base of the gorge and a permanent pool. If you turn right and walk for a short distance you'll reach a small, picturesque waterfall, if you turn left there is a lovely and flat walk downstream to **Rock Arch Pool** (3 km return). **Hamersley Gorge** is another delightful spot, although on the far western border 100 km from the visitor centre. This is a large, open gorge with dramatically folded rock walls in shades of purple, green and pink. Fortescue River flows through the gorge, creating beautiful pools and waterfalls. If you head upstream you'll pass a deep 'spa' pool on the way to the fern-lined **Grotto** (1 km, difficult). To get a bird's-eye perspective on the whole landscape you can climb **Mount Bruce**, WA's second highest mountain at 1235 m. This is the island peak visible from the western end of Karijini Drive and the track is a long but rewarding slog up the western face (9 km, six hours return).

Marble Bar (250 km from Auski Roadhouse) is a tiny Outback town with a wide main street of corrugated iron buildings proudly claims to be the hottest town in Australia, which is not exactly a strong selling point. The town is surrounded by spectacular Pilbara scenery of low spinifex-covered ranges and dark red ironstone ridges. Just outside Marble Bar is the beautiful rock bar of jasper across the Coongan River that gives the town its name and **Chinaman's Pool** nearby where you can swim.

THE PILBARA LISTINGS

Tom Price
$$-$ Tom Price Tourist Park, 2 km from town, T9189 1515. Self-contained A-frame units, 4-bed dorms in dongas, and a campers' kitchen and shop.

Karijini National Park
$$$-$ Auski (Mujani) Roadhouse, T9176 6988, on the Great Northern Highway, 265 km from Port Hedland, 200 km from Newman. On the northeastern border of the park, the roadhouse is a coach stop and a useful meeting point for tours. 20 comfortable motel rooms, budget twins without en suite, and powered and unpowered sites. Internet access available.

$$$-$ Karijini Eco Retreat, Savannah Campground, off Weano Rd, T9425 5591, www.karijiniecoretreat.com.au. This is the only commercial accommodation within the park and 100% Gumala Aborigine owned. There are deluxe en suite eco tents with king or twin beds, campsites and a communal kitchen. Guided walks.

Camping
Dales Camping Area, 10 km east of the visitor centre, is a simple campground. Dingoes are common here, so ensure you store all food in your vehicle.

Tom Price
Pilbara Gorge Tours, T9188 1534, www.pilbaragorgetours.com.au. Runs half- ($125, children $60) and full-day ($145, children $60) 4WD tours to the main attractions of Karijini National Park.
West Oz Active, T0438 913713, www.westozactive.com.au. For a more extreme Karijini experience, trips include hiking, climbing, swimming and abseiling. Prices range from around $140-220.
Willis Walkabouts, T8985 2134 www.bushwalkingholidays.com.au. Good 14-day camping tours departing from Tom Price into the Karijini National Park (it is in 2 sections and participants can choose to do one or both).

PARDOO ROADHOUSE TO BROOME

This is one of the most tedious stretches of road in WA, particularly the last 300 km or so. There are sections where the vegetation struggles to get above knee-high, and the endless flat vista can be quite mesmerizing. Take plenty of water, even if you don't plan on any stops, and allow a full day. Pardoo ① *150 km from Port Hedand, T9176 4916, www.pardoo.com.au*, (**$$-$**), has rooms, fuel 0600- 2200, a bar, a small range of supplies and serves meals until 2000. Drinkable (bore) water is available (20 litres maximum) and there is also a campsite with a pool. The roadhouse is close to the junction with two unsealed roads. The main place of interest is **Eighty Mile Beach**, 10 km (unsealed) off the highway and 105 km from Pardoo. The beach stretches as far as the eye can see in either direction and slopes gently down to the water, and is a favoured fishing spot though not recommended for a swim. Adjacent to the beach is the **Eighty Mile Beach Caravan Park**. Sandfire Roadhouse ① *T9176 5944*, 140 km from Pardoo, is the last before the junction with Broome Road, 290 km up the track, so make sure you have enough fuel.

THE KIMBERLEY

The far north of the state is called the Kimberley, an area larger than Germany with a population of 30,000. It's a wild and rugged region of gorges and waterfalls, cattle stations and diamond mines, spectacular coastline and ancient Aboriginal art. The Kimberley is part of Australia's tropical north with a summer monsoon that throws a green cloak over the grassy plains and scrub covered ranges, and turns the rivers into powerful torrents. During the dry season the rivers shrink to a series of pools, waterfalls slow to a trickle and heat and humidity drop to a comfortable level. There are only three major roads in the Kimberley and just one of them is sealed – the Great Northern Highway from Broome to Kununurra. Broome is a sophisticated coastal resort of entirely unique character, while Kununurra, on the eastern edge of the state, is surrounded by beautiful Kimberley range country and fertile land fed by the Ord River. The Gibb River Road connects the same towns and provides access to the region's most beautiful gorges in cattle station country but this is a challenging dirt route. There are many places so remote that you can only see them by boat, plane or 4WD, such as the extraordinary western coast, the Mitchell Plateau, Buccaneer Archipelago and the beehive domes of the Bungle Bungle Range.

→BROOME AND THE KIMBERLEY COAST

Turquoise water, red cliffs, white sand and green mangroves; Broome (population: 13,700) is a place full of vivid colour and tropical lushness, with an interesting history and composition quite unlike any other Australian town. It was established on the shore of Roebuck Bay in the 1890s as a telegraph cable station and a base for pearl shell merchants and their divers. The first pearl divers were Aboriginal, then later Malaysian, Indonesian, Chinese or Japanese. Consequently the people of Broome are a unusual mix of Aboriginal, Asian and European heritage. When plastic buttons were invented in the 1950s Broome survived by learning to produce cultured pearls and has since prospered, not only on the profits from the world's largest and most lustrous pearls, but also, more recently, from tourism. Refined and expensive resorts at Cable Beach have brought the town much attention and sophistication, and although it is probably true that Broome has lost some of its unique character, it remains a fascinating oasis and a very enjoyable place to spend a few days.

ARRIVING IN BROOME
Moving on   From Broome the Great Northern Highway heads east across the foot of the Dampier Peninsula and then forks, giving the traveller a choice of two very different routes to the Northern Territory. The northerly fork heads up to Derby (see page 156) and the Gibb River Road (see box, page 158), while directly east the Great Northern Highway curls around the bulk of the Kimberley, skirting the deserts to the south; see page 156.

PLACES IN BROOME
Chinatown is the oldest part of town and is still the main focus of the town. Carnarvon Street and Dampier Terrace are lined with architecture that is characteristic of the town and its history. Australian corrugated iron and verandas are blended with Chinese flourishes such as red trims and lattice. Modern boats now use the jetty at the Deep Water

Port but two luggers survive and can be seen at **Pearl Luggers** ① *T9192 0022, www.pearlluggers. com.au, Mon-Fri 0900-1630, Sat 0900-1500, daily tours (call to check times), $20, children $10, concessions $16.50,* at the other end of Dampier Terrace. This is the best place to learn about the pearling industry of the old days. The commercial **Monsoon Gallery** ① *corner of Hamersley and Carnarvon Sts, T9193 5379, www.monsoongallery.com.au, May-Sep Tue-Sat 1000- 1700, Oct-Apr Tue-Sat 1000-1600, free,* is housed in a fine old pearling master's residence and is worth a visit to see an example of early Broome architecture as well as the fine collection of art and jewellery. About 1 km south is the **Broome Historical Museum** ① *67 Robinson St, T9192 2075, www.broomemuseum.org.au, Jun-Sep Mon-Fri 1000-1600, Sat-Sun 1000-1300; Oct-May daily 1000-1300, $5, children $1, concessions $3,* which houses a small but well-arranged and quite fascinating collection of artefacts, memorabilia and photographs charting the whole history of the European and Asian colonists.

Not far away is **Town Beach**, a small shallow bay with warm golden sand and Broome's amazing opaque turquoise water, fringed by a low rocky headland on one side and mangroves on the other. This is the best place to see the phenomenon called **Staircase to the Moon**, when the moonlight shines on pools of water left behind by the tide to create the illusion. Pick up a monthly visitor guide from the VIC for 'staircase' dates and tide times. In the **Shell House** ① *76 Guy St, T9192 1423 (also at 23 Dampier Terr, which is open year-round), May-Sep Mon-Fri 0900-1600, Sat 0900-1300,* the owners display their

compact collection of 6000 shells from hundreds of mostly local species. **Gantheaume Point** is a jumble of red rock stacks that make a striking contrast to the turquoise sea beyond. It is a lovely place to watch the sun set, although the light for photography is best in the morning. It is also one of many areas around Broome where fossilized **dinosaur footprints** can be seen in rock shelves. They are just at the base of the cliff but can only be seen at very low tide, which only happens once or twice a month (the VIC will be able to advise). Around the corner, **Reddell Beach** runs along the southern edge of the peninsula. It is known for interesting rock formations and sheer pindan cliffs above the beach. Cable Beach is a perfect, long, wide, white-sand beach, 6 km from the town centre, which faces west and the setting sun. The classic way to watch the sunset at Cable Beach is, unlikely as it may sound, on the back of a camel. It is a relatively safe place to swim and there is usually a lifeguard patrol in winter. A small beach shack hires out surf and boogie boards.

In the centre of the cluster of tourist resorts at Cable is **Broome Crocodile Park** ⓘ *Cable Beach Rd, T9192 1489, www.malcolmdouglas.com.au, Apr-Nov Mon-Fri 1000-1700, Sat-Sun 1400-1700, daily feeding tour at 1500 plus an extra guided tour Mon-Fri at 1100; Dec-Mar daily feeding tour at 1600, $30, children $20, concessions $25,* the public arm of a large commercial crocodile farming operation. Dozens of pens hold hundreds of crocs and alligators from five species, but mostly the big estuarine (or saltwater) crocodiles of northern Australia. The tours are fascinating.

DAMPIER PENINSULA

Forming a large triangle north of Broome, the Dampier Peninsula is a huge area and home to several Aboriginal communities. Access is limited but some communities offer tours and accommodation, an excellent way to spend time with Aboriginal people and see the peninsula. The land is entirely covered in long grass and spindly trees but the coastline continues Broome's spectacular blend of red cliffs, white beaches and chalky blue sea. Just one dirt road traverses the peninsula from Broome to its tip at Cape Leveque (220 km) and it's a shocker. Ruts, sand, rocks and pools of water make this a road for high-clearance 4WD vehicles only (usually closed in wet season).

The first turn-off, shortly after leaving the sealed road, leads to the **Willie Creek Pearl Farm** ⓘ *T9192 0000, www.williecreekpearls.com.au, half-day tours $90, children $45, including 37-km transfer from Broome, or $50, children $25, self-drive to Willie Creek (4WD recommended),* on a wide tidal inlet at the bottom of the Dampier Peninsula. It is the only Broome pearl farm that receives visitors and that is because it's actually a demonstration farm, nowhere near the valuable commercial beds. A quick boat trip enables visitors to see how the oysters are suspended in the creek and the tour ends with a look at the finished product in the showroom. On the edge of Roebuck Bay, 25 km from Broome, is **Broome Bird Observatory** ⓘ *T9193 5600, www.broomebirdobservatory.com, $5, children free, bookings essential for tours and accommodation,* one of the best places in Australia to see migratory shorebirds and also a peaceful place to stay, with chalets and rooms ($$$-$). Regular two-hour tours are held that explore the mangroves or bush and may include seeing the migrations, depending on the time of year.

Following the Cape Leveque road for about an hour, the next stop is **Beagle Bay community** ⓘ *call into the office when entering the community, T9192 4913, gold coin donation.* The unusual church was built in 1917 and is notable for its altar, walls and floor lined with pearl shell. Fuel is sometimes available, but there's no accommodation.

Continuing north for about 50 km, you'll reach the Aboriginal community of **Lombadina** ① *T9192 4936, day visitors $10 car, payable at office or craft shop*, a former mission settlement. The local Bardi people, many of them still Catholics, offer the best range of accommodation and tours, including fishing and whale-watching charters (July-October), mud crabbing and bush walking and 4WD tours. **Kujurta Buru** (T9192 1662, www.kujurta buru.com.au) runs the **Dampier Peninsula Transfer Service** which travels between Broome and the major communities.

Cape Leveque lies at the end of the road, capped by red cliffs, rocky coves and white beaches. You can stay here, in a resort owned by Aboriginals or in beach shelters. On the eastern side of the peninsula is **Mudnunn community** ① *T9192 4121*, who allow unpowered camping and sometimes run mud-crabbing tours in the mangroves ($55), which can be a memorable experience. The route east across the foot of the Dampier Peninsula to Derby passes through a flat country of grass and woodland. The main stop is the Willare Bridge roadhouse. After 15 km the road divides, heading east to Fitzroy Crossing (220 km), for the Great Northern Highway (see below) or north to Derby (42 km), the starting point of the Gibb River Road (see box, page 158).

DERBY

Derby sits on a narrow spur of land surrounded by tidal mud flats, close to where the mighty Fitzroy River flows into King Sound, 220 km from Broome. The entrance to the sound is a maze of a thousand islands, the **Buccaneer Archipelago**, a spectacular area to explore by boat or plane. The town was one of the earliest in the Kimberley, established in 1883 as a port for wool and pearl shell exports, and used until recently to ship zinc and lead from mines near Fitzroy Crossing. The unusual D-shaped jetty has been constructed to cope with one of the highest tides in the world (11.8 m). Although the town has few attractions for visitors, its position at the start of the Gibb River Road (see box, page 158) and close to the spectacular Kimberley coast means that tours and cruises from Derby are very good value. On the way into Derby stop and have a look at the impressive 1500-year-old Boab Prison Tree, thought to have held Aboriginal prisoners captured by pearling 'blackbirders'. Derby also has a large supermarket, camping store, car rental agencies, ANZ, ATM and fuel. The **VIC** ① *Clarendon St, T9191 1426, T1800 621 426, www.derbytourism.com.au, Mon-Fri 0830-1630, Sat-Sun 0900-1300 (Jun-Aug Sun open until 1600)*, is efficient.

→GREAT NORTHERN HIGHWAY

The Gibb River Road is one of Australia's great Outback drives but if time or resources compel you to take the sealed highway route this is not necessarily second-best option. This long run between Derby and Kununurra is split into two very different scenic sections. The first 550 km to Halls Creek are frankly pretty tedious and have little to distract the traveller. (There no services in the first 260-km stretch from Derby to Fitzroy Crossing until Fitzroy Crossing.) **Halls Creek** is a popular stopover and offers a small but broad range of accommodation options. The 365-km stretch between Halls Creek and Kununurra has far more striking scenery than that of the Gibb River Road; indeed it is one of the most scenic bits of road in the whole country, and it also gives you a chance to see the magnificent **Purnululu National Park** (the **Bungle Bungles**). If conditions allow, consider taking the Gibb River Road for 120 km (62 km sealed) to the Windjana Gorge turn-off. The Leopold Downs Road passes Windjana Gorge and Tunnel Creek (see box, page 158) before rejoining the Northern Highway just 42 km west of Fitzroy Crossing. There are a couple of creek crossings, but it is usually okay for 2WD during the dry season.

FITZROY CROSSING AND AROUND

On the banks of one of the Kimberley's greatest rivers, 395 km from Broome and 290 km from Halls Creek, the small town of Fitzroy provides services and supplies for the mining and pastoral industries and more than 30 Aboriginal communities in the area. The main appeal for visitors is the beautiful Geikie Gorge, the only gorge in the Kimberley that can be reached by sealed road. There's an excellent **VIC** ① *T9191 5355, Mon-Sat 0800-1700 (Apr-Sep), Mon-Fri 0900-1700 (Oct-Mar)*, just off the highway.

Geike Gorge National Park ① *0630-1830 (Apr-Nov), no fees, no camping, toilets, BBQs, is 20 km from Fitzroy Crossing*, has 30-m cliffs which are studded with fossils and caves, and regular annual flooding scours the lower walls creating a striking line of clean white limestone below orange and grey rock. The gorge is best seen on a boat cruise, on which you can also see freshwater crocodiles and lots of birdlife. CALM run a one-hour cruise that examines geological and natural features. Darngku Heritage Cruises (www.darngku.com.au) offer a more intimate look at the gorge from the perspective of the traditional owners, the Bunaba people. Their 5½-hour tours include walks, bush tucker, demonstrations of fire-lighting or spear making and other aspects of Aboriginal culture. There are also a couple of short walks along the riverbed. The river walk leads from the gazebo to the sandbar and you may see basking crocodiles and birds (20 minutes return). The Reef Walk (3 km, one hour return) heads upstream along the base of the rocks (where fossils can be seen) until you reach the dramatic West Wall. Follow the river bank back for good views of the East Wall.

HALLS CREEK AND AROUND

A far better stop on the highway than Fitzroy, Halls Creek has a good range of facilities and is 545 km from Derby. The **VIC** ① *corner Great Northern Highway and Hall St, T9168 6262, T1800 877 423, www.hallscreektourism.com.au, Apr-Aug daily 0700-1700, Oct-Mar 0800-1700*, is on the main highway in the centre of town. Some 16 km west of Halls Creek is the junction to the unsealed **Tanami Track**, which leads to the **Wolfe Creek Meteor Crater**, the second-largest of its kind in the world at over 900 m across. About 300,000 years old, it's also one of the best preserved on the planet. As a diversion off the main highway it's a big effort, and you should consider flying over it instead, but the side-trip off the Tanami involves only about 40 km of rough driving. The Tanami continues on its way to Alice Springs, frequently accessible by 2WD, though you should check first with the police at Halls Creek (T9168 6000), or Main Roads WA (T138 138). The road's chief difficulty is the scarcity of roadhouses – be prepared to go 700 km without a fill-up.

PURNULULU NATIONAL PARK (THE BUNGLE BUNGLES)

① *Open Apr-Dec only; visitor centre 0800-1200, 1300-1600. Park fee $11 car, from camping $7 per adult. Unless you have a sturdy 4WD you'll need to take a tour. For more information contact CALM in Kununurra, T9168 4200. The park is 160 km from Halls Creek and 105 km from Warmun.*

GOING FURTHER

GIBB RIVER ROAD

This legendary unsealed Kimberley road is both an experience and a challenge. It was created in the 1960s as a way for the cattle stations of this region to get their stock to Derby and Wyndham ports. Although now used more frequently by travellers, the alarming sight of a huge cattle road train barrelling along in clouds of dust is still common. The Gibb River Road traverses 660 km between Derby and Kununurra (about 250 km shorter than the highway route, but it takes much longer because of the condition of the road) and passes through remote range country and grass plains, threaded with creeks, gorges and waterfalls. Part of the Gibb River Road experience is also staying at the cattle stations along the way. There are also good campsites close to several beautiful gorges.

Remember this is a rugged road though, and travelling it is less than comfortable. Dusty and bone-jarring conditions means a 4WD is essential and you should allow at least four days. If you don't have your own vehicle there are plenty of operators offering adventure tours (contact the VIC in Broome, www.broomevisitorcentre.com.au, or Kununurra, page 162). Road conditions vary along the route, during the season and from year to year so it is essential to check current conditions before setting out with **Main Roads WA** ① *T138 138, www.mainroads.wa.gov.au*. Generally the road is only passable in the dry season (May-November) and the eastern section is much rougher and more corrugated than the western section. Vehicles need to be in excellent condition and you'll need to carry extra fuel, water and spare wheels. For more information see the *Gibb River and Kalumburu Roads Travellers Guide* ($5), produced every year by the Derby Tourist Bureau, which lists current facilities. Available from Derby and Broome VICs, it can also be ordered by phone. If the worst happens, for road rescue from Derby call T9193 1205, or from Kununurra T9169 1556. The website www.exploroz.com has some good information, tips and travellers' comments.

DERBY TO WINDJANA GORGE

The western half of the Gibb River Road (GRR), a distance of 145 km, is both the easiest and the most interesting. The road starts 6 km south of Derby and is sealed for 62 km. The next 57 km to the Windjana Gorge turn-off is a wide gravel road, usually fairly smooth and fine for a 2WD. The striking **Windjana Gorge National Park** is on Leopold Downs Road, 20 km south of the GRR turn-off. Dark-grey fluted stone forms impressive cliffs above the plains, broken by a narrow gap where the Lennard River has carved a gorge into the range. The broad sandy river banks are lined with trees and provide a basking spot for a large population of freshwater crocodiles. Swimming is not recommended. You can follow a sandy path up to the end of the gorge (3½ km one way) although the most pleasant area is close to the entrance, by Bandingan Rock, the large white rock in the river that the Bunaba linked with the spirits of babies. There is a campsite nearby with fine views of the cliff face, as well as showers (cold) and toilets.

Tunnel Creek National Park, where the creek has carved a 750-m tunnel through the Napier Range, is 35 km further south on the same road. During the dry season the water level in the tunnel varies between waist and knee high but it's good fun on a hot day to take a torch and wade through the cold pools in the tunnel; look out for bats and rock art. For more information contact CALM in Broome, T9195 5500.

WINDJANA GORGE TO THE KALUMBURU ROAD

Shortly after the Windjana turn-off the Gibb River Road passes through the narrow Yammera Gap in the Napier Range. Continuing east through open grassland the road slowly ascends into the red-sandstone King Leopold Ranges, named after the Belgian king. Within these ranges, Mount Hart Wilderness Lodge, 200 km from Windjana Gorge, 110 km from Kalumburu Rd, offers comfortable homestead accommodation. Deep and narrow **Lennard Gorge**, 7 km east then reached by a rough 8-km access road (4WD only for the last few kilometres), has waterfalls and rock pools to swim in. Another 23 km east is the turn-off for **Bell Gorge**, which is one of the most beautiful here. It is 29 km down a rocky road. There are lovely secluded campsites by Bell Creek; otherwise camp at Silent Grove (19 km from GRR) which has showers (cold). Pick up a tag at Silent Grove for Bell Creek sites. Back on the main road it is only 7 km to Imintji Store, with groceries, diesel and a mechanics (T9191 7471).

Leaving the ranges behind, you shortly pass the turn-off for **Mornington Wilderness Camp** ① *T9191 7406, T1800 631 946, www.australiawildlife.org*. This private wildlife sanctuary, although 100 km off the GRR, is well worth a visit for its stunning river and gorge scenery and wildlife tours. There are luxurious safari tents, camping, restaurant and tours. On the northern side of the GRR is **Charnley River Station** ① *T9191 4646, www.charnleyriverstation.com*, a working cattle station with a campsite, self-catering accommodation, more beautiful gorges, swimming spots and rock-art sites. **Galvans Gorge**, 35 km after the homestead turn-off, is one of the most accessible gorges. Park by the gate and it's an easy 10-minute walk to an idyllic swimming hole under a small waterfall.

The next stop, 20 km east, is an essential one. **Mount Barnett Roadhouse** (T9197 7007), sells the only fuel between here and El Questro, 324 km east. There are also showers and camping permits to nearby Manning Gorge. An hour's walk from this campsite gets you to a rock platform over the river and impressive falls. **Barnett River Gorge** is 22 km east of the roadhouse and provides more swimming within a shorter walk (five to 20 minutes) but note that the 5 km access road is very rough. A further 10 km past the gorge turn-off, **Mount Elizabeth Station** ① *T9191 4644, www.mountelizabethstation.com*, is an interesting place to stay, and is a working cattle station with a homestead (B&B) and camping. The junction of the Gibb River Road and Kalumburu Road is another 68 km to the east.

KALUMBURU ROAD TO THE PENTECOST RIVER

Only 240 km of the Gibb River Road remains but if any stretch of road is likely to test your patience, it will be this very corrugated one. There are no places to stop or to camp except for the station stays and the scenery is less interesting until you reach the imposing bluffs of the Cockburn Range on the far side of the Pentecost. There are a few 'jump-ups' or steep hills in the next 40-50 km: make sure you keep well to the left on these hills as you can't see what is hurtling in the opposite direction. The last stop before crossing the Pentecost (9 km further east) is Home Valley Station (T8296 8010, www.hvstation.com.au), with campsites and hot showers. Note that the Pentecost riverbed crossing can be waist-deep in water at the beginning of the season, so seek advice before attempting it. There are also plenty of salties in this river so walking across it to check the depth is not recommended!

The magnificent landscape of Purnululu National Park, most commonly just called the Bungles, is still little known and it is not easy or cheap to visit but utterly unforgettable if you do. The most striking feature of this park are the sandstone 'beehive' domes of the Bungle Bungle range, found in the southern area of the park, and part of a landscape formed 360 million years ago. The domes are striped with orange and grey bands that are astonishingly regular across the whole formation. The Piccaninny Creek bed winds through this surreal landscape of rippled rock, unlike any other in Australia. The western part of the range is a long, imposing wall of conglomerate rock up to 200 m high, eroded into deep, narrow chasms full of palm trees. Aboriginal people have lived here for at least 20,000 years and it contains many significant cultural and archaeological sites closed to the public. Until the 1980s the Bungles were known only to the Aboriginal owners and a few cattle drovers. Then in 1983 a German documentary crew filmed aerial footage of the park and when these images of the Bungles were screened in Australia the television station was deluged with callers wanting to know where this incredible place was. In 1986, the first visitors were allowed into the area and 1800 people drove into the Bungles on a track so rough that it took 12 hours to travel the 50 km. The same track now takes around three hours but it is still a rough 4WD-only road that keeps the numbers of visitors low. In 2001 about 25,000 people visited the park but over 200,000 took scenic flights over it. Around the time of the declaration of the national park in 1987 the government intended that the park be jointly managed by CALM and traditional owners. However management terms have still not been agreed and the process complicated by dispute between the Jaru and Kija people, both claiming ownership of certain areas of the park. Negotiations and court cases are continuing. In the meantime, the park was nominated for World Heritage Listing in 2003 and this will also influence its future development.

The main activity in the Bungles is walking and you do need to be fairly fit and agile to see what the park has to offer, although the beehive domes are easily seen within a short distance of the Piccaninny car park. Most trails involve walking on pebbles or over boulders so make sure you take sturdy footwear. At the northern end of the park, **Echidna Chasm Trail** (2 km return) leads up a creek bed into the high walls of the chasm, narrowing to just a few metres across. **Froghole Trail** (1 km return) is a more open walk, past huge boulders of conglomerate and lush vegetation to a dry waterfall and semi-permanent pool. If you don't have time to do all of the walks, take the **Mini-Palms Trail** (5 km return) which offers elements of both Echidna and Froghole. This lovely walk follows a pebbly creek bed into an large oasis of palms surrounded by high domes. After climbing up past large boulders, the trail reaches a platform overlooking a narrow chasm. At the southern end of the park, the **Piccaninny Creek** area is surrounded by beehive domes. The main walk is **Cathedral Gorge Trail** (3 km return), heading between the domes into a an enormous bowl-shaped cavern and a shallow pool. The **Domes Trail** (1 km) is a loop off Cathedral Gorge Trail, just after the car park, providing more views of domes. The best walk, though, is simply to follow the dry bed of Piccaninny Creek until you have had enough and return, for this provides spectacular perspectives on the domes the whole way. If you take plenty of water, food and camera film this can easily occupy you for a whole day (14 km return to the 'elbow'). This route is also the start of the **Picaninny Gorge Trail** (30 km return) for experienced walkers. It's 7 km from the car park to the mouth of the gorge (the 'elbow'), then another 8 km along the gorge to the pools and side gorges, or 'fingers', at the end. Camping is allowed at the gorge but there are no facilities so you must carry in a fuel stove. To walk this trail, you must register and pay for your campsite at the visitor centre close to the entrance. The main park camping areas, Kurrajong and Walardi, have toilets, water and firewood.

WARMUN (TURKEY CREEK ROADHOUSE)

Warmun is an Aboriginal community, just northwest of Purnululu National Park and 200 km from Kununurra. It has an excellent art gallery, **Warmun Arts Centre** ① *T9168 7496, www.warmunart.com, Mon-Fri 0900-1600, but may be closed for special viewings; weekends by appointment only*. The Warmun community artists produce bold, streamlined images using natural ochres and pigments in coarse form that gives their work a textured surface. Their distinctive paintings usually sell for several thousand dollars and attract much international interest. Facilities for visitors are found at the Warmun Roadhouse (www.warmunroadhouse.com.au). On the way to Kununurra, after about 100 km, look out for a small 'scenic lookout' sign and turn-off. This leads after a short distance to a parking area with spectacular views over the Ragged Range.

EL QUESTRO

Less than 50 km off the main highway is **El Questro Wilderness Park** and a further 16 km (4WD recommended) south is El Questro ① *www.elquestro.com.au*, a million-acre cattle property, which is a friendly, down-to-earth place run as a wilderness park (effectively a private national park complete with rangers) offering accommodation, restaurants and tours. Deep-red gorges, natural springs, major rivers, Aboriginal rock art and loads of wildlife are all part of the El Questro experience. You need at least two days at El Questro. Note that some sights are only accessible to 4WD vehicles and all visitors must buy a Wilderness Pass Permit ($20), valid for a week.

WYNDHAM AND AROUND

Sitting at the wide, flat confluence of five of WA's biggest rivers, run-down Wyndham is surrounded by some spectacular hill ranges and the most concentrated population of crocs in Australia. It is split into two centres: Wyndham Port and, 4 km inland, the main town with most of the few facilities. A road east of the main town leads up Bastion Hill to **Five Rivers Lookout**, actually a series of lookouts. The views from both are breathtaking, especially at sunrise and sunset. Reached by a short road not far from the Wyndham turn-off is the **Grotto**, a deep and narrow chasm with a waterfall at one end (wet season only) and a permanent waterhole at the bottom, reached via 150-odd steps. A good spot for a swim and a picnic. On the other side of the highway, closer to Wyndham, reached via 10 km of unsealed roads, is the **Parrys Lagoon Nature Reserve**, a huge network of lily-covered pools on the wide flood plain that attracts dozens of species of resident and migratory birds. Boardwalks make the most of a truly magical spot.

→KUNUNURRA AND AROUND

WA's northeastern outpost, Kununurra (population: 5000) is 910 km from Derby and 510 km from Katherine (NT). Surrounded by range country and the bountiful waters of the Ord River, Kununurra has the most picturesque setting of any town in the Kimberley. Built in the 1960s as a service town for the Ord River Irrigation Scheme, the town has matured into a confident and growing community supported by agriculture, diamond mining and tourism. The river is dammed to the south of Kununurra, forming Lake Argyle, Australia's largest inland waterway, and holding back the wet-season water so the Ord can flow steadily all year around. The lake and river lie beneath the Carr Boyd Ranges, typically red-rugged, Kimberley sandstone, and are strikingly beautiful. A boat or canoe trip from Lake Argyle to Kununurra along the upper Ord River, through 55 km of ranges, gorges and lush greenery, is one of the WA's highlights and should not be missed. Comfortable accommodation, services and a wide range of tours make Kununurra an ideal base for exploring the East Kimberley.

PLACES IN KUNUNURRA

On Kununurra's eastern border, the **Mirima National Park** ① *park entry fee $11 per car, no camping, no water*, 2 km from town, is a delightful pocket of rich-red sandstone outcrops, with similarities to the Bungle Bungle range. If you have limited time this beautiful park (plus a cruise on the Ord River) will show you the best of Kununurra's scenery. There are two short walks in Hidden Valley, an oasis of beehive domes and ridges among boabs and ghost gums. There's a loop walk (400 m) from the car park focusing on native plants, and a lookout trail (800 m) off this loop which climbs up a ridge overlooking the valley and the town. The lookout in the park is a fine place to watch sunset or sunrise, as is **Kelly's Knob**, the steep-sided hill just north of town. The lookout is at the end of Kelly Road, a short walk up from the car park. Kununurra's western border is formed by the **Diversion Dam**, a span of radial gates that hold back the Ord River and feed water to the irrigated plains around the town. About 16,000 ha are under cultivation and the main produce is sugar cane and fruit crops such as melons, bananas, and mangoes. From the town, Ivanhoe and Weaber Plain Roads head north into the farming area and it is possible to visit melon and banana farms, and the wonderful **Hoochery** ① *T9168 2467, www.hoochery.com.au, daily 0900-1600, distillery tours on the hour 1100 and 1400, $12, Oct-Apr Mon-Fri 0900-1600, Sat 0900-1200*, a cane distillery and barn bar selling a smooth Ord River Rum and a beautiful chocolate and coffee Cane Royal.

Below the Diversion Dam, the **Lower Ord** flows out to Cambridge Gulf, and despite damming and irrigation 80 per cent of the Ord's flow still reaches the sea. Saltwater crocodiles are found in this lower part of the river as they can't get above the dam, to the waters called **Lake Kununurra**. This lake and its many lagoons are a lush series of waterways, full of birds, fish and freshwater crocodiles. Unusual striped rock found only on an island in Lake Argyle is polished and sold at the **Zebra Rock Gallery** ① *Packsaddle Rd, 15 km from town, T9168 1114, www.zebrarock.biz, Apr-Oct 0800-1700, Nov-Mar 1000-1500*, on the western bank of Lake Kununurra, opposite the 'sleeping buddha' hill. Zebra rock souvenirs are also available in town. If you follow the river upstream from here for 55 km you'll reach **Lake Argyle** but by road the lake is 70 km south of town. To the south of the lake, Argyle Diamond Mine is the largest diamond producer in the world, producing about 30 per cent of the global supply, and is known for its coloured diamonds. Pink, cognac and champagne Argyle diamonds can all be seen in local jewellery shops. The vast open-cut mine can be visited on an in-depth tour.

The friendly and very efficient VIC ① *T9168 1177, T1800 586 868, www.visitkununurra.com, May-Sep Mon-Sat 0800-1700, Sun 0900-1500, Sep-Mar Mon-Fri 0900-1600, Sat 0900-1200*, is on Coolibah Drive, the main loop road in the town centre. The **Kununurra Hotel** ① *37 Messmate Way, T9168 0400 and T1800 450 993, www.hotelkununurra.com.au*, (**$$$**) has various air-conditioned rooms, a pool, laundry facilities, an on-site restaurant and bar. From the town 4WD, flight, canoe and boat tours head out to sights such as the Ord River, Lake Argyle, the Argyle Diamond Mine, The Bungles, El Questro Wilderness Park and Wyndham.

KEEP RIVER NATIONAL PARK

A laid-back border with WA, 55 km from Kununurra, Keep River has more in common with the rugged landscape around Kununurra than most of the Territory scenery to the east. The park's chief attractions are the **Nganalam Art Site** and the long, shallow sandstone **Keep River Gorge**, both about 25 km off the highway and accessed by unsealed 2WD roads. There are walking tracks and walking notes at both sites but the main walk is Keep River Gorge Walk. Due to seasonal flooding of the Keep River, parts of the park, particularly the gorge, are often closed in the wet season. There is a quarantine checkpoint at the WA border where officers will check for illegal fruit. For more information contact the Keep River ranger, T9167 8827.

TIMBER CREEK

ⓘ *230 km from Kununurra.*

This small settlement had its beginning as a stores depot for the cattle station the size of a small country in the **Victoria River** region but is now little more than a refuelling stop on the highway and a base for trips into the Gregory National Park. However, if you have time a boat cruise on the Victoria River with Max's Boat Tours, it is well worth it. If you intend to visit the national park head for the Parks and Wildlife Commission office at the western end of town for information.

GREGORY NATIONAL PARK

ⓘ *No park fees, for more information contact Parks and Wildlife Timber Creek, T8975 0888. Bullita Homestead 55 km south of Timber Creek.*

Remote and rugged, most of Gregory is difficult to access without a 4WD. The park encompasses dramatic large-scale scenery of escarpments and flat-topped ranges above plains of open woodland. Divided into two sections, the western Gregory sector offers rough 4WD routes to explore former cattle stations and joins up with the Buchanan Highway to the south. **Limestone Gorge** is an attractive camping area with a billabong generally said to be safe to swim in and a good ridge walk with views of East Baines River valley. The gorge has unusual limestone karst formations, fossil stromatolites, and calcite rock that looks like a frozen waterfall. The unsealed road is sometimes accessible by 2WD in the dry, but check road conditions at the Timber Creek park office. Back on the highway, about halfway between the two park areas is **Kuwang Lookout**, giving fine views over Stokes Range. The spectacular eastern sector of the park is a much smaller area, around the Victoria River, and accessible to 2WDs. **Joe Creek Walk** (one hour loop) takes you to the escarpment wall by way of Livistonia palms and Aboriginal art. The Escarpment Lookout walk (1½ hour return) climbs to the top of Stokes Range for views of the valley and Victoria River gorge. Beware of estuarine crocodiles in Victoria River – no swimming. The cheapest fuel stop around here is at the Victoria River roadhouse, 190 km before Katherine and in the midst of the spectacular eastern section of the Gregory National Park. The roadhouse makes an excellent base for exploring this part of the park and serves cheap scran. Here are a few walking trails, including the excellent Joe Creek Walk.

Around 85 km before Katherine on the Victoria Highway is the turn-off for **Flora River Nature Park**. Canoeing and fishing is allowed on the river but no swimming as estuarine crocodiles are found here. The rare pig-nosed turtle also lives in the river.

THE KIMBERLEY LISTINGS

WHERE TO STAY

Broome

Broome has easily the widest range of accommodation north of Perth. The following is a small selection of what is available. Contact the VIC for other options, and if you're around for a while consider a spell out on the Dampier Peninsula (see page 155). Book well ahead for the peak Apr-Sep season. If coming in Oct-Mar shop around for some excellent deals.

$$$$ Broome Town B&B, 15 Stewart St, T9192 2006, www.broometown.com.au. A centrally located boutique B&B designed and built by the owners. The spacious rooms have been tastefully furnished, all with en suite, a/c and TV. The friendly hosts serve up an excellent breakfast. Massage and spa therapies are also available. Recommended.

$$$-$ Kimberley Klub YHA, Frederick St, T9192 3233 and T1800 004 345, www.kimberley klub.com. A superb large hostel, and very much a party destination. Modern, well maintained and clean, it centres around a large open-plan games, dining and pool area. Facilities include a bar and cheap café, Wi-Fi, bike and scooter hire, volleyball and badminton courts and well-equipped kitchen. Beds in spacious 6- and 10-bed dorms, plus a few doubles and a fully self-contained room. Recommended.

WHAT TO DO

Broome

Astro Tours, T0417 949958, www.astrotours.net. Heads about 10 km out of Broome once or twice an evening up to 4 nights a week (Fri-Sat at 1800, Mon and Wed at 2000) between Apr-Oct. Its guided 2-hr tour of the night sky is both animated and fascinating, one of the country's very best, and 8 telescopes means plenty of viewing time, $75.

Aussie Off Road Tours, T9192 3617, www.aussieoffroadtours.com.au. Brad Bayfield runs 1- to 3-day 4WD tours in the Kimberley. All meals are homemade and included.

Broome Kayak Adventures, T1300 665888, www.broomeadventure.com.au. 3-hr kayak trips in and around Turtle Bay.

Kujurta Buru Aboriginal Cultural Tours, 640 Dora St, T9192 1662, www.kujurta buru.com.au. Broome through Aboriginal eyes – tours can include bush tucker, bush medicines, weapon throwing, learning about hunting techniques and traditional foods. Half-day (3-hr) tours depart Mon-Fri at 0900 and cost $77, children $38.50.

Pinnacle Tours, T9192 8080, www.pinnacletours.com.au. This outfit heads out on day and night 4WD trips to the Dampier Peninsula, as well as offering 1-day trips for those with less time.

Sentosa, T9192 8163, www.sentosa charters.com. Offers full-day fishing trips from $235. Bait, gear, refreshments and lunch provided. Also offers whale-watching tours in season.

DREAM TRIP 3:
Darwin→Uluru→Adelaide 21 days

GOING FURTHER

DREAM TRIP 3
Darwin→Uluru→Adelaide

The Northern Territory is a neat rectangle of land in the northern heart of Australia with a ragged coastline of mangroves, tidal flats, islands and sky-blue ocean. The state is divided into two halves by climate and environment, each almost the opposite of the other.

The northern part of the state, prosaically called the Top End, is a tropical region of wetlands, waterfalls and powerful rivers. It is a state of extraordinary landscapes, many protected within some of the country's finest national parks. In the Top End you can see some of the world's best rock art, cruise among waterlillies and crocodiles in Kakadu National Park or swim under the waterfalls and rock walls of Litchfield and Nitmiluk national park.

The Northern Territory's centre is classic Outback country and its stark beauty is considered as Australian as the beach. The desert sand is paprika red and the ancient low hill ranges are weathered to a harmonious rust colour. The centre is the place to experience the space and silence of Australia while walking around majestic Uluru, to feel small amid the immensity of the Outback or marvel at the night-time brilliance of the stars.

'The driest state in the driest continent' is a remark South Australians often make with a certain pride in their endurance of such an unforgiving land. In the central deserts is the opal mining town of Coober Pedy, whose inhabitants have dealt with the desiccating heat by burrowing underground. South of Coober Pedy are the Flinders Ranges, ancient folds of weathered rock, best known for Wilpena Pound, a vast circle of mountains that tilts at the sky like city ramparts.

Two-thirds of South Australia's population lives in Adelaide, an island of easy-going sophistication where locals make the most of the climate by spending a large part of their lives at outdoor cafés. The city is surrounded by the wine regions of Barossa, McClaren Vale and Clare. Just south of Adelaide is Kangaroo Island, a sanctuary of wild beauty, teeming with native animals.

DARWIN

In the minds of southerners Darwin will always be the last frontier: the home of nefarious characters and fugitives. But if anything has been constant in this city it is change. Bombarded by cyclones and destroyed by Japanese bombs, Darwin has had to shed its skin as regularly as a snake since 1869. The result is a modern, tropical city of spreading trees and palms, tall apartment blocks and neat suburbs. The population of Darwin has doubled in the last 30 years, making it a young and multicultural city, as befits a place closer to Singapore and Jakarta than to Canberra. The city centre is contained within a narrow peninsula at the eastern entrance to Darwin Harbour, a body of topaz-blue water twice the size of Sydney's harbour. North of the city centre, residential suburbs spread up the coast bordered by mangroves and yellow cliffs. Along the coastline are some of the most enjoyable activities: sunset markets on Mindil Beach, a cruise from Cullen Bay marina or fish and chips at Stokes Hill Wharf. Small, informal and friendly, Darwin operates at a relaxed pace and caters well for travellers.

→ARRIVING IN DARWIN

GETTING THERE AND AROUND
Darwin is serviced by all the major national airlines with regular flights from most of the major cities in the country, and is also an international airline destination in its own right. It is possible to get between the major centres by air. The **airport** ① *T8920 1811, www.darwinairport.com.au*, is 11 km from the centre. **Airport Shuttle** ① *T8981 5066, www.darwinairportshuttle.com.au, $14 for 2 sharing, cheaper for more passengers*, meets all incoming flights and picks up from hotels on request for departures. A taxi costs roughly double, $30, including the $3 exit toll. The airport has ATMs, foreign exchange, tourist information and car hire. **The Ghan** ① *T132147 (in Australia), T8213 4592, www.greatsouthernrail.com.au, train service operates from Perth, Melbourne and Sydney.* The easiest way of getting around the NT is under your steam, but a surprising amount can be seen by combining public bus transport (essentially the Greyhound coach network, www.greyhound.com.au) with Darwin bus and other local tour operators. In the popular dry season a constant northerly wind kicks in on many days, making life miserable for cyclists travelling south. Drivers should check out www.ntlis.nt.gov.au/roadreport for road conditions if travelling on unsealed roads or during the wet season.

TOURIST INFORMATION
Northern Territory Tourist Commission (NTTC) has a useful website, www.australiasoutback.co.uk. The NTTC produces useful free brochures that can be ordered online or collected from VICs. Also on the NTTC website are smartphone apps. Drivers should look at www.exploroz.com which has a detailed guide to planning a 4WD trip. Bookings and packages for NT travel and tours can be found at www.territorydiscoveries.com, the commercial arm of the NTTC. If you're in Sydney, Australia's **Northern Territory and Outback Centre** ① *28 Darling Walk, Harbour St, next door to the Chinese Garden, Darling Harbour, T9283 7477, daily 1000-1800,* is a good resource. *Camping Guide to the Northern Territory*, complied by Lewis and Savage of Boiling Billy Publications, is a very useful rundown of 150 campsites and facilities in the region's national parks and reserves.

There is plenty to do in Darwin (population: 79, 000) but you'll need to get about a bit as many of Darwin's best attractions are located away from the city centre, up around Fannie Bay and on the airport ring road. It is well worth having a stroll around the Esplanade and Parliament House area though, as this is the only place in Darwin where you get a real sense of its history, as well as lovely views of the harbour.

CITY CENTRE AND BICENTENNIAL PARK

One of the city's most popular attractions is **Aquascene** ① *20 Doctors Gully Rd, T8981 7837, www.aquascene.com.au, $15, children $10, see website for feeding times* , at Doctors Gully. It started 40 years ago with a local tossing scraps to fish in this pretty cove and has developed into a fish visitation of almost biblical proportions. Every day at high tide, milkfish, mullet and other species arrive to feed on bread thrown by tourists. There are also gardens of tropical orchids and rainforest.

From Doctors Gully the foreshore **Bicentennial Park** runs along the west side of the city centre right around to the commercial wharves at the southern end. Popular with locals and tourists alike, there are lookouts over the harbour, war memorials and large grassy areas. There is a path through the park, close to the cliff edge, but it is worth deviating from this for a quick look at Lyons Cottage and Old Admiralty House on the Esplanade. **Lyons Cottage** ① *corner of the Esplanade and Knuckey St, T8832 9933, Mon-Fri 0900- 1700, Sat-Sun 0900-1400, free*, was built in 1925 to house staff of the British-Australian Telegraph Company; the cottage is also known as BAT (British Australian Telegraph) House. A stone bungalow of classic colonial design for tropical conditions, it now houses exhibitions of the early European and Larrakia history of Darwin. There is also a retail and tourist outlet run by the not-for-profit Aboriginal Bush Traders. **Old Admiralty House** is on the opposite corner. This is not open to visitors but is of interest as it is one of very few pre-war (1937) houses that survived both bombing and cyclones, and is a fine example of tropical architecture. Continuing towards the wharves, the unusual modern edifice of **Parliament House** ① *Mitchell St, T8946 1512, public areas open daily 0800-1600, free tours run every Sat at 0900 and 1100, May-Sep also on Wed at 1030, bookings not necessary*, looms up ahead. Built in 1994, it stands on the site of the former post and telegraph office destroyed by the first bombing raid on Darwin in 1942. It has a fine reception hall with an interesting display on state political history, good views of the harbour, a café and craft shop. The building also houses the **state library** ① *T8999 7177, Mon-Fri 1000-1700, Sat-Sun 1300-1700, good for catching up on foreign newspapers*.

Following the road around, the charming white gabled building opposite is **Government House** (1879). On the same side of the road, about 50 m further, is **Survivors Lookout**, where you can see historical photographs of Darwin. The elegant stone buildings nearby are the former police station and courthouse buildings (1884), now used by the government administrator, and one of a small cluster of old buildings surviving at this southern end of the city centre.

Deep underneath here are five long, wide tunnels, built between 1943 and 1945 as bombproof storage tanks for naval and commercial shipping fuel. Although they were completed too late to be of strategic use, and never saw a drop of oil, two have been

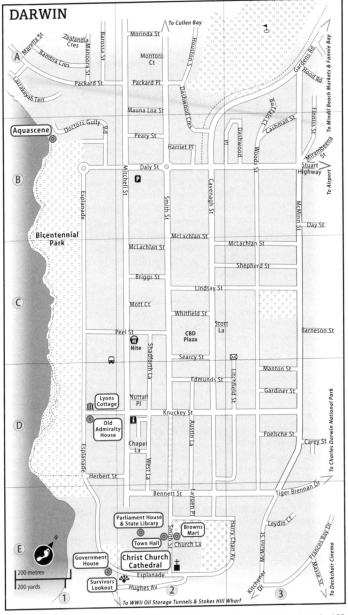

DARWIN

Marella St
Zealandia Cres
Bambra Cres
Barossa St
Manoora St
Larrakeyah Terr
Packard St

To Cullen Bay

Morinda St
Montoro Ct
Packard Pl
Houston St
Gardens Rd
Hood Rd

To Mindil Beach Markets & Fannie Bay

A

Mauna Loa St
Dashwood Cres
Dashwood Pl
Cashman St
Finniss St

Aquascene

Doctors Gully Rd
Peary St
Harriet Pl
Daly St
Woods St

Mirambeena St
Stuart Highway

To Airport

B

Esplanade
Mitchell St
Smith St
Cavenagh St
McMinn St
Day St

McLachlan St
McLachlan St

Bicentennial Park

McLachlan St
Briggs St
Shepherd St

C

Mott Ct
Lindsay St
Whitfield St
Stott La
Barneson St

Peel St
CBD Plaza

Nite
Searcy St
Lichfield St
Manton St

Shadforth La
Edmunds St
Gardiner St

Lyons Cottage
Nuttall Pl

Old Admiralty House
Knuckey St
Austin La
Foelsche St

D

Chapel La
West La
Carey St

To Charles Darwin National Park

Esplanade
Herbert St
Bennett St
Laguen Pl
Tiger Brennan Dr

Leydin Ct

To Deckchair Cinema

Harry Chan Av
McMinn St
Kitchener Dr
Frances Bay Dr

Parliament House & State Library
Smith St
Browns Mart
Church La

Town Hall

Government House
Christ Church Cathedral

E

200 metres
200 yards

Survivors Lookout
Esplanade
Hughes Av

To WWII Oil Storage Tunnels & Stokes Hill Wharf

1   2   3

heritage listed and are open to the public as the **WWII Oil Storage Tunnels** ① *accessible from both the Esplanade and Kitchener Drive, T8985 6333, daily May-Sep 0900-1600, Oct-Apr 1000-1300, $6, children $3.50.* The largest is 171 m long, 5 m high and 4½ m wide, and has pictures of Darwin during the war set every 10 m or so along its length.

If you walk back towards the city along Smith Street, **Christ Church Cathedral** on the corner is an example of the damage caused by Cyclone Tracy in 1974. The porch is all that remains of the original 1902 building, now joined to an incompatible modern cathedral. Further up, on the left, the **Town Hall** (1883), is another casualty of the cyclone, but opposite **Browns Mart** ① *www.brownsmart.com.au*, dating from 1885, managed to survive and is now used as a theatre venue.

STOKES HILL WHARF

As well as a great collection of cheap eateries, there are two sea-themed visitor attractions at the point at which this wharf meets the shore. **Indo Pacific Marine** ① *29 Stokes Hill Rd, T8981 1294, www.indopacificmarine.com.au, Apr-Oct 1000-1600 (rest of year for Nov-Mar), $22, children $10, evening tour and buffet at 1900 Tue, Wed, Fri and Sun, $110,* consists of about 20 water tanks of varying sizes, each containing a self-sustaining coral-based ecosystem. Detailed displays on marine environments, and a film about coral evolution and behaviour, make this a fascinating visit (allow at least an hour). Seeing the systems at night, when the corals are at their most active, is even better, but can only be done in conjunction with a pricey wine-and-seafood buffet.

GEORGE BROWN DARWIN BOTANIC GARDENS

① *Gardens Rd, Fannie Bay, T8981 1958, daily, Geranium St and Gardens Rd gates open 0700-1900, Orientation Centre daily 0800-1600, plant display house 0730-1530, free. Bus route 4 along Gilruth Av, then a 5-min walk to the entrance on Gardens Rd.*
The Botanic Gardens, established in 1886 as a botanical experiment and now devoted to relaxation and conservation, have suffered over the years from cyclones, wildfires and bombings. Managed by the NT Parks and Wildlife Commission, the gardens have undergone redevelopment to bring them up to the standard of other state capital botanic gardens. One of the best areas is the rainforest gully, with a waterfall, ponds and lush understorey of palms (of which the gardens has 450 species), cycads and bamboo. A plant display house exhibits orchids, bromeliads and other tropical plants. There are several interesting self-guided walks including one illustrating Aboriginal plant use and short walks among the mangroves and coastal plants on the bay side. In the southern area of the gardens there is an excellent playground and a natural amphitheatre, often used as a venue for plays or musical performances.

MUSEUM AND ART GALLERY OF THE NORTHERN TERRITORY

① *19 Conacher St, T8999 8264, http://artsandmuseums.nt.gov.au/museums, Mon-Fri 0900-1700, Sat-Sun 1000-1700, free. Bus routes 5 and 10 then a 1-km walk, or bus route 4 and a 500-m walk.*
This large modern museum and art gallery, in a tropical garden on the foreshore overlooking Fannie Bay, has a fine collection of Aboriginal art including bark paintings from Arnhem Land, totems and paintings from the Tiwi Islands and contemporary acrylics. It also showcases Southeast Asian and Pacific art and culture. There is an excellent imaginative

display of Northern Australian geology and fauna in the **Transformations Gallery**, which documents the impact of Cyclone Tracy on the city in 1974, including a spooky room in which to listen to howling wind. The unusual **Maritime Gallery** houses a collection of boats from the Top End and Southeast Asia, including canoes, a pearl lugger, Indonesian perahu and other traditional fishing craft. You can also visit Sweetheart, the 5-m stuffed estuarine crocodile, named after Sweet billabong where he lived in the 1970s and used to attack the outboard motors of dinghies and toss fishermen out of their boats. The museum and art gallery also hosts regular touring exhibitions, check the website for details. There is also a great café here; see box, page 174.

FANNIE BAY GAOL
ⓘ *East Point Rd, 1000-1700, free. Bus route 4.*
The first gaol in Darwin was on the corner of Mitchell Street and the Esplanade but the locals weren't fond of prisoners being quite so visible so a new gaol was opened in 1883 out at Fannie Bay, which at that time was miles away from civilization. Like most of Darwin, the gaol has been rebuilt many times following cyclones and bombing so the only old buildings are the original cell block and the stone Infirmary, built in 1887. Most of the buildings are corrugated iron sheds with mesh wire cells built in the 1950s and 1960s. The gaol was closed in 1979 and its prisoners transferred to Darwin Prison at Berrimah.

EAST POINT RESERVE
East Point is the northern pincer of the headlands that form Fannie Bay and covers nearly 200 ha. This was one of Darwin's main defensive placements during the war but it is now a recreation reserve. A path follows the water's edge out to the point and a walk or cycle here is a fine place to take in wonderful views over the pale-turquoise water of the bay to the tower blocks of the city centre; Dudley Point is a particularly good spot to watch the sunset. The reserve is a good place to go wildlife spotting; you can see wallabies, bandicoots and brushtail possums and there are over 130 species of birds. There is a 30-minute circular route along a mangrove boardwalk, which starts from the car park at the northern end of Lake Alexander.

On the foreshore are barbecues and picnic tables, while there is a swimming area on the saltwater Lake Alexander, where it is safe to swim year round. You can swim from the calm sandy beaches of the reserve but it is not advised during October to May because of the dangerous box jellyfish.

The gun emplacements and command post at the point have been turned into the **Darwin Military Museum** ⓘ *T8981 9702, www.darwinmilitarymuseum.com.au, daily 0930-1700, $14, children $5.50, bus routes 6 and 8 plus a 3-km walk or taxi ride,* which boasts an impressive collection of weapons and a fascinating interactive display and multimedia exhibition on the bombing of Darwin; the city was bombed 64 times between 1942 and 1944. The museum also has an outdoor collection of anti-tank and anti-aircraft guns and military vehicles. Those interested in tracking down Second World War historic sites throughout the Territory should pick up the *Historic Trail* brochures available at the museum. There is also a café and a shop here.

AUSTRALIAN AVIATION HERITAGE CENTRE

ⓘ *557 Stuart Hwy, T8947 2145, www.darwinsairwar.com.au, daily 0900-1700, $35, children $17.50, bus route 8.*

One of the country's best aircraft museums, the AHC is in one massive hanger built to house Darwin's very own cold-war era B-52 bomber, permanently on loan from the United States Air Force; there is only one of two of these gigantic aircraft outside the US. Aside from this giant, the core of the 18-aircraft collection is connected with the Second World War and Darwin's role in the conflict, from a life-size model Spitfire to the remains of several Japanese, Australian and American planes. Knowledgeable staff are happy to conduct impromptu tours if they're not busy and there are regular screenings of aviation films.

CROCODYLUS

ⓘ *815 McMillans Rd, Berrimah, T8922 4500, www.crocoduluspark.com.au, daily 0900-1700, guided crocodile feeding tours 1000, 1200, 1400, 1530, $25, children $12.50. Bus route 5 then 1-km walk.*

Arguably the best of the Top End crocodile parks, if only for the incredibly detailed, fascinating and graphic crocodilian museum which will tell and show you everything you ever wanted to know about crocs, and a lot more you didn't want to know. The main park comprises a series of breeding and rearing pens, two large enclosed lagoons and several other enclosures housing a variety of indigenous and exotic wildlife, including over 1000 crocodiles, lions, tigers, monkeys, dingoes, reptiles, kangaroos and wallabies. The best way to see the park is on one of the entertaining guided feeding tours.

→LITCHFIELD NATIONAL PARK

ⓘ *www.litchfieldnationalpark.com. 170 km from Darwin.*

Following the Arnhem/Kakadu Highways circuit through Kakadu (see under Kakadu National Park, page 175) southeast of Darwin will bring you out at Pine Creek on the Stuart Highway. Hence unless you backtrack – or for some reason are unable to undertake the Kakadu circuit – you'll miss Litchfield National Park southwest of Darwin. We describe it here for those who are able to spare the time to seek it out.

This lovely park is one of the most popular in the state, thanks to its proximity to Darwin and its accessibility. It encompasses a sandstone plateau called the Tabletop Range and it is the water cascading off the range that gives Litchfield its main feature. The plateau's sandstone holds wet-season water releasing it gradually to create year-round waterfalls and rock pools, although naturally all the falls are far more impressive during the wet season. All the major sights can easily be seen in a day but an overnight camp will make the most of the experience.

Entering from Batchelor, the first stop is a field of tombstone-like magnetic termite mounds, built on a north-south axis to regulate the internal temperature of the mound. To regulate your own temperature take your swimming gear to the next feature, **Buley Rockholes**, a stunning series of small rock pools, that eventually flow into **Florence Falls** downstream. A 1½-km walk along the riverbank connects the two or you can drive. There is large plunge pool at the bottom of the 15-m falls and this is a quiet place to swim as you have to walk 500 m downhill to reach it. **Tolmer Falls** drop into a deep, sheer-sided gorge to a pool, but can only be viewed from above, as it is the protected habitat of orange horseshoe and ghost bats. The Tolmer Creek walk loops back to the car park from the lookout (1½ km) and is well worth doing for the views of the upper gorge. **Greenant Creek** is a quiet picnic area and the start of a 3-km return walk to Tjaetaba Falls (no swimming). The most popular falls are **Wangi Falls**, accessible by a short path. These double falls make an idyllic swimming spot, with a good walk (1½ km loop) up through tropical monsoon forest to the head of the falls. There is also a kiosk at the falls, phones, a picnic area and campsite.

Few people visit **Walker Creek**, the last site on the road north, but this is a magical place if you like bush camping. A series of eight and secluded sites, situated beside falls and deep rock pools, are strung along 2 km of the creek and must be reached on foot. There are powered sites here. Four-wheel drives can also get to the **Lost City**, a collection of sandstone towers. The gravel road north to Berry Springs should be sealed shortly, allowing a loop from Darwin via the Territory Wildlife Park. Park notes and a road condition report available at the entry point west of Batchelor. For more information contact the park offices in Batchelor, T8976 0282.

DARWIN LISTINGS

WHERE TO STAY

In the wet season, look at a few rooms before choosing. In the busy dry season book ahead and check exactly what room and facilities you are getting. Most hostels offer a refund for some or all of the airport shuttle if you stay 2 or more nights and offer a free light breakfast.

$$$ Darwin City B&B, 4 Zealandia Cres, T8941 3636, www.darwinbnb.com.au. Very welcoming B&B with pretty en suite double rooms, garden pool and large covered breakfast and chill-out area. Also have 2 self-contained apartments 5 mins' walk away. Recommended.

$$$-$$ City Gardens Apartments, 93 Woods St, T8941 2888, T1800 89 1138 www.citygardensapts.com.au. Centrally located, spacious and well-equipped self-contained units, with full kitchens, a/c and Wi-Fi, set on 2 storeys around a courtyard pool. Each has double and twin bedrooms.

$$-$ Banyan View Lodge, 119 Mitchell St, T8981 8644, www.banyanviewlodge.com.au. One of the city's smaller and quieter options with dorms, singles and twins and shared or en suite bathrooms. Optional a/c. Communal facilities are a little institutional but there's a large and peaceful tropical garden with a spa and a pool. Free internet. Operated by YWCA.

$$-$ Chilli's, 69a Mitchell St, T8941 9722, www.chillis.com.au. Twins, doubles and dorms make up this lively, large hostel in the heart of the backpacker area. All rooms have sinks, a/c and lockers. Communal facilities are mostly large alfresco balconies, including 2 spas on a rear sun deck and use of a pool in a nearby sister hotel. Wi-Fi. Price includes breakfast.

RESTAURANTS

Darwin's cuisine is influenced by the city's proximity to Asia and its large Asian population. There are countless small noodle outlets in the city and its regular markets. Fresh fish and seafood is also a feature of most menus and Darwin is a good place to try local treats such as barramundi. Although there are some excellent upmarket restaurants in the city, the population is too small to support many of them and the defining feature of Darwin eating is its excellent value for money, especially at the Asian food halls, markets or Stokes Hill Wharf. Open-air street dining is becoming more common but the humidity of the 'build up' and wet season mean that many patrons prefer to eat indoors for half the year anyway. All opening hours indicated are for the dry season. Some establishments will close earlier during the wet season.

$$$ Hanuman, Holiday Inn Esplanade, 93 Mitchell St, T8941 3500, www.hanuman.com.au. Mon-Fri 1200-1430 and 1830-2130 , Sat-Sun 1830-2230. A smart Asian restaurant serving fine authentic Indian, Nonya and Thai cuisine. Recommended.

$$$ Pee Wees at the Point, Alec Fong Lim Dr, T8981 6868, http://peewees.com.au. Daily 1730 till late. This sophisticated contemporary restaurant hovers above Fannie Bay in East Point Reserve, with spectacular water views. Dishes with an emphasis on local seafood are served in a light and open space.

$ Cornucopia, next to the Museum and Art Gallery of NT, see page 170, www.cornucopia darwin.com.au. Daily 0900-1700. This café makes the most of its superb position overlooking the bay with a large outdoor terrace. Fine meals range from weekend brunches to healthy salads. Fabulous cakes. and coffee. Recommended.

KAKADU NATIONAL PARK

Kakadu is one of Australia's great treasures. The forested lowlands of open eucalypt – covering some 80 per cent of the park – meet the South Alligator River in the middle of the park and it is this river that provides some of Kakadu's most beautiful areas, the billabongs and wetlands. The entire river system is protected within the park, from its catchment area in the stone country of the Arnhem Land plateau to the mudflats and mangroves on the coast. The wetlands areas are full of birdlife – the jabiru stork, sea eagle, heron and grey crane – which can be seen at the Mamukala Wetlands, Anbangbang Billabong and at Yellow Waters, where you can also glide among the wildlife on a boat cruise. At the end of the dry season when the water recedes, there are impressive concentrations of wildlife at these spots. In the eastern section of the park, the escarpment towers above the floodplain, scored with secret gorges harbouring rainforest and rare animals and cascading with waterfalls in the wet season.

Only a fraction of this terrain is accessible and is best seen by flying over it, but those areas of stone country you can explore are simply captivating. To name a few: the waterfalls and plunge pools of Jim Jim Falls, Twin Falls, Maguk and Gunlom, but the escarpment also contains extraordinary rock art, testifying to the inseparable nature of the spiritual and material connection between Kakadu and its indigenous people. The main sites are at Ubirr and Nourlangie, both are of outstanding natural beauty, and contain images that range from many thousands of years to just a few decades old. Although few Aboriginal people now live in Kakadu, it's a different story in Arnhem Land. About 20,000 people live in an area the size of Victoria, and only 10 per cent are Balanda or Managa (non-indigenous people).

→VISITING KAKADU

GETTING THERE

Kakadu is best seen with your own transport, though it is possible to see the park at your own pace using public transport and the local tours and still experience much of the best that Kakadu has to offer. Qantas flies to Gove (Nhulunbuy) every two weeks on a Thursday from Darwin, and a shuttle bus meets every flight. Greyhound runs a service three times a week (Friday, Monday and Wednesday) from Darwin during the dry season to Kakadu Resort, Jabiru and Cooinda, leaving at 0630. There are a couple of excellent day tours from Kakadu into the nearer parts of Arnhem Land, and a couple of overland multiple-day tours from Darwin up to the Cobourg Peninsula. Most trips and tours into the area involve flying from Darwin to either the Cobourg or Gove peninsula. Jabiru, the main gateway to the park, is 250 km from Darwin and 220 km from Pine Creek.

TOURIST INFORMATION

Entry fee $25 per person (valid for 14 days), under 16s free. The park is managed by its Aboriginal owners and Parks Australia. As many Aboriginal people still live in Arnhem Land entry is controlled by a permit system but some areas may be visited on tours or with a 4WD. For permit information, contact the Permits Officer on T8938 1140, kakadu.permits@environment.gov.au. Permits can take up to a week to process. For extensive information see www.kakadu.com.au; it has maps, details of walks and tours, and a useful visitor guide available as a downloadable PDF. Within the park is the informative Bowali Visitor Centre (see under Jabiru below) and the excellent Warradjan

Aboriginal Cultural Centre (see page 178). For advice on swimming in the park and crocodiles, see www.kakadu.com.au.

(see page 178)

→NORTHERN KAKADU

FROM MARY RIVER TO JABIRU

From Mary River the border of Kakadu National Park is reached quite quickly, though there's a fair way to go before the good stuff. The first real attraction of the park is the boardwalk and lookout over the **Mamukala Wetlands** on the South Alligator floodplain. Mamukala is a tranquil place to see birdlife, but can feel a bit distant from the action – take binoculars if possible. The best time to visit these wetlands is September-October when thousands of magpie geese are concentrated here. There is a 3-km loop walk from the car park (mostly through woodland). Mamukala is 90 km from Annaburroo.

JABIRU

Named after the black-necked stork, this small town was created in the 1970s to house and service workers from the Ranger Uranium Mine nearby. Uranium was found in Kakadu during geological surveys in the 1950s, a time when the British and Australian governments were offering rewards for uranium discoveries to feed the development of atomic weapons. It is now the main gateway to the park and is also home to many of the park's rangers, hospitality workers and tour operators. It has a surprisingly good range of facilities.

The excellent **Bowali Visitor Centre** ① *5 km by road from Jabiru, or 2 km on foot, T8938 1120, daily 0800-1700*, is the main point of park information for visitors. The centre features an imaginative display on the history, management, flora and fauna of the park. A small theatre shows films about Kakadu every 30 minutes and it is well worth trying to catch the one featuring the late Bill Neidjie, known as 'Kakadu Man'. Bowali has an information desk, maps etc. Also here is the **Marrawuddi Gallery** ① *same contact details and opening hours as Bowali, free*, selling a good range of Aboriginal arts and crafts, books and souvenirs, while next door is an outdoor café.

UBIRR

① *Apr-Nov 0830-sunset, Dec-Mar 1400-sunset (but check first, as the road may be flooded).*
Although well off the beaten track, Ubirr is one of the most beautiful areas in the park and shouldn't be missed. The rock overhangs of Ubirr were used by Aboriginal people as campsites close to the rich food resources of the river and floodplain and as a canvas for recording those resources and their creation myths. A 1-km loop walk wanders through several rock art sites that include spirit figures and animals such as the thylacine, extinct in this area for several thousand years. By the Main Gallery is a short, steep track to the top of the outcrop and from here the views of the wetlands and escarpment are breathtaking; especially half an hour before sunset when golden light intensifies the green vegetation and orange-grey rock. Unfortunately hordes of chattering tour groups descend at the same time but it is still worth it.

BORDER STORE

Nearby to Ubirr, is Border Store, 40 km from Jabiru and 3 km from Ubirr. Here, the East Alligator River forms the border of Arnhem Land and the only way in is across **Cahill's**

Crossing, a tidal ford that is impassable for six months of the year (permits are required to enter Arnhem Land). If you intend to cross the river you'll need to check the tides chart here. Border Store is the starting point for tours into Arnhem Land and has a few facilities.

There are two good short walks close to the river. The **Manngarre Walk** starts from the riverside car park opposite the Border Store and passes through monsoon rainforest (1½ km loop). The more striking **Bardedjilidji Walk** winds through layered sandstone stacks, weathered into mushrooms shapes, caves and tunnels (2½ km). To reach this one take the riverside path from Cahills Crossing to the upstream boat ramp car park and keep walking south along the road until you reach the walk car park.

→CENTRAL KAKADU

NOURLANGIE

Nourlangie Rock, 12 km off the highway and 36 km from Jabiru, is best known as a rock art site but it is also a spectacular feature of the landscape, more dramatic than Ubirr. The sheer southern wall rises at least 100 m above the plain, the orange sandstone striped with black water lines. Below this wall a walking trail leads to the most visited site, **Anbangbang rock shelter and gallery**. As recently as the 1950s this shelter contained a paperbark bed, stone scrapers, blades, used bits of ochre and burial parcels. Such items were stolen from many areas of Nourlangie in the 1970s when tourists began to arrive. The famous paintings at Anbangbang, of Namargon the lightning man and X-ray like family groups, are significant because they are among the last rock paintings done in Kakadu. Painted in 1964 by the master artist Najombolmi (also known as Barramundi Charlie) they represent the end of a tradition that began perhaps 20,000 or more years ago. Further along the path, the **Gunwarddehwardde Lookout** provides the park's best views of the escarpment, including the three pillars that are the sacred site of Namargon.

There are many other layers of older paintings at Nourlangie, and many inaccessible sites, but if you are interested in rock art don't miss the little-visited **Nangaluwurr** site on the northern side of the rock. It requires a 2½-km return stroll through woodland to get to this overhang but it contains many fascinating paintings, such as a sailing ship, ancient hand prints and a Namandi spirit carrying dillybags to hold its victim's body parts. To get there, take the first unsealed road to the left on the road to Nourlangie. The lily-covered **Anbangbang Billabong** sits under the western face of the rock and is a picturesque place for a picnic or break, especially in the late afternoon when the wall lights up. A 2½ km walk follows the edge of the billabong but the best views are to be had from the first few picnic tables along the access road. There are also good views of the western end of Nourlangie from **Nawulandja lookout**, a large rock on the other side of the billabong (600 m climb).

JIM JIM AND TWIN FALLS

If these falls were more accessible they would probably be as famous as Uluru itself. **Jim Jim Falls** drop from a sheer 200-m cliff into a dark, tight bowl of rock and the plunge pool below. The huge boulders that lie scattered along the creek bed below the pool are all covered when the falls become a torrent in the wet season but must be clambered over to reach the falls during the dry (1 km). Often by the time Jim Jim falls are open there is just a trickle falling over the edge but the scale of the escarpment wall here is impressive enough. The falls are 70 km off the highway, 115 km from Jabiru and 82 km from Cooinda.

Twin Falls, a further 10 km down the track, are simply magical. The sandstone of the escarpment breaks down into soft white sand so, unlikely as it seems, the falls and their emerald-green plunge pool are fringed by a beautiful wide beach, within an amphitheatre of rock walls and falls. What makes this spot even more idyllic is that to reach it you need to swim, paddle or canoe about 1 km through the clear, cold pools of the gorge. Several operators run tours to both falls and you can also drive yourself, although the track, 4WD only, becomes very rough towards the end and includes a 500-m deep creek crossing to get to Twin Falls. There are crocodile warning signs near both falls; park authorities go to a lot of effort to trap and remove any estuarine crocodiles before they open the area. You can swim at the Jim Jim Falls at your own risk, but the Twin Falls are definitely not safe for swimming. There is a bush campsite near Jim Jim Falls.

WARRADJAN ABORIGINAL CULTURAL CENTRE

ⓘ *1 km from Gagudju Cooinda Lodge, T8979 0051, daily 0900-1700.*

Just before Cooinda, this distinctive centre is built in the shape of its namesake, the warradjan or pig-nosed turtle, and also represents the way Aboriginal people communicate with each other – sitting in a circle. It is one of the best centres of its kind in Australia, with attractive and innovative ways of describing the indigenous cultural environment of Kakadu. It not only explains Aboriginal uses and management of the land's resources but manages to give an insight into their way of thinking and concerns for the future. One of the highlights is a model that illustrates the complex rules and relationships of Aboriginal 'skin' groupings. A theatre shows videos about Kakadu and the centre has a shop selling expensive art and craft work.

COOINDA AND YELLOW WATER

Cooinda, the most southerly of the commercial centres within the park boundaries, 60 km from Jabiru, and also the closest to Jim Jim and Twin falls, is essentially the **Gagudju Cooinda Lodge**. Lodge facilities include accommodation (including camping), fuel (including LPG gas), shop, internet, bar and restaurant. During the wet season the lodge contracts its activities to the shop, fuel and minimal accommodation and eating. **Yellow Water Wetlands**, at the confluence of Jim Jim Creek and the South Alligator River, is a large area of billabongs, flood plains, paperbark swamps and river channels. It is one of the prettiest areas in the park but the best thing about Yellow Water is that there are regular boat cruises allowing you to get right in among the wetlands. It is an excellent way to see lots of birds and crocodiles at close range and the wetlands are wonderfully serene. Egrets, sea eagles, whistling kites, jacanas, pelicans and rainbow beeeaters are all commonly seen among the grass and waterlillies. There is a 2.6-km boardwalk across the flood plains to a platform on Home Billabong for those who want to take the wildlife in at their own pace.

→SOUTHERN KAKADU

GUNLOM

ⓘ *40 km unsealed from the highway, turn-off 10 km from Mary River.*

Southern Kakadu is the home of the Jaowyn people and is confusingly known as the **Mary River** area. The river forms the southwestern boundary of Kakadu but it is also part of the Mary River National Park to the north. The beautiful stone country of the escarpment is close to the highway here but despite its stunning beauty few, except locals, come here. The Jaowyn call this area Buladjang, the place of powerful and dangerous creation ancestor Bula, also translated as 'sickness country'. Jaowyn believe that if people disturb Buladjang country they will become unwell and their knowledge of their land has been vindicated by science. The area of sickness country corresponds almost exactly with areas that land surveys have shown to contain unusually high concentrations of uranium, arsenic, mercury and lead. In the 1953 a major deposit of uranium was found at Coronation Hill (Gimbat) and during the 1950s and 1960s a total of 13 gold and uranium mines were being worked in southern Kakadu, much to the distress and fear of the Jaowyn, until there was a world oversupply of uranium. By the 1980s, when proposals were made to mine Coronation Hill for gold, palladium and platinum, Aboriginal people had more of a political voice and after an extensive inquiry the Commonwealth government decided against mining in favour of the cultural and environmental values of the area. Most Jaowyn now live in the Katherine-Pine Creek region but continue to be involved in the management of the park.

Heading south the first attraction is **Maguk** (Barramundi Gorge), although the 12-km track to this pretty gorge is 4WD only. A 1-km walk through monsoon rainforest and paperbarks leads to a plunge pool and small waterfall. It is a fine place for a swim (although see the advice on crocodiles on the park website www.kakadu.com.au), you may see fish and freshwater crocodiles, and there is a bush campsite. After another 42 km, past the unexceptional **Bukbukluk Lookout**, is the turn-off for Gunlom, one of Kakadu's best camping spots. It is about 40 km to Gunlom but the unsealed road is usually fine for 2WD in the dry season (check road conditions at Bowali Visitor Centre, see page 176). After 13 km on the Gunlom Road is **Yurmikmik** car park, the startpoint for several good walks. Yurmikmik lookout (2½ km from the starting point) has views over the ridge country and the Marrawal Plateau. **Motor Car Falls** (4 km from the start) drop over a high orange and black streaked sandstone wall to a large plunge pool. The falls are named after the Chevy that a miner managed to drive up the track as far as Motor Car Creek in 1946. From here the trail becomes unmarked but after crossing the bridge over the creek you can follow an old vehicle track to **Kurrundie Creek**, then drop south for 800 m to Kurrundie Falls (6 km from the start). This is another lovely plunge pool swimming spot and can make an excellent overnight walk. For more details pick up park notes from Bowali Visitor Centre (see page 176) and if you intend to leave the track also take a topographic map and compass. Camping is allowed at sites near Motor Car Falls and Kurrundie Falls but you must obtain a permit from Mary River Ranger Station (just north of the southern entry booth) or Bowali Visitor Centre. After walking from Yurmikmik, continue on to the comforts of **Gunlom** campground (where there are showers and toilets). One of the pleasures of camping here is that it is only a few hundred metres from a delightful plunge pool below a high dark rock wall. You can also climb to the top of the falls, from where there are great views of the South Alligator Valley and more magical green rock pools to swim in. If you have a 4WD there is one more stunning spot to find, considered one of the most beautiful gorges in the park and way off the beaten track. **Jarrangbarnmi** or Koolpin Gorge is accessible from the Gunlom Road. An unmarked trail follows the gorge of faulted and folded Kombolgie sandstone for a few kilometres, involving rock hopping, scree, rapids, rock pools and waterfalls. Access to this remote gorge is limited so a permit and access key must be obtained from the southern entry booth or Mary River ranger station.

KATHERINE TO THE RED CENTRE

Though a part of the great plateau that separates the western Top End from Arnhem Land, the southwestern corner is protected not by Kakadu National Park, but by its southern state-run neighbour, Nitmiluk. The centrepiece is the magnificent succession of connected gorges known collectively as Katherine Gorge. The town of Katherine sits on the banks of its namesake river a little further downstream and is the last major town on the Stuart Highway before Alice Springs. There aren't many diversions on the long drive down other than millions of termite mounds, though the crystal-clear springs of Mataranka and the ruddy globes of the Devil's Marbles are well worth stopping for. The vast tracts of land either side of the highway – scrubby pastoral land and baking desert – are interrupted by just two sealed roads. From Katherine the Victoria Highway carves through the impressive bluffs of the eastern Gregory National Park before following the Victoria River to the Western Australia border, and from Tennant Creek the Barkly Highway heads over to Queensland.

→KATHERINE

On the southern bank of the Katherine River, at the junction of the major routes north and west and 310 km from Darwin, Katherine is a service town for the pastoral industry and nearby Tindal air force base, as well as for travellers heading to Nitmiluk National Park (see page 181). The town and river were named by explorer John McDouall Stuart in 1862, after a friend's daughter, but his favourable reports of the area led to the issuing of pastoral leases and dispossession of the local Jawoyn people. The Jawoyn managed to retain strong cultural links to their country but it took another century before their land ownership was legally recognized in 1989. In 1998 the entire town was flooded to the eaves. Few businesses had flood insurance so recovery has been slow but the townspeople are proud of enduring this disaster and '98 flood levels are marked all over town.

ARRIVING IN KATHERINE
Moving on If driving, fill up with fuel before leaving Katherine.

Tourist information The friendly and efficient **VIC** ① *Katherine Terrace, T8972 2650, visitor@ktc.nt.gov.au, May-Oct Mon-Fri 0830-1800, Sat-Sun 0900-1400, Nov-Apr Mon-Fri 0830-1500, Sat-Sun 0900-1300,* has information on the whole region. See also www.visitkatherine.com.au.

PLACES IN KATHERINE
On the southwest edge of Katherine, **Springvale Homestead** ① *Shadforth Rd, 8 km from town, T8972 1355, 0800-1730, free, guided tour daily at 1500 (May-Sep),* is one of the oldest pastoral properties in the state, built in 1879, close to natural springs. The property is now a caravan park but the small homestead still stands, although damaged by the 1998 flood, and contains a few display boards on its history. The Alice Springs–Darwin railway line crosses the river by Springvale. About 3 km upstream the **Low Level Nature Reserve** is a

pretty area by the low river crossing where locals swim, fish and picnic. Better for swimming though are the small clear pools of **Katherine Hot Springs** ⓘ *Riverbank Drive, T8972 5500, 24 hrs, free,* around 2 km to the north. These palm-fringed springs lie on a narrow tributary of the river and are a tepid 32°c, best experienced on a cool evening with the stars twinkling above. About 1½ km from the post office is **Katherine School of the Air** ⓘ *101 Giles St, T8972 1833, www.schools.nt.edu.au/ksa, tours Mon-Fri 0900, 1000, 1100 (Mar-Oct), $5, children $2,* where visitors can learn how children in remote areas are educated by radio, mail and internet. The school serves 800,000 sq km of Northern Australia. Tours include listening to live radio lessons, a film and talk by school staff. **Katherine Museum** ⓘ *Gorge Rd, T8972 3945, www.katherinemuseum.com, daily 0900-1600, $7.50, children $3.50, concessions $5,* is a further 1 km past the school, in the former airport buildings. The museum has interesting displays on the early days of Katherine and the town's regular floods but the centrepiece is a De Havilland Gypsy Moth, owned by Dr Clyde Fenton, one of Australia's first 'flying doctors'.

The tropical **Cutta Cutta Caves Nature Park** ⓘ *1 km off the Stuart Highway, T8972 1940, http://www.parksandwildlife.nt.gov.au, daily 0830-1630, tours daily on the hour 0900-1500 (not 1200), except Feb-Mar, best time to visit is May-Aug, $17.50, children $8.75 (cash only),* 30 km south of Katherine, is a protected area of limestone karst covering 1500 ha. The caves have good collections of sparkling cave decorations, including stalactites and stalagmites. There is also a short walk through tropical woodland, which is good for birdwatching, and a small visitor centre.

→NITMILUK NATIONAL PARK

Nitmiluk protects some of the most majestic gorge scenery in Australia, as well as dozens of waterfalls and permanent waterholes created by the rivers carving their way through the plateau. The park is owned by the Jawoyn people and jointly managed with the Parks and Wildlife Commission. The main feature is Katherine Gorge, actually a series of connected gorges that dog-leg their way across the landscape, some with sheer walls as high as 70 m. The Katherine River flows through this gorge for 13 km but unless it is very high, which usually happens at some point between January-April, each section is separated by dry rocky sections which have to be negotiated by boat-cruising visitors and canoeists alike.

VISITING NITMILUK NATIONAL PARK

The park's main entrance is 30 km northeast of Katherine. The Nitmiluk Visitor Centre is here and has displays, a café, shop and tour desk. For more information see http://www.parksandwildlife.nt.gov.au or T8972 1886. Tours include boat, helicopter and canoeing.

PLACES IN NITMILUK NATIONAL PARK

The most spectacular of the gorges are the long, narrow second gorge, Katherine Canyon, and the slightly less impressive but far less visited fifth gorge. Aboriginal rock art is found throughout the park, and is most easily seen on the impressive walls above the rapids between the first and second gorges. The gorges can seem like one huge waterfall when the water's flowing, but this is usually only for a few hours after local heavy rain. Another site worth visiting is Edith Falls, 62 km north of Katherine (20 km off the highway). This is a picturesque series of gorges and low falls cascading into an enormous pool. There are over 130 km of great walking trails in the park, but don't visit without taking a boat cruise, or preferably hiring a canoe.

Although the gorges are best viewed from the water, there are walks which allow views from the rim down some of the canyons, and occasional access to the river itself. The hour-long **Lookout Walk** gets to the top of the first main bluff, **Crocodile Rock**, and is well worth the effort if you have some time to fill or you're there around sunset. To see the view down **Katherine Canyon** (the second gorge) you should take the slightly more challenging **Butterfly Gorge Walk** (12 km, four hours return). Overnight options include **Smitt Walk Rock**, which reaches the start of the first gorge, and **Eighth Gorge Walk**. The 45-km **Jatbula Trail** from the visitor centre to **Edith Falls** is generally considered a four to five day walk. It is allowed in this direction only, although walkers can go as far as **Crystal Falls** and then retrace their steps (three to four days). For another full day's walk head out and back to the waterfall and pool at **Northern Rockhole**, the first major point of interest on the trail. At Edith Falls itself there is a lovely short walk, **Leliyn Loop**, on the plateau that circumnavigates the main pool and crosses Upper Falls with fine views and lots of swimming spots along the way.

→KATHERINE TO TENNANT CREEK

The journey south from Katherine is 665 km long, straight and mostly of little interest to those travelling through, which makes almost any stop a welcome diversion. After Mataranka the vegetation gets sparser and more stunted and population centres smaller and further apart, their hotels becoming ever more rustic.

MATARANKA
Mataranka lies just west of the thermal springs of **Elsey National Park**, a beautiful and popular oasis. This small highway town, 105 km from Katharine, is also associated with the classic Australian novel *We of the Never Never* by Jeannie Gunn, based on her experiences as the mistress of nearby Elsey Station in the early 1900s. Mataranka has a surprisingly good range of facilities including ATMs at the pub and supermarket, an internet bureau and post office. There are two main area of springs within the park, also the headwaters of the Roper River which flows east to the Gulf of Carpentaria. **Bitter Springs** is the most natural and beautiful spring with pools of emerald-green water among a forest of palms, northeast of the township along Martin Road. Homestead Road leads to Mataranka Homestead and access to **Rainbow Spring**, feeding Thermal Pool. Though it doesn't appear very natural, it is located within a striking forest of tall palms and paperbarks. Rainbow Spring pumps out a volume of water roughly equivalent to an Olympic-size swimming pool every hour at 34°C into the Waterhouse and Roper rivers, ensuring a year-round flow. A great walk is to follow the path along the riverbank from the Mataranka Homestead to Mataranka Falls (16 km), past swimming holes, beaches and parrots. Canoes can be hired at the campground for a 4-km canoe paddle downstream to the falls.

LARRIMAH

This tiny settlement, one of several on the highway that grew up during the Second World War and 75 km from Mataranka, was the rail terminus for the Alice Springs line. Men, stores and equipment had to get off here and travel by road to Darwin, consequently it became a busy staging post and many units were stationed here. Now, for most people it's simply a roadhouse stop.

DALY WATERS

Daly Waters, 90 km from Larrimah, was a lonely telegraph repeater station until the 1930s when an enterprising couple set up a shop and aerodrome. By 1934 it had become a refuelling stop for Qantas international flights to Singapore and became an increasingly busy air and mail centre. A hotel was built for overnight stays in 1938 and the 3-km side-trip off the highway is well worth the effort to check out the **Daly Waters Pub** (http://dalywaterspub.com), the best and friendliest of the 'Outback' pubs along this part of the Stuart Highway.

DALY WATERS TO TENNANT CREEK

ⓘ *A distance of 400 km.*

There are small settlements or roadhouses at least every 100 km on this stretch of highway running through the prime cattle country and Aboriginal communities of the Barkly region. **Newcastle Waters** is one of the largest cattle stations in the territory and once the junction of three major overland stock routes. Cattle drovers used the station township to rest and replenish supplies just as truck drivers hauling loads of cattle now frequent the roadhouses. The township, 3 km off the highway, is worth a visit to see the Drovers Memorial and the few rusting corrugated iron buildings that once housed a pub, store, repeater station, school and post office. **Elliott**, the largest settlement between Katherine and Tennant Creek, was established as an army camp during the Second World War. The Djingili and Mudbura people of the Barkly Tablelands live in the town and on Murranji land nearby, which was successfully claimed in 1990.

There are two further stopping options during the next 250-odd km, Renner Springs and Banka Banka before the **Three Ways Roadhouse**, some 25 km north of Tennant Creek, where the Barkly Highway heads off to Queensland.

→TENNANT CREEK AND AROUND

TENANT CREEK

Tennant Creek, 505 km from Alice Springs, has an attractive setting by the McDouall (or Honeymoon) Ranges and makes a useful stop for travellers. As well as several interesting local sights it sits just south of the junction of the Barkly Highway to QLD and 100 km north of the beautiful Devil's Marbles (see below). Set up as the site of an overland telegraph station in 1872, Tennant Creek stood in splendid isolation for over 60 years until gold was found in the region in 1932, kickstarting Australia's last gold rush. Almost all the facilities and services lie on the highway, called Paterson Street, which runs through the town centre.

As very little alluvial gold was ever found here, and due to the difficulty of extracting gold from the local ironstone ore in the later years, most mining has been carried out by companies rather than individuals. **Battery Hill Mining Centre** ① *Peko Rd, 1½ km from the town centre, T8962 1281, daily 0900-1700*, named after the government stamp battery that has been operating here for decades, has exhibits about the 1930s gold rush. There are daily tours of the battery and underground mine, and the site also includes an interesting mining museum, minerals collection and the opportunity to do a bit of gold panning. The Tennant Creek VIC is also here. **Lake Mary Ann**, 5 km north of town, was created in the 1980s as a recreational area. Well maintained, it still fulfils that role and is easily the best spot around town for a picnic and for spotting water birds. You can visit the **Tennant Creek Telegraph Station Historical Reserve** ① *just off Stuart Highway, 10 km north of town, to access the buildings ask for a key at the Tennant Creek VIC, located at the Battery Hill Mining Centre, see above.* Built in 1872, the station formed part of the 3600-km Overland Telegraph Line which provided a telegraphic link to Britain. The small compound of solid stone buildings is in good repair and there are interpretative signs, ranger-guided walks May to September and self-guided walks at the site.

DAVENPORT RANGE NATIONAL PARK

Davenport Range National Park lies east of the Devils Marbles (see below), and marks the boundary between the traditional lands of the Warumungu, Alyawarre and Kaytetye people. It is also the only national park between the markedly different environments of central Australia and the Top End. These low, arid-looking ranges have many permanent waterholes, attracting lots of birdlife, and other animals. The Park is located 90 km southeast of Tennant Creek.

VISITING DAVENPORT RANGE NATIONAL PARK

A 4WD is essential for all routes into the park. There are no tours into the park and it is a remote, rugged area suited to experienced off-roaders only. Access is by two main routes: via Stuart Highway, turn off at Bonney Well along the Kurundi–Epenarra road, or – for a more scenic, but slower route – turn off at Taylor Creek along the Murray Downs–Hatches Creek road. A third option is the Frew River Loop 4WD Track, to the Old Police Station Waterhole. This is a demanding 17-km/two-hour track for experienced 4WD drivers only. Visitors may only visit Whistleduck Creek and the Old Police Station Waterhole. Roads in the park may be flooded from December to March. To find out about local road and weather conditions phone the police station in Alekerenge (Ali Curung) T8964 1959. See www.parksandwildlife.nt.gov.au for more information.

KARLU KARLU (DEVILS MARBLES CONSERVATION AREA)

Karlu Karlu (translated as 'round boulders' in Aboriginal), 105 km south of Tennant Creek, is a vast area of bizarre-looking, gigantic granite boulders. The Devils Marbles Conservation Area was officially returned to its Aboriginals traditional owners in 2008 and is a registered sacred site. Many boulders seem to balance precariously on the slab below but if you look closely at the base you can see that the boulder and base are joined, and are in fact the same piece of rock that has simply eroded into these forms. There is a short loop walk by the main car park but it is worth taking the time to walk more extensively over the whole reserve and climb on top of the larger groups for good views of the plain. The boulders look wonderful at sunrise and sunset. There is a bush campsite on the eastern side of the reserve, with tables, toilets and fireplaces (BYO wood and water, camping fees payable in cash only).

KATHERINE TO THE RED CENTRE LISTINGS

WHERE TO STAY

Katherine

The town has a plentiful supply of budget accommodation. The dedicated backpacker hostels are all very friendly and helpful.

$$$ BIG4 Katherine Holiday Park, Shadforth Rd, T8972 3962, T1800 501984, http://katherine-low-level-caravan-park.nt.big4.com.au. One of half a dozen caravan parks. This one is superb; shady and spacious, 5 km from town. En suite a/c cabins, large pool, poolside bar and great facilities. Camping from $28 per site. Recommended.

$$$-$$ Best Western Pine Tree Motel, Third St, 8972 2533, http://pinetree.bestwestern.com.au. Bland but comfortable with a pool and licensed bistro.

$$$-$$ Knotts Crossing Resort, corner of Giles and Cameron streets, T8972 2511, www.knottscrossing.com.au. Pleasant resort includes a wide range of motel rooms, self-contained units, cabins and powered sites with private en suite. Also pools, kiosk and bistro.

$ Coco's, First St, T8971 2889. This small place has just 10 beds in single-sex rooms, and a couple of tents ($11 per person) in the garden available if it's busy, making for an intimate, homely atmosphere. Owner Coco's long friendship with many talented local Aboriginal artists and musicians can make a few days stay here a rich experience.

Tennant Creek and around

$$ Tourist's Rest, corner of Windley and Leichhardt streets, T8962 2719, www.touristrest.com.au. Small, friendly backpackers with dorms, doubles, good kitchen, lounge, pool and sociable courtyard space. Also good deals on Devils Marbles tours.

TO ALICE SPRINGS

Just 9 km south of Karlu Karlu is the tiny settlement of **Wauchope**, with a pub ① *T8964 1963, http://www.wauchopehotel.com.au*, providing fuel, food and rooms. A further 26 km south, **Wycliffe Well** is another roadhouse settlement but unusually it claims regular visits from UFOs. Test your gullibility at the Wycliffe Well Holiday Park caravan park ① *T8964 1966, www.wycliffe.com.au*, a roadhouse and small store. There are further services at **Barrow Creek**, site of a former telegraph station. There is also a nice old pub here ① *T8956 9753*. **Aileron** ① *T8956 9703, www.aileronroadhouse.com.au*, is the last roadhouse before Alice (125 km).

THE RED CENTRE

To many visitors Alice Springs is simply the town that you arrive at before visiting the 'rock' and leave scant time to explore. It is often assumed that 'the Alice' is just up the road from Uluru so it can come as quite a surprise that Alice is actually a long, long way from the rock (435 km) and amidst the impressive MacDonnell hill ranges. Although the town is the Territory's second largest, it is comparatively tiny, but its history, location and local geography combine to make it of considerable interest. Alice Springs lies in the geographical heart of Australia – a region known simply as the 'Centre' – and the locals proudly call themselves 'Centralians' rather than 'Territorians'.

→ALICE SPRINGS

The southern entrance to 'the Alice' is through the grand gateway of Heavitree Gap, a natural break in the MacDonnell Ranges. Once inside, neat streets, shopping malls and swimming pools appear in the middle of the Outback. Around 100 years ago the only pool in town was the waterhole named Alice Springs (population 28,000) in the Todd riverbed by the telegraph station. Winding through the town the sandy bed of the river, lined with river red gums, is a reminder of the extremities of the region. It flows so rarely that when the locals hold their annual boating regatta they have to carry their boats downstream. Today the town survives as an administrative and service centre and a base for tourism. It also serves as a meeting point for Aboriginal people from many communities in the Northern Territory and South Australia. The local people are Arrernte (pronounced Arr-un-ter) who know the area as Mparntwe, a site of caterpillar dreaming. Aboriginal culture is heavily promoted in the town and there are shops full of Aboriginal art, but the divide in the black and white communities seems is all too obvious. However, for visitors it is a convenient base for exploring the beautiful spots in the surrounding ranges and there are several fascinating sights in the town itself.

ARRIVING IN ALICE SPRINGS
Getting there *The Ghan* rides to and from Adelaide; book on www.great southernrail.com.au. Alice Springs is 1490 km from Darwin and 1530 km from Adelaide.

Getting around There are plenty of local buses run by ASbus/Buslink ① T8952 5611. For timetables, visit the bus station at Railway Terrace or see www.transport.nt.gov.au. A hop-on, hop-off tourist bus is run by Alice Wanderer Centre Sightseeing ① *T1800 722 111, T8952 2111, www.alicewanderer.com.au, $44, children $28, 0900-1600*. Plenty of operators run trips around the area.

Moving on Which way you head from Alice will depend on the time available to you and whether you are able to travel on unsealed roads, the latter being the major factor. If you're limited to the tarmac then (after, perhaps an excursion along the West McDonnells) you will need to head south from Alice through the Heavitree Gap and down to Eldunda to turn onto the Lasseter Highway, the road to Kings Canyon and Uluru.

If you're able and keen to tackle a bit of unsealed driving then the route along the West MacDonnells to Glen Helen, past Gosse Bluff and around the Mereenie Loop Road to Kings Canyon is considerably more interesting.

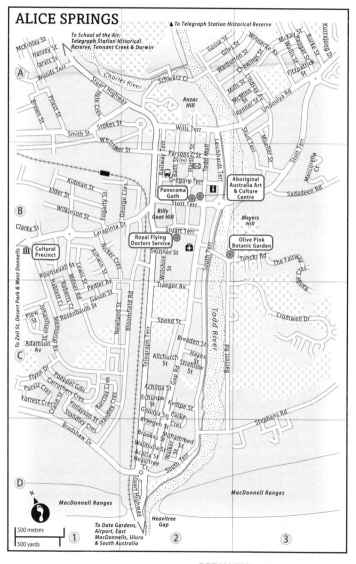

PLACES IN ALICE SPRINGS

Alice Springs is surrounded by many natural attractions but also has a surprising number of interesting sights in town. The difficulty will be in deciding what can be fitted in. There is a lookout at the top of **Anzac Hill** overlooking the town centre towards Heavitree Gap which is a good place to get your bearings and the **Olive Pink Botanic Garden** or **Date Gardens** are pleasantly shady green places to relieve the eye of dry red earth.

Telegraph Station Historical Reserve ① *4 km north of town, signposted from Stuart Highway or walk along the sandy trail next to Todd River from town or take the hop on-hop off bus (see Getting around above), T8952 3993, historical precinct daily 0800-1700, $8.50, children $4.50, entry fee includes guided tour; rest of reserve 0800-2100, free*, sits above the shady banks of the Todd River. Built in 1872, the telegraph station is the best preserved along the Overland Telegraph Line. The cool stone buildings have been restored to the way they looked around 1900 and reflect the self-sufficient lifestyle of the tiny community. Displays in the station buildings detail the history of the site. After functioning as a telegraph station for 60 years, the buildings were turned into a school for aboriginal children. There is also a kiosk and pleasant picnic sites by the riverbed with free barbecues.

Alice Springs School of the Air ① *80 Head St, signposted from Stuart Highway, 3½ km north of the town centre, T8951 6834, Mon-Sat 0830-1630, Sun 1330-1630, $6.50, children $4.50, bus route 3, stop 11*, grew out of the 1930s Outback radio technology pioneered by the Royal Flying Doctors Service. Regular chats over the RFDS radio frequency, usually operated by women on the station, came to be known as the 'galah session' after the screechy, chattering parrots. The idea was naturally extended to giving children school lessons and in 1959 Alice Springs was the first school on-air of the 16 schools now operating. Children who live in remote Outback areas receive lessons via webcams and the internet. The Alice Springs school services only 130 primary school students in an area of 1.3 million sq km. Students can see other children in their 'class' as well as the teacher and this helps to allay loneliness and isolation. Visitors can watch a teacher give a lesson from the studio and listen to the children's responses, and watch a short film explaining what life is like for the students.

Wholly Aboriginal owned and operated, **Aboriginal Australia Art and Culture Centre** ① *86 Todd St, T8952 3408, www.aboriginalart.com.au, 0800-1700, free, tours $82.50, 0830-1230*, is a welcoming and relaxed place to learn about Aboriginal culture and chat to a few local Southern Arrernte people. The centre has an art gallery and a small museum. This is one of few places in town where an Aboriginal perspective can be heard and some of the shocking European acts of the past are documented. Didgeridoo lessons (1400 daily, $11, one hour) guarantee a good laugh trying to get a sound out of the thing. The lively and interesting morning tours take visitors for a bush walk to learn about the relationship between the Arrernte and the landscape, followed by tea and damper, a dance performance, and a bit of boomerang and spear throwing.

Royal Flying Doctors Service ① *Stuart Terrace, T8952 1129, www.flyingdoctor.net, Mon-Sat 0900-1600, Sun 1300-1600, tours every 30 mins, $5.50, children $2.20*, is a much loved Australian institution. The service provides medical care for people in remote inland areas over a chunk of Australia larger than Western Europe. The Alice Springs base is one of 20 in the country that between them operate 45 aircraft at a cost of about $50 million a year. Tours include a short video, a talk outside the radio control room and a stroll around a small museum. There is also a lovely garden café and a souvenir shop. The service runs almost entirely on donations and grants so any money spent here benefits the service.

The white castellated tower of **Panorama Guth** ① *65 Hartley St, T8952 2013, Mon-Sat 0900-1700 all year, Sun 1200-1700 Mar-Nov, $5.50, children/concessions $3.30*, sits above the flat streets of the town where it has been a landmark since it opened in 1975. This 360° panorama of Central Australia is the work of Dutch painter Henk Guth and the complex includes more of his landscapes and some work of the Hermannsburg school. There is also an unusual collection of strange Aboriginal artefacts such as emu feather boots.

Just outside town is the **Cultural Precinct** ① *Larapinta Drive, 15-min from town, T8951 1120, www.nt.gov.au/dam, Araluen Centre Box Office T8951 1122, 1000-1700. $8, children and concessions $5*, which encompasses several museums and galleries. Built on the site of the town's first aerodrome, the precinct has been designed to fit around seven sites and trees sacred to Arrernte women. Some of these sites are signposted on a path through the sculpture garden linking the buildings. The **Araluen Centre** has four galleries that show exhibitions of Aboriginal art from the Central Desert region and contemporary art by Northern Territorians. The highlight is the annual **Desert Mob** exhibition held in September featuring Central Australian Aboriginal art, which attracts buyers from all over the country. There is also a permanent exhibition on the work of Albert Namatjira, his teacher Rex Batarbee and others of the Hermannsburg School. Araluen's theatre is Alice Springs' main performing arts venue. **Museum of Central Australia** has a collection to effectively illustrate and explain the features of the Central Australian environment such as the meteorite craters of Gosse Bluff and Henbury. In the same building is the **Strehlow Research Centre**, a collection gathered by TGH (Ted) Strehlow, son of a Hermannsburg missionary. Ted Strehlow learned Arrernte languages from his childhood playmates and later spent many years studying and recording Arrernte culture. He was entrusted with the care of 1200 Arrernte men's sacred ceremonial objects and these along with his research are now preserved in the Research Centre. The Cultural Precinct also includes a small **Aviation Museum** and **Memorial Cemetery**, where Albert Namatjira's grave can be found.

Desert Park ① *6 km west of town, Larapinta Drive, T8951 8788, www.alice springsdesertpark.com.au, 0730-1800, $18, children $9, concessions $9*, sits below the West MacDonnell Ranges. It is an extraordinary place that should not be missed by any visitor. In the words of BBC wildlife supremo, David Attenborough: "there is no museum or wildlife park in the world that can match it". The park features plants that are grown in their natural landscape such as woodlands or sand country, and is populated by animals dependent on that habitat. The traditional use and management of the landscape by Aboriginal people is also explained, highlighting how all desert dwellers are dependent on each other for survival. Two kilometres of walking trails pass through different habitats, aviaries and kangaroo and emu enclosures. Highlights are the Bird of Prey theatre at 1000 and 1530, the 'Changing Heart' film, and the outstanding nocturnal house where creatures such as bilbies and thorny devils can be seen easily. Facilities include a café, picnic and barbecue area and wheelchair and stroller hire. **Desert Park Transfers**, T8952 4667, runs a shuttle bus to the park and can pick up from accommodation.

→WEST MACDONNELL RANGES

① *Entry to the park, which is free, is possible at several points between Alice Springs and Redbank Gorge. There are many well-marked walks from the various gorges, the best being at Serpentine and Ormiston in the west, and Trephina in the east. They vary from 10 mins to a full* day, but hikers should always wear a hat and sunscreen, and carry plenty of water (4 litres a day). If doing a longer walk on your own, let someone know your plans.

Standing up to 800 m above the central plain, the MacDonnells are a series of rounded, rusted hill ranges punctured by a series of gaps, gorges and chasms, some with permanent waterholes, a boon to wildlife, indigenous people and sweaty tourists alike. To the west of Alice Springs a long section of the ranges has been declared West MacDonnell National Park.

LARAPINTA DRIVE

Simpsons Gap, 24 km from Alice Springs, is the best spot for seeing black-footed rock wallabies, though the waterhole is out of bounds. There is a **parks visitor information area** ① *T8955 0310*, and toilets. Rangers run nature walks here most of the year at 1000 on Saturday, Sunday and Monday for 30 minutes. A 23-km cycle path from Alice is partly cross-country. Gates are closed 2000-0500. The turn-off for **Standley Chasm** ① *0900-1700, $5.50, children and concessions $4.50*, is 40 km from Alice, and the chasm itself another 9 km. This sheer gully, just a few metres across, is known for catching the sun on both sides for just a few minutes in the middle of each day. There is a takeaway and shop, toilets and shaded tables.

NAMATJIRA DRIVE

Access to **Ellery Creek Big Hole**, 90 km from Alice Springs, is via a 2-km unsealed road. This soaring gap has a large, permanent waterhole, the first of three where swimming is allowed. Camping is also permitted ($3.30 per person) and there are basic toilets and fireplaces. **Serpentine Gorge** is a few kilometres further on. Here, several semi-permanent waterholes are strung out along a winding, steep-sided gorge, with an entrance straight out of Jason and the Argonauts. A waterhole guards this and an approach was forbidden by local Aboriginal law, except during times of extreme drought. Access isn't easy. The 3½-km drive in is unsealed and rough, and then it's another 1½-km walk. Swimming is forbidden, so a blow-up mattress with a length of string attached is required to get across – this is all well worth the effort, however. Alternatively, make the 10-minute climb up the eastern bluff to catch the grand view into the gorge and to the ranges to the south. Just before Glen Helen is the turn-off to popular **Ormiston Gorge**, 8 km down the sealed road. This has the best visitor set-up of any of the accessible gorges. The campground ($6.60 per person) has barbecues, toilets, drinking water and showers, and a parks visitor centre ① *T8956 7799, 0800-1700*. Swimming is allowed in the permanent waterhole. The gorge is wide and high with impressive rounded bluffs, and a colony of shy wallabies. There are several good walks from the campground, including the enjoyable three-hour **Ormiston Pound** loop walk. Map and walkers guides from the visitor centre.

GLEN HELEN

The 700-km-long **Finke** is one of the Centre's principal river courses, capable of high and forceful flows, but normally a dry bed. During its more than 100-million-year existence it has cut a series of dramatic red gorges and bluffs through the landscape. One of these is Glen Helen, 132 km from Alice Springs and 114 km unsealed from Hermannsburg, which is also important as one of the river's six permanent waterholes. Visitors who make it this far can stay at the **Glen Helen Resort**, see page 195. You can see the sights from a helicopter if you wish. From Glen Helen the road crosses the Finke and then immediately becomes unsealed. At this point is a **lookout**, the best one easily accessible in the ranges, with extensive views to the north and the unusually craggy **Mount Sonder**. The last campground west is 20 km further on at the awesome 4WD only **Redbank Gorge**. After this the road curls south, past **Gosse Bluff**, to its western junction with Larapinta Drive and the Mereenie Loop Road, permits required.

HERMANNSBURG

This settlement, 125 km from Alice Springs, was the first Aboriginal mission in the Northern Territory, established by Lutherans in 1877, on the lands of the Western Arrernte (or Aranda) people. Control of the mission lands was handed back to the original owners in 1982 under the Aboriginal Land Rights Act and is now a strong Aboriginal community with very few residents of European origin. The town is particularly well known for the skill of its artists. In the early days of the mission, the famous Aboriginal painter **Albert Namatjira** was taught how to paint European-style landscapes and quickly developed his unique style and talent. Many of Namatjira's descendants and relatives continue to paint in his distinctive style and the Hermannsburg Potters have become well regarded for their coiled pots, painted and decorated with features of the Hermannsburg landscape. **Hermannsburg Heritage Precinct** ⓘ *T/F8956 7402, 1000- 1600, $4.50, children $3, concessions $3.50, includes self-guided tour and a cuppa, art gallery $3.50*, preserves the buildings of the mission and an art gallery showing the work of Namatjira and his school. The mission is a fascinating and delightful place to explore, shaded by tall gum trees and scattered with cool whitewashed stone buildings. There is also a rustic tea room in the former Pastor's house where you can have tea and scones (quite a surreal experience as you gaze out in the heat over the compound walls to the rough-looking township and desert beyond). Local art and the work of the Hermannsburg potters is also on display at reasonable prices.

FINKE GORGE NATIONAL PARK

The course of the **Finke River**, fresh from its exertions at Glen Helen, reappears to the visitor just west of Hermannsburg. A 4WD-only track follows the course south of the town, and continues down to the Ernest Giles Road, though only the first stretch is recommended unless you are an experienced and well-equipped off-road driver. This first section heads on down to **Finke Gorge** and **Palm Valley**, which is a vibrant and permanent oasis that shelters many wonderful remnant plant species, including the red cabbage palm. This really is a magical place to spend a couple of nights and there is a small campground just short of the valley with facilities including toilets, water and barbecues. No entry fee and no camping fee. For more information contact Parks and Wildlife NT, T8951 8211.

MEREENIE LOOP ROAD

This unsealed road offers a northerly short-cut between Alice Springs and Kings Canyon. Though it can sometimes be negotiated by 2WD with care and good preparation this isn't recommended, and trailers and caravans are asking for trouble. The road passes through the **Haast Bluff Aboriginal Land Reserve**, country less flat and forbidding than along the longer sealed route, and frequently passes close to the bases of several undulating ranges. Near the far end of the road a left-turn leads to **Glen Helen**, see page 190, with an optional 4WD only side-trip to **Gosse Bluff**, a 5-km wide comet crater with tall walls. There are picnic facilities here, but no camping. The road becomes sealed just before **Hermannsburg**, see page 191. A travel permit is required for the loop which is available for $2.20 on the day of travel from Kings Canyon Resort, Hermannsburg supermarket, Glen Helen Resort or the VIC in Alice Springs.

→WATARRKA NATIONAL PARK

ⓘ *No entry fee, for more information contact Parks and Wildlife NT, T8951 8211. The park is 300 km from Yulara.*

Enclosing the western part of the George Gill Range and its impressive western bluff, **Carmichael Crag**, Watarrka is best known for **Kings Canyon**, the upper reaches of which culminate in sheer red walls, 100 m high. Some of these are finely patterned by horizontal bedding planes and vertical water stains, others by myriad tiny cracks creating a resemblance to ancient Egyptian hieroglyphs. The ranges consist of pale Mereenie sandstone, its surface rusted everywhere to fantastically rich reds and oranges. As well as the main canyon, relentless weathering has created dozens of cool refuges from the arid plains below, such as waterholes and lush valleys like the **Garden of Eden**. These harbour rare plants such as cycads, a remnant Gondwanan species. On top of the ranges a regular grid of weaknesses have been weathered down to hundreds of beehive domes, which range from the size of a car to the size of a house. The park is named after a native cat linked to a dreaming route of the local Luritja people along Kings Creek. There is a ranger talk and slide show about the park, nightly at the resort from May to October. The best time to visit is between April and September. Water, picnic tables, gas barbecues can be found at Kings Canyon and Kathleen Springs. There is no camping however.

LURITJA ROAD TO LASSETER HIGHWAY

The sealed **Luritja Road** connects the Lasseter Highway with the **Watarrka National Park** and **Kings Canyon**. After 65 km is the junction with the 100-km unsealed Ernest Giles Road, a 4WD 'short-cut' between Kings Canyon and Alice Springs, though it is never graded and very rough. Soon after this the red bluffs of the **George Gill Range** appear on the right-hand side. In the lee of these, 40 km short of Kings Canyon, is **Kings Creek Station**, with accommodation, food and tours.

WALKS IN WATARRKA

The main walk in this park, the **Kings Canyon Walk**, is superb. It begins with a climb up rock steps to the rim of the canyon. Once on the plateau the track winds through striking domes of red sandstone towards the end of the canyon. A short sidetrack leads to a lookout point giving some of the finest views on the walk. Standing on the edge of sheer rock walls you face the canyon's 100-m high south face. Returning to the main track, after a short distance steps lead down to a bridge over the **Garden of Eden**, a lush waterhole lined with palms and eucalypts, to the far side of the canyon. The track then swings south to bring you to the edge of the main wall visible from the lookout. Leaving the rim, the track passes by countless domes, sometimes called the **Lost City**, and descends to the car park (6 km, three hours). The terrain is uneven but once the rim is reached the walk is easy and flat. There is little shade so try to start the walk by 0800, earlier in summer. There is a shady short walk about halfway up **Kings Creek**, leading to a lookout point with views of the canyon walls from below (2½ km, one hour return). **Kathleen Springs**, is a similar walk, leading to a spring-fed waterhole. It is possible to walk from Kathleen Springs to Kings Canyon on the **Giles Track** (22 km, two days) but this should only be attempted in cool weather, and walkers must register with the Overnight Walkers Scheme, T1300 650730.

→EAST MACDONNELL RANGES

After visiting the West MacDonnells, the eastern ranges come across as an interesting surprise. The overall impression of ancient red rock is the same, but there is much less of the uniformity. There are many more smaller and more tortured formations that interrupt the horizon, and dense woodland crowds some of the even, wider valleys. Access is via the **Ross Highway**, which leaves the Stuart Highway just south of the Heavitree Gap. After 10 km and 18 km respectively are two impressive gaps, **Emily and Jessie**, with semi-permanent waterholes (swimming is not allowed) and a small amount of Aboriginal rock art. Both have basic toilets and picnic sites. **Corroboree Rock** is a further 30 km. This is a semi-circular 5-m slab of weathered but resistant sandstone, standing vertically on a very small hill. It is very sacred to the Arrernte people and visitors are asked to be respectful and keep their distance. The highlight is undoubtedly the **Trephina Gorge**, which can be reached by an 8-km unsealed road, 70 km from Alice. Here visitors will find a wide watercourse which has carved-out long, low and vivid red cliffs. The approach road passes under the much higher cliffs of **Trephina Bluff**. There are several walks from the gorge campground. The sealed highway ends at **Ross River Resort**. Just before Ross River is the turn-off to **Arltunga Historical Reserve**, 35 km down an unsealed road. This was the site of a mini goldrush in the early 1900s and the abandoned underground mines, stone ruins and small cemetery are easily accessible. A dozen kilometres past Ross River, on a 4WD only track, is **N'Dhala Gorge**, best known for its cultural significance to the Arrernte people. There are thousands of rock carvings in the gorge, most engraved in the last 2000 years, with a few as old as 10,000 years.

→SOUTH OF ALICE SPRINGS

CHAMBERS PILLAR AND EWANINGA ROCK CARVINGS
It takes a special trip or an expensive tour to visit **Chambers Pillar**, a 40 m high remnant column of colourful layered sandstone. It's 150 km from the **Maryvale** turn-off near the airport. Fuel is availabe in Maryvale. The road is unsealed the whole way, most of it recommended for 4WD only, and the final 30-odd km are definitely 4WD only. If you do head this way, the **Ewaninga Rock Carvings** are about 25 km south of the airport. Several Aboriginal images, of undetermined age, have been carved into rocks on the edge of a small claypan. They can be viewed via a 20-minute loop walk.

ALICE SPRINGS TO ERLDUNDA
The Stuart Highway slips through **Heavitree Gap** then takes the more or less direct route south. The turn-off to **Rainbow Valley** is 77 km from Alice, then 22 km down an unsealed road. This jagged semicircle of cliffs in the James Range are made up of clearly differentiated layers of sandstone and provide a colourful sight, particularly at sunset. **Henbury Meteorites Conservation Reserve** is 18 km down the very poor unsealed Ernest

Giles Road. The reserve encompasses 12 craters, all caused by fragments of the Henbury Meteor which crashed in from space, broke up and hit the ground about 4700 years ago. The largest crater is 180 m across and there are walking tracks around this and several others. Erldunda, a resort-style roadhouse 200 km from Alice Springs, marks the junction with the Lasseter Highway, the road to Uluru and King's Canyon.

→MOUNT CONNOR

Soon after the Luritja Road/Lasseter Highway junction are the first glimpses of what most travellers take to be Uluru, but is, in fact, Mount Connor, an impressive flat-topped mesa that's over twice the size of 'the rock', 160 km from Erldunda and 75 km from Yulara. It is on the Curtin Springs cattle station, which operates the friendly Curtin Springs pub and cookhouse (www.curtinsprings.com), which has accommodation, serves food and is the basis for some great tours, either on a camel or 4WD.

ALICE SPRINGS AND AROUND LISTINGS

Where to stay

Alice Springs

Alice has numerous, virtually all have a swimming pool, and most offer free airport/ station pick-ups. Backpackers are well catered for with lots of hostels and other budget options. Book ahead though.

$$ Winter Sun, Stuart Highway, T8952 4080, www.wintersun.com.au. A caravan park 2 km north of town. Good facilities, including a pool. All cabins have a/c.

$$-$ Alice Lodge Backpackers, 4 Mueller St, T8953 1975, T1800 351925, www.alice lodge.com.au. This small hostel is friendly, relaxed and clean. All rooms a/c, but some are in caravans. A stiff walk out.

$$-$ Alice Springs YHA, Parsons St, T8952 8855, www.yha.com.au. This is the most central hostel. Once an outdoor cinema, the hostel still screen nightly films under the stars. There are 6-bunk, 4-bunk and double rooms, all with a/c.

Good-sized communal areas around a pool and travel agency with good value tours. Clean, secure, but no parking.

$$-$ Annie's Place, 4 Traeger Av, T8952 1545, www.anniesplace.com.au. Sets the standard in hostel accommodation. With 128 beds it's big enough to have excellent facilities, including a pool, a bar, $5 evening meals, tour desk and internet café, but small enough to retain a good buzz. All 6-bed dorms and most doubles are en suite, and a/c.

West MacDonnell Ranges

$$$-$$ Glen Helen Resort, Glen Helen, T8956 7489, www.glenhelen.com.au. A/c motel rooms, basic bunk rooms, safari tents and campground. Restaurant, bar, pool and natural swimming hole, fuel and tours.

What to do

Alice Springs

There are a host of companies eager to whisk travellers off into the bush with a 4WD tour. Contact the VIC for a comprehensive list.

Adventure Tours, T1800 068886, T8132 8230, www.adventuretours.com.au. One of the largest companies in the region, with a wide choice of options to suit all pockets, including a 3-day Uluru package from $355.

Wayoutback, T1300 551510, www.wayoutback.com.au. This outfit gets closer than most to the raw experience and have exclusive access to two of the major cattle stations between Yulara and Kings Canyon. Their 5-day 'Kangaroo Dreaming' 4WD trip is $975 and takes in Uluru, Kata Tjuta, Kings Canyon and West MacDonnell Ranges, using bush camps and visiting an aboriginal community.

West MacDonnell Ranges

The Larapinta Trail has been marked out along the 220 km spine of the West MacDonnells, with 13 sections linking the accessible gorges. The easier sections are 1-3 (Alice to Standley Chasm) while sections 8-12 are more challenging (Serpentine Gorge to Redbank Gorge). Walking the trail should only be attempted Apr-Oct and even then walk in the cool of early morning or late afternoon. The Alice Springs tourist office has a full range of maps and brief guides. For transport to trail heads contact Trek Larapinta, www.trek larapinta.com.au. Long-distance walkers are strongly advised to register with the Parks & Wildlife Commission, T8951 8250, www.parks andwildlife.nt.gov.au. For more advice talk to the knowledgeable staff at Lone Dingo in Alice Springs, T8953 3866, http://lonedingo.com.au. They hire equipment.

ULURU (AYERS ROCK) AND AROUND

The grand, haunting bulk of Uluru, the country's most famous landmark, is close to the geographical centre of Australia and is often called the 'red heart'. Perhaps 'soul' would be a better word as even staunch atheists will readily acknowledge the profound feeling of spirituality it elicits; a natural cathedral rising above the surrounding bush and spinifex-covered plains. The horizon is broken only by Kata Tjuta, a more subtle and secretive formation. Beyond these huddled hills the dry plains spread further, though still not unbroken. Mount Connor, a beautifully symmetrical mesa twice the size of Uluru and sometimes mistaken for it, also stands proud on the flat landscape. A couple of hundred kilometres north, the George Gill range of hills are outliers of the MacDonnells and famous for Kings Canyon, part of the Watarrka National Park. Another of the country's most impressive sights, a walk around the rim should not be missed.

→ULURU-KATA TJUTA NATIONAL PARK

ⓘ *T8956 2299, daily approximately 1 hr before to 1 hr past sunset, $25 for a 3-day pass.*
This national park contains **Uluru**, the red rock rising from the plain in the centre of the continent still widely known as Ayers Rock (though the name changed over a decade ago). 'Nearby', over the spinifex-covered plains and ancient low sand dunes, lie the domes of **Kata Tjuta**, gently curving red hills leaning in closely like heads drawn together in conversation. For over 20,000 years this landscape has been revered by the Aboriginal inhabitants of the area and is now part of one of Australia's most popular national parks, receiving around 400,000 visitors a year. The park received its first tourists in the 1950s and 1960s. In 1985 the government handed the title deeds of the park to the local Pitjantjatjara and Yankunytjatjara Aboriginal people, recognizing that their continual use and custodianship of the land constituted legal ownership. These people, known locally as **Anangu**, decided to lease the park back to the government and manage it jointly with Parks Australia. The park is further protected by its World Heritage listing, received for its outstanding natural and cultural values.

ULURU-KATA TJUTA CULTURAL CENTRE

ⓘ *1 km from Uluru, T8956 3138, 0700-1800 (Nov-Mar), 0700-1730 (Apr-Oct).*
The cultural centre, built in 1994, is where the Anangu teach visitors about their culture, Tjukurpa and management of the park. It's a very pleasant, cool and spacious place with plenty of shaded areas to picnic or rest. The two buildings represent Kuniya (woma python) and Liru (poisonous snake), ancestral beings of the Tjukurpa linked to the southern side of Uluru. The entry tunnel represents aspects of Anangu life and leads to the park information desk where visitors can pick up park notes and other publications and find out more about tours, events and ranger activities. The complex also includes high-quality arts, crafts and souvenirs and a café with a close view of Uluru. All businesses are Aboriginal-owned although few Anangu are visible. This is because they tend to be fairly shy and reserved people who find the attention of thousands of visitors hard to face.

ULURU (AYERS ROCK)

Uluru is recognized as the largest monolith (or single rock) in the world and is right up there on the 'wow factor' scale. It is 3 km long and rises abruptly 340 m above the surrounding plain. It has a loaf-shape from a distance but closer up it reveals sharp vertical ridges, muscular curves, and caves eroded into evocative shapes. The beautiful form is enhanced by the deep-red colour of the rock, caused by the rusting of one of its minor constituents, iron. The colour becomes particularly rich at sunrise and sunset when light from the red end of the spectrum is reflected from the surface, making it glow as if molten. Uluru was named Ayers Rock in 1873 after a South Australian politician by explorer William Gosse, the first European to climb it, but reverted to its original name when park ownership was handed back to the Anangu. It is surrounded by trees and bushes and has the feel of an oasis even in high summer. There are several walks close to the base starting from the large Mala car park, but the main facilities are concentrated at Uluru-Kata Tjuta Cultural Centre.

→YULARA

Yulara is a large and friendly resort complex, strategically built between low dunes so as not to intrude on the Uluru landscape 20 km away, but with easy access to the Uluru-Kata Tjuta National Park in mind. It has a monopoly on accommodation in the area and the price of a bed here is high – but then so are the standards, particularly the exceptional levels of service. There are half a dozen hotels of varying styles and facilities, all built on the periphery of a loop road. Between two of these, **Emu Walk** and **Lost Camel**, is the 'resort centre' a set of shops, services and cafés surrounding a spacious, sunny courtyard. These include a good-sized supermarket, post office, bank and ATM, and art galleries and a souvenir shops. The best gallery is **Mulgara**, in Sails hotel. There are several lookouts around the resort, all with views over to Uluru with a glimpse of Kata Tjuta in the distance, the best being the one at the coach campground. The **visitor centre** ① *T8957 7377, between Desert Gardens and Emu Walk, 0830-1900*, has an extensive interpretative centre. Uluru is 435 km from Alice Springs and 735 km from Coober Pedy.

KATA TJUTA ('THE OLGAS')

① *Mount Olga: 1066 m. 48 km from Yulara, 48 km from Uluru.*

The domes of Kata Tjuta lie to the west of Uluru, visible across a low sand plain. Although they are less well known than the great rock in the distance, they are easily as beautiful, if not more so. The Anangu name means 'many heads' and there is something curiously lifelike about the smooth, high domes huddled together. Between them cool, deep valleys have the mystery and silence of a cathedral and indeed the area is sacred to Anangu. However, the Tjukurpa stories of Kata Tjuta are considered men's business and cannot be revealed to the uninitiated. There are two short walks and a sunset viewing area at the western end where visitors linger over the intense red colour of the domes at the end of the day. This area has a few picnic tables and is a quieter spot than the sunset area at Uluru. Sunrise is best seen from the dune viewing area, 25 km from the Kata Tjuta turn-off, facing the southern edge of the rocks.

WALKS IN ULURU

The **Base Walk** at Uluru circumnavigates the entire rock, combining two shorter tracks, the Mala and Mutijula walks. It is a fascinating walk allowing a close look at rock formations, rock art and waterholes passing through surprisingly lush vegetation in some areas. There are a few shelters to rest under and a drinking-water tank at the halfway point (9½ km, two to three hours). The **Mala Walk** (2 km, one hour return) focuses on the journey of the ancestral Mala, the wallaby. A free guided walk is conducted daily by a ranger who explains the significance and features of Uluru. It starts from the Mala Walk sign at the Mala car park (0800 October-April, 1000 May-September). The **Mutitjulu Walk** (1 km, 30 mins) leads to a waterhole that is the home of Wanampi, an ancestral watersnake, and looks at the features left behind by Kuniya, woma python, and examples of rock art. It is accessible from the Mutijulu car park, just to the east of the main junction. The **Liru Walk** leads through mulga woodland from the cultural centre to the Mala car park (2 km one way). There are two walks at Kata Tjuta, one of which is the best in the park. The **Valley of the Winds** is a spectacular circuit walk through the deep valleys between the western domes. The walk heads over uneven terrain to Karu Lookout, a peaceful clearing near a creek, and then swings south. Turning east again the track passes through a beautiful canyon to Karingana Lookout with views of the domes beyond. The track follows the base of the left dome back to Karu Lookout (7½ km, three hours). This track is closed beyond the first lookout from 1100 on days when the temperature is forecast at 36°C or more. The **Walpa** (Olga Gorge) **Walk** leads to the end of the narrow, high gorge and is an attractive easy walk (2½ km, one hour return). Visitors to Kata Tjuta are asked not to leave the path or climb the domes. At both Uluru and Kata Tjuta there are several rock features considered sacred sites by the Anangu that cannot be photographed or touched but these are all clearly signposted or indicated by double lines (no stopping) on the road.

ULURU LISTINGS

Where to stay

Yulara

Accommodation should be booked in advance at any time of year, but particularly Mar-Nov. This even applies to campsites. All reservations are directed through the office in Sydney, T02 9339 1040, www.voyages.com. au. Rates can be lower by booking special deal/combination package. Ayers Rock Resort includes all the following places.

$$$$ Desert Gardens, T1300 134 044, www.ayersrockresort.com.au. A slightly less expensive alternative to **Sails**. Rooms are less luxurious and have decidedly less character. The pool is available to all resort guests.

$$$$ Emu Walk, as **Desert Gardens**. This hotel provides the upmarket self-contained option. Apartments are extremely spacious, well-equipped and worth considering for groups or large families.

$$$$ Sails in the Desert, as **Desert Gardens**. This uber-luxurious hotel is the 5-star flagship. The incredible suites, with Uluru views, are worth every cent.

$$$$-$ Outback Pioneer Hotel & Lodge, as **Desert Gardens**. Provides most of the 'budget' options and the buzziest nightlife. Relatively basic but comfortable en suite double rooms vary in price and amenities, some have kitchenettes. Backpackers have the option of 4-bed or 20-bed single-sex

dorms. Cleanliness in rooms, kitchen and shower block, and quality of service are on a par with the rest of the resort. The pool is available to all resort guests.

$ Resort Campground, has the cheapest double-bed option and the few cabins also have a kitchenette, though no en suite. Camping on the grassed lawns is $36 per couple for a non-powered site.

Watarrka National Park

$$$$ Kings Canyon Resort, at the end of Luritja Rd, 6 km from King Canyon, T9426 7550, T1300 863248, www.voyages.com.au. This straddles the main road, with the reception and the more expensive hotel accommodation and restaurant on one side, and the campground, budget rooms, bar and café, internet kiosk, fuel and small expensive store (open 0700-1900) on the other. Other facilities include a pool and tennis court. Lawned campground sites from $19 each. At sunset, drinks are served at the Sunset Viewing Platform, overlooking Uluru.

$$$ Kings Creek Station, Lasseter Highway, T8956 7474, www.kingscreekstation.com.au. 36 km from Kings Canyon, this working cattle and camel station has camping areas (from $19.50 per person) and canvas 'safari' cabins available, plus pool. The station runs quad and camel safaris, as well as helicopter flights.

What to do

Yulara

Most tours do not include the park entry fee. The central tour booking office is in the resort centre, T1300 134044. Aerial tours are amazing and recommended. Kata Tjuta is particularly striking from the air.

Ayers Rock Scenic Flights, www.ayers rockresort.com.au. The best budget option, particularly for longer tours.

Frontier Camel Tours, coach campground, www.cameltours.com.au. Sunset rides into the national park, includes drink and refreshments.

Professional Helicopter Services, T8956 2003, www.phs.com.au. Flies over Uluru or Kata Tjuta or both (30-min Uluru-Kata Tjuta flight $275) and also operates trips to Kings Canyon.

STUART HIGHWAY VIA COOBER PEDY

→FROM THE RED CENTRE TO MARLA

From Erldunda it's a (relatively – about 250 km) short run down to the Marla Roadhouse. From Marla, there's the choice of either continuing down the tarmac of the Stuart Highway to Coober Pedy and then Port Augusta (and a 100 km-odd backtrack up to the Flinders) or of taking the unsealed (but usually very well graded) Oodnadatta Track that heads out further west and leads more directly to the ranges (see box opposite). If you're in a hire vehicle then it will need to be 4WD if you want to take the track.

KULGERA
The geographical centre of mainland Australia, 75 km from Erldunda, 415 km from Coober Pedy, is formally located 150 km to the east on the unsealed road to Finke. There's a roadhouse and fuel too here.

MARLA
Marla, 180 km from Kulgera and 235 km from Coober Pedy has a roadhouse and hotel, **Kulgera**, T8670 7001, www.marla.com.au, **$$**. Fuel and supermarket are open 24 hours. As well as motel-style rooms there are powered and unpowered camping and caravan spots available, and there's a pool and many other facilities.

From Marla it's 80 km to the **Cadney Homestead roadhouse**. Just before the roadhouse is a rough unsealed road that leads after about 100 km to the **Painted Desert**, a series of multi-coloured mesas similar to the Breakaways but on a much grander scale.

BREAKAWAYS
The highway then passes through the bulk of the opal fields and then out onto a 130-km stretch to the Breakaways, flat-topped mesas (hills) in a stony desert north of Coober Pedy which have featured in movies such as *Mad Max III* and *The Adventures of Priscilla, Queen of the Desert*. Access is via an unsealed loop road that heads around to Coober Pedy (about 20 km longer than the straight tarmac route) along the **Dog Fence**, which stretches for 5300 km across South Australia, NSW and Queensland and was built to keep dingos out of sheep country. The Breakaways Reserve and Dog Fence can only be reached on unsealed roads (2WD but impassable after rain) so those without transport or in a hire car will need to take one on a tour from Coober Pedy. An entry permit is required from Coober Pedy VIC or shelter at Lookout One. It is signposted from Stuart Highway, 23 km north of Coober Pedy. The circuit is about 70 km return.

→COOBER PEDY

One of Australia's more unusual Outback towns, Coober Pedy has been settled by opal miners, many of whom live in homes underground to avoid the baking heat, adding to the alien nature of this harsh, arid landscape. Opal was 'discovered' by gold prospectors in

GOING FURTHER

The Oodnadatta Track to Marree

The unsealed Oodnadatta Track follows a route taken by the dogged explorer, John McDouall Stuart, who first crossed Australia from Adelaide to Darwin in 1862. It was his third attempt and in two years of trying he only had a scant three months restocking supplies in Adelaide. Stuart is thought to have followed the advice of local Aboriginal people because the route is also an ancient Aboriginal trade route and follows a line of mound springs. The availability of water meant that the Overland Telegraph Line in the 1870s and the Central Australian Railway in 1890 also followed this route. The Oodnadatta testifies both to the detailed knowledge Aboriginal people had of their land and to the tough determination of European pioneers. It can be passable for 2WD and is frequently graded, though it usually gets rutted and difficult after rain. Outback driving rules apply. A Westprint map is available.

OODNADATTA

Oodnadatta, 210 km from Marla, was the Ghan's railhead for a few decades from 1890 until the late 1920s, though it is now difficult to imagine the hustle of transferring passengers, luggage and freight onto long camel trains for the exhausting onward journey to Alice. The spectacle is evoked to some degree in the old station, which is now a mostly photographic museum depicting the town's century or so of existence. A key can be picked up from the roadhouse. The frontier spirit may have gone, but this is still an evocative spot. The town has adapted well to its new clientele and the pub and roadhouse cheerfully cater for the visitors.

WILLIAM CREEK TO MARREE

This route covers a distance of a distance of 205 km. William Creek is a major overnight and refuelling stop. It consists of a pub and café and a small outdoor museum of rocket and engine parts. There are a places to stay, a general store and some tours on offer.

Lake Eyre is actually two lakes, the northern and southern parts only linking when they fill with water, which last happened in 1974. If it does happen to be full, or nearly so, it is worth making the trip to the shores of the northern lake. There's a signposted 4WD-only track on the right about 10 km south of William Creek. Just past the Mound Springs, there is an oasis at Coward Springs. This former rail siding is being carefully restored by the owner, who has built a small, pleasant campground. A flowing bore provides the water for a novel spa bath among the reeds of a small wetlands area. Day visitors are welcome. Lake Eyre South is usually dry and the salty surface glitters on the horizon.

MARREE

Marree (population 250) is the biggest town on the track and is 370 km from Coober Pedy and 520 km from Birdsville. The town has a historic hotel and two small roadhouses, both with cafés and basic groceries. Scenic flights are available from the town. One option overflies Lake Eyre, another passes over the Marree Man, a 5-km-long detailed 'drawing' of an Aboriginal figure 70 km west of Marree, the origin of which remains a mystery. From Marree, you can head 120 km south to Leigh Creek, one of the gateways to Flinders Ranges (see page 209).

1915, although local Aboriginal people had long been aware of the coloured stone here, and miners soon began to descend on the area. The rough-and-ready community changed little until the road from Adelaide to Darwin was sealed in 1987, and then the town began to attract large numbers of tourists. Opals and tourism are big business now and tough the town's edges have been smoothed considerably since the isolation of earlier days, car wrecks and junk still litter parts of the town and more eccentric locals have been known to use their explosives for more than just mining. Coober Pedy is 535 km from Port Augusta and 730 km from Yulara.

PLACES IN COOBER PEDY

There are many places in town to see former mines and dugout homes. One of the best is the Old Timers Mine, a mine dug by hand in around 1916. It is a warren of low curving drives, some filled with displays on early mining methods or seams of opal in situ. The trail also leads through an old-style dugout and the former family home of the **Goughs** ① *T8672 5555, www.oldtimersmine.com, 0900-1700. $7.50, children $3.50*, who still run the mine. Although larger and less intimate, **Umoona** ① *Hutchison St, T8672 5288, www.umoonaopalmine.com.au, 0800-1900, tours 1000, 1200, 1400, 1600, entrance free, tours $8, children $4*, is another interesting mine museum complex. It stands out for its entrance tunnel which has an excellent display on the geology and history of the area and a good short film called 'The Story of Opal'. Guided tours include the film, mine, hand and machine dug homes and an Aboriginal Interpretative Centre. There are several underground churches in the town such as the **Catacomb Church** ① *Catacomb Rd, off Hutchison St, visitors welcome*, a hand-dug former mine that was extended into the shape of a cross and turned into a church. It has a charming simplicity that the parishioners explicitly link to the earliest days of Christianity. The **Serbian Othodox Church** ① *Flinders St, off Hutchison St, 1600-1700, donation appreciated*, is a grander affair dug by tunnelling machines with an impressive curved ceiling and unusual modern windows.

The real attractions of Coober Pedy are simply the eccentricities of local homes, the detritus of film sets left lying around and the cone-shaped mounds of mine tailings on the barren red landscape. The best way to see the place is just to drive around a bit or take one of the tours. Start at the **Big Winch Lookout** where there are good views and some interesting homes nearby. Things to look out for are **Jewellery Shop Road**, where anyone can 'fossick' through the piles of dirt for opal, and the **Cemetery**, with Carl Bratz's keg-topped grave. The fees are cheap at the **Golf Course**. There's not a blade of grass on the 'green' and golfers take their putts on a dirt surface greased with sump oil. Note that visitors cannot enter a **mining field** unless on a guided tour. This is because the fields are riddled with 1½ million open shafts about 1-m wide and 25-m deep. The warning signs are not an exaggeration – tourists have been killed by falling down shafts while taking photos.

The **VIC** ① *District Council offices, Hutchison St, T8672 5298, www.opalcapitalof theworld.com.au, Mon-Fri 0900-1700*, is itself a mine of information.

→STUART HIGHWAY SOUTH FROM COOBER PEDY

From Coober Pedy the road enters the **Woomera Prohibited Area** and there is little of interest for the next 250-km stretch. Glendambo, an extended roadhouse, is the first chance for fuel and supplies. The unrelenting golden red continues on, covered in a bright blue Australian sky (though after heavy rains the vegetation creates a carpet of vibrant greens, dotted with flowery yellows, purples and reds – this place can surprisingly seem like a meadow in springtime). After 110 km the community of **Pimba** and Spuds roadhouse are a welcome sight. Pimba marks the only junction with a sealed road before Erldunda, in the Northern Territory.

Once much larger, the Woomera Prohibited Area is chunk of desert about the size of England that extends west of Woomera to the Western Australian border and north as far as Cadney Homestead. It was surveyed and declared a prohibited area in 1946-1947 to allow the British to begin missile and rocket testing here. From its beginnings till 1982 **Woomera**, 7 km from Pimba and 180 km from Port Augusta, was the main residential town for those working in the various facilities in the Woomera Prohibited Area. The developments by **Kistler**, and the takeover of most of the facilities by **British Aerospace** has, however, rekindled interest. The sparkling, clean town now features a fascinating **Missile Park and the Heritage Centre** ① *T/F8673 7042, 0900-1700, museum $5.30, children and concessions $3.30.* The park is an impressive static display of a couple of dozen missiles, rockets and aeroplanes. The centre comprises a café, excellent VIC, 10-pin bowling alley and a small but interesting museum that recounts the history of the test facilities.

→PORT AUGUSTA

Port Augusta lies on the fringe of South Australia's vast Outback, at the head of the Spencer Gulf, 305 km from Adelaide and 530 km from Coober Pedy. It is surrounded by arid plains relieved by the pale blue of the gulf and the ranges of the Flinders rising in the near distance. Known as the crossroads of Australia, the large town forms the junction of the major road and rail routes north to Darwin and west to Perth, so many people whistle through every day. There is a high Aboriginal population, with about 4000 Aboriginal people from the ranges and the 'lands' Aboriginal-owned territory to the west residing in the town. Some interesting sights and useful services make Port Augusta well worth a stop. The VIC ① *T8641 0793, www.portaugusta.sa.gov.au, Mon-Fri 0900-1730, Sat-Sun 1000-1600*, acts as a booking service for the Flinders, Outback and Northern Territory.

On Flinders Terrace, is one of the state's most interesting interpretative centres, the **Wadlata Outback Centre** ① *$8.95, children $5.50, concessions $7.95*, housed in the same building as the VIC. The centre takes visitors through a 'tunnel of time', from the ancient geology of the area and the beliefs of the Aboriginal inhabitants, to the European explorers, the early days of Port Augusta and present day industries and endeavours. The display is particularly strong on the dreaming stories and culture of local Aboriginal people and is well worth a couple of hours. Next door is the **Fountain Gallery** ① *Mon-Fri 0900-1630, free*, a venue for touring exhibitions. A few kilometres north of town on the Stuart Highway to Darwin is the **Arid Lands Botanic Garden** ① *Mon-Fri 0900-1700, Sat-Sun 1000-1600, free. tours Mon-Fri at 1100 (Apr-Oct) or 0930 (Nov-Mar), $5.95, children $4.50, call T8641 1049 to book.* Covering more than 200 ha, the garden aims to conserve and display native flora from the arid zone. The gardens also have wonderful views of the Flinders Ranges so visitors can wander along the paths to enjoy the view or sit in the café inside the eco-friendly rammed-earth visitor centre.

Quiet, friendly **Quorn**, gateway to the Flinders Ranges and 41 km from Port Augusta, has often been used as a film location for films set in the nostalgic Australian past. It was established as a railway town on the narrow-gauge line built in 1879 from Port Augusta through the **Pichi Richi Pass** to service the settlements north of Quorn and link to the Ghan train to Alice Springs. Volunteers maintaining the Pichi Richi line operate a variety of steam trains to Port Augusta every weekend and some weekdays from March to December, T8648 6598. There are some excellent walks in the low ranges to the west and south of the town. There is a VIC ① *Seventh St, T8648 6419, www.flinders ranges.com, 0900-1700.*

There are three principal peak walks near the town, all accessed via unsealed roads. From the shortest to the longest they get progressively more difficult but also more rewarding. **Devil's Peak** is on private land to the south. This is a no-nonsense, two-hour return ascent to one of the area's most distinctive peaks. The final 300 m climbs steeply past the towering summit bluff and onto the 45° shelf that crowns the peak. Views are in every direction, including Spencer Gulf, Mount Brown and the central Flinders. It is closed in fireban season (November to April). **Dutchmans Stern** (820 m) is part of a conservation park of the same name and native fauna and flora are much more in evidence. It's a three-hour return hike or four-hour loop result in similar views. Mount Brown (970 m) is the summit of the large horseshoe ridge to the east of Devil's Peak. The best ascent walk is an eight-hour loop – providing you don't get lost, which is easy to do as both the path and summit are indistinct.

Willochra Plain around Quorn and the country north to Hawker is littered with the stone remains of the homes and stations of 19th-century pastoralists. The most extensive ruins are those of **Kanyaka** station, 38 km north of Quorn, where 70 workers and their families lived. It is possible to wander around the site, about 1 km off the main road by Kanyaka Creek. Subtler evidence of the region's original inhabitants can be seen at **Yourambulla Caves**, where there are simple rock paintings and good views to the south and west on a 3-km loop walk, 10 km south of Hawker.

Hawker, once a railway town, has survived thanks to its position at the junction of the highway north to Leigh Creek and the road from Port Augusta to Wilpena. With a low backdrop of the Yourambulla Range, it has some enduring heritage buildings and a few key services that make it a useful place to replenish supplies before moving on. Tourist information and petrol can be found at **Hawker Motors**. The cavernous **General Store**, over the road, seems to stock practically everything. The solid stone post office on the main street, Wilpena Road, also houses a **parks office** ① *T8648 4244*, with useful brochures and maps on the Flinders Ranges.

STUART HIGHWAY VIA COOBER PEDY LISTINGS

Where to stay

Coober Pedy

There are plenty of places to sleep underground but also rooms for those who may feel claustrophobic. The underground rooms are usually airy with high ceilings but the lack of a window and natural light can feel strange.

$$$$ Desert Cave Hotel, Hutchison St, T8672 5688, www.desertcave.com.au. Dominating the main street is this 5-star hotel, with rooms above and below ground (specify which you'd like when booking). The general facilities are excellent, especially the pool and spa.

$$$ Mud Hut, St Nicholas St, T8672 3003, www.mudhutmotel.com.au. 28 a/c rooms, all above ground in modern rammed-earth brick buildings, split between standard motel-style doubles and self-contained units.

$$$ Radeka Down Under, Oliver St, T8672 5223, www.radekadownunder.com.au. In this former opal mine are a fascinating range of rooms from the virtually fully underground suite to budget doubles and the warren of completely subterranean hostel dorms. Good bar and common rooms. Clean and comfortable with a Mediterranean air. Recommended.

$$-$ Opal Cave, Hutchison St, T8672 5028, www.opalcavecooberpedy.com. This place has rooms with 4 bunk beds in each with basic facilities.

$ Riba's, 4 km south on the William Creek Rd, T8672 5614. A caravan park which has some underground campsites ($15 per person) and budget rooms. There are also a few other large caravan parks around Coober Pedy.

What to do

Coober Pedy

Just about every hotel, motel and caravan park offers a day or half-day tour to the sights on the town's periphery and the Breakaways. See the VIC for full listings.

Desert Diversity and Mail Run, T8672 5226, www.desertdiversity.com. An excellent way to get into the deep Outback easily and safely. Day tours with the Mail Run, which delivers mail every Mon and Thu to cattle stations on a 600-km triangle between Coober Pedy, William Creek and Oodnadatta, travelling on unsealed roads and the Oodnadatta track ($195). There is time to stop for short walks, photos and chats with locals. Recommended.

Opal Air, T8670 7997, www.opalair.com.au. Offers scenic flights over the Breakaways at sunset ($90, 30 mins). Longer options include flights to Lake Eyre, Dalhousie Springs, Uluru (Ayers Rock) and Alice Springs (half-day flights from $285).

FLINDERS RANGES

The Flinders Ranges cover several hundred kilometres of rugged, hill country, and are made accessible to visitors via several national, state and private parks. In the north the Arkaroola and Gammon Ranges parks are accessible on to those with 4WD or (privately owned) hardy 2WD vehicles, with Leigh Creek being the main access point if you're coming south off the Oodnadatta. The Flinders Ranges National Park itself is also mostly 4WD territory, but the majestic Wilpena Pound is accessible (via Hawker) on sealed roads. To the south, the small parks around Quorn and – on the way to the wine regions – Mount Remarkable National Park (see page 212) are all well worth a visit.

South Australian painter Sir Hans Heysen described the Flinders Ranges as 'the bones of nature laid bare' and there is much geological truth in his observation. The forces that have shaped this region make the Flinders among the most striking and fascinating of Australian mountain ranges. Coloured bands of stone, twisted and folded layers of rock and deep jagged gorges are typically beautiful Flinders forms. In the Southern Flinders, rich farming lands and small historic towns such as Melrose and Quorn rise to low forested hills. The covering of vegetation drops away in the Central Flinders to reveal the spine of the ranges among increasingly arid land dotted with the ruins of 19th-century pastoral properties. At its heart is the magnificent amphitheatre of Wilpena Pound, a feature easily as dramatic and inspirational as Uluru to the north. The Northern Flinders begins to have an outback quality as services become remote and roads rougher. The Gammon Ranges and Arkaroola Sanctuary enclose a secretive jumble of peaks and precious waterholes sheltering wildlife. The area offers superb bushwalking and cycling on the Heysen and Mawson Trails, and peaceful bush camping, wildlife spotting and photography.

VISITING FLINDERS RANGES

Getting there To check unsealed road conditions see www.transport.sa.gov.au, or T1300 361033.

→FLINDERS RANGES NATIONAL PARK

The most commanding and beautiful landscapes of the Flinders Ranges are found in this national park which is also a compact and accessible area. The remarkable geological formation of **Wilpena Pound**, a ring of serrated mountains, loops north to become the Heysen Range, flanked by the lower peaks of the ABC range. Creeks have cut deep gorges into the tilting red rock of the Heysen Range and score the surrounding soft valleys with dry stony beds bordered by river red gums. It is magnificent walking country but there are also incredibly scenic drives that roll around the valleys under the walls of the pound. In spring the land is a verdant green, then in summer the lush vegetation disappears and the mountains take on a harsh red in the intense sunlight. At any time of year the royal purples, reds and golds of the ranges and ramparts of the pound are best revealed at dawn and dusk. Thriving wildlife and good bush-camping spots also make this park one of South Australia's most popular and treasured.

PLACES IN FLINDERS RANGES NATIONAL PARK

The easiest way into the pound is to take the shuttle bus from the resort ($3.50 return approximately every 1½ hours daily). The short journey leaves an easy 1½ km walk to the lowest gap in the pound walls, **Wangarra Lookout**, via the Hills Homestead. The highest peak in the Flinders and best-known pound viewpoint is **St Mary Peak** (1170 m). This challenging trail heads north-west outside the walls to the saddle, ascends via a sidetrack to the summit, and then descends into the pound basin to return by the Hills Homestead route (21 km, nine hours). **Mount Ohlssen Bagge** is a good alternative to St Mary Peak, providing wonderful views over the entire pound to the **Elder Range** with much less effort. The trail is steep but short with some rock hopping near the top (6 km, three hours return). On the southeastern edge of the pound is an enormous boulder, **Arkaroo Rock**, with 15,000-year-old Aboriginal cave paintings. A short walk leads to the rock where signs explain Adnyamathanha dreaming. It is also a good place to see the **Chace Range**

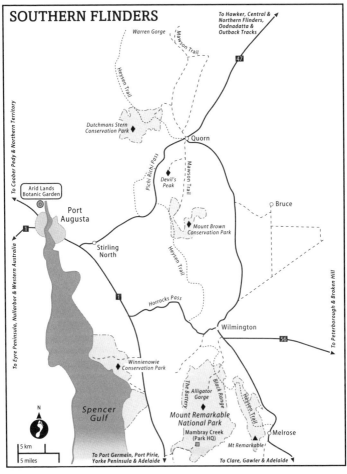

opposite at sunset (3 km, 1½ hour return). To the north there are two good walks at Bunyeroo, a easy walk through the pretty, intimate **Bunyeroo Gorge** with near-permanent waterholes (7 km, three hours return), or the **Bunyeroo-Wilcolo Creeks** loop walk (9 km, four hours), through the valley and ABC Range with good views of

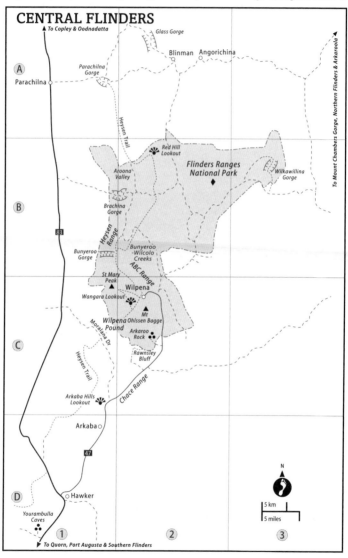

CENTRAL FLINDERS

To Copley & Oodnadatta

Glass Gorge

Blinman   Angorichina

Parachilna
Gorge

(A)

Parachilna

Heysen Trail

To Mount Chambers Gorge, Northern Flinders & Arkaroola

Red Hill
Lookout

Flinders Ranges
National Park

Aroona
Valley

Wilkawillina
Gorge

Brachina
Gorge

(B)

83

Heysen Range

Bunyeroo
Gorge

Bunyeroo
-Wilcolo
Creeks

ABC Range

St Mary
Peak

Wilpena

Wangara Lookout

Mt
Ohlssen Bagge

Wilpena
Pound

Moralana Dr

Arkaroo
Rock

Heysen Trail

(C)

Rawnsley
Bluff

Chace Range

Arkaba Hills
Lookout

Arkaba

47

N

5 km

5 miles

(D)

Hawker

Yourambulla
Caves

To Quorn, Port Augusta & Southern Flinders

1   2   3

Wilpena Pound. On the northern park border at Aroona, a favourite of painter HansHeysen, **Red Hill lookout** gives fine views over the valley, Heysen and ABC Ranges (9 km, four hours return). On the eastern boundary of the park is **Wilkawillina Gorge**. This peaceful gorge is 45 km from Wilpena so it doesn't see many visitors but is well worth a visit if you have the time. There is also the chance to see a colony of rock wallabies there. The trail follows the creek bed past tranquil pools and red rock faces similar to those of Brachina Gorge (23 km, 10 hours return). For those wanting a longer walk, the section of the **Heysen Trail** from Parachilna Gorge to Wilpena Pound is a magnificent four to five day walk offering incredible mountain views and peaceful bush camping.

→BLINMAN TO ARKAROOLA

The tiny village of Blinman, the prettiest in the central Flinders, and the highest settlement in the state (650 m), is a former copper-mining town, surrounded by low hills stripped bare of trees to feed the smelter furnaces. A drive around the **Glass Gorge** loop is recommended as is the wonderful **Blinman Pools** walk from Angorichina. This is a linear walk along Parachilna and Blinman creeks, past shady gums and sheer gorge walls to two sets of pools (12 km, four hours return).

The shortest route to the northern ranges from Blinman is via the rough, unsealed roads to the east, which allows a 4WD-only side trip to the impressive **Chambers Gorge**. Heading west up the highway you have the choice of enjoying the magnificent mountain scenery of **Glass Gorge** or the idyllic **Parachilna Gorge**, with camping spots by the riverbed. **Parachilna** is nothing more than a country pub, and its associated hostel but this is one of the best pubs in the state and shouldn't be missed, **Prarie Hotel**. Further north the **Beltana Roadhouse** marks the central turn-off, and shortest route (8 km), to **Beltana township**, now a charming relic with old stone and tin houses which makes for an interesting wander.

Leigh Creek, 65 km from Parachilna, is a service town for the massive open-cut coal mines nearby that feed the Port Augusta power station. About 5 km north, at **Copley**, is the turn-off to Arkaroola and the Bush Bakery and Quandong Café, an essential stop with the best food for many kilometres, open Easter to November. The friendly caravan park also provides tourist information, local maps and Desert Park Passes. The pub has the last ATM for hundreds of kilometres. About 55 km east of Copley is **Iga Warta** ① *T8648 3737, www.igawarta.com*, an environmental and cultural interpretative centre owned by a local Adnyamathanha family. It is a superb place to learn about the land and culture of the Flinders from this wonderfully warm family. Visitors can go for walks to look at bush tucker, land features or rock art sites, make wooden tools, or simply chat around a campfire. Accommodation is available in tents and swags and delicious homemade set meals are served up every breakfast, lunch and dinner. If possible ring in advance to arrange a visit but it is also okay to drop in and see what activities are on offer or camp overnight. Prices are negotiated according to requirements but expect to pay around $100 a day for camping, food and activities. Transfers can be arranged from the **Prairie Hotel** at Parachilna, see above.

As the ranges approach the Outback they become appropriately more and more rugged. Gammon Ranges and Arkaroola Wilderness Sanctuary enclose countless peaks and ranges, all with a fascinating beauty. It is wild, arid country that is difficult to access but this is part of its appeal. The rough unsealed roads mean that far fewer visitors reach this area than those drawn to the softer ranges of the Central Flinders. Only experienced walkers and 4WD vehicles will be able to penetrate its depths but the accessible waterholes and gorges are some of the most peaceful and striking in the entire ranges. The nearest VIC to the region is at **Leigh Creek** ① *T8675 2723, lcvic@internode.on.net, Mon-Fri 0900-1600, Sat-Sun 1000-1400,* but the main contacts are staff at Balcanoona and Arkaroola. The Northern Flinders Ranges are 105 km from Leigh Creek and 130 km from Blinman.

GAMMON RANGES NATIONAL PARK
① *T8648 4829, www.parks.sa.gov.au. Sometimes closed to cull feral animals.*
This park is sandwiched between Arkaroola to the north and Nepabunna and Nantawarrina Aboriginal land to the south and also includes a corridor of land out to the saltpan of Lake Frome. Gammon means 'place of red ochre' to the Adnyamathanha people who believe Arkaroo, a giant serpent, formed the ranges, gorges and waterholes as he snaked down to drink at the salt lake, and there are painting sites and rock engravings within the park. Europeans had used the land for sheep and cattle grazing since 1857, until the park was declared about 20 years ago, and have left their mark in the station buildings, tracks and hoof-damaged terrain. The park headquarters are at Balcanoona, where walking pamphlets, maps and advice can be obtained from the rangers. Rangers are not always available but RGS walk brochures can be collected from a box outside. Try to call ahead for advice, rangers will return all calls if the office is unattended. Most of the park is only accessible to experienced bushwalkers.

The park's most popular walk is at **Weetootla Gorge** where there is a permanent spring and delightful pools fringed with ferns and mosses. Starting from Weetootla Trailhead the track follows Balcanoona Creek to the spring (4 km) and then continues in a loop to Grindell Hut (6 km) and back to the campground via Weetootla Gorge (18½ km, 7½ hours). Ask the rangers for details of more rugged terrain.

ARKAROOLA WILDERNESS SANCTUARY
Arkaroola encompasses much of the most rugged of the Flinders' ancient mountain ranges. There are many beautiful waterholes, especially at **Echo Camp** and **Nooldoonooldoona**, although **Bararranna** and **Arkaroola** are also lovely paces. There are also many species of birds and rare native animals such as the pretty yellow-footed rock wallaby. The former sheep station provides comfort amid a magnificent wilderness, though the extremely rocky, rough roads make even short trips slow and jolting. If finances are limited don't miss the stunning **Acacia Ridge** walk. Arkaroola also has an **Observatory** ① *daily after sunset, $25, 1 hr,* to take advantage of the bright night sky. Arkaroola Village is 30 km from Balcanoona.

FLINDERS RANGES LISTINGS

Where to stay

$$$$-$$$ Rawnsley Park Station, T8648 0030, www.rawnsleypark.com.au. This property has a great location close to the southern wall of Wilpena Pound near Rawnsley Bluff and is a relaxed unsophisticated place with plush eco-villas, a homestead for 2 couples with its own pool, holiday units, a bunkhouse and a caravan park with cabins and vans. The complex also has a shop, restaurant, bike hire, and some good walking and cycling trails.

$$$$-$$$ Wilpena Pound Resort, T8648 0048, www.wilpenapound.com.au. Just outside the northern walls of the pound, consisting of attractive low timber and mud-brick buildings by Wilpena Creek. Accommodation in smart motel rooms or the vast camping area ($22 for 2). Some rooms have kitchenettes and there are camp BBQs. Restaurant, bar or snacks from the well-stocked shop. The shop also has an internet kiosk, ATM and sells fuel. The motel pool is available to non-room guests for $2.

$$$-$ Skytrek Willow Springs Station, 21 km northeast of Wilpena Pound, T8648 0016. Sheep station with self-contained, converted workers' and shearers' cottages sleeping from 2 to 17. Fairly basic but very good value. There are many bush-camping areas in the park ($25 per couple) with basic toilets, fire ring and BBQ. Washing and cooking facilities are at the main station. Skytrek 4WD trips are also available.

$$-$ Merna Mora, T8648 4717, www.merna mora.com.au. A working sheep and cattle station just off the highway at the western end of the Moralana drive. Self-contained a/c units are available, with good sunset views of the pound, backpacker accommodation, a powered campsite and bush camping.

What to do

Dedicated walkers should talk to staff at the park information centre where topographic maps are available.

Rawnsley Park Station, see above. Scenic flights last 1 hr organized from the resort.

Skytrek Willow Springs Station, see above. Skytrek is a scenic 65-km 4WD loop route on private station land, the highlight being the lookout at Mount Caernarvon (921 m).

Wilpena Pound Resort, see above. Runs tours to the main gorges; a full day to Blinman and Parachilna is $280, which includes lunch.

PORT AUGUSTA TO ADELAIDE

Covering 16,000 ha of the Southern Flinders Ranges, the Mount Remarkable National Park includes some of the highest points of the Flinders south of Wilpena Pound. Further south still is the Barossa Valley, a wide plain and soft folds of hills scattered with gum trees and neatly dressed in ribbons of green vines. It is reminiscent of Europe but the clear light, the muddy green of eucalypts and the corrugated tin roofs and verandahs make this an unmistakably Australian landscape. The Clare Valley, a long and narrow valley in the Mount Loftus Ranges, surrounded by tall gum trees and softly rounded hills, is not the biggest wine-producing area in South Australia but has more than its fair share of small 'boutique' wineries; wine drinkers have been well catered for here since the arrival of the Jesuits in 1851.

→MOUNT REMARKABLE NATIONAL PARK

The park is best known for Alligator Gorge, a sheer-sided canyon of considerable depth that it is possible to walk through if dry. The park encloses a loop of ranges, including the Black Range on the eastern side and The Battery to the west, and is heavily forested. There are extensive views of farming plains from the high points and it's easy to spot parrots and wallabies in the shady valleys and gorges. Emus are common sights, but resist the temptation to feed them as they can become aggressive. The park is 130 km from Clare and 60 km from Quorn.

PLACES IN MOUNT REMARKABLE NATIONAL PARK

The Mount Remarkable park headquarters are located at **Mambray Creek**, on the western side of the park close to the main Adelaide to Port Augusta highway (A1). The town is the major trailhead for walks and has the main park camping ground. This is very popular during school holidays and will be fully booked well ahead by South Australians. There are some lovely circuit walks through woodland here, all clearly signposted, particularly the demanding **Mount Cavern Trail** (11 km, six hours) and the **Hidden Gorge Trail** (18 km, seven hours) and there is also a linear day-walk to **Alligator Gorge**. Alligator Gorge is in the north of the Mount Remarkable National Park and is its most spectacular feature. From the Blue Gum Flat picnic area, a long flight of stone steps leads to the floor of the gorge at a point called the Terraces where the river spills over slabs of deep-red rock. A short walk leads down to the Narrows where the gorge walls close in to just a few metres across. Here you'll find **Alligator Lodge**. The gorge is 12 km down a rough unsealed road from the turn-off, about 1 km south of Wilmington.

The oldest town in the Flinders and one of the most appealing is **Melrose**, nestled at the foot of Mount Remarkable itself and a favourite among walkers. Shaded by giant gums and overflown by large flocks of corellas and cockatoos, this small, quiet town is home to a string of historic buildings. From the town centre there is an easy direct walk to the summit of Mount Remarkable (six hours return), with superb views to the east for much of the ascent. This route follows the Heysen Trail which continues over the summit to head north-west along the spine of the Mount Remarkable Range.

The wineries in Clare Valley receive fewer visitors than Barossa or McClaren Vale and consequently offer a more relaxed and involved tasting experience and the setting is also beautiful. Burra appears like a mirage out of the low bare hills some 40 km to the east of Clare. It was a very successful mining town in the mid-19th century and is the state's most interesting historic mining site. Evidence of the area's mining legacy can also be found in the picturesque settlements of Auburn and Mintaro.

WINERIES

There are over 40 wineries in the Clare Valley, almost all along or just off the main highway that runs between Clare and Auburn. **Mt Horrocks** ① *The Old Railway Station, Curling St, Auburn, T8849 2202, www.mounthorrocks.com, Sat-Sun 1000-1700*, is a small winery also serving light lunches. **Quelltaler Estate** ① *Quelltaler Rd, Watervale, T8843 0003, www.annieslane.com.au, Mon-Fri 0830-1700, Sat-Sun 1100-1600*, is a large 1854 winery with multi-award winning wines. **Sevenhill Cellars** ① *College Rd, Sevenhill, T8843 4222, www.sevenhill.com.au, Mon-Fri 0900-1700, Sat-Sun 1000-1700, guided tour at 1400 on Tue and Thu, $7.50, 1¼ hrs, book in advance*, is the oldest winery in the valley, set up and still run by Jesuits. There is a museum, and bikes are available for hire. **Skillogalee** ① *Hughes Park Rd, Sevenhill, T8843 4311, www.skillogalee.com.au, wines $19.50-$70, restaurant open daily for lunch*, has the award-winning Riesling and good shiraz. This winery stands out for its superb food served on old farmhouse verandah overlooking the vines. Self-catering accommodation is also available. **Stringy Brae** ① *Sawmill Rd, Sevenhill, T8843 4313, www.stringybrae.com.au, wines $22-24, by appointment only*, has a café, **Waldie's Shed**, a lovely spot to try excellent Riesling and have cheese or antipasto, overlooking the dam and vines.

→BAROSSA VALLEY

The Barossa is one of Australia's best wine regions and one of its oldest. The main towns, Nuriootpa and Tanunda, lie along the backbone of the valley, while picturesque Angaston is just to the east over the ranges in a small valley all its own. The area was settled by wealthy English free settlers who found the valley's soil and climate were ideal for vineyards. They were joined by Silesian Lutherans fleeing religious persecution in the 1830s. Their traditional methods of curing meats, baking and making relishes, pickles and jams have survived, along with the distinctly Lutheran architecture, and prized by visitors as much as the excellent wines.

Sitting on the valley floor, **Tanunda** is the heart of the Barossa and has a busy and prosperous feel. Near the town centre is the site of the original 1843 settlement named Langmeil, which was on the eastern side of town, next to the North Para River. Several neat and narrow Lutheran churches survive and the quiet roads off Murray Street hide many historic houses. Leaflets on a heritage town walk can be picked up from the **Barossa Wine and Visitor Centre** ① *Mon-Fri 0900-1700, Sat-Sun 1000-1600, T8563 0600, visitorcentre@barossa.sa.gov.au, 66-68 Murray St*.

WINERIES

There are over 50 wineries in the Barossa Valley, mostly clustered around Nuriootpa and Tanunda. A representative sample are mentioned below. As in most wine regions, the smaller wineries are often the most interesting and rewarding to visit, but are infrequently visited by organized tours.

Bethany ① *Bethany Rd, T8563 2086, www.bethany.com.au, Mon-Sat 1000-1700, Sun 1300-1700*, is the site of the oldest Tanunda settlement and the view over the valley is worth the trip alone, but the whites aren't bad either. **Elderton** ① *Tanunda Rd, T 8568 78788586 7878, www.eldertonwines.com.au, Mon-Fri 0900-1700, Sat-Sun 1100-1600*, is a friendly modern winery with some superb reds. **Kaesler** ① *Barossa Valley Way, T8562 4488, www.kaesler.com.au, tastings daily 1000-1700*, is a small winery in interesting 19th-century farm buildings with a fine Shiraz. **Langmeil** ① *Para Rd, T8563 2595, www.langmeilwinery.com.au, daily 1030-1630, tour at midday, free, 45 mins*, is the site of the second Tanunda settlement. Some of the smooth reds here are made from their vines which are over 150 years old. **Penfolds** ① *Tanunda Rd, T8568 8408, www.penfolds.com, daily 1000-1700*, is steeped in history and tradition. As well as casual tastings, the real buff can book a private Ultimate Tasting Experience with 24 hours' notice, see the website for details. **Peter Lehman** ① *Para Rd, T8563 2500, www.peterlehmannwines.com, Mon-Fri 0930-1700, Sat-Sun 1030-1630*, is a very pleasant winery with lawns and picnic areas. **Richmond Grove** ① *Para Rd, T8563 7303, www.richmondgrovewines.com, daily 1030-1630, Sat-Sun 1030-1630, tours 1430, $7.50, 45 mins*, is a large winery with good Riesling. A short country walk from here runs through the next two wineries and past 150-year-old vines. **Rockfords** ① *Krondorf Rd, T8563 2720, www.rockfordwines.com.au, daily 1100-1700*, is a very friendly small winery where hand-picked grapes are crushed, pressed and fermented in the traditional manner using 100-year-old equipment to make some of the finest reds in the valley. Visit in March or April to see this fascinating process in full swing. **Seppelt** ① *Seppeltsfield, 36 Cemetery Rd, T8568 6200, www.seppelt.com.au*, is a huge, historic winery, with immaculate grounds, barbecues and picnic areas. **St Hallett** ① *St Hallett's Rd, T8563 7000, www.sthallett.com.au, daily 1000-1700*, has the bargain, smooth and light *Poacher's Blend* white. **Turkey Flat** ① *Bethany Rd, T8563 2851, www.turkeyflat.com.au, daily 1100-1700*, is a very friendly small winery and their wines are extremely sought after, with many selling out fast. Try the renowned *Butcher's Block* blended red.

ADELAIDE AND AROUND

Some Australians feel it's no coincidence that Adelaide rhymes with staid and it is true that there is something intrinsically 'proper' about the city. Adelaide is clean and wholesome, the streets are neat and straight, and it doesn't have the grimy organic jumble of backstreets that some of the other state capitals do. When settlers bought land in South Australia they intended to stay and so the early stone civic and private buildings in the centre possess a well-crafted solidity, although these are now overshadowed by the usual collection of modern office blocks and skyscrapers. Colonel Light's visionary town plan gives a sense of space. The trees of the surrounding Park Lands and the Hills are almost always visible at the end of the street.

All this well-kept tidiness doesn't mean Adelaide is dull. Actually it's one of the most liveable cities in Australia. The wonderful climate has allowed a café culture to flourish, and the arts scene is thriving, with two festivals of international standing. Public transport is plentiful and easy to use, the clean white beaches just a short tram-ride away. And if the flat, open country palls, then the spectacular steep-sided Adelaide Hills are only 20 minutes' drive away. To top it all off the Barossa Valley, McLaren Vale and Fleurieu Peninsula are all easy day trips.

→ARRIVING IN ADELAIDE

GETTING THERE

Adelaide is serviced by all the major national airlines with regular flights to most of the major cities in the country. The **airport** ① *Sir Donald Bradman Dr, T8308 9211, www.adelaideairport.com.au,* 8 km from the city centre, has separate domestic and international terminals, plus a separate small terminal for **Emu Airways**. A taxi between the city centre and airport will cost about $22. The public JetBus service is the cheapest way to travel between the centre and airport. You can buy a MetroTicket; prices start at just $3. The privately run **Skylink Airport Shuttle** ① *T1300 383783, $12,* operates half-hourly (hourly early morning and evenings) between 0550 and 2155.

The Ghan and *Indian Pacific*, T8213 4592, www.greatsouthernrail.com.au, train services operate some days to Perth and Darwin. The Railway Station on North Terrace, between the city centre and North Adelaide, is for local services only; interstate trains run from the **Adelaide Parklands Terminal** ① *off Richmond Rd, Keswick, 3 km to the west of the city centre.* The Skylink Airport Shuttle, see above, links the station with airport and city centre while a taxi to the city will cost around $15.

GETTING AROUND

The city centre is compact so is easily explored on foot. See www.adelaidemetro.com.au and www.cityofadelaide.com.au for planning journeys on public and private transport. A free Adelaide Connector bus links the centre with North Adelaide and features a bus running on 100% solar energy. Another free bus service, the 99c, runs in a loop around the centre. A tram runs from the Central Business District to the suburb of Glenelg and is free for some of its route. Adelaide is very bike-friendly city, with dedicated bike lanes and flat roads. The city council runs a free bike hire scheme; see www.cityofadelaide.com.au for details.

TOURIST INFORMATION

The VIC ① *corner of Rundle Mall and James Place, T8203 7611, www.cityofadelaide.com.au*, runs guided walks Monday to Friday at 0930. You can also pre-book a free 'greeter', a volunteer who will spend two to four hours with you, helping you to get to know Adelaide. The greeter service is available daily 0900-1700.

→PLACES IN ADELAIDE

Starting at East Terrace and heading west, cultural pilgrims will first encounter the **Botanic Garden and Ayers House Museum** ① *eastern end of North Terrace, T8222 9311,*

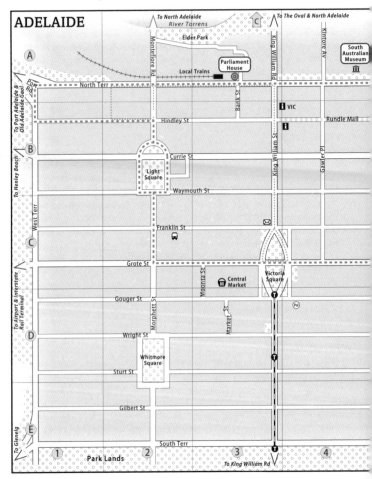

www.botanicgardens.sa.gov.au, Mon-Fri 0800 and Sat 0900, closes daily 1700-1900, depending on time of year, free, guided tours daily 1030. It makes for a tranquil retreat from the city, where you can wander around the lake and under long tunnels of wisteria or lie on the lawns under huge shady trees. It's interesting to compare the jewel-like 19th-century Palm House and the spaceship-like conservatory housing tropical rainforest species. Also worth a look is the *Cascade* near the Bicentennial Conservatory, a beautiful sculpture of a breaking wave, built with plates of glass. There is also a fine restaurant, café and a kiosk.

Cross the road from the Botanical Gardens for the 19th-century **Ayers House Museum** ① *288 North Terrace, opposite the hospital, T8223 1234, www.ayershousemuseum.org.au,*

Tue-Fri 1000-1600, Sat-Sun 1300-1600, entry by guided tour only, every 30 mins, 1 hr, $10, under-12s free, concessions $8, once owned by Sir Henry Ayers, a self-made man who emigrated from England to Australia and made his fortune from his interests in the Burra copper mine. He was made premier seven times, and his house reflects the life of a high-society politician.

The impressive complex on the eastern edge of the Botanic Garden, the **National Wine Centre** ① *corner of Botanic and Hackney roads, T8313 3355, www.wine australia.com.au, daily 0900-1730, free guided tours daily 1130, tastings $17-$34,* is a showcase for Australian wine. The cellar has a capacity for 38,000 bottles and it also includes a working vineyard planted with 500 vines representing typical Australian varietals. There is also a tasting gallery and Wine Discovery Exhibition. A wine tourism information desk supplies detailed information on visiting each Australian wine region and, naturally, a vast selection of wines are for sale.

The National Aboriginal Cultural Institute, **Tandanya** ① *Grenfell St, near the intersection with East Terrace, T8224 3200, www.tandanya.com.au, daily 1000-1700, free entry to galleries, free guided tour Thu 1130, other tours $5-$10,* is housed in a monumental building. Converted in the 19th century from an electricity substation, the place continues to hum with energy. Tandanya aims to promote a better understanding of Aboriginal people and culture mainly through visual and performing arts. The large gallery space houses changing exhibitions with a core of permanent works and there are cultural performances Tuesday to Sunday at noon, $5, children $3. Very welcoming staff, high-quality exhibitions and a shop make this an excellent place to learn about Aboriginal culture, art and history. **Tandanya Café** has cheap 'bush tucker'-influenced meals and live music or jam sessions at weekends.

Back on the north side of the road, the **Art Gallery of South Australia** ① *T8207 7075, www.artgallery.sa.gov.au, daily 1000- 1700, free, tours daily 1100 and 1400, audio guides also available*, is an elegant classical-style building similar to Parliament house, built in 1898. The gallery houses some of the country's finest colonial art. There are also fine collections of Rodin bronzes, Aboriginal dot paintings, Southeast Asian ceramics, modern art and European art dating from the 16th century, as well as a good café and art bookshop.

Next to the Art Gallery, the main building of the **South Australian Museum** ① *T8207 7500, www.samuseum.sa.gov.au, daily 1000- 1700, free*, is a duplicate of the State Library's Jervois Wing, with a long low extension tacked onto it. The museum has displays relating to natural history and anthropology, the highlights being a fascinating Pacific Cultures Gallery and an exhibition on the life of the Antarctic explorer Douglas Mawson. The exhibition includes the sledge Mawson sawed in half and dragged for many miles in agony, silent film footage shot in Antarctica by Frank Hurley and many specimens collected there. The museum's flagship is the **Australian Aboriginal Cultures Gallery**, an absorbing presentation of the world's largest collection of Aboriginal artefacts, sound recordings, photographs and manuscripts. Other facilities include an excellent café and bookshop, the Information Centre and the Science Centre.

NORTH ADELAIDE

Only a 10-minute walk north of the centre, North Adelaide is a leafy suburb full of beautiful 19th-century stone cottages. Some of Adelaide's best cafés, restaurants and pubs are clustered in this small heritage area, especially along O'Connell Street and Melbourne Street, and there's also a welcome concentration of good pubs. After walking the pedestrian-friendly streets of Colonel Light's town layout you may want to join him in admiring the view at **Light's Vision**. Head towards North Adelaide on Montefiore Road, passing the gracious **Adelaide Oval**, one of world cricket's favourite venues. A statue of Light stands on a rise overlooking the city where he is said to have often stood while forming a picture of the city's future layout in his mind.

GLENELG

Just 10 km from the city centre, and easily accessible by road, tram or bus, Glenelg is Adelaide's favourite seaside playground. Known locally as 'the bay', Glenelg has a very modern feel despite some stately 19th-century civic buildings and the fact that it was the first mainland settlement in South Australia. Jetty Road follows the line of the jetty and white sand beach and is the focus of the town's restaurant and night life. It also carries trams (free for the section along Jetty Road) all the way to the city centre. This is a bustling seaside suburb, particularly on Sundays in summer, when it becomes thronged with swimmers, promenaders, rollerbladers, shoppers, or diners at pavement tables. The **Old Gum Tree**, where Governor Hindmarsh formally proclaimed the settlement of South Australia still stands in a reserve 15 minutes' walk from the jetty.

Bayside Discovery Centre ① *T8179 9508, daily 1000-1700, free but donations welcome*, in the Town Hall, has a display on the colonial history of South Australia and the early days of Glenelg. The VIC ① *foreshore, T8294 5833, http://glenelgsa.com.au/information, daily 0900-1700 summer, 1000-1600 winter*, has guides to historic walks and cycle rides.

GLENELG TO PORT ADELAIDE

From Glenelg the broad, white sand beach runs about 20 km north to the outer harbour. Almost the entire stretch is lined with beachfront housing, holiday units, and bed and breakfasts. By far the best of the beach suburbs along here is **Henley**, which has a few restaurants and cafés encircling the small square that sits adjacent to the town jetty. A couple of kilometres north of Henley lies **Grange** where, in between his various adventures, Captain Charles Sturt built his home, The Grange. Still there, it is now run as a Sturt Museum ① *800 m west on Jetty St, T8356 8185, tours Fri-Sun 1300-1700, small admission charge*, by a private trust. **Semaphore** is a particularly good family destination with lots of cafés, a waterslide, carousel, mini steam train, public barbecues and children's playground.

→SOUTH OF ADELAIDE

MCLAREN VALE

The McLaren Vale is a lush, gently rolling stretch of countryside bounded to the north by the Adelaide outer suburbs, 40 km from the city centre. One of the oldest Australian wine regions west of New South Wales, the McLaren tradition begins with the English adventurer John Reynell arriving with vines bought at Cape Town, en route from Devon in 1838. The vale wineries specialized early in red wines, and the area is well known for its Grenache, Merlot and particularly Shiraz, though some wineries have experimented with whites such as Chardonnay and Sauvignon. The area is particularly good value with many very good wines under $20. Most of the wineries are clustered around the bustling town of McLaren Vale, which is spread along 2 km of the busy Main Road. The excellent VIC, McLaren Vale & Fleurieu Visitor Centre ① *T8323 9944, www.fleurieupeninsula.com.au, 1000-1700*, is at the eastern end of Main Road and will help with accommodation and tour bookings. The complex also includes the pleasant **Stump Hill Café** and **McLaren Vale Regional Wine Cellar**, which offers tastings and expert advice on which wineries will suit your palate.

There are over 50 wineries in the region. This is a sample of the most interesting, mostly boutique establishments. **Chapel Hill** ① *Chapel Hill Rd, T8323 8429, daily 1200-1700*, sited on a small hillcrest with good views over much of the vale, is a converted chapel serving as the cellar door. Good reds, particularly the special edition *Vicar's Blend*. **Coriole** ① *Chaffeys Rd, T8323 8305, Mon-Fri 1000-1700, Sat-Sun 1100-1700*, is a small family owned business with an award-winning Sangiovese, serves cheap ploughman's platters in the relaxed vine-covered rustic courtyard. Recommended. **d'Arenberg** ① *Osborn Rd, T8323 8206, daily 1000-1700*, family owned since 1912, is a medium-sized winery with one of the biggest ranges and some of the most respected wines in the vale. The cellar door and associated seriously expensive restaurant are in a specious renovated farmhouse. **Maglieri** ① *Douglas Gully Rd, T8383 2211, daily 1000-1630*, regularly wins national and international awards. **Marienberg** ① *Main and Chalk Hill Rd, T8323 9666, 1000-1700*, established by Australia's first female winemaker, is now owned by the Hill family. The

Reserve Shiraz is particularly sought after. In the town centre, it has a good restaurant attached. **Scarpantoni** ① *Scarpantoni Dr, McLaren Flat, T8383 0186, Mon-Fri 0900-1700, Sat-Sun 1100-1700,* has a good range with whites unusually coming to the fore. **Wirilda Creek** ① *McMurtrie Rd, T8323 9688, daily 1100-1700,* is an eco-friendly, rustic winery built almost entirely with recycled materials.

→KANGAROO ISLAND

Kangaroo Island, with high rugged cliffs on the calmer north coast and long sandy beaches on the stormier south, is Australia's third largest island, around the size of Sussex. Wildlife has thrived in this habitat, 'unmanaged' for several thousand years, in fact it is so 'native-friendly', some species have been deliberately introduced, such as the koala which is now almost ubiquitous. Patient visitors may also see platypus, echidna. Marine life is equally diverse and diving is enhanced by the 50-odd ships that have come to grief on the rocky coasts here. First charted simultaneously by Matthew Flinders and Frenchman Nicolas Baudin in 1802, sealers and escaped convicts ruled the island until official colonization began in 1836. Little freshwater and unexpectedly poor soils have, however, kept the very friendly population low, and today it numbers only 4,500. A welcome consequence is the ease with which several parks and wilderness protection areas have been declared over the last century.

PENNESHAW

This very small modern township, 56 km from Kingscote, is home to the Sealink ferry terminal and the island's main VIC. It is also one of two places on the island where fairy penguins can be seen and walking tours go from the **Penguin Interpretative Centre** ① *T8553 1103, 2030, 2130 nightly, $6, children/concessions $4.50.* The boardwalk can be trodden for free during daylight hours, but the little fellas are pretty elusive then. There is a sandy beach to the east of the ferry terminal. The helpful Gateway Visitor Centre ① *Howard Ave, T8553 1185, www.tourkangarooisland.com.au, Mon-Fri 0900-1700, Sat-Sun 1000-1600,* five minutes' walk west of town.

DUDLEY PENINSULA

Turning left just past the VIC, the unsealed Willoughby Road runs south-east with occasional beach turnoffs. The last two lead to car parks on opposite sides of the **Chapman River**, a good spot for picnicking, swimming, fishing and canoeing. Both sandy banks lead down to the beach on wide **Antechamber Bay**, but it is not very sheltered and swimming is not advised. **Cape Willoughby Lighthouse** ① *T8553 1191, tours 1130, 1230, and 1400 minimum, 45 mins, $10.50, children $6.50, concessions $8,* marks the termination of the road, some 25 km from Penneshaw. The lighthouse sits on an exposed headland with waves pounding at the base of the cliffs. Accommodation is available in two of the self-contained weatherboard keepers' cottages. To the west of Penneshaw, Hog Bay Road passes **American Beach**, **Browns Beach** and **Island Beach** in quick succession. **Pennington Bay** is another long white beach, the most accessible of the ones along the wilder southern coast, and popular with surfers.

AMERICAN RIVER AND CYGNET RIVER

American River is less a township, more a loose collection of homes and holiday accommodation along the western neck of **Pelican Lagoon**. There's no beach but the land rises away from the shore and there are some terrific views. Canoes and fishing tackle can be hired, and yacht cruises can be booked at Rendezvous ① *T8553 7150, daily 0800-1700*, a shack on the wharf. Kingscote Airport is a few miles inland at tiny Cygnet River.

KINGSCOTE TO SNELLING BEACH

As the island's biggest town, Kingscote has the only large supermarket and a number of facilities not available elsewhere, most of which can be found along the main shopping street, Dauncey Street. The town is a good base for seeing the island. Pelican feeding takes place daily at the wharf, around 1700.

Emu Bay, 17 km northwest of Kingscote on sealed roads, is a 4-km arc of pristine white sand beach with a few holiday homes clustered around the western end. From here the unsealed North Coast Road snakes through grazing land away from the sea until it reaches **Stokes Bay**, which in itself appears rocky and uninviting, but a short walk between a series of huge boulders to the east magically reveals an almost perfect long sandy beach. **Snelling Beach**, at the bottom of a narrow river valley, has no facilities except toilets but is a very good swimming and fishing beach. The last beach before the parks is **Western River Cove**, where a footbridge leads to a sandy cove.

THE SOUTH COAST

Cape Gantheaume Wilderness Protection Area is a large dense region of mallee scrub, untouched and unmanaged. On its northern border is the **Murray Lagoon**, the largest wetland habitat on the island and home to thousands of swans, geese and ducks amongst more than 100 bird species to be found here. There is a small **Parks Office** at Murray Lagoon, with details of the accessibility of the short lagoon walks, T8553 8233. It is possible to trek around the wild coast of the Cape from **D'Estrees Bay** to **Bales Bay**, but the route is largely unmarked, there are no facilities, fresh water or return transport. Only experienced bushwalkers should consider this.

Seal Bay is one of the island's main attractions, where Australian sea lions come to rest on the long sandy beach, bordered by high dunes, after three days at sea. This colony is the last remnant of an enormous population of seals almost hunted to extinction on Kangaroo Island. A wander on the beach is only permitted with a national parks tour guide but you can get up close. The sea lions can also be viewed from extensive boardwalks. Further to the west is another beautiful white beach at **Vivonne Bay**, where the Harriet and Eleanor rivers flow into the sea. Swimming is safe at the western end, near the jetty, but there is a strong undertow in the rest of the bay. This is a popular surfing and fishing spot and there is a basic campground halfway down the dirt track signposted to the jetty. Petrol and supplies are available from the **Vivonne Bay Store** on South Coast Road, 0800-2000 during summer, as per custom during winter. Yarraman Ridge here offers horse riding, kayaking, dune buggying, and hire out sail, surf and snorkel equipment.

Kelly Hill Caves are unusual in being buried under a series of sand dunes and, unlike true limestone, the bedrock above is porous. This has led to some weird and wonderful cave decoration which is eerily beautiful. An excellent 18-km return hike from Kelly Hill Visitor Centre passes through the bush of the **Kelly Hill Conservation Park**, past freshwater

Adelaide

The upmarket hotels are found on North Terrace and South Terrace, both pleasantly situated next to the Park Lands, although North Terrace is closer to the action. The mid-range hotels and apartments are to be found in the centre of the city, between Gouger and Hindley streets, with a few interesting B&Bs on the fringes. A string of anonymous motels lines Glen Osmond Rd. There are many backpacker hostels in the city centre. Rooms become scarce during the Adelaide Festival of Arts in Mar (even years) and Womadelaide in Feb (odd years). North Adelaide Heritage Group, T08 8267 2020, www.adelaideheritage.com, have a wide array of heritage properties dotted around the city from the unique **Fire Engine Suite** to the cosy **Café Suite B&B**.

Centre, north and beachside

North Adelaide has many lovely B&Bs and, apart from being under the main flight path is a civilized, tranquil place to stay.
$$$$-$$$ East End Astoria Apartments, 33 Vardon Av, T1300 858607, www.ozihotels.com.au/adelaide/astoria.ph. Modern, self-contained and minimalist apartments with balconies. Great location. Free parking.
$$$-$$ Big 4 Adelaide Shores Caravan Park, 1 Military Road, West Beach, T1800 444 567, T08 8355 7320, http://adelaide-shores-caravan-resort.sa.big 4.com.au. Standard reliable facilitation of a Big 4 in a beachside location.

Adelaide Hills

$$$$ Thorngrove Manor, 2 Glenside Lane, Stirling, T08 8339 6748, www.slh.com/thorngrove. A member of the prestigious Small Luxury Hotels of the World this is a Victorian gothic revival building complete with fantasy turrets and towers in the Adelaide Hills. Sumptuous rooms and suites all adorned with period antiques. Restaurant complete with butler service.
$$$-$$ Mount Lofty Railway Station, Sturt Valley Rd, Stirling, T8339 7400, www.mlrs.com.au. Sleep in a double-bed waiting room or en suite office and tuck into a continental breakfast out on the platform. Options sleeping up to 6 or 2 in the Club Saloon. 3.5-star self-catering facilities make this a good value option.

Kangaroo Island

$$$ Kangaroo Island Wilderness Resort, South Coast Rd (Hwy 49), Flinders Chase via Kingscote, T08 8559 7275, www.kiwr.com. Located at the southeast corner this all-in-one retreat is a good mid-range option. Eco lodge rooms and motel-style suites with bath or spa. Guest-only restaurant, shop and petrol.

lagoons and over steep sand dunes to reach the **Hanson Bay beach**. This superb white sandy beach stretches away to cliffs in the distance with huge breakers rolling in from the Southern Ocean. Allow nine hours and inform a ranger of departure and return times. A little further along the South Coast Road on the left is the entrance to Hanson Bay Sanctuary. Donate $1 to walk up the driveway, wild koala sightings virtually guaranteed.

Restaurants

The world-class Central Market should not be missed, as much for its happy vibrant atmosphere as the quality of the produce. Cafés and restaurants tend to be grouped along streets. Rundle St draws the in-crowd and although there are some gems, many establishments concentrate on style rather than substance. Gouger St is known for more consistent quality. On weekday lunchtimes and Fri nights, take your pick from one of the two cafeteria-style Asian food markets on either side of Moonta St for seriously cheap food and a lively atmosphere. Hutt St has less choice but the wide tree-lined avenue provides a more relaxed setting. Some of the city's best cafés, restaurants and pubs are to be found on O'Connell and Melbourne streets, many with pavement tables.

$$$ The Summit Restaurant and Café, Summit Rd, Mount Lofty, T08 8339 2600, www.mtloftysummit.com. Café open daily 0900-1700. Restaurant open daily 1200-1500 and Wed-Sun from 1800. Situated on the edge of the Adelaide Hills and summit of 710 m Mount Lofty offering fine views across the city. Both a café and restaurant serving Modern Australian cuisine.

$$$ Universal Wine Bar, 285 Rundle St, T08 8232 5000, http://www.universal winebar.com.au. Mon-Sat 1200-1500, 1800-2230. Extensive international showcase wine list complements simple but very effective modern Australian cuisine.

$ Lucia's, inside the Central Market, T08 8231 2260. Mon-Thu 0730-1700, Fri 0730-2100, Sat 0730-1500. A constantly busy traditional Italian that's been going strong for over 40 years. Brilliant breakfasts, sandwiches and coffee if you haven't time for the pizza or pasta.

FLINDERS CHASE NATIONAL PARK

ⓘ *$7, children $4, concessions $5.50. Visitor Centre, Rocky River, T8559 7235, 0900-1700 Sep-May, 1000-1700 Jun-Aug, park passes and accommodation must be paid for here and park rangers consulted if you plan any serious walking.*

Together, the Flinders Chase National Park and the Ravine des Casoars Wilderness Protection Area constitute the largest area of untouched native bushland in Australia and cover the entire far western end of the island. Set amidst stands of manna and sugar gums, **Rocky River** is the park's headquarters. Around the complex are picnic and barbecue areas, and various short bush walks where sightings of koalas and kangaroos are quite likely. One of the best walks leads through the forest to a series of boardwalks over pools. Platypus may be seen in the pools here around dawn.

From Rocky River the sealed road twists its way 15 km down to the south coast through virgin mallee bush to the small peninsula of **Cape du Couedic**, home to a large colony of New Zealand fur seals basking in the shadow of the impressive **Admirals Arch**. Some 6 km to the east are the equally impressive **Remarkable Rocks**. A rough unsealed road heads west from Rocky River. The right-hand turn after 7 km is the Shackle Road to Cape Borda and soon after a left turn leads the short way to **Snake Lagoon**. From the campsite a 1½-km walk heads first through thick young mallee scrub over a low limestone ridge to the Rocky River itself. At this point a boardwalk crosses the riverbed, and in the dry season there is a slim chance of seeing platypus. The path follows the shallow ravine to the ocean and a small beach. A direct return will take about 1½ hours, but a longer circular option is to follow the cliff top to the right (northwest) for 2½ km to **Sandy Beach**, take the marked track inland back to the road and use the road to return to Snake Lagoon camping ground. Allow three to four hours. The road continues for another 15 km to **West Bay**, a beautiful and particularly isolated beach bordered by two long headlands.

At **Cape Borda**, the northwesterly tip of the island, some of the highest cliffs in South Australia soar nearly vertically out of the ocean. **Cape Borda Lighthouse** ① *T8559 3257, tours 1100, 1230 and 1400 minimum, 45 mins, $10.50, children $6.50, concessions $8*, built in 1858, has a colourful history, much of which is revealed by the daily tours and small museum. Just to the south is the **Ravine Des Casoars**, where a steep trail winds down the ravine to a rivermouth beach with adjacent caves. Fairy penguins sometimes shelter here, but a torch is needed to see them. Nearby is a sheltered beach, hemmed in by high cliffs, at **Harveys Return**, a 25-minute walk down a very steep incline from the park campsite of the same name, where you can swim in the exceptionally clear water.

DREAM TRIP 4:
Melbourne→Tasmania→Sydney 21 days

Melbourne and around 2 nights, page 227

Great Ocean Road 2 nights, page 241
2 hrs (150 km) by car from Melbourne
(starting at Lorne and going as far
as Warrnambool)

Tasmania: Hobart 1 night, page 245
1 hr 15 mins by plane from Melbourne

Freycinet National Park 1 night,
page 251
2 hrs 45 mins (190 km) by car from Hobart

Launceston 1 night, page 252
2 hrs 30 mins (175 km) by car from Freycinet
National Park

Cradle Mountain 1 night, page 254
2 hrs 35 mins (180 km) by car
from Launceston

Strahan 1 night, page 258
2 hrs (140 km) by car from Cradle Mountain

Hobart 1 night, page 245
4 hrs (300 km) by car from Strahan

Melbourne 1 night, page 227
1 hr 15 mins by plane from Hobart, Tasmania

Wilsons Promontory 1 night, page 259
3 hrs (230 km) by car from Melbourne

Bairnsdale 1 night, page 260
2 hrs 50 mins (200 km) by car from
Wilsons Promontory

Thredbo 2 nights, page 264
4 hrs 50 mins (390 km) by car
from Bairnsdale

Canberra 1 night, page 264
2 hrs 30 mins (180 km) by car from Thredbo

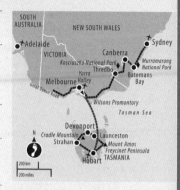

**Batemans Bay for Murramarang
National Park** 1 night, page 267
2 hrs (150 km) by car from Canberra

Jervis Bay 1 night, page 269
1 hr 43 mins (115 km) by car from
Batemans Bay

Sydney 3 nights, page 35
2 hrs 50 mins (190 km) from Jervis Bay

GOING FURTHER

The coastal route page 262
Bairnsdale to Batemans Bay

DREAM TRIP 4
Melbourne→Tasmania→Sydney

Almost the size of Great Britain and home to 5.5 million, Victoria is Australia's smallest and most populous mainland state. Despite its size it is incredibly diverse, with mountains, deserts, rainforest, beaches and plains. The state also has a rich historical heritage, multicultural people and the large sophisticated city of Melbourne. To the west is the iconic scenery of the Great Ocean Road, whilst to the east, the moist green fields of Gippsland on the coast meet the perfect sandy coves of Wilsons Promontory.

From Melbourne, you can fly to Tasmania, a heart-shaped island state, about the size of Ireland. It's a magnificent wilderness, covered in mountains and rainforest, bordered by a dramatic coastline of cliffs and meandering peninsulas. More than a third of Tasmania is protected by a World Heritage Area, national parks and forest reserves, including the breathtaking Cradle Mountain-Lake St Clair National Park.

Back in mainland Australia, the southeast coast in NSW has unspoiled beaches and stunning scenery; the Sapphire Coast idles its way from the Victoria border and has one of the best coastal parks in NSW, Ben Boyd National Park. Beyond here, heading north towards Sydney, are the little-known coastal towns of Jervis Bay, Batemans Bay and Narooma are gateways to some great parks. Inland is Canberra, the capital of Australia, with more trees per square metre than Kew Gardens. Also inland are the Snowy Mountains and Australia's best skiing and snowboarding resort, Thredbo.

Sydney has come a long way since January 1788, when Captain Arthur Phillip declared the entire continent a British penal colony. Where once were sorry-looking shacks full of desperate convicts stands a forest of glistening modern high-rises. In their shadow, hordes of cosmopolitan city workers have every reason to be proud of their beautiful city, one that, in their eyes, is the 'real' capital of Australia.

MELBOURNE AND AROUND

Melbourne has always been impressive, right from its earliest days when it was the largest, wealthiest and most refined city in the country. This former wealth, reflected in the ornate 19th-century architecture and spacious public gardens, has also bred an innate confidence and serious sophistication that gets right up the noses of Sydneysiders. By the same token, Melbournians see their New South Wales cousins as insufferably brash and hedonistic.

The Victorian capital is the most European of Australia's cities. Its laneway cafés are filled with the chatter of cosmopolitan urbanites, and its famously damp, grey weather lends the city an air of introspection lacking in other state capitals. Melbourne is also known as the events capital of Australia, with such high-profile annual extravaganzas as the Melbourne Cup (Spring Carnival) and Grand Prix, together with major showcases like the Commonwealth Games in 2006, all raising the international profile of the city – and sending Sydney quietly green with envy.

→ARRIVING IN MELBOURNE

GETTING THERE

Melbourne's **Tullamarine airport** ① *20 km northwest of the city, www.melair.com.au,* has both domestic and international flights. Terminal facilities include car hire, bank ATMs, currency exchange and a **Travellers' Information Desk** ① *T9297 1805, open almost 24 hrs,* which provides accommodation and tour bookings as well as general information. One thing you will not find at Melbourne Airport is a rail or underground link to the city centre, with the **Skybus** ① *T9335 2811, www.skybus.com.au,* being the principal budget option. It runs every 10 or 15 minutes 24/7 between the International terminal and the Spencer Street (Southern Cross) Coach Station (one way $17, return $28, 20 mins) in the city centre. Tickets can be bought on board or from the information desk. A taxi between the airport and the city costs around $50.

The Southern Cross Coach Station is the terminus for all national services operated by **Greyhound** ① *T1300 473946, T9642 8562, www.greyhound.com.au,* state and interstate services operated by **V-Line** ① *T136196, www.vline.com.au* and by **Firefly Express Coaches** ① *T1300 730740, www.fireflyexpress.com.au,* from Adelaide and Sydney.

Flinders Street Station is the main terminus for metropolitan **Metro** train services, but is also the station for **V-Line** Gippsland services. Southern Cross Station is the main terminus for all other state **V-Line** services. All interstate trains, *The Overland, Ghan* (via Adelaide) and *XPT,* also operate from Southern Cross. For information on New South Wales (NSW) services refer to Great Southern Rail, www. gsr.com.au, and Cityrail, www.cityrail.com.au; for Queensland (QLD) refer to Queensland Rail, www.qr.com.au.

GETTING AROUND

All metropolitan services are operated by Public Transport Victoria (PTV, also refered to as Metlink) and if intending to use public transport it's a good idea to head for the **Met Shop** ① *ground floor, Melbourne Town Hall, 103 Swanston St, Mon-Fri 0900-1730 Sat 0900-1300.* The shop has useful maps of tram, bus and train routes and timetables. For all train, bus and tram information, T131638 or refer to www.metlinkmelbourne.com.au and www.viclink.com.au.

Currently the ticketing system surrounding the Melbourne public transport system and trains, trams and buses combined has, to put it diplomatically, 'major issues'. Ask your average Melbournian commuter about it and they will laugh and shake their heads. Traditionally a single Metcard fare system covered trains, trams and buses. Three zones covered greater Melbourne, but you would rarely need anything other than a Zone 1 ticket as this covered everything within about 10 km of the city centre. The city operated a system of saver cards. Most services operated every day, from early morning to around midnight.

This system was set to change with the introduction of the new and reputedly state-of-the-art 'Myki' ticketing system in 2010. But its development and introduction was nothing short of disastrous and has been plagued with technical and financial

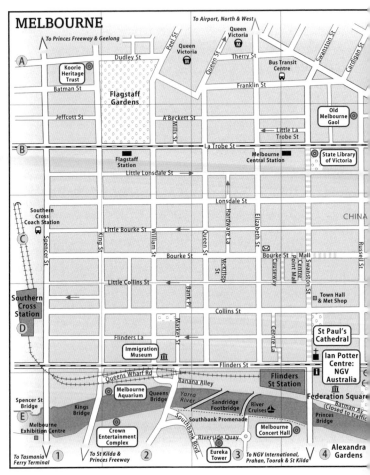

problems. So the best current travelling advice is to consult the Visitor Information Centre or Metshop as soon as you can upon arrival for the latest details. Rumour has it a special visitor or tourist-oriented Myki will be made available.

MOVING ON

From Melbourne, you can first head west to the Great Ocean Road, see page 241, before returning to Melbourne to take a flight to Tasmania. If you have extra time, you could consider taking the ferry (nine hours). For flight and ferry information for Tasmania, see Getting there, page 243. After a return flight back to Melbourne, head east towards Wilsons Promontory and then on to Sydney, see page 268.

TOURIST INFORMATION

Melbourne Visitors' Centre ① *Federation Sq, corner of Flinders St and St Kilda Rd, T03-9658 9658, www.visitmelbourne.com.au, 0900-1800,* offers information, brochures and bookings for Melbourne and the rest of the state. Also event ticketing, multilingual information and an ATM. The VIC runs one of the world's few **Greeter and Ambassador Services** ① *T9658 9658, www.thats melbourne.com.au/greeter,* where local volunteer 'Ambassadors' (in distinctive red attire) are staked around the city centre to offer advice, while 'Greeters' take visitors on a free sightseeing walk of the city centre. Greeters and visitors are matched by interests and language (over 30 languages spoken). There are also information booths in the Bourke Street Mall and Flinders Street Station. Melbourne has a useful telephone interpreting service, offering assistance in communication in over 100 languages, T131450 (24 hours).

→CITY CENTRE

Melbourne has some of the best museums, galleries, gardens and architecture in the country and recent developments will ensure that the city continues to possess the most impressive spread of cultural and sporting facilities in Australia. The main tourism and urban development areas within and on the fringes of the Central Business District (CBD) are Federation Square, Southbank and Docklands. Fed Square (as it is dubbed) is the most obvious and the most celebrated. Considered a city icon, it encompasses an entire city block next to the Yarra River and Flinders Street Station. The central plaza contains space for 10,000 people, and the square buzzes with restaurants, galleries and shops. In addition, the National Gallery of Victoria on the ground floor (which is one of two major venues) highlights the importance of arts to this city. Clearly in view beyond Fed Square is the Melbourne Cricket Ground, which is another great city icon. Often referred to as the 'G', it is Australia's most famous sporting venue. There is a well-developed walkway between the cricket ground and Fed square that has seen many a colourful procession over the years of both the victorious and the defeated.

FEDERATION SQUARE AND THE NATIONAL GALLERY OF VICTORIA

Whether by design or location, or indeed both, Federation Square has become the main focus for visitors to Melbourne, and no matter what your movements around the city centre it always seems to draw you back. Initiated as an international architectural design competition in 1996, and finally opened in October 2002 at the mind-boggling cost of $450 million, it remains one of the most ambitious construction projects undertaken in Australia. Covering an entire block, the ultra-modern city square is an intriguing combination of angular plates, steel girders and plate glass, all cleverly housing restaurants, cafés, performance spaces, the main VIC and the supremely well-endowed **Ian Potter Centre: NGV Australia** ① *T8620 2222, www.ngv.vic.gov.au, daily 1000-1700, free except for special exhibitions*, which is one of two sites of the National Gallery of Victoria. This site houses the largest collection of Australian art in the world. Across the river, at 180 St Kilda Road, is the revamped **NGV International** (same details as NGV Australia), where the international collections are displayed. Especially impressive is the 19th-century European section, purchased during Melbourne's boom period.

IMMIGRATION MUSEUM

① *Old Customs House, 400 Flinders St, T131102 or T9927 2700, www.immigration. museum.vic.gov.au, 1000-1700. $10, children and concessions free.*

A few blocks west of Fed Square is the late 19th-century former Customs House, which seems an appropriate spot for an immigration museum due to the relationship between this part of the riverbank and the city's earliest immigrants. Melbourne's culture has been heavily influenced by immigration, but this museum focuses on how the experience affected the migrants. Personal stories are told using photographs, recordings and letters, and there is even a mock ship to illustrate voyage conditions. Regular travelling exhibitions also explore the history and culture of migrants. Should you start suffering from information overload then you can always migrate to the onsite café.

EUREKA TOWER SKYDECK

① *Riverside Quay, Southbank, T9693 8888, www.eurekalookout.com.au, daily 1000- 2200, $17.50, children $10 (The Edge Experience an additional $12, children $8).*

Until mid-2006 Melbourne's tallest building was the 253-m Rialto Towers on Collins Street, but now, almost in its shadow and across the river, the Eureka Tower has surpassed it by 47 m. There is an impressive observation deck on the 88th floor. But it doesn't end there. Attached to the tower is 'The Edge', in essence, a see-through glass box that extends 3 m from the building's façade. Additional unique and impressive touches include walls that start opaque then gradually clear and soothing music that turns to the sound of grinding metal and breaking glass. There are also great views from the **Sofitel Hotel**, which takes up floors 35 to 50. The rooms are suitably impressive and there is also an excellent, if expensive, café and restaurant up on the 35th. If the budget doesn't allow for a sky-high meal then catch the lift up anyway for a brief glimpse, and make sure you pop to the toilet when you do.

MELBOURNE AQUARIUM
ⓘ *Yarra riverbank, T9923 5999, www.melbourneaquarium.com.au, open 0930-1800, $35, children $21.50, concessions $24.*

The Aquarium features the creatures of the Southern Ocean and offers the chance to get as close to these as most people would wish. Via a glass tunnel, visitors step into the Oceanarium, a large circular room with thick perspex walls. Sharks, stingrays, turtles and fish swim around and above you, so close that you can count the rows of teeth in the mouth of a 3-m-long shark. Several times a day divers get into the tank and feed the fish, and visitors can do the same (the sharks are kept well fed so they don't eat their tank mates). It is pricey, however: certified divers pay $279 and non-divers (who must complete a two-day resort dive course) $399.

In keeping with other aquaria around the world Melbourne has added penguins to its live and flippered inventory with the regulation King and Gentoo's providing the 'cool'. For $290 (14+ years only) you can don Antarctic snow gear and take a 45-minute tour of the interior before sitting in amongst them.

The Aquarium also has a simulated rollercoaster ride, café and shop.

MELBOURNE MUSEUM AND THE ROYAL EXHIBITION BUILDING
ⓘ *Carlton Gardens, 11 Nicholson St, T131102, www.melbourne.museum.vic.gov.au, 1000-1700, $10, children and concessions free.*

Due north of Fed Square is the vast and striking Melbourne Museum. Opened in 2000, it uses the most advanced display techniques to make the museum lively and interesting. Major exhibitions come and go, with some permanent features. The **First Peoples** looks at the history of Aboriginal people in Victoria since white invasion.The **Mind and Body Gallery** examines humans in exhaustive detail, perhaps more than is palatable for the squeamish. Other highlights include the **Melbourne Story**, with its focus on the social history of Melbourne and Victoria, **Bugs Alive**, with its colourful inventory of live insects and spiders, creatures with a far larger footprint (and even more impressive dentition) in **Dinosaur Walk**and the **Children's Gallery**, where the little darlings can check out their own weight and height in 'wombats'. The museum also has an excellent shop and lots of eating choices.

Facing the Melbourne Museum, and in striking architectural contrast, is the Royal Exhibition Building, a Victorian confection built for the International Exhibition of 1880. At the time it was Australia's largest building and grand enough to be used for the opening of the first Federal Parliament. The Victorian Parliament sat here for 26 years until it was able to move back into the Victorian Parliament House (see below). The building is still used as an exhibition centre, and the museum occasionally runs tours.

OLD MELBOURNE GAOL

ⓘ *Russell St, T8663 7228, www.nattrust.com.au, 0930-1700, $23, children $12, concessions $18.*

Near Carlton Gardens is Melbourne Gaol, built in the 1850s when Victoria was in the grip of a gold rush. Like Tasmania's Port Arthur, the design was based on the Model Prison at Pentonville in London, a system of correction that was based on isolation and silence. The three levels of cells now contain stories and death masks of female prisoners, hangmen and some of the 135 people hanged here. Visitors can also see the scaffold on which bushranger Ned Kelly was hanged in 1880, as well as his death mask and a set of Kelly Gang armour. The gaol comes alive on night tours when a tour guide acts as a prisoner from 1901 to explain the history of the gaol.

STATE LIBRARY OF VICTORIA

ⓘ *328 Swanston St, corner of La Trobe St, T8664 7000, www.slv.vic.gov.au, Mon-Thu 1000-2100, Fri-Sun 1000-1800.*

Designed by Joseph Reed, who also designed the Town Hall and Exhibition Building, the doors behind the grand classical portico opened in 1856 with 3800 books chosen by the philanthropist Sir Redmond Barry. In 1913 a domed reading room was added, modelled on London's British Library and the Library of Congress in Washington. The library exhibits some of the treasures in its collection, such Audubon's *Birds of America* (the library's most valuable book) and Ned Kelly's armour. The grassy forecourt is a popular meeting place for students and also serves as a sculpture garden.

KOORIE HERITAGE TRUST

ⓘ *295 King St, T8622 2600, www.koorieheritagetrust.com, Mon-Fri 1000-1700, Sat 1000-1600, donation.*

On the northwestern fringes of the CBD is the Koorie Heritage Trust. 'Koorie' is the collective name given to the Aboriginal people of southeastern Australia. The trust preserves and celebrates the 60,000 year-old history and culture of the Koorie people of Victoria from their own viewpoint. The centre has some hard-hitting history displays on the shocking results of the arrival of Europeans in 1835. There are also exhibitions of contemporary art and crafts by local Koorie people, an extensive reference library and a small shop selling some original and reproduction art.

PARLIAMENT HOUSE

ⓘ *Spring St, T9651 8568, www.parliament.vic.gov.au, tours Mon-Fri when Parliament is not sitting, 40 mins, free. Call for sitting details.*

Due south of Carlton Gardens stands the extravagant colonnaded Parliament House, at the head of a group of government buildings and the manicured parkland of the Fitzroy and Treasury Gardens (see below). It was built at the height of the gold rush in 1856 and this is reflected in its grandeur and interiors lavished with gold. Victoria's Parliament House was also the first home of the Australian Parliament after Federation in 1901. When parliament is not sitting tours are offered at regular intervals during the day; visit the website or call for more details.

FITZROY AND TREASURY GARDENS

Some Melbournians consider these gardens the best in the city for their small scale, symmetry and avenues of European elm trees. Nearby you can find **Cook's Cottage** ① T9419 5766, 0900-1700, www.cookscottage.com.au $5, children $2.50, concessions $3, a tiny stone house that used to belong to Captain James Cook's family and was transported from England in 1934 to commemorate the centenary of the State of Victoria. After sunset many possums come out of the trees in Treasury Gardens and are often fed by visitors.

MELBOURNE CRICKET GROUND AND THE NATIONAL SPORTS MUSEUM

① Jolimont St, T9657 8888, www.mcg.org.au, 0930-1630 (tours run from 1000-1500 on days without events), $20, children and concessions $16.

For some sports fans the 'G' – as the ground is universally known – approaches the status of a temple. Built in 1853, the ground became the home of the Melbourne Cricket Club and has hosted countless historic cricket matches and Aussie Rules (Australian football) games as well as the 1956 Olympics, rock concerts and lectures. Tours of the MCG are one of Melbourne's most popular attractions and include walking into a players' changing room, stepping on to the 'hallowed turf' and visiting the members' swanky Long Room. An extended tour ($30, child $24) also includes entry to the National Sports Museum (Gate 3, $20, children $16) a conglomerate of the Australian Gallery of Sport, Olympic Museum, Australian Cricket Hall of Fame and exhibitions on Aussie Rules and extreme sports. Interesting highlights include Don Bradman's cricket bat, Ian Thorpe's swimming costume, Cathy Freeman's running outfit, Olympic medals and memorabilia and the original handwritten rules, drafted in 1859, of the Aussie Rules game.

SOUTHBANK

Melbourne's Southbank is the heart of the cultural and entertainment precinct. At the western end the vast, shiny **Crown Entertainment Complex** – more commonly known just as 'the casino' – includes an enormous casino, hotel, cinema, over 35 restaurants, around 20 bars and nightclubs, and boutiques. To the west, beyond the Spencer Street Bridge, is the **Melbourne Exhibition Centre**, and the new precinct redevelopment surrounding it. On the river alongside the precinct is the *Polly Woodside*, an 1885 Belfast-built iron barque, which until recent years served as the main feature of the former Melbourne Maritime Museum.

At the eastern end of Southbank, by Princes Bridge, is the newly refurbished **Victorian Arts Centre** ① T1300 182183, www.theartscentre.net.au, Mon-Fri 0700-late, Sat 0900-late, Sun 1000-last show, comprising the circular Concert Hall and the Theatres Building crowned by a steel net and spire. The arts centre also has free galleries, a café and a quality arts shop. It is possible to tour the complex. One of the most pleasant ways to see Southbank and the impressive border of the CBD is from the river. Many operators offer river cruises in front of Southgate; the cruises depart regularly and generally last about an hour, costing about $28.

BOTANIC GARDENS

① Birdwood Av, South Yarra, T9252 2300, www.rbg.vic.gov.au, Apr-Oct daily 0730-1800; Nov-Mar 0730-2030, free. Visitor Centre Mon-Sat 0900-1700, Sat-Sun 0930-1700.

The gardens are a large oasis just to the south of the CBD. Bordered by busy roads with the city's skyscrapers looming above, it's not easy to forget that you're in a city, but the emerald lawns, ornamental lakes and wide curving paths provide a soothing respite from crowds and concrete. The main entrance is at Observatory Gate, where there's a visitor centre and the **Observatory Café**. A quieter and more upmarket tearoom, **The Terrace**, is by the lake. Check the Visitors' Centre for daily events, details on all the gardens' main features and in summer the outdoor theatre and cinema shows. There are several themed and specialist walking tours on offer. Consult the centre or visit the website for the latest details.

→INNER SUBURBS

The city centre has traditionally been thought of by visitors as the area enclosed by the circle tram, but it is far better to think of Melbourne city as a collection of inner city villages. Just to the north are Carlton, Fitzroy and Collingwood. Their proximity to the city meant that these were among the first areas to be developed as it expanded rapidly during the gold rush. **Carlton** is best known for being an area where Italian immigrants settled. It's now a middle-class area where yuppies enjoy the Italian food and cafés of Lygon Street. The neighbouring **Fitzroy** also has some fine boom-time domestic architecture but had become a slum by the 1930s. Cheap rents attracted immigrants, students and artists and the area gradually gained a reputation for bohemianism. Brunswick Street is still lively and alternative although increasingly gentrified. The alternative set now claim Smith Street in **Collingwood**, just a few blocks to the east, as their own. Johnston Street, crossing Brunswick, is the centre of Melbourne's Spanish community. These areas are the liveliest of the Melbourne villages and have some of the city's best cheap eating, edgy shopping, colourful street art and raw live music venues.

Just to the west of the CBD is a vast area known as **Docklands**, as big as the CBD itself. This was the city's major port until the 1960s when containers began to be used in world shipping and vast holding sheds were no longer needed. The area has undergone some massive redevelopment in the last 10 years or so, transforming the area into an attractive waterfront precinct for inner city offices, apartments, restaurants, shops and entertainment venues. The flagship is the Etihad Stadium, a major venue for Aussie Rules football matches and Rugby League games. It is a great venue for a walk and views across the CBD.

Southeast of the centre, **Richmond** is the place to come for Vietnamese cuisine and offers the inner city's best range of factory outlet shopping on Bridge Road and Swan Street. Greeks populated the suburb before the Vietnamese and the community is still represented in the restaurants of Swan Street. South of the river, **Toorak** and **South Yarra** have long been the most exclusive residential suburbs and this is mirrored in the quality of the shops and cafés at the northern end of Chapel Street. The southern end becomes funkier and less posh as it hits **Prahran**, where Greville Street is full of second-hand clothes shops, bookshops and cafés and Commercial Street is the centre of the city's gay community. These suburbs are among the most fashionable and stylish and unsurprisingly Chapel Street is a wonderful destination for clothes shopping.

Down by the bay **St Kilda** has a charm all of its own. An early seaside resort that became seedy and run down, it's now a cosmopolitan and lively suburb but still has an edge. Only the well-heeled can afford to buy here and though some of them aren't too keen on living next to the junkies and prostitutes still seen on Grey Street, the picturesque foreshore makes this the most relaxed of the inner suburbs and a great place to base oneself for a few days. Here also is **Luna Park** ① *Cavell St, T9525 5033, www.lunapark.com.au, mid- Apr until mid- Sep Sat-Sun 1100-1800 and mid-Sep until mid-Apr Fri 1900-2300, Sat 1100-2300, Sun 1100-1800, from $43.95, children $33.95 and family $133*, a fairground with some impressive rides and an unmistakable front door.

The rural area northeast of Melbourne is promoted as a Valley of the Arts for its past and present links with artists' communities. A path winds along the Yarra River from the city centre to **Eltham** (25 km) so hiring a bicycle is a good way to explore these leafy and tranquil areas beyond the city. An important stop along the way is the **Heide Museum of Modern Art** ① *7 Templestowe Rd, Bulleen, signposted from Eastern Freeway, T9850 1500, www.heide.com.au, Tue-Fri 1000-1700, Sat-Sun 0900-1700, $14, children free, concessions $10*, the former home of art patrons John and Sunday Reed during the 1930s and 1940s. The museum is set in beautiful bushland by the river and includes a sculpture garden with works by Anish Kapoor and Anthony Caro. The gallery has an exceptional collection of modern Australian art and hosts temporary exhibitions of contemporary art.

If you have your own transport and want to see something unique and Australian, head to the Bellbird Picnic Area (off Yarra Boulevard, location Melway 2D K6). You'll see a vast array of bizarre furry Christmas tree decorations there in the form of the largest **Flying Fox (fruit bat) colony** in Victoria.

→AROUND MELBOURNE

There is great variety of scenery and many activities around Melbourne, so even if you are short of time you can still see something of the state's attractions within a day. The Yarra Valley is a beautiful wine region with some of the most sophisticated cellar doors and accompanying restaurants in Australia. Nearby, Healesville has a wonderful wildlife sanctuary, and just beyond there is a very scenic winding drive through forest and ferns on the way to Marysville. The once beautiful sub-Alpine village of Marysville was effectively razed during the 'Black Saturday' bush fires of 2009, with the loss of 47 lives and almost all man-made structures. Although the bush is regenerating, and the village is being slowly rebuilt it is a sad testament to the devastation that bush fires can cause. Local natural sights still worth seeing include the 84-m Steavenson Falls (4 km from Marysville).

Heading south, the Dandenongs is a fine area in which to walk or drive through towering mountain ash forests, and if you're lucky you might just see an elusive lyrebird. The Mornington Peninsula, often just called 'the bay', has some great beaches as well as diving or swimming with dolphin trips, and the penguins of Phillip Island are among the region's most popular attractions.

MORNINGTON PENINSULA

This is Melbourne's beach playground, where you can swim with dolphins, dive and sail, visit some world-class vineyards, play some of Australia's best golf courses, or take a trip to French and Phillip Islands. Both the peninsula's popularity and its proximity to Melbourne have resulted in a suburban sprawl creeping down as far as Rye, but beyond this things improve dramatically. The pristine south coast is protected by the Mornington Peninsula National Park; and the beaches and cafés of Sorrento and Portsea can make for a memorable stay.

Just east of the coastal suburb of Dromana is **Arthur's Seat**, a 300-m-high hill in Arthur's Seat State Park with striking views over Port Phillip Bay. At the top there are some pleasant, easy walks in the state park, as well as the Seawinds Botanic Gardens and a maze.

Near the tip of Mornington's curving arm is **Sorrento**, its shore lined with jetties, boats and the odd brightly coloured bathing box. The town has been popular for seaside

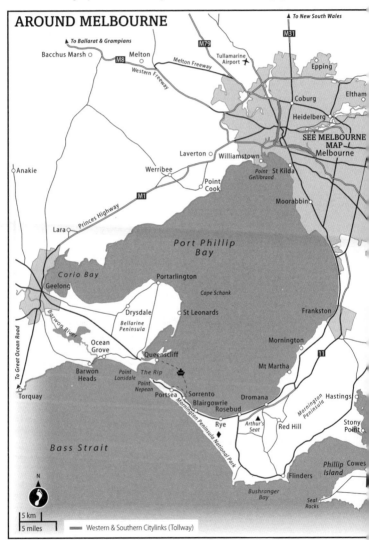

AROUND MELBOURNE

holidays since the 1880s and consequently has many fine old limestone buildings along the main street, Ocean Beach Road. The Back Beach at Sorrento is also one of the best in the state with everything from views to rock pools ideal for snorkelling. A few kilometres further on is **Portsea**, a small suburb frequented by wealthy Melbournians and boasting the stunning Portsea Back Beach. Both Sorrento and Portsea are full of stylish cafés, pubs and shops. **Point Nepean** is the long, tip of the Mornington Peninsula, where it's possible to explore the gun emplacements, tunnels and bunkers of **Fort Nepean** ① *T5984 6014, 0900-1700, $10, children $3.90.* From the Visitors' Centre there is a short drive to Gunners car park; from here you can walk to the fort, about 3.5 km, with magnificent views over Bass Strait and the Bay, or you can take the visitors' transporter ($10, children $7). Bike hire is also available from $20.

This long, straight strip of **Mornington Peninsula National Park** stretches from Portsea down to Cape Schank, protecting the last bit of coastal tea tree on the peninsula and the spectacular sea cliffs from the golden limestone at Portsea to the brooding black basalt around Cape Schank. There are picnic areas and a lighthouse at the cape and some good walks. There are also regular tours of the light station, and the lighthouse keepers' cottages have been renovated for holiday letting. There is a short walk with excellent views from the Cape Schank car park out to the end of the cape. For a longer walk, Bushrangers Bay Track is a great coastal route along the cliffs to the sublime and picturesque Bushranger Bay, ending at Main Creek (45 minutes one way).

The Mornington Peninsula is also well known for its world-class **vineyards**. Mornington wine production dates back to 1886 but was not begun in earnest until the early 1970s. The region is recognized as the home of Australian Pinot Noir, with around 200 vineyards and 50 cellar doors, many with quality restaurants or cafés attached. If you're short of time, don't miss what is arguably the most lauded of all the

MELBOURNE LISTINGS

WHERE TO STAY

$$$$ The Prince, 2 Acland St, St Kilda, T9536 1111, www.theprince.com.au. Sleek boutique hotel, the height of hushed minimalist luxury with its own spa. The 40 en suite rooms are seriously stylish and the pool and deck one of the city's finest posing spots. The smart fine dining restaurant, **Circa**, is well regarded, while the basement **Mink** bar plays the tune to an Eastern bloc theme with leather couches and more varieties of vodka than a Russian distiller on speed.

$$$$ Robinsons in the City, 405 Spencer St, T9329 2552, www.robinsonsinthecity.com.au. A quality 4-star 6-bedroom boutique B&B in a former 1850s bakery. Contemporary decor, queen or king suites. Parking available with pre-booking.

$$$$-$$$ Jasper, 489 Elizabeth St, T8327 2777, www.jasperhotel.com.au. Modernity without excess and close to Victoria Markets. Good value double, twin and 2-bedroom suites. Pool, cable TV, Wi-Fi and an affordable restaurant. The hotel also supports local artists through a dynamic foyer gallery. Discounted parking nearby.

$$$$-$$$ Villa Donati, 377 Church St, T9428 8104, www.villadonati.com. Charming and good value 4½-star boutique hotel located 2.5 km from the city centre. Chic, classy rooms with a mix of European and Asian furnishings. Fine café-style breakfast. On-street parking.

$$$ Pensione Hotel, 16 Spencer St, T9621 3333, www.pensione.com.au. Good value mid-range hotel only metres from Southern Cross station. Attractive rates can often be secured for their 'Petite Doubles'.

$$$-$ Melbourne Big4 Caravan Park, 265 Elizabeth St, Coburg, T1800 802678, www.melbournebig4.com.au. Takes a bit of finding but the best (and one of the very few) quality motor parks in the city. Not overly expensive, good facilities and within a 10-min walk to the tram or train lines to the CBD.

$$$-$ Nunnery Accommodations, 116 Nicholson St, T9419 8637, www.nunnery.com.au. Friendly, funky backpacker hostel in a rambling Victorian terraced house with a seriously comfortable front lounge. Free linen, breakfast and lots of laid-on activities. Range of doubles, twins, 3-beds and cheaper 12-bed dorms. There is also quality boutique accommodation available in Fitzroy.

peninsula's vineyards, **Montalto** ⓘ *33 Shoreham Rd, Red Hill, T5989 8412, www.montalto.com.au.* The VIC in Dromana can provide full details and tour options.

Peninsula Hot Springs ⓘ *Springs Lane, T5950 8777, ww.peninsulahotsprings.com, daily 0730-2200, from $30,* is one of the most popular and unexpected attractions on the peninsula. Located in a peaceful bush setting just south of Rye, the 17-ha complex hosts a range of indoor and outdoor pools, a day spa and a café. Recommended.

Melbourne is foodie heaven. It boasts an incredible variety at inexpensive prices. In fact, the choice of restaurants can be overwhelming. A quarter of all Melbournians were born outside Australia and there are roughly 110 ethnic groups living in the city who have enriched Melbourne cuisine. Such is the breadth and quality of cuisine that the city can now claim to be ahead of Sydney – much to the latter's chagrin. The best option is to head for an 'eat street' or area known for a particular cuisine, such as Brunswick St in Fitzroy or the Vietnamese restaurants of Richmond, and stroll up and down to see what appeals. During the day look out for the Mon-Fri business lunches at some of the fancier restaurants: starter, main course and glass of wine for $25-35. Despite the vast number of seats, try to book in summer and at weekends.

City centre eating tends to be lunch-based. For greater choice in the evening most people head for the inner suburbs, although Chinatown (Little Bourke St) and the Southbank remain busy dinner spots. There are cheaper options on Russell St. Hardware Lane, to the west of Elizabeth St, has a strip of restaurants and cafés that buzz at lunchtimes. Centre Lane, off Collins St, at first glance looks like a grimy dark alley but is one of the best places in the city centre for a cheap lunch.

$$$ Flower Drum, 17 Market Lane, T9662 3655, www.flower-drum.com. Mon-Sat 1200-1500, 1800-2300, Sun 1800-2230. Considered by many to be the best Chinese restaurant in Australia and well worth the painful hit to the wallet. The finest Cantonese cuisine in a light, elegant dining room, impeccable service and an excellent wine list. The Peking duck must be tried. Expect to spend about $160 for 2 without wine. Recommended.

$$ Cutler and Co, 55 Gertrude St, Fitzroy, T9419 4888, www. cutlerandco.com.au. Dinner Tue-Sun from 1800; lunch Fri/Sat from 1200; bar Tue-Sun 1600-midnight. Multi award-winning restaurant/bar owned by celebrity chef Andrew McConnell. His former restaurant Three, One, Two in Carlton was his prelude to Cutler and Co and his success continues unabated. Set in a former metalwork factory, the architecture successfully marries both the old and new creating a chic atmosphere that is both informal and relaxed. The brilliantly imaginative and inventive cuisine offers one of Australia's best dining experiences, provided you can get a booking!

$ Pellegrinis, 66 Bourke St, T9662 1885. Mon-Sat 0800-2330, Sun 1200-2000. Melbourne's original Italian café – it opened in 1954 and hasn't really changed much since then. It still remains a vibrant, crowded small space serving wonderful coffee and cheap pasta dishes.

YARRA VALLEY AND AROUND

The Yarra Valley is one of Victoria's best known and most visited wine districts, but not content with creating great wine some of the wineries here have restaurants of the highest standard, and dining rooms and terraces that rank amongst the most striking and scenic in the country. In summer the valley gets very busy, particularly at weekends. Just east of the valley is another excellent reason to visit – Healesville Sanctuary, the best native wildlife park of its kind in Australia.

There are 40-plus wineries in the valley, most of which offer food. This is just a sample. **Rochford-Eyton** ⓘ *Maroondah Highway, T5962 2119, www.rochford wines.com, wines $20-50, cellar door daily 1000-1700, lunches 1200-1500*, is striking for its modern architecture and has a fine dining room overlooking a lake. The excellent Merlot and the expensive modern Australian cuisine are regarded by many as the best in the valley. In summer, outdoor classical concerts add to the experience. At **Yering Station** ⓘ *38 Melba Highway, T9730 0100, www.yering.com, wines $15-50, cellar door 1000-1700, lunches daily*, tastings and Yarra Valley produce are held in an old farm building, but don't miss a stroll around the new restaurant and cellars. This graceful sweep of stone and glass has the feel of a Bond movie, and the massive terrace has huge views. **McWilliam's Lilydale** ⓘ *Davross Court, T5964 2016, wines $20-25, cellar door daily 1100-1700, flexible lunch hours*, is a small and very friendly winery with an octagonal conservatory dining room and vine-hung garden gazebo, both looking out over vines and gum woods. There are simple cheap platters and cook-it-yourself barbecue meals. The salad bar is balanced by the scrumptious puddings. **Domaine Chandon** ⓘ *Maroondah Highway, T9739 9200, wines $25-50, cellar door daily 1030-1630*, is part of the Möet group, with a stylish but relaxed tasting room with a high arched window looking out over the valley. A small savoury platter is served with each $5-10 glass of bubbly. A couple are good for a snack lunch. There are no free tastings. Finally, **Long Gully** ⓘ *Long Gully Rd, T9510 5798, wines $15-30, cellar door daily 1100-1700*, is a small easy-going winery with a very picturesque setting in its own mini-valley, making excellent and good value wines. Picnickers are welcome on the cellar door balcony.

Healesville Sanctuary ⓘ *T5957 2800, www.zoo.org.au, 0900-1700, $25.40, children $13, concessions $19.60. A few buses daily from corner of Green St and Maroondah Highway, Healesville, Mon-Fri from 0925, Sat 0858, Sun 1133*, 4 km from the little town of Healesville, on Badger Creek Road, is devoted to the conservation, breeding and research of Australian wildlife. The appeal of this place is seeing animals being so well cared for, including species that are almost impossible to see in the wild, including Tasmanian devils, platypus, the endangered orange-bellied parrot, the lyrebird and Leadbeater's possum. The sanctuary has 30 ha of bushland with Badger Creek running through its centre. Visitors walk along a wide circular path (1.5 km), taking side loops to see the creatures that interest them. Highlights are the Animal Close-Up sessions, held several times a day, when you can get as close as is legally allowed to wombats and koalas. The star exhibit is the World of the Platypus, a nocturnal tunnel with glass windows where you can watch the little fellas swimming and hunting. The most recent addition to the zoo is the Australian Wildlife Health Centre. An impressive multi-million dollar facility, it cares for sick or injured native wildlife from all over Victoria and offers the visitor a unique live view of the working veterinary hospital.

GREAT OCEAN ROAD

The three great natural attractions of Australia are often said to be 'the road, the rock and the reef'. The 'road' is the Great Ocean Road, which runs west from Anglesea, round the treacherous Cape Otway, to Warrnambool. It is truly one of the great coastal routes of the world and has everything, from stylish villages such as Lorne and Apollo Bay, backed by a lush hinterland of forests and waterfalls inhabited by glow worms and platypuses, to Port Campbell National Park, whose famous golden rock stacks are seared into the minds of most travellers long before they see them for real.

VISITING THE GREAT OCEAN ROAD

Getting around The road is congested all year, but especially in summer, when there is a procession of slow coaches. If you can, plan a route from west to east to avoid it all. Most traffic and tours travel west from Melbourne along the Great Ocean Road, then return eastwards to the city along the faster inland route, the Princes Highway.

Tourist information The **VIC** ① *Princes Hwy, Little River, north of Geelong, T1800 620888, www.visitgreatoceanroad.org.au, 0900-1700*, is for the whole region, from Geelong to Port Fairy. There are also numerous VICs en route including Torquay, Surf City Plaza, Beach Road, T5261 4219 and Apollo Bay, 100 Great Ocean Road, T5237 6529.

THE ROUTE

Start off at **Lorne**, a glamorous coastal town of classy boutiques and fine restaurants surrounded by the thick forest, rivers and waterfalls of Angahook-Lorne State Park. Next up is **Apollo Bay**, a relaxed and friendly town and a good base from which to explore the **Otway National Park**, just to the west. Among the highlights of Otway National Park is Maits Rest Rainforest Walk. The towering mountain ash surrounding the upper edges of the gully are also impressive. Koala, swamp wallabies and yellow-bellied gliders live in the park, along with the rare spot-tailed quoll. The best place to see koala is in the roadside bush around the turn-off (left) to Blanket Bay Campsite, which in turn is along the main road to the Otway Lightstation. Note how the local overpopulation of koalas has devastated parts of the bush with whole tracts of trees now dead or dying.

West of the cape the sheer limestone cliffs have been eroded into a series of huge rock stacks, sculpted by the elements themselves into a series of arches, caves and tapering sails. The most famous group of stacks, the **Twelve Apostles**, was dramatically reduced to 11 when one of the stacks collapsed into the sea in June 2005, an event witnessed by a group of tourists (minus video camera, unfortunately). The most fascinating area of this stretch of the road is beautiful Loch Ard Gorge, named after the ship that was wrecked on Mutton Bird Island in 1878, killing 52 people on board. There is a walk from a lookout over the wreck site to the gorge and beach and then to the cemetery.

Beyond Port Campbell are more rock features, The Arch, London Bridge and The Grotto. The latter is probably the most interesting but London Bridge is famous for losing the arch connecting it to the mainland in 1990 and leaving some astonished tourists stranded on the far side. Adjoining Port Campbell, beyond the tiny settlement of Peterborough, is the Bay of Islands Coastal Park, an area of countless striking rock stacks. At Warrnambool the Great Ocean Road meets the Princes Highway. Only a stone's throw from here is the long, curving

GREAT OCEAN ROAD LISTINGS

Where to stay

$$$$ Chris's Beacon Point Restaurant and Villas, 280 Skenes Creek Rd, 5km before Apollo Bay, T03-5237 6411, www.chrissbeaconpointrestaurantandvillas.street-directory.com.au. Set in the Otway Ranges overlooking the ocean this is a firm favourite for both accommodation and dining. Self-contained luxury studio or 2-bedroom villa. Quality à la carte dining, with seafood and Greek cuisine a speciality.

$$$$-$$$ Cape Otway Lighthouse, T03-5237 9240, www.lightstation.com. For something a bit different check out this large residence in the old keeper's cottage. It has 4 comfortable bedrooms and lounges with sofas and open fires, as well as the incredible position. Also 2 cheaper studio rooms for couples.

$$$ Merrijig Inn , 1 Campbell St, Port Fairy, T03-5568 2324, www.merrijiginn.com. Beautifully restored and maintained 1841 homestead B&B. Great value accommodation consisting of 4 charming ground floor suites and 4 small, cosy attic rooms.In-house à la carte restaurant and bar. Open daily to non-guests, bookings essential.

$ DSE Blanket Bay Campground, 7 km from Cape Otway Lighthouse. Without doubt one of the best campgrounds along the Ocean Road. Forming the first overnighter on the Great Ocean Walk it offers great sites with fire pits and toilets – and the odd bower bird, wallaby and koala! Arrive early and avoid during peak holidays.

What to do

Go West, T1300 736551, www.gowest.com.au. This is one of the best day tours along the Great Ocean Rd. It picks up from about a dozen Melbourne backpacker hostels between 0715 and 0820 every day, returning about 2130. Tours cost around $125.

Wildlife Tours, T1300 661730, www.wildlifetours.com.au. This has similar options with a day tour of the Great Ocean Rd from $99. Both companies offer a 2-day tour of the Great Ocean Rd plus the Grampians for around $199, and have backpacker bus routes to Adelaide and Sydney.

Lady Bay, with some of the coast's best swimming and boogie-boarding beaches, and the rugged low headlands and tiny bays that stretch away from the breakwater at its western end. The Thunder Point Coastal Walk runs along the top of these cliffs and at low tide offers the opportunity to wade out to Middle Island, with its rocky outcrops, caves and small fairy-penguin rookery. Just to the east of the town, across Hopkins River, there is a very good opportunity for seeing southern right whales from the free viewing platforms at Logans Beach (between mid-July and mid-September).

If you have the time, want to shed a few kilos and get really intimate with the coastline (and the odd koala) then consider doing the new Great Ocean Walk. Considered Victoria's premiere walking track, it stretches 104 km from Apollo Bay in the east to The Twelve Apostles. It can be tackled in whole or in part with a wide range of accommodation choices along the way, from luxury B&Bs to remote beachside campsites. For more information, consult Parks Victoria, the local Visitor Information Centres and the dedicated website.

TASMANIA

This heart-shaped island state, about the size of Ireland, is usually forgotten by mainland Australians, left off maps and omitted from the itineraries of visitors. There are no vast, flat plains here, no red dusty interior, no searing heat or enormous distances to travel. Instead, much of the island is a magnificent wilderness, covered in mountains and rainforest, bordered by a dramatic coastline of cliffs and meandering peninsulas. More than a third of Tasmania is protected by a World Heritage Area, national parks and forest reserves. Tasmania's isolation has also helped preserve many species of wildlife and flora that are now extinct on the mainland. It is a place made for adventure where almost every outdoor activity is possible, from rock climbing and kayaking to diving and bushwalking.

→ARRIVING IN TASMANIA

GETTING THERE
Budget airline **Jetstar**, T131538, www.jetstar.com, fly in to both Hobart and Launceston daily. Flights are also available to and from Sydney. To a lesser extent and for a similar fare or less try **Tiger Airways**, www.tigerairways, T03 9999 2888. Tiger also offer flights from both Melbourne and Sydney to Hobart. **Ferry TT-Line**, T1800 634 906, www.spiritoftasmania.com.au, operates year-round conventional car ferries, all called the *Spirit of Tasmania*. They sail from Station Pier, Port Melbourne, Victoria, and Devonport (13 hours). Overnight evening sailings from Melbourne daily, with a morning service subject to demand, but frequent in summer. A similar schedule operates for the return leg. Vehicle and passenger prices vary according to season and almost constant marketing campaigns. But being a monopoly and regardless of 'the spin' it is expensive. Be prepared to pay between around $1000 and $2000 (return) if you are a couple with a camper trailer (depending on cabin accommodation). Note you cannot of course sleep in your vehicle.

GETTING AROUND
There are a couple of backpacker bus operators offering full-island tours, including the locally owned **Under Down Under**, T1800 064 726, www.underdownunder.com.au.

TOURIST INFORMATION
The VICs in Hobart, Launceston, Devonport and Burnie provide information and bookings for their local area and the rest of the state. Other offices provide information only on the local area. The government-funded **Tourism Tasmania**, www.discovertasmania.com, is a useful site and lists the Visitor Information Centres. **Service Tasmania**, T1300-135513, www.service.tas.gov.au, provides Tasmanians with one-stop shopping for government services. It is mostly aimed at local residents but can be useful to visitors as offices usually stock regional and topographic maps, and sell national park passes. Most Tasmanian towns have a Service Tasmania office. *Travelways*, www.travelways.com.au, is an excellent free newspaper, listing all accommodation.

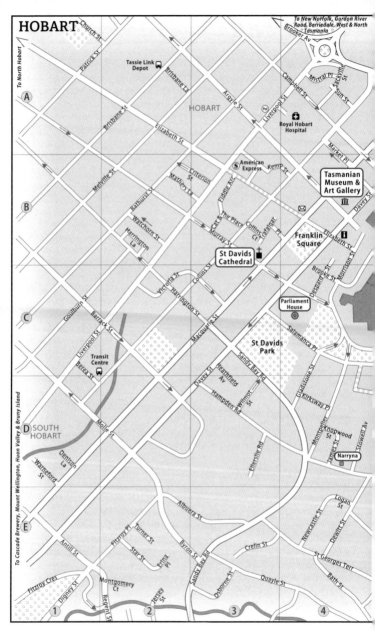

HOBART

To North Hobart

Church St

To New Norfolk, Gordon River
Road, Berriedale, West & North
Tasmania

Brooker Av

Patrick St

Tassie Link
Depot

Brisbane La

Brisbane St

Argyle St

Campbell St

Mistral Pl
Jackville

Sun St

A

HOBART

Liverpool St

Royal Hobart
Hospital

Market Pl

Elizabeth St

Melville St

Criterion
St

Mathers La

American
Express

Kemp St

**Tasmanian
Museum &
Art Gallery**

Davey St

B

Bathurst St

Fiddle Arc

Collins St

Trafalgar

Franklin
Square

Elizabeth St

Watchorn St

Harrington
La

Car & The Place

Murray St

**St Davids
Cathedral**

Brooke St

Morrison St

Victoria St

Collins St

Harrington St

Despard St

**Parliament
House**

Salamanca Pl

C

Goulburn St

Barrack St

Macquarie St

**St Davids
Park**

Gladstone St

Kirksway Pl

Liverpool St

Berea St

**Transit
Centre**

Davey St

Heathfield
Av

Sandy Bay Rd

Montpelier

Knopwood
St

James St

Narryna

D

SOUTH
HOBART

Denison La

Molle St

Hampden Rd

Whitmor

Fitherlie Rd

Stowell Av

Warneford St

Logan
St

Albuera St

Newcastle St

E

Antill St

Fitzroy Pl

Turner St

Star St

Erina
Pl

Byron St

Sandy Bay Rd

Crelin St

Devitt St

St Georges Terr

Bath St

Fitzroy Cres

Digney St

Montgomery
Ct

Regent St

Jersey
St

Osborne St

Quayle St

To Cascade Brewery, Mount Wellington, Huon Valley & Bruny Island

To North Hobart

(1) **(2)** **(3)** **(4)**

NATIONAL PARKS

Much of the scenery of the island state is protected by national parks, some of which comprise the Wilderness World Heritage Area. They are managed by the **Tasmanian Parks and Wildlife Service** ① *T1300 135513, www.parks.tas.gov.au.* There is an entrance fee for all parks of $24 per vehicle per day, or $12 for pedestrians, cyclists or passengers in vehicles with nine seats or more. Most visitors staying more than a couple of days will find it well worth while investing in a vehicle ($60) or personal ($30) holiday pass which covers entry for two months, available at any Parks and Wildlife office or station, Service Tasmania offices and many Australian travel agents. **Forestry Tasmania** ① *T6233 8140, www.forestrytas.com.au,* also manages vast areas of the state and provides access to many scenic locations. There are generally no entrance fees to state forests except for specific attractions such as the Air Walk Camping in state forests is limited but usually free.

→HOBART

Like most harbour cities the best way to enter Hobart (population: 195,000) is by sea. A fine white arch spans the Derwent River and houses spread up the surrounding foothills. The docks are lined with honey coloured stone warehouses with the modern city buildings rising behind, framed by the imposing bluff of Mount Wellington. Most visitors today enter by the 'back door', through suburbia along the highway, and don't immediately see the grandeur of the city's fine Georgian architecture and harbour. The city is at its liveliest during the Sydney to Hobart Yacht Race. This legendary race starts in Sydney on Boxing Day when about 150 yachts head south for the four-day journey to Hobart. It is a tough challenging race so when the yachts arrive safely at

ON THE ROAD
A walk on the wild side

Tasmania has the best long-distance walking in Australia, with tracks along wild, rugged coast, through spectacular craggy mountain ranges, long white-sand beaches and thick bush and forest. For most treks walkers need to be well prepared and entirely self-sufficient, although the popular six-day Overland Track (see box, page 248) does have basic huts. Tasmania may not be very big by Australian standards, but it's still not a good place to get lost and the Parks and Wildlife Service hires out EPIRBs (emergency electronic beacons) for $10 a month. The best book on walking on the island is *100 Walks in Tasmania* by Tyrone T Thomas, though *South West Tasmania* by John Chapman is indispensable for taking to the challenging tracks such as the South Coast Track. There is good information on the Parks and Wildlife website and maps can be bought or ordered from Tasmanian Map Centre. *Tasmanian Tramp*, a magazine produced by the Hobart Walking Club, publishes interesting articles on walking in Tasmania and is available at bookshops.

On arrival the following all have excellent hire services and give sound advice. In Hobart, Camping World, T6234 3999, jollyswagmans@bigpond.com; in Launceston, Launceston City Youth Hostel, T6344 9779; and in Devonport, Backpackers Barn, T6424 3628.

Constitution Dock the sailors and the city are ready to party. The Hobart Summer Festival is held during January, incorporating the race finish and the week-long Taste of Tasmania, and there is no better time to experience the spirit of the city. In more recent years (and in particular with the opening of David Walsh's 'alternative' Museum of New and Old Art, see below) Hobart has also enjoyed resurgence and a growing international reputation for the arts.

ARRIVING IN HOBART

Getting there The airport is 18 km northeast of the city centre. The **Airporter Shuttle** meets every flight and makes hotel pick-ups, T1300 385511. It costs $17, children $13 (return $30/23) and takes 30 minutes). A taxi costs around $50. The Transit Centre on Collins Street is the main terminal for the airport shuttle.

MUSEUM OF OLD AND NEW ART

ⓘ *655 Main Rd, Berridale, T6277 9900, www.mona.net.au, Wed-Mon 1000-1800, also Tuesdays in January free.*

Opened in January 2011 'MONA' is no ordinary museum of art. Not ordinary at all. For a start it is the brainchild of local gambling multimillionaire and art collector David Walsh and therefore lacks what he would call 'the wank' surrounding the vast majority of lauded establishments. It is also quite remarkable in its architectural design, with much of the complex being deep underground. A visit here (and you will need more than one) is an experience that beggars any attempt at detailed description, since your reaction inevitably becomes so unique and so personal - which is exactly Walsh's aim. As you might expect Walsh's own collection forms a large part of what is ultimately a diverse range of works from some of the most controversial domestic and international artists of the era from Brett Whiteley and Sidney Nolan to Pablo Picasso and Damien Hirst. Most describe what they see (or the experience of it) as deeply moving or awe inspiring, others describe it as shocking, while some take one look and hate the place so much they vow never to return and remain suffused with complete bewilderment - something no doubt Walsh would describe as 'job done'! One very interesting feature in itself is the use of modern technology in the manner in which you view the art; armed with an iPod and headphones it opens up access (and personal choice) of sound, interviews with artists and, yes, lots of information surrounding each piece, which has cheekily been headed as 'the wank'!

The site it is also home to the **Moorilla Estate Winery and Cellar Door** (known for excellent Pinot Noir), the French-accented fine dining restaurant **The Source**, a wine bar and micro-brewery.

There is a market every Saturday afternoon during the summer months and live music or entertainment events that are proving very popular.

TASMANIAN MUSEUM AND ART GALLERY
ⓘ *T6235 0777, www.tmag.tas.gov.au, 1000-1700, free, tours Wed- Sun 1430.*
Just north of Franklin Square is the magnificent Tasmanian Museum and Art Gallery, the former Customs House and of unusually elaborate classical revival design with its pillars, balustrade and dome. Inside are small but significant collections of art and artefacts that display the island's fauna and flora, indigenous Australasian culture and history, the convict era and Tasmania's European heritage. The café is a good spot for a coffee and a snack.

AROUND ST DAVID'S PARK
From Franklin Square head along Davey Street, past many fine old buildings, to St Davids Park. This was the original burial ground for Hobart and contains the grave of the first governor, David Collins, and many interesting plaques on a memorial wall. To the right of the park is **Parliament House**. This fine late-Georgian building was constructed by convicts around 1840 and was used as the Customs House until 1856 when Tasmania became self-governing and needed a home for its parliament. A short distance north of the park, on the corner of Murray Street and Macquarie Street, **St Davids Cathedral**, is not particularly old – its foundation stone was laid in 1868 – though both the organ and the Bishops's Throne pre-date it. The latter was made for the 1842 Westminster Abbey consecration of Francis Russell Nixon, Tasmania's first Bishop. An interesting side chapel houses a small museum notable for its collections of regimental colours and small carved stones donated by cathedrals around the British Isles and the old empire.

THE WATERFRONT
The area around the docks makes for a pleasant stroll. Opposite the Museum and Art Gallery is **Constitution Dock**, where many of the Sydney-Hobart yachts tie up after the race. Continue along Davey Street, past **Victoria Dock**, usually crowded with fishing boats, to Hunter Street. Turn right down **Hunter Street** passing many fine Georgian warehouses. This street was originally an island where all cargo and convicts were unloaded. In 1820 a causeway was built to the shore and land reclaimed after which the area developed into a busy industrial wharf. There are signs explaining the history of this area halfway down the street, after looking at these turn right and walk over the bridge past the docks to **Elizabeth Street Pier**. There are several excellent seafood

The Overland Track

This is the classic Tasmanian walk, through an area of alpine wilderness unlike any other in Australia. The Overland Track is about 80 km from Dove Lake to Lake St Clair, traversing a high plateau in the heart of Tasmania scoured and shaped by ice ages. In every direction lie distinctive and unusual mountain peaks and ranges, sheer columns and cliffs of dark dolerite. In fact the side trips on this walk are a peak bagger's dream, including Mount Ossa (1617 m), Tasmania's highest mountain. The walk winds through a varied landscape of open moorland, glacial tarns and rainforests of myrtle, deciduous beech and sassafras. There are also streams and waterfalls, stands of snow gums and native pines and flowering heath. It is undoubtedly among the finest of Australian walks and an unforgettable experience.

Like most of the Tasmanian wilderness the Cradle Mountain-Lake St Clair National Park is subject to severe and changeable weather. Walkers must have warm and waterproof gear and be prepared for all conditions. Snow is not unusual in summer. The walk is best done in November-April, although February-March are the ideal months as they have relatively stable weather and are less busy than December-January when most Australians have long holidays. The colours are richest in autumn when the weather is more dicey but the leaves of the native deciduous beech turn a golden copper. The walk itself takes about five days but there are many wonderful side trips, including the unmissable Labyrinth, and there's always the possibility of being held up by bad weather so walkers should allow about 8-10 days. To start from Cradle Mountain is the usual route as the track is generally downhill to Lake St Clair and ends enjoyably with a ferry trip.

Walkers must be entirely self-sufficient, carrying in all food, a fuel stove and camping equipment. There are basic huts along the way but a tent must be carried, as huts may be full. The standard map for this walk is the Cradle Mountain-Lake St Clair National Park Map & Notes ($10) available at the park centres at both ends. If requested, park staff can mail out an Overland Track Pack including this map, the Overland Track Walkers Notebook (describing each section and its geology, flora and fauna) and a general bushwalking guide to the World Heritage Area.

It is possible to walk the Overland Track with a guide and in considerable comfort. Tasmanian Expeditions, T1300 666856, www.tasmanianexpeditions.com.au, run a catered walk. Cradle Mountain Huts Walk, T6392 2211, www.cradlehuts.com.au, use their own private, relatively luxurious and eco-friendly cabins (from $2800, November-May).

For comprehensive access and walks information contact the Parks and Wildlife Service (Cradle Mountain), T6492 1110, www.parks.tas.gov.au

restaurants at the pier. Continue along this area, known as Franklin Wharf, to **Brooke Street Pier** where there are several offices for companies running ferry cruises.

BATTERY POINT

Just south of the docks are the Georgian warehouses of **Salamanca Place**, opposite Princes Wharf. These warehouses have been restored and turned into galleries, studios, shops and restaurants. This is Hobart's most attractive area and a fine place to stop for a coffee or lunch. Heading east you'll reach **Kellys Steps** which lead behind the warehouses to **Battery Point**, a historic suburb full of former fishermen's cottages and merchant's houses. At the top of the steps turn left into McGregor Street and follow it down to **Princes Park**. Retrace your steps to McGregor Street and take the first left up Runnymede Street. This leads to **Arthurs Circus**, an unusual green surrounded by quaint cottages. Continue in the same direction to reach **Hampden Road**, the main shopping street of Battery Point lined with interesting domestic architecture. At No 103 is **Narryna** ① *T6234 2791, Tue-Fri 1030-1700, Sat-Sun 1230-1700, closed Jul, $6, children $3, concessions $5*, a former Georgian merchant's home and now a museum of domestic life as it was in the early days of Hobart.

MOUNT WELLINGTON

Hobart walkers have many fine Tasmanian mountains to climb but they are fortunate to have one of the best right under (or rather above) their noses. At 1270 m Mount Wellington is not one of the highest of the country's peaks, but rising straight up from sea level it is the impressive centrepiece of Hobart's dramatic backdrop. There are no facilities at the top except for a thankfully enclosed lookout. The wind gets very strong at the summit and the wind-chill factor can make it 10°C colder than down in the city. The views are, however, well worth the effort with most of the city and much of the Derwent Valley visible on a clear day. One difficulty for visitors is the lack of public transport. For the latest listings for private shuttle buses contact Mt Wellington Descent, T6274 1880, www.mtwellingtondescent.com.au or the VIC. Mount Wellington Descent also offer an exhilarating way of experiencing the peak – and the road down – by mountain bike, from $75.

There are two main walking routes to the summit. From Fern Tree take the Middle Track to the junction of Radfords Track and head right for The Springs. From there the Pinnacle Track climbs for 1½ km to a junction with the Organ Pipes Track. Ignore this and continue up to the Zig Zag Track. It's very steep but the views provide a good excuse to catch your breath. From the plateau a short track leads north to the summit and lookout (8 km, 3½ to four hours). The track from Cascades, behind the brewery is longer but passes right underneath the spectacular dolerite columns of the Organ Pipes. Head along Old Farm Road past a vehicle barrier to Myrtle Gully Track. This is a lovely section through ferns next to a stream. After about 2 km on this track, and a steepish climb out of the gully, there is a junction with a rough dirt road. Turn left and continue a short distance to Junction Cabin, at the crossroads of several tracks. Take Hunters Track up to Pinnacle Road and cross the road to find the Organ Pipes Track. This is the most dramatic part of the walk, some of the pipes have vertical faces 120 m high. The track meets the Pinnacle Track, and this and the Zig Zag Track should be followed to the summit. To return by the same route makes this walk about 16 km (6½ hours) but to descend to Fern Tree is shorter and offers more variety (12 km, five hours). Both of these walks are fairly challenging and are exposed near the summit so should only be attempted in fine weather. The mountain is subject to changeable and severe weather so walkers should be prepared with adequate clothing, food and topographic map. *Mount Wellington Walk Map & Notes* is widely available in Hobart.

Connected to its northern neighbour the Forestier Peninsula by a pinch of sand, the Tasman was selected in 1830 to become the British Empire's principal prison-within-a-prison. Macquarie Harbour had become unworkable and the Tasman Peninsula was not only close to Hobart but was easily sealed off from the rest of the island and had one of the best natural deep-water ports in Van Diemen's Land. If possible, plan to spend a few days on the peninsula as it has some of the most spectacular coastal cliffs in the state and is wonderful territory for walkers, climbers and divers alike.

Port Arthur ① *T1800 659101, www.portarthur.org.au, 0830-dusk, $32, children $16, concessions $27, ghost tour $25, children $15, 1½ hrs, bookings essential*, is a name that evokes horror to most Australians both for its reputation as a place of abject misery for convicts and for a tragic day in 1996 when many staff and visitors were killed and wounded by a lone gunman. The penal settlement was named after Tasmania's Governor Arthur, a severe and devout man who believed that criminals suffered from a 'mental delirium' and conceived a system of punishment that would allow them to earn their own redemption. Many visitors are surprised by the extent of the historic site which was once a busy self-sufficient working community. About 12,500 convicts served time in Port Arthur, about a sixth of all those condemned to Van Diemen's Land, and at its height during the 1840s and 1850s many thousands of people lived here including staff, soldiers and their families. Even though relatively few buildings survived the bushfires and demolitions of the two decades after Port Arthur closed in 1877, there are still more than 30 historic buildings open to visitors. Whilst the prisoners lived in abject misery, the staff and their families enjoyed the setting and facilities, and the harbour, green lawns and crumbling ruins are quite beautiful. The church, gardens and Commandant's home lend the place the air of an English village and it would have been easy to forget the prisoners in later years as they were locked up in the chilling solitary confinement of the Separate Prison. Built in 1849 and modelled on Pentonville, this cruciform building drove many convicts insane and the extraordinary chapel illustrates well just how merciless this attempt at prison reform was. The entrance fee includes an orientation tour and a short boat trip around Point Puer, where boys were kept separately from the corrupting influence of hardened crims, and the Isle of the Dead.

Near the wharf, by the remains of the Broad Arrow Café, there is a poignant memorial garden dedicated to the 35 people killed here and nearby in 1996 (staff ask that visitors refrain from asking them about the incident). Allow at least half a day, preferably more, to explore the site. If staying overnight don't miss the ghost tour. If ghosts do exist there is no more likely place to find them and the guides make the stroll by lantern as scary as possible. There are cafes, picnic tables and a shop on site.

Just north of Eaglehawk Neck is a scenic lookout over the lovely Pirates Bay and Tasman National Park. At the northern end of the bay is the **Tessellated Pavement**, a rock slab that has vertical and horizontal lines scored into it, making it look like cobblestones. **Eaglehawk Neck** itself is a scrawny bit of sand barely 50 m wide. There are some remains here of soldiers' barracks, relics of convict days when dogs were chained across the narrowest part of the peninsula to pounce on escapees. Just south of Pirates Bay are **Tasman Blowhole**, only worth seeing when there are high seas, **Tasman Arch** and **Devils Kitchen**, both high sheer cliffs skirted by boiling surf. The **Tasmanian Devil Park** ① *Arthur Highway, Taranna, T6250 3230, www.tasmaniandevilpark.com, 0900-1700, $32, children $16, Devil feeding daily at 1100, Kings of the Wind daily 1115*, focuses on wildlife rescue and rehabilitation and native animals such as devils, quolls, possums and parrots can be seen on the 900-m park walk. A bird of prey show is one of the main attractions.

Tasman National Park, along the eastern and southern edges of the peninsula, encompasses some of Tasmania's most dramatic coastal scenery and is much more accessible than the isolated south-west coast. The main walk in this area is the **Tasman Coastal Track** from Tasman's Arch to Cape Pillar (three to four days), following the coast to the turquoise water and white sand of Fortescue Bay, then heading inland to reach the end of the cape. Alternatively start at Devil's Kitchen and walk to Tatnells Hill (four hours return), or continue to Fortescue Bay (17 km) where there are good campsites. Both of these walks include waterfalls, wildflowers and extensive cliff-top views. From Fortescue Bay there is a magnificent four-hour walk to **Cape Huay**. South of Port Arthur are yet more wonderful coastal walks. There is a track out to **Cape Raoul** along high and exposed coastal cliffs and an excellent short walk to **Mount Brown** and the sparklingly white and isolated **Crescent Bay** beach (three hours). Beach lovers will also enjoy **Lagoon Beach**, a surf beach hidden by high dunes at the north western tip of the peninsula. There is an easy 3 km walking track from Lime Bay. These walks are well marked but for more detail see the *Tasman Coastal Track Map & Notes*, available from map shops in Hobart.

Facilities on the peninsula are concentrated in the small service town of **Nubeena**, with just a store at Port Arthur that also doubles as a post office, takeaway and petrol station. The Port Arthur visitor centre doubles as a regional **VIC** ① *T1800 659101, www.portarthur.org.au, 0900-1700*.

→FREYCINET NATIONAL PARK

① *T6257 7000, www.parks.tas.gov.au. Information and maps are available from the Park Visitor Centre and East Coast Interpretation Centre close to the park border.*

One of Australia's great national parks, Freycinet is best known for **Wineglass Bay**, a perfect arc of aquamarine sea with a fine rim of white sand. The bay is hidden from view on the eastern coast of the park and the half-hour climb over a low saddle to the Wineglass Bay lookout is one of Tasmania's most popular short walks. On the western side the rugged red-granite domes of the **Hazards** range stand shoulder to shoulder between two low sandy necks. Beyond are the forests, rocky coves and remote beaches of the mountainous southern peninsula and **Schouten Island**. The park also includes a narrow coastal strip to the north, protecting the Friendly Beaches, miles of pristine white sand and sparkling clear water. Other lovely spots on the east coast of the park are **Cape Tourville** and **Sleepy Bay**, which is great for snorkelling, although beginners may prefer the more sheltered water at beautiful **Honeymoon Bay**.

All walks start from the walking track car park at the end of the sealed road. The classic walk is the short walk to the Wineglass Bay lookout (one hour return). To extend this walk continue down to the beach for the **Wineglass Bay-Hazards Beach circuit** (11 km, five hours). Just before reaching the beach a track off to the right leads across the swampy isthmus to Hazards Beach. Then heading north, the track continues up the beach and around the coastline back to the car park. The Hazards are less than 500 m but provide wonderful views. With care , well equipped and in the right conditions it is possible to walk to the summit of **Mount Amos** (454 m) for the best views of Wineglass Bay and the peninsula (three hours return). Do not attempt in bad weather. These day walks can be combined for an overnight circuit walk to the summit of **Mount Graham** (579 m) along easy formed tracks and beaches.

→LAUNCESTON, DEVONPORT AND AROUND

This area is one of the most populous areas of Tasmania and also encompasses diverse and spectacular countryside. Launceston itself is a gracious river city, notable for its lovely Cataract Gorge right in the heart of the city. To the north are the tame agricultural lands of the Tamar Valley, an expanding wine region, with a small remnant of bush at the tip, the Narawntapu National Park, which is known for its scores of grazing wombats. To the east is the dramatic dark plateau of Ben Lomond, one of few Tasmanian mountains that has a road up to the summit, albeit an alarming one. Devonport provides the first glimpse of Tasmania for many visitors and as a busy industrial port city it gives little indication of what is to come. However, just south of Devonport and clearly visible on a cloudless day, are the magnificent mountain ranges of the Great Western Tiers. The cliffs of the Tiers mark an abrupt drop from the Central Plateau to the fertile plains below. Farmers settled the area around Sheffield and Mole Creek and thought it so idyllic they named some parts of it Paradise, Promised Land and No Where Else. The fertility and gentle climate of the north coast mean it is one of the more populous areas of Tasmania but most visitors will hardly notice this. Great walking, forest, waterfalls, caves and wildlife can all be found.

LAUNCESTON

Launceston is an attractive little city of gardens and historic buildings surrounded by the hills at the head of the Tamar Valley, 173 km from Coles Bay and 98 km from Hobart. It is an important second city and a useful base for travellers. Established in 1806, it is Australia's oldest provincial centre and contains some of the country's best examples of Edwardian and Federation architecture. The Cataract Gorge is in the heart of the city and is surrounded by acres of parkland. The city celebrates the riches of the area with the Tamar Valley Festival of the Senses in mid-February. The festival celebrates food, wine, music and theatre with a three-day party in City Park. The VIC ① *12-16 St John St, T1800 651 827,www.visitlauncestontamar.com.au, Mon-Fri 0900-1700, Sat 0900- 1500, Sun 0900-1500*, handles bookings and information for the north of the state.

PLACES IN LAUNCESTON

To see a sample of the city's architecture, walk east from City Park along historic Cameron Street. At the junction of St John Street is the elaborate post office and the grand, white Town Hall with its Corinthian columns. Walk through the civic centre, cross Charles Street and continue along Cameron to see some wonderful terraces. A cruise up the Tamar is also a fine way to get acquainted with the area.

Queen Victoria Museum and Art Gallery ① *2 Wellington St, T6323 3777, www.qvmag.tas.gov.au, 1000-1700, free; planetarium shows Tue-Sat 1500, $5, children $3*, has Tasmania's finest colonial art collection, featuring the works of John Glover and Tom

Roberts, and is housed in a complex at the Inveresk Railyards on the far side of the river. The museum's natural sciences and zoology collections are housed separately in Wellington Street and if you haven't managed to spot a Tasmanian tiger in the wild they include a stuffed specimen. There is also a planetarium here projecting images of the southern sky. Also at the railyards on Sundays is the **Inveresk Market**, a community market with art, food and bric-a-brac stalls and live bands. Launceston also has several places to look at contemporary art and design. **The Design Centre of Tasmania** ① *corner Tamar and Brisbane streets, T6331 5506, 0930-1730, $2.20*, features Tasmania furniture, regular design exhibitions and a shop with high quality craftwork. Next door is the **Wood Design Collection** ① *T6334 6558, Mon-Fri 0930-1730, small entry fee*, displaying what the state's finest craftspeople can do with Tasmania's beautiful timbers such as Huon and Sassafras. It was established with funding from Forestry Tasmania in 1991 and grows every second year when the best new work is selected and purchased from the Wood Design Biennial in Hobart. Art and craft of a different kind can be found at the **National Automobile Museum** ① *86 Cimitiere St, parking in Willis St, T6334 8888, Sep-May 0900-1700, Jun-Aug 1000-1600, $12, $6.20 children*, which has a collection of British and European vintage and veteran classic cars, sports cars and motorcycles. All of the cars are on loan so the collection changes regularly as the owners take their cars out for a spin or on tour.

CATARACT GORGE RESERVE

① *Chairlift daily 0900-1630, Jul-Aug 1000-1600. $12 return, children $8.*

The gorge that drains the South Esk River into the Tamar is one of the most spectacular on the island, a long, wide chasm with steep sides of tiered, jumbled rock, and ridiculously accessible; the entrance is only a 10-minute walk from the city centre. The gorge extends inland for about 1 km before widening out into a huge grassed and forested natural amphitheatre at the centre of which is a wide stretch of water, First Basin. Just above this is Alexandra Suspension Bridge which allows a pleasant three-hour circular walk from the mouth of the gorge at Kings Bridge. This walk starts up the steep, winding Zig-zag Track to the First Basin, from there across the bridge to the reserve's main kiosk and restaurant at Cliff Grounds, and then back along the flat Main Track, at the base of the gorge's northern wall, to Kings Bridge. Further walks radiate out from Cliff Grounds. There is a car park at the rise where the reserve meets the outer suburbs at Basin Road, and from here a chairlift operates across First Basin to Cliff Grounds. Further walks radiate out from Cliff Grounds, some taking in lookouts, and one heading a further couple of kilometres upriver to the disused **Duck Reach Power Station**. At Cliff Grounds comprise a small takeaway kiosk open during the day, a restaurant (open Tue-Sun 1200-1430, Tue-Sat 1630-2000), and toilets. The 51 and 52 buses drop-off at the bottom of Basin Rd, then a 10-minute walk.

DEVONPORT

Sprawling between the mouths of the rivers Don and Mersey, 100 km from Launceston and 50 km from Burnie, Devonport is a major commercial port as well as the home dock of the Bass Strait and Sydney ferries, *The Spirits of Tasmania*. It is a practical city that lacks the fine colonial architecture of Launceston and Hobart, but there is a pleasant foreshore area and it is possible to walk from the Mersey River to the Don River. From the VIC, head north past the Maritime Museum and out to Tiagarra and the lighthouse at Mersey Bluff.

Maritime Museum ① *Gloucester Av, T6424 7100, Tue-Sun 1000-1600, small entry fee*, recounts Devonport's long connection to the sea as both port and shipyard. This former harbourmaster's house still has its original signal mast and lookout from pre-radio days. The museum has displays on maritime and local history. **Tiagarra** ① *Bluff Rd, T6424 8250, 0900-1700, small entry fee*, is an Aboriginal keeping place on the site of a young men's hunting ground. The museum has a fairly dusty, static display but has some interesting exhibits such as a rare stone axe and photographs of Tasmanian Aboriginals. There is also a walking track around the bluff past about a dozen fascinating rock engravings. Staff welcome visitors wanting a chat about Aboriginal culture and history and offer free beverages in the mornings. The VIC ① *Formby Rd, T6424 4466, www.devonport tasmania.travel, 0900-1700; in summer from 0730.*

→WILDERNESS WORLD HERITAGE AREA

The Wilderness World Heritage Area covers one fifth of Tasmania, virtually the whole of the southwest corner, and was proposed and negotiated by the Federal Government in the early 1980s, partly as a way of blocking the state government's moves to dam the Franklin River. The region is split into a number of parks and reserves, but these mark human boundaries and do not define particularly different physical areas. It is a gloriously rugged region, covered in thick bush and low but craggy mountains that can swallow unwary or ill-prepared walkers, never to be seen again. The Wilderness is traversed by just one road and penetrated a certain way by a couple more. Other than these the only ways of really seeing region are by air or by tackling one of the great walking tracks. The Overland is generally regarded as the most dramatic track through the area, but not the most challenging, and so is by far the most popular; see box, page 248. It is frequently cited as the most memorable long-distance walk in Australia.

CRADLE MOUNTAIN
① *T6492 1110, www.parks.tas.gov.au, 0800-1700 (1800 in summer), standard park entry fees apply. It's 181 km from Launceston and 91 km from Devonport.*

The most famous and beautiful of Tasmania's mountains, Cradle Mountain is set in a narrow ridge of jagged dolerite peaks at the northern end of the Cradle Mountain-Lake St Clair National Park. Often wearing a balaclava of cloud, visitors must be fortunate to see the mountain on one of about 30 clear days a year. The surrounding country of striking mountains, alpine moorland, glacial lakes and forested valleys offers some of the most spectacular wilderness walking in the world as well as accessible short walks. Parks and Wildlife operate a visitor centre, about 7 km from Dove Lake, where visitors can pick up a free guide to short walks in the area and obtain information and advice on the park. The centre also sells topographic maps, guide books and some cold-weather clothing. The merchandise is cheaper here than elsewhere in the village and all profits are returned to the park.

There are many lovely short walks in the area around the park centre and **Cradle Mountain Lodge** but Dove Lake and Cradle Mountain are the main attraction. The **Dove Lake Circuit** (6 km, two hours) stays close to the shore of the lake and covers easy terrain accessible to all. When the mountain is visible and the surface of the lake unruffled this is an impossibly beautiful walk and is still worth doing, even in less than ideal conditions. There is also a more challenging **upper circuit** that allows views over the park in every direction. For the best views a walk to **Hansons Peak** or **Marions Lookout**, on the western side of the lake, is recommended (both about two hours return). **Crater Lake** and **Lake Lilla** also make for picturesque short walks. The Lodge shop (open daily 0900-1700) hires out waterproof jackets and trousers by the day.

LAKE ST CLAIR

At the southern end of the **Cradle Mountain-Lake St Clair National Park**, Lake St Clair fills a basin carved out by glaciers many thousands of years ago and lies between formidable mountain ranges covered in forest down to the shoreline. This finger lake is about 11 km long and 2 km wide and, at 167 m deep, is the deepest lake in Australia. A walking track follows the length of the shore providing tranquil views of Mount Olympus, the Traveller Range and pointy Mount Ida. However, the most leisurely way to see the lake is to take the ferry from Cynthia Bay in the south to Narcissus Bay in the north, where walkers are collected, and return. The park facilities are based at **Cynthia Bay** where there is a striking modern park centre with interpretative displays on the geology, history and fauna of the park. Park rangers often provide guided walks, talks and slide shows in the busy summer season. There is also a café overlooking the lake and an accommodation booking office. The park centre ① *T6289 1172, www.parks.tas.gov.au, 0800-1700 Mar-Nov, 0800-1900 Dec-Feb, standard park fees apply*, is opposite the cafe.

Lake St Clair is the end of the **Overland Track** for many walkers but it is also a fine walking destination for shorter walks ranging from one hour to two or three days. Walkers should be prepared for all weather conditions with warm and waterproof layers of clothing. One of the most popular walks begins with catching the ferry to **Narcissus Bay** then returning to Cynthia Bay on foot via the Overland Track along the lake shore (five to seven hours walking). On a fine day don't miss the walk to the summit of **Mount Rufus** (1416 m), from which you can see most of the peaks of this national park as well as many in the Southwest National Park. For experienced walkers, spending a few days in the **Labyrinth and Acropolis** area is recommended, only a day's walk from Narcissus Bay. This is a high, relatively level area that has been heavily glaciated, full of lovely tarns and closely surrounded by rugged cliffs and peaks. Walking expert Tyrone T Thomas describes this area as a 'world treasure'. For details consult walking guides and topographic maps and discuss plans with staff at the park centre. The *Lake St Clair Day Walk Map* is available at the park centre.

→THE WEST COAST

Like so much of Tasmania the west coast has been shaped by the elements. Subject to the fierce gales of the 'Roaring Forties' the coast has huge seas, high rainfall and the interior is covered in dense impenetrable forest. Although Tasmanian Aboriginals are known to have lived in this area and survived on its resources, European settlers only penetrated the west for the purposes of punishment and commerce. The whole coast has just one sheltered natural harbour, though it happens to be one of Australia's biggest – over 30 km long by 10 km wide. It was inside Macquarie Harbour that colonial authorities decided to build a penal settlement, at the ends of the earth and entered through 'Hell's Gate'. Later, the pretty village of Strahan was founded inside the harbour by loggers and fishermen and is now the main drawcard of the west coast for cruises up the magnificent

TASMANIA LISTINGS

Where to stay

Hobart and Richmond

$$$ Battery Point Manor, 13 Cromwell St, T6224 0888, www.batterypoint manor.com.au. This B&B has 8 huge, individual en suite rooms with harbour views, a cheerful, sunny dining room and very friendly hosts. A 2-bedroom cottage is also available.

$$$ The Richmond Barracks, 16 Franklin St, Richmond, T03 6260 2453, www.richmond barracks.com. Three beautifully restored self-contained heritage cottages in a former barracks. Enjoy all the comforts the former colonial officer could only have dreamt about!

$$-$ Hobart Airport Tourist Park, 1 Holyman Av, Cambridge, T1800 441 184. A new facility in a convenient location for both city and airport. Cabins and vans of a good standard. Camp kitchen and airport shuttle.

$$-$ Montgomery's, 9 Argyle St, T03 6231 2660, www.montgomerys.com.au. Smart, contemporary en suite rooms, budget doubles, and excellent backpacker dorms (YHA), each with linen, heater and phone.

East Coast

$$$$-$$$ Freycinet Lodge, Freycinet National Park, T1800 420 155, www.freycinet lodge.com.au. Around 60 timber cabins and the lodge are tucked away in bush facing Coles Bay. The lodge organizes lots of daily activities such as nocturnal wildlife walks, and has a bar and 2 restaurants open to all.

$$ Pub in the Paddock, 24 km out of St Helens the road slips back down to Pyengana, T6373 6121, www.pubinthepaddock.com.au. The pub is an 1880s homestead, first licensed in 1901, with a cosy, rustic but smart front bar and bistro and 6 good value double rooms.

Cradle Mountain

Cradle Valley has some superb expensive accommodation but little for those on a budget. Book as far in advance as possible for the Dec-Easter period and visit midweek in summer.

$$$$-$$$ Peppers Cradle Mountain Lodge, T03 6492 2100, www.cradlemountain lodge.com. 98 luxurious cabins with woodfires (but no TV, phone, or cooking) dotted around a large wooden alpine lodge. The lodge has quiet reading rooms, a bar, and every conceivable facility such as massage, sauna, bike hire, internet, wilderness slide shows, guided walks and nocturnal wildlife-spotting tours.

$$$-$ Cradle Mountain Tourist Park, T03 6492 1395, www.cosycabins.com.au. This is the only option for camper vans and tents. It is well facilitated but overpriced. Simple self-contained cabins, a large campground, basic alpine huts and a large warm kitchen. Bookings essential in summer, even for campsites.

West Coast

$$$$ Risby Cove, The Esplanade, Strahan, T03 6471 7572. www.risby.com.au. Former sawmill now housing chic 1 or 2-bedroom suites, in-house café/restaurant and art gallery, all overlooking the waterfront. Restaurant open daily 0700-1800.

$$$ Franklin Manor, Esplanade, T6471 7311, www.franklinmanor.com.au. Luxurious traditional boutique hotel. Cosy guest lounges, deep-red-walled dining rooms with log fires and dark wood furniture, and 14 en suite rooms. Meals are expensive, uncomplicated but delicious, and complemented by one of the state's best wine lists. Bookings required.

$$$ Renison Cottages, 32-36 Harvey St, Strahan, T03 6471 7057. Www.renison cottages.com.au. Four stylish, former miners cottages in a quiet bush setting close to the town centre. Fully self-contained, open fires and bath/spas.

Restaurants

Hobart

$$ Boathouse, Cornelian Beach, T6228 9289. Daily 1200-1500, Mon-Sat 1800-2130.Wonderful, solitary location on the lawns of this small bay. The large dining room is modern, sophisticated but relaxed and makes the best of the location. The food is an interesting medley of dishes and includes good veggie options. Superb value cheap lunches.

$$-$ Mures, between Constitution Dock and Victoria Dock. Something of a Hobart landmark, the ground floor is a large fish and chip café and fresh fish shop, open daily 0800-2100. The first floor is a significantly more refined seafood restaurant, open daily 1200-1430, 1800-2130.

$ Jackman and McRoss, 57 Hampden Rd, Battery Point, T6223 3186. Daily 0730-1700.This café-bakery makes the best bread in Hobart and a breakfast of fresh croissants here in the simple wooden cottage is a must, if you can get in the door. For lunch try the pies, sandwiches and tarts.

What to do

Hobart

Hobart Historic Tours, T03-6238 4222. Various local walk options departing from the Travel Centre, corner Davey & Elizabeth streets. Tue-Sat 1500, Sun 0930. Pub tour departs 1700, from $30.

Lady Nelson Tall-ship,Elizabeth St Pier, T03-6234 3348, www.ladynelson.org.au. Local cruises at weekends aboard the 1798 tall-ship, from $25.

West Coast

Rafting Tasmania,T03-6239 1080. www.raftingtasmania.com. Founded by Graham Mitchell, one of the first 50 people to raft the Franklin and has done more than 100 trips. The company now runs 5-, 7- and 10-day trips Nov-Apr for 4-8 people ($1750-$2700). The experience of a lifetime.

World Heritage Cruises,The Esplanade. T03-6471 7174, www.world heritagecruises.com.au. Well-established operator offering half-day cruises up the Gordon River, from $99, child $50.

East Coast

Freycinet Adventures, Coles Bay, T03-6257 0500,www.freycinetadventures.com.au. Extensive range of guided kayak trips from 3 hrs to 4 days, from $95. Also offer independent kayak hire from $55 per day and a water taxi service.

Gordon River and to the convict ruins on Sarah Island. Just inland are the small, quiet towns of Queenstown, Rosebery, Zeehan and Tullah, established as mining and 'hydro' towns and providing routes north and east.

STRAHAN

Hugging the small bay of Risby Cove, a tiny inlet on giant Macquarie Harbour, Strahan began in the 1870s as a convenient base for those wanting to plunder the area's considerable resources, first the Huon timber cutters, the 'piners', and then the miners who ran a railway to Strahan from Queenstown. Now it is the convenient and hugely popular base for those wanting simply to see the region's quite astounding natural beauty. Pretty as it is, there is actually little to see and do in the small town itself, though a stroll around the cove is always satisfying and there is a wonderful 40-minute return walk to **Hogarth Falls** from the Peoples Park. The VIC ① *the Esplanade, T6471 7622, strahan@tasvisinfo.com.au, 1000-2000 from Nov-Apr, 1100-1800 otherwise, interactive display $2, children free*, incorporates a superb interactive display on the controversial aspects of local Aboriginal, convict and environmental history.

   Macquarie Harbour, Tasmania's largest natural harbour, was missed by the earliest explorers but discovered by Captain James Kelly in 1815 during his circumnavigational search for commercial resources. **Huon pine** was his major find here, a tree particularly popular with shipwrights for its bug- and worm-resistant oils. Coal was found shortly after and this combination made the harbour irresistible to the colonial authorities, who were looking for a suitably profitable site for a 'prison-within-a-prison'. A penal settlement was established on tiny **Sarah Island** in 1822, a name that was soon feared by the British Empire's convict and criminal communities. The narrow mouth of the harbour was nicknamed **Hells Gate** by the prisoners and hell it certainly was for many, leading to frequent escapes and suicides-by-proxy. The decision to relocate Tasmania's principal punishment station to Port Arthur meant closure for the settlement in 1833. Ten years later the settlement briefly re-opened as a probation station, but for 40-odd years the harbour saw little human activity other than a few piners. Today a small **fishing** fleet operates out of Strahan, and several tourist vessels use the harbour to cross from Strahan to Sarah Island and cruise up the magnificent rainforest-shrouded banks of the **Gordon River**, the western gateway to the Franklin-Gordon Wild Rivers National Park. To the west of town an unsealed road threads through the **Henty Dunes** to the long **Ocean Beach**. From here it is a 8-km walk up the beach (or unsealed drive) to Macquarie Heads and a view of Hells Gate. There are basic camping and picnic facilities here. A few kilometres north of Strahan the highway also briefly touches the dunes, some of the biggest in Tasmania at up to 30 m high.

INLAND TO SYDNEY

Lying east of Melbourne and extending from the mountains to the coast, Gippsland is the rural heartland of Victoria, a rich landscape of rolling green dairy pasture. In the far south is the main attraction, Wilsons Promontory, a low range of forest-covered granite mountains, edged with isolated sandy bays and golden river inlets and marked only by the occasional walking track. Carefully maintained as a wilderness, the 'Prom' offers intimate encounters with wildlife and is a stunning place to walk, swim, camp or simply laze about. In the centre of the region, the Gippsland Lakes system forms the largest inland waterway in Australia, where every small town has jetties festooned with yachts and fishing boats. Heading inland, the landscape rises to the Snowy Mountains.

→WILSONS PROMONTORY NATIONAL PARK

The 'Prom', as it is known by Victorians, is one of the state's top attractions, with granite-capped mountains covered in forest sloping down to the purest of white sand beaches and tannin-stained rivers meandering down to the sea. The northeastern region is a wilderness area only accessible to bushwalkers and boats. The park's most accessible beaches and bushwalks are on the western coast near Tidal River, the only 'settlement', where parrots, wombats and kangaroos roam (and fly) around freely. The year 2005 saw two notable events on the Prom, first in summer when wildfires decimated the region, and then, ironically, the first snowfalls for years in August. The notorious fire season of 2009 saw further and more extensive outbreaks, but now regeneration is in full swing.

AROUND THE PARK

The park offers dozens of trail options. **Squeaky Beach**, **Picnic Bay** and **Whisky Bay** can be reached by very short walks from car parks but the best walk is to all of these beaches from Tidal River along the coast (9 km return). The best views of the Prom are from the top of **Mount Oberon**. The walk up from Telegraph Saddle car park, 3.5 km from Tidal River, is wide and easy with a few rock-cut steps at the top (7 km, two hours return). Sunrise is the best time for photographs of Norman Bay below. A good spot for sunset is Whisky Bay. A very popular day walk from the same car park is the track to **Sealers' Cove** (9.5 km, 2½ hours one way) passing through thick rainforest to the eastern side of the Prom. The cove has a long arc of golden sand, tightly fringed by bush. There is a basic campsite at Sealers' Creek. The cove is beautiful but the walk has little variety and the return leg can feel like a bit of a slog. A more interesting day's walk is the **Oberon Bay** loop that also starts from Telegraph Saddle (19 km, six hours). There is also an extended walk (38 km, two to three days) to the lighthouse that sits on a great dome of granite on the southern tip of the promontory. The **Lighthouse Trek** can be done independently or from October to May with a ranger guide ($300-450, including accommodation and meals). At the lighthouse you can stay in cottages that are equipped with bunks, kitchen and bathroom. The cottages can be booked by the bed or exclusively for groups (**$$**).

The break between central and eastern Gippsland is marked by a series of connected lakes, separated from the sea only by the long thin dune system of the eastern end of Ninety Mile Beach. This strip of sand, designated the Gippsland Lakes Coastal Park, is accessible only by boat and is relatively unspoiled, even in peak season. The main service town in the area is Bairnsdale, but there are some pretty settlements dotted around the margins of the lakes, and Metung is particularly picturesque. Soon after Yarram is the turning to Woodside Beach, which marks the start of Ninety Mile Beach, the long golden stretch of sand that curves all the way to Lakes Entrance.

MOVING ON

After the Gippsland Lakes Coastal Park, there are two options. You can either continue along the coastal route, via the Ben Boyd National Park and the Sapphire Coast (see box, page 262), or take the inland route to the Snowy Mountains (see opposite), then take the road to north via Buchan, heading towards Jindabyne, after Bairnsdale. This route goes to the Kosciuszko National Park, the ski resort of Thredbo and then Australia's capital, Canberra, before rejoining the coastal route at Batemans Bay.

VISITING THE LAKES

Sale, the administration centre for Gippsland, has all the usual services available but offers few attractions for visitors. The **VIC** ① *Princes Highway, T1800 677520, www.destinationgippsland.com.au, 0900-1700,* is just west of the town centre. **Bairnsdale** is the largest town in the Lakes area, though it isn't actually on a lake shore itself. It is worth stopping here for the Aboriginal **Krowathunkalong Keeping Place** ① *Dalmahoy St, T5152 1891, Mon-Fri 0900-1200 and 1300-1700, (small charge)* , which features chillingly frank descriptions of the brutal Gunnai massacres that took place in Gippsland during the 1830s-1850s. The excellent **VIC** ① *240 Main St, T1800 637060, www.destination gippsland.com.au, 0900-1700,* will help with information and bookings for the whole Lakes region as well as Bairnsdale.

Paynesville hugs a stretch of lake shore facing **Raymond Island**, a small haven for wildlife, especially koalas, with one of the country's most concentrated wild populations. It's not a park, however, and the Paynesville township effectively extends across the car ferry (every half an hour, $10 return, pedestrians free) to claim a portion of the island as a suburb. Further offshore, **Rotamah Island** is home to a **Bird Observatory** ① *T131963, rotamah@i-o.net.au.* Camping is possible; contact the observatory.

Metung is on a small spit only a few hundred metres wide, giving it the feel of a village surrounded by water. Most of the homes spreading up the low wooded hill to the rear overlook Bancroft Bay, lined with yachts and jetties. Well-heeled visitors are catered for here, with a couple of good restaurants, wonderful day and sailing options and some luxurious accommodation options.

Standing at the only break in the long stretch of dunes that separate the Gippsland Lakes from the sea is **Lakes Entrance**. Once a small fishing village, it has become a traditional Victorian coastal holiday resort, known for its pleasant and varied scenery, range of accommodation, eateries and water-based activities.

Over the footbridge is the **Entrance Walking Track**, a leisurely and rewarding two-hour return stroll through dunes and bush to **Ninety Mile Beach** and **Flagstaff Lookout**. Wyanga Park Winery runs popular day and evening cruises from the town's Club Jetty on their launch, the *Corque*. The **VIC** ① *corner Marine Pde and the Esplanade, T1800 637060, discovereastgippsland.com.au, 0900-1700.*

→THE SNOWY MOUNTAINS

Though the idea of anything covered in snow may seem totally incongruous to most people's image of Australia, the Snowy Mountains are as much a part of the country as the Great Barrier Reef. The 'Snowies' contain the highest elevations of the Great Divide, which are protected by Kosciuszko National Park (pronounced 'Kozzie-usko'), the state's largest. The park offers a fragile sanctuary to numerous rare plant and animal species. In spring, vivid displays of wild flowers carpet the slopes where the snows have melted and, in autumn, the bark of the gnarly snow gums take on a range colourful hues. Cooma, in the Monaro Plains south of Canberra, is often considered the capital of the Snowies.

KOSCIUSZKO NATIONAL PARK
At over 600,000 ha, the Kosciuszko National Park is the largest in New South Wales and certainly one of the most beautiful. Home to the continent's highest peak, the 2228-m Mount Kosciuszko, the famous Snowy River and the country's best skiing and snowboarding resorts, the park also offers a plethora of year-round mountain activities, such as hiking, mountain biking, whitewater rafting, horse trekking and fishing. And with much of the park being wilderness, it also offers sanctuary to many rare native plants and animals. Jindabyne, at the eastern fringe of the park, is the main satellite town for the skiing and snowboarding resorts and has a huge range of accommodation and restaurants.

Visiting Kosciuszko National Park To get to the ski fields, the 8-km long **Skitube** at Bullock's Flat, 20 km east of Jindabyne (Alpine Way), connects Thredbo Valley with Perisher Blue Resort and the summit of Blue Cow Mountain. It operates daily in winter on the hour from 0900-1500. A shuttle bus service runs between Jindabyne and Thredbo. There is the **NPWS Snowy Region Visitors' Centre** ① *just off Kosciuszko Rd, Jindabyne, T6450 5600, www.environment.nsw.gov.au, daily 0900-1600.*

Places in Kosciuszko National Park At a height of 1680 m the **Perisher Resort** is the largest in the Southern Hemisphere and incorporates the Perisher Valley, Mount Blue Cow, Smiggin Holes and Guthega. There are 50 lifts and over 90 runs from advanced to beginner as well as trails suitable for cross country skiing. The resort is very well facilitated with plenty of mainly upmarket accommodation, eateries and ski hire/retail outlets. The VIC in Jindabyne has full accommodation listings and prices of lifts and lessons. Access is via the Kosciuszko Road west of Jindabyne. The road is fully sealed but snow chains may be required in winter. The main service stations in Jindabyne offer chain hire. National park day vehicle fees apply. Shuttle services by road vary from season to season. Contact the VIC for the latest schedules. The other transport alternative is the Skitube.

GOING FURTHER

The coastal route

The Yalmy Road continues inland from Gippsland Lakes Coastal Park down to **Orbost**, sitting at the point at which the Snowy River meets the Princes Highway. Though well placed to capitalize on the considerable tourist traffic, the small town offers little to the traveller except the cheapest petrol and last decent supermarkets until well into NSW, and a helpful **VIC** ① *The Slab Hut, Nicholson St, T5154 2424, 0900-1700.*

MARLO AND CAPE CONRAN

The tiny fishing community of Marlo at the mouth of the Snowy River is a popular long-weekend destination for Victorians, with a variety of caravan and cabin accommodation but few facilities aside from a couple of small grocery shops, one doing takeaways, and an impressive pub with guesthouse facilities. There are several good marked walking trails around Cape Conran, where two beautiful sandy beaches are generally fine for swimming. Camping is available.

CROAJINGOLONG NATIONAL PARK

This wonderful park, a narrow strip south of the Princes Highway that runs for 100 km west of the state border, is best known for its long stretch of wild coastline, but it also has eucalyptus forests, rainforests, granite peaks, estuaries and heathland. The remoteness of the park has led to a wide diversity of flora and fauna, with over 1000 native plants and more than 300 bird species, and it has been recognized as a World Biosphere Reserve.

Point Hicks was the first land in Australia to be sighted by the crew of Captain's Cook's *Endeavour* in 1770 and mainland Australia's tallest lighthouse was built here in 1890. The track to Point Hicks (2.25 km) starts at the end of the road past Thurra River campsite, and passes Honeymoon Bay. There are fantastic views from the top of the **lighthouse** ① *T5156 0432, www.pointhicks.com.au, tours 1300 Fri-Mon*, and southern right whales are often seen just off shore in winter. It is possible to walk the coast from **Bemm River** right over the NSW border into the **Nadgee Nature Reserve**. Trekking on the wild beaches makes up the bulk of the experience, but walkers will also encounter a range of spectacular coastal scenery. There are a number of campsites with facilities along the route, though water can get scarce and walkers need to carry a couple of days' supply. Numbers are restricted on all stretches of the trek, and permits are required. Contact the Cann River or Mallacoota Park's Victoria office ① *T5161 9500, www.parkweb.vic.gov.au.*

MALLACOOTA

Perched on the edge of the Mallacoota Inlet and the sea, Mallacoota is a beguiling and peaceful place. Surrounded by the Croajingolong National Park and a long way from any large cities, it's a haven for wildlife, particularly birdlife. The quiet meandering waters of the inlet are surrounded by densely forested hills. To the south are several beautiful coastal beaches, like **Betka Beach**, a popular local swimming beach. Spectacular layered and folded rocks can be seen at **Bastion Point** and **Quarry Beach**. There are numerous opportunities for coastal walks, bushwalking, fishing and boating.

The **Mallacoota Walking Track** is a 7-km loop, signposted from the main roundabout. To explore the inlet by water there are several options. Motor boats, canoes and kayaks can be hired from the caravan near the wharf. Several cruising boats are also based at the wharf: visit their kiosks for bookings. There are magnificent views of the area from **Genoa Peak**; the access road is signposted from the Princes Highway, 2 km west of Genoa. Further afield is tiny **Gabo Island**, home to one of the largest fairy penguin colonies in the country, plus one of the highest lighthouses. For local information, contact the **VIC** ① *main Wharf, T5158 0116, www.visitmallacoota.com.au, 0900-1700.*

BEN BOYD NATIONAL PARK

Sheer wilderness, beautiful coastal scenery, sublime walks, strange, colourful geological features, great campsites and even a remote lighthouse all combine to make the Ben Boyd National Park one of the best coastal parks in NSW. The 9490-ha park straddles Twofold Bay and the fishing village of Eden.

In the northern section of the park, the principal feature is **The Pinnacles**, a conglomerate of white and orange, sand and clay that has eroded into strange pinnacle formations over many thousands of years. They can be reached on a short 500-m-circuit walk from the car park off the 2 km Haycock Road, which is partly sealed and signposted off the Princes Highway. To the north, at the end of Edrom Road (16 km, signposted off the Princes Highway), is **Boyd's Tower**, which though very grand, never served its intended purpose as a lighthouse. Below the tower a clearing looks down to clear azure waters and the strange volcanic convolutions of the red coastal rocks. Another diversion off Edrom Road, to the west, takes you to the remains of the **Davidson Whaling Station**, created in 1818 and the longest-running shore-based station in Australia, ceasing operations in 1930. Further south off Edrom Road an unsealed, badly rutted road leads to the delightful and wildlife-rich **Bittangabee campsite** (15 km, then 5 km on the left).

Back on the main track the Disaster Bay Lookout is worth a look before the track terminates at the 'must-see' **Green Cape Light Station** (21 km). Surrounding by strange, rust-coloured rocks, pounded by surf and home to laid-back kangaroos, it is a wonderful place to find some solitude. **City Rock**, accessed down a short badly rutted track, off the lighthouse road, is signposted also well worth seeing. The wave action against the rock platform is dramatic and a favourite haunt for sea eagles. The superb but demanding (30 km) **'Light to Light' Walking Track** connects the Green Cape Light Station with Boyd's Tower, passing the **Bittangabee** and **Saltwater Creek** campsites along the way. It is one of the best and most remote coastal walks in NSW.

SAPPHIRE COAST

From the Victorian border to Narooma is a region known as the Sapphire Coast. Just south of Narooma, in the shadow of Gulaga Mountain, are the quaint and historic villages of **Central Tilba** and **Tilba Tilba**. Now classified by the National Trust, they boast many historic cottages and also offer some of the South Coast's best cafés and arts and crafts outlets. Ask for a self-guided heritage leaflet from the VIC in Narooma. They can also provide listings for numerous cosy B&Bs in and around the two villages. **Tilba Valley Wines Vineyard** ① *off the Princes Highway, 5 km north of Tilba Tilba, T4473 7308, www.tilbavalleywines.com, open from 1000*, produces Shiraz, Semillon and Chardonnay.

At 1760 m **Charlotte Pass** marks the end of the Kosciuszko Road and the start of various high alpine walks including the 12½-km one-way walk to the summit of Australia's highest mountain, Mount Kosciuszko. In winter the Charlotte Pass Ski field is the most remote with four lifts and a scattering of chalets and lodges. The area is also particularly good for cross-country skiing, and in summer it is a top spot for mountain walks. In the heart of the national park, halfway between Tumut and Cooma, are the **Mount Selwyn ski fields** (1490 m), which are the cheapest, but the least well facilitated. There are about a dozen lifts and runs particularly suitable for children and families. Cross-country trails are also plentiful. **Selwyn Snow World Centre** ① *T6454 9488, www.selwynsnow.com.au*, offers indoor and outdoor activities for kids, with attractive half or full day programmes. For information surrounding Charlotte Pass refer to Perisher Valley sources. For Mount Selwyn information, T1800-641 064, www.selwynsnow.com.au. An All Day Lift Pass at Mount Selwyn costs from $62, child $34 (under 15 years). Hire prices for skis/boots/poles, from $45 per day and for snowboards/ boots $50. Lift pass and lesson deals from around $92. The VIC in Jindabyne or Tumut can assist with accommodation listings and bookings.

Wandering around the Alpine-style mountain village resort of **Thredbo**, 32 km west of Jindabyne, in either winter or summer feels most un-Australian. Set in a beautiful river valley and shadowed by the Crackenback Mountain Range, it feels a million miles from the sun-baked outback, surf beaches or bustling east coast cities. Sadly, the name Thredbo is eternally associated with a tragic event in August 1997, when a landslip devastated the village and claimed 18 lives. Thredbo however prefers to put that episode behind it and today is considered a very progressive village and the best ski and snowboarding resort in the country. Things don't grind to a halt after the snow disappears, because in summer Thredbo becomes an alpine walking centre.

When it comes to skiing Thredbo is considered the best venue in the country. Not only is the resort exceptionally well facilitated, but also the fields themselves are also highly regarded with numerous lifts taking you to a wide range of runs. Night skiing is also available. A Lift-only Day Pass costs from $110 (two-day $165) child $62, while a one-day Lift and Lesson Pass costs from $158. There are plenty of ski hire outlets in the village or at the main lift terminals.

In summer Thredbo also offers a whole host of activities from alpine walking and fishing, to biking and golf. The Valley Chairlift stays open in summer allowing walkers to reach the higher elevations. Thredbo offers walkers the shortest route to the summit of Mount Kosciuszko (6½ km one-way, lookout 2 km one-way). The ski lift takes out 1930 m, leaving only 298 m of elevation. Guided summit and sunset walks are also available.

For a full list of the many activity and accommodation options, visit the excellent **VIC** ① *6 Friday Drive, T1300 020589, T6459 4100, www.thredbo.com.au.*

→CANBERRA

Derived from the Aboriginal word *Kamberra* (meeting place), Australia's capital is, sadly, one of the most underrated cities in the world. It has been described in many ways – mostly derogatory – with adjectives like artificial, boring and mundane to the fore. Thanks to architect Walter Burley Griffin's deliberately spacious and perhaps overly well-facilitated layout of endless parks, tree-lined circular roads, lakes and highways almost as wide as they are long, the city lacks a certain intimacy. Also, it is too modern to have developed a real sense of history and suburban character, or even a seamy underbelly, and is infested with politicians and civil servants, but surely that is no reason to dismiss it. To further add to its woes the region suffered some horrific bushfires in February 2003 that hit with remarkable speed and ferocity across the city fringes costing several lives and numerous homes. But if you can ignore the negative publicity and all that you may have heard about little Canberra and the ACT, it's actually a very nice place. A bit like rural England, with more trees per square yard than Kew Gardens. There are highways that are so well designed they've never seen a traffic jam, the climate is pleasantly cool with distinct and colourful seasons, and the quality of its national treasures and architecture is comparable with any other city of its size in the world.

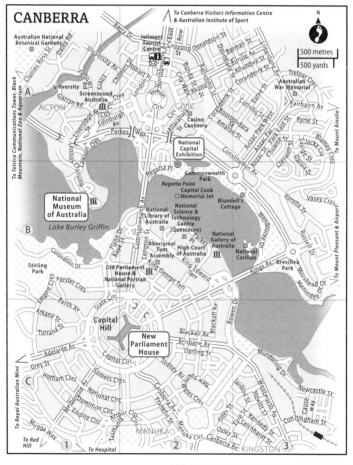

ARRIVING IN CANBERRA

Getting around   An efficient bus service runs throughout the city. A sightseeing bus tour is a good way of experiencing the sights, particularly if you are short of time. Cycling is a great way to get around the city, with numerous purpose-built cycleways and a fairly flat topography. The VIC can supply more detail and maps.

Moving on   From Canberra you can head east and then southeast towards the coast and Batemans Bay; see the Batemans Bay to Sydney section opposite.

Tourist information   The VIC ① *330 Northbourne Av, 3 km north of the centre, T1300 554 114, T6205 0044, www.visitcanberra.com.au, Mon-Fri 0900-1700, Sat-Sun 0900-1600*, can provide detailed information and detailed city maps.

PLACES IN CANBERRA

If you're short of time don't miss the National Museum, the New Parliament Building and the National Capital Exhibition, all of which are neatly contained within the National Triangle, or Parliamentary Triangle. Although the temptation is to head straight for the Triangle's crowning glory, the New Parliament Building, start your tour instead at the **National Capital Exhibition** ① *Regatta Point, Commonwealth Park, T6272 2902, www.nationalcapital.gov.au, 0900-1700, free,* which imaginatively outlines the fascinating history of the nation's capital from its indigenous links to today's intriguing landscaped metropolis. The views across Lake Burley Griffin are memorable.

Completed in 1988, **New Parliament House** ① *T6277 5399, www.aph.gov.au, 0900-1700, guided tours every 30 mins from 0900,* is the architectural showpiece of Canberra and one of Australia's great man-made wonders, like Sydney's Opera House and Harbour Bridge. Where else in the world is there such a building with its lawn on the roof? Once you have trampled all over it and taken in the angles, perspectives and views you can then turn to the interior. Along with more fascinating architecture the interior hosts precious Australian art and craft, including Arthur Boyd's impressive *Shoalhaven Tapestry.* When Parliament is sitting, access is allowed to 'Question Time' in the House of Representatives and begins at 1400. Tickets are free; make bookings through the Sergeant of Arms office.

Facing Lake Burley Griffin, in the heart of the National Triangle, is the **Old Parliament House** completed in 1927, hub of the nation's political life until the New Parliament House took over in 1988. Immediately outside is the Aboriginal Tent Embassy that serves as a pertinent reminder that the Aboriginal people of Australia were living here for tens of thousands of years before the first acre of land was ever purchased. Sitting proudly on the shores of Lake Burley Griffin, the **National Museum of Australia** ① *Lawson Crescent, T1800 026132, www.nma.gov.au, 0900-1700, free (admission charge to some specialist displays),* is superb, with a range of exciting displays and themed galleries that convey all things 'Aussie', all beautifully designed and presented.

BATEMANS BAY TO SYDNEY

The coast south of Sydney has its fair share of beautiful unspoiled beaches and stunning coastal scenery. Overshadowed by Sydney and the north coast, it has pretty much been left alone and few visitors have any idea that this little corner is as beautiful as anywhere else in NSW.

EUROBODALLA COAST

The Eurobodalla coastal region stretches from Batemans Bay in the north to Narooma in the south. The bustling seaside resort of **Batemans Bay** provides an ideal stopover along the coastal Princes Highway. Most of the Bay's beaches are located southeast of the town centre and if you have time it is worth heading that way. Tomakin and Broulee offer the best surf and fishing sites and jet skis can be hired on Coriggan's Beach. On the river you can take a leisurely three-hour cruise upstream to the historic riverside village of Nelligen. The area offers some excellent sea kayaking. There are numerous excellent dive sites around the Bay. Just off the Princes Highway near the town centre is the very helpful **VIC** ① *T1800 802528, T4472 6900, www.eurobodalla.com.au, 0900-1700.*

Nestled on a headland in the glistening embrace of the Wagonga River Inlet and surrounded by rocky beaches, national parks and the odd accessible island, **Narooma** has all the beauty and potential activities for which the south coast is famous. The biggest attraction is **Montague Island**, about 8 km offshore. Officially declared a nature reserve and administered by the National Parks and Wildlife Service, Montague has an interesting Aboriginal and European history and is crowned by a historic lighthouse built in 1881. But perhaps its greatest appeal are the colonies of fur seals and seabirds – including about 10,000 pairs of fairy penguins – that make the island home. Between October and December humpback whales can also be seen on their annual migration.

Back on the mainland the immediate coastline has some interesting features including **Australia Rock**, which as the name suggests, looks like the outline of Australia. It is however not the rock that plays with the imagination but a hole in its middle. Access is via Bar Rock Road beyond the golf course, at the river mouth on Wagonga Head. Further south **Glasshouse Rocks** is another interesting geological formation. On the western side of town the Wagonga Inlet offers fishing and river cruises. The **VIC** ① *off Princes Highway, T1800 240003, T4476 2881, www.eurobodalla.com.au, 0900-1700,* is at the northern end of town.

MURRAMARANG NATIONAL PARK

① *Day-use vehicle entry costs $11, pedestrians free. Access to Pebbly Beach is via Mt Agony Rd (unsealed) right of the Princes Highway 10 km north of Batemans Bay. Depot Beach and Durras North are accessed via North Durras Rd off Mt Agony Rd. Pretty Beach and the Murramarang Aboriginal Area are accessed via Bawley Point and Kioloa on Murramarang Rd (sealed) off the Princes Highway 16 km south of Ulladulla.*

The 11,978-ha Murramarang National Park is most famous for its tame and extremely laid-back population of eastern grey kangaroos. Here they not only frequent the campsites and the foreshore but on occasion are even said to cool off in the surf. The park is a superb mix of forest and coastal habitat that offers a host of activities from swimming, surfing and walking to simple socializing with the resident marsupials. Of the beaches and campsites, **Pebbly Beach** and **Depot beach** are the most popular spots, but **Durras**

INLAND AND COASTAL ROUTES TO SYDNEY

Where to stay

Wilsons Promontory National Park

The Prom is so popular that accommodation is allocated by ballot for Dec-Jan (including campsites). Even at other times, weekends may have to be booked a year in advance. Also, check out www.promaccom.com.au.

$$$ Tingara View Tea House and Cottages, 10 Tingara Close, Yanakie, T131963/T5687 1488, www.prom country.com.au/tingaraview. 3 pretty, colonial-style 1-room cottages with lovely views, cooked breakfast served in main house, also dinner and afternoon tea.

$$$-$$ Park cabin/campsite, T5680 9555, wprom@parks.vic.gov.au. The best place to stay is within the park itself. Good range of options, including cabins, units and huts.

Camping in the park is fantastic. There is an (unbookable) international campers area available for 1-2 nights.

Gippsland Lakes

In Bairnsdale there are a couple of caravan parks, and several motels and B&Bs. Accommodation may be plentiful in Lakes Entrance, but if you're travelling over Christmas and Jan, book well ahead.

$$$$-$$$ Déjà Vu, just to the north of Lakes Entrance over the lake on Clara St, T5155 4330, www.dejavu.com.au. This modern, glass-filled, hosted B&B, set in 7 acres of wild lakeside country, has rooms with private lake-view balconies, and the first-class service is friendly and attentive, with some unexpected and unusual flourishes. Also a couple of suitably alluring self-contained properties fronting the lake. Book well in advance. Lovely.

$$$ BelleVue, 201 Esplanade, Lakes Entrance, T5155 3055, www.bellevuelakes.com. A cracking little daytime café and decent

mid-range seafood restaurant help make this very comfortably furnished, family-run motel stand out from the crowd.

$ Riviera Backpackers, 669 Esplanade, Lakes Entrance, T5155 2444, www.yha.com.au. Very well-run and well-equipped YHA hostel with a good-value range of rooms, including doubles (some en suite). Cheap bike hire, pool. Friendly and knowledgeable owners.

Canberra

The VIC has listings and a bookings service, T1300 554 114, www.visitcanberra.com.au.

$$$$ Kurrajong, 8 National Circuit, Barton, T6234 4444, www.hotelkurrajong.com.au. One of the capital's best boutique hotels. It is well positioned between the lively suburb of Manuka and the National Triangle.

$$$-$$ Canberra City YHA, 7 Akuna St, T6248 9155, www.yha.com.au. One of the best budget options, costing more than your average hostel but worth it. Kitchen, bar, pool and spa.

Eurobodalla Coast

The VIC in Batemans Bay has full listings. There are several other motor parks on the beachside along Beach Rd southeast of the centre.

Batemans Bay

$$$$-$$$ Comfort Inn Lincoln Downs, Princes Highway (on the right just beyond the bridge heading north), T4478 9200, www.lincolndowns.com.au. Excellent hotel with full facilities .

$$$-$ Shady Willows Holiday Park, Old Princes Highway, corner of South St, T4472 4972, www.shadywillows.com.au. Backpackers and those in campervans should head here. It incorporates a YHA with dorm or onsite caravans for couples, fully equipped kitchen, pool, internet, bike hire.

Murramarang National Park
$$$$-$ Eco-Point Murramarang Resort,
Banyandah St, South Durras, T4478 6355,
www.murramarangresort.com.au. A top spot
and although not in the park itself it has its own
tame kangaroos and some sublime coastal
scenery. Luxury cabins, powered and
non-powered sites, pool, bar/restaurant, camp
kitchen, activities and canoe and bike hire.
$ NPWS campsite, Pebbly Beach, T4478
6023, www.nationalparks.nsw.gov.au. Good
facilities, with hot showers and fire sites. A
warden collects fees daily. It's often busy so
book ahead.

Jervis Bay
$$$$ Paperbark Lodge and Camp,
605 Woollamia Rd, T4441 6066, info@
paperbarkcamp.com.au. An excellent
eco-tourist set-up in a quiet bush setting with
luxury en suite tent units, camp fire, good
restaurant, tours and activities. Book ahead.

Shoalhaven Coast
$$$$-$ Rest Point Garden Village, Browns
Rd (5 km south of Shoalhaven), T4421 6856,
www.nowracaravanpark.com.au. The most
modern motor park in the area with a range of
accommodation including powered and
non-powered sites.

North, south of Depot Beach and Pretty Beach to the north, is also great. There is a network of coast and forest walks available including the popular 'Discovery Trail' off North Durras Road, which skirts the edge of **Durras Lake**. There is also a fine coastal track connecting Pretty Beach with Pebbly Beach.

SHOALHAVEN COAST
The area of Shoalhaven extends from Batemans Bay to Nowra. The true magic of the Shoalhaven coast begins to be revealed, with some of the best beaches and national parks in the state, on the stretch leading up to and around Jervis Bay. If you have time you may also like to consider a detour inland to Kangaroo Valley and the Morton National park (Fitzroy Falls) or others that explore the coast in more detail. The VIC can provide all the details. Nowra is home to the **Shoalhaven VIC** ① *corner of Princes Highway and Pleasant Way, T1300 662808, T4421 0778, www.shoalhaven.nsw.gov.au, 0900-1630*, as well as the **NPWS office** ① *55 Graham St, Nowra, T4423 2170*.

JERVIS BAY AND AROUND
Jervis Bay is a deep, sheltered bay that sits neatly in the embrace of the Beecroft Peninsula to the north and the exquisite Booderee National Park to the south. It is blessed with stunning coastal scenery, beautiful white beaches, a marine park with world-class dive sites and even a resident pod of over 60 playful dolphins, all of which combine to earn it the quiet reputation as the jewel of the NSW South Coast. Local information is available from **Huskisson Trading Post** ① *1 Tomerong St, Huskisson, T4441 5241, www.tourism jervisbay.com.au, 0900-1700*.

The old shipbuilding town of **Huskisson** (known as 'Husky') and its neighbour **Vincentia** are the two main settlements on Jervis Bay and form the gateway to the bay's water-based activities. The diving in the **Jervis Bay Marine Park** in particular is said to be second only to the Great Barrier Reef and is well known for its marine variety and water clarity. A few companies offer activities like whale and dolphin watching.

Booderee National Park ① *day fee (including and per car) costs $10 and camping fees (from $10-$20) must be paid on top of that, so if you intend staying overnight it does add up*, formerly known as the Jervis Bay National Park, takes up almost the entire southern headland of Jervis Bay and is, without doubt, one of the most attractive coastal national parks in NSW. Owned and administered by a collaboration of Parks Australia and the Wreck Bay Aboriginal Community, it offers a wealth of fine, secluded beaches, bush walks, stunning coastal scenery and a rich array of wildlife. Not to be missed are **Green Patch Beach**, the further flung **Cave Beach**, a good surf spot, and **Summercloud Bay**. The walking track to **Steamers Beach** (2.3 km) is also recommended although there are many fine options to choose from. Another unique attraction in the park is the 80-ha **Booderee Botanic Gardens** ① *Mon-Fri 0800-1600, Sat-Sun 1000-1700, free with park entry fee*, created in 1952 as an annexe of the Australian National Botanic Gardens in Canberra. There are over 1600 species centred on the small freshwater Lake McKenzie, with most being coastal plants more suited to the local climate. There are a number of short walks and nature trails. The VIC ① *Village Rd, T4443 0977, www.booderee.np.gov.au, 0900-1600*, at the park entrance, can supply detailed information about the park, its attractions, walks, amenities and its scattering of great campsites. Provisions can be bought at the general store ① *0700-2100, or 1900 outside school holidays*, in Jervis Bay Village, off Jervis Bay Road, which is within the park boundary.

MOVING ON
To Sydney

From Jervis Bay, it's another 200 km, or two hours and 52 minutes, to Sydney. See page 35.

PRACTICALITIES

INS AND OUTS

→BEST TIME TO VISIT AUSTRALIA

One of the joys of Australia is that at any time of year there are considerable chunks of territory where the weather is just about right. The converse, of course, is that those particular about their destination need good timing. The peak season, broadly speaking, in the southern third of the country is mid-December through to the end of January. This is high summer and school holidays, and also when the airlines hike up their fares from Europe and North America. Practically every form of accommodation on the coast, from Shark Bay in the west, right around the south to the Gold Coast in the east, gets booked out – months in advance in the most popular spots. The northwest of WA (Pilbara and Kimberley) and the QLD coast get particularly busy May-September. The exception to the standard tourist seasons is whale-watching, possible at many southern coastal spots from March-October.

Being a southern hemisphere continent, the seasons, such as they are, are reversed. As a general rule, the further north you travel, and the further in time from July, the hotter it gets. And hot means very hot: days over 40°C regularly occur in high summer in the arid regions, and even cities as far south as Perth and Adelaide often get '30-over-30' (over 30°C for 30 consecutive days). Australia is the driest continent, excluding Antarctica, and virtually nowhere further than 250 km inland gets more than an average of 600 mm of rain a year. About half the continent, in a band across the south and west, gets less than 300 mm and much of it is desert. The only areas that get high rainfall are the north QLD coast, western coast of VIC, the highlands in TAS and the southwest tip of WA.

Watch out for school holidays, when some areas get completely booked out. They vary from state to state (www.australia.com for details), but broadly speaking they cover the whole of January, a week or two around Easter, two to three weeks in June-July and the same in September. During these times you are advised to book accommodation well in advance.

→GETTING TO AUSTRALIA

AIR

There are international flights direct to Melbourne, Sydney, Brisbane, Cairns, Darwin, Adelaide and Perth and it is quite possible to have different points of arrival and departure that complement your intended itinerary. If there is not a direct flight to your primary choice there will usually be a same-day connection from Sydney or Melbourne. It is usually possible to book internal Australian flights when booking your international ticket, at lower prices than on arrival. Some do not even require a stated departure and arrival point. If you have any plans to fly within New South Wales or Queensland check this out prior to booking. Fares depend on the season, with prices higher during December and January unless booked well in advance. Mid-year sees the cheapest fares. Qantas, www.qantas.com.au, is Australia's main international and domestic airline and flies from most international capitals and major cities. That said, with the advent of the global financial crisis, competition is fiercer than ever, and Qantas is struggling in international and domestic markets against other airlines like Emirates, V Australia and Tiger Airways. Most other international major airlines have flights to Australia from their home countries.

Airport information   Melbourne, Sydney, Brisbane and Cairns are the main airports on the east coast and all have excellent services. All the main airlines fly to these airports with regular connections from international and national destinations. Facilities are good and include banks, ATMs and tourist offices where help is on hand with booking accommodation and organizing tours and transport. All the airports offer regular and efficient connections with the city centres either by coach or rail. That said, Melbourne still lacks a fast rail link relying solely on the vehicular. See the respective sections for further details or refer to www.melbourneairport.com.au; www.sydneyairport.com.au and www.bne.com.au.

Perth Airport, 10 km east of the city centre, has two terminals – domestic and international. With no direct link between the two, transfers are via the perimeter highways. The domestic terminal, Brearley Avenue, has a wide range of services including ATMs, Travelex foreign exchange, luggage lockers, cafés and all the major car hire firms. The international terminal, Horrie Miller Drive, is slightly further out. Facilities are just as comprehensive, the Thomas Cook foreign exchange counters remaining open before and after all flights.

Flights from Europe   With the advent of the global financial crisis and increased competition between carriers airfares to Australia remain reasonable. Now, it is the strength of the Australian dollar that is of more concern to almost all foreign visitors. The main route, and the cheapest, is via Asia, though fares will also be quoted via North America or Africa. The Asia route usually takes 20-30 hours including stops. There are no non-stop routes so it's worth checking out which stopovers are on offer. Stopovers of a few nights do not usually increase the cost of the ticket appreciably. The cheapest return flights, off season, will be around £950, with prices rising to at least £1100 around Christmas.

Flights from North and South America   There are direct Qantas flights from Los Angeles to Brisbane and Sydney, and from Vancouver and New York to Sydney. Connections to Melbourne and Cairns are available from Auckland. The cost of a standard return in the high season from Vancouver starts at around C$1800, from New York at US$1900 and from Los Angeles at US$1500. Flights take around 11 hours. There are also direct flights from Buenos Aires to Sydney.

→TRANSPORT IN AUSTRALIA

Public transport in and around the state capitals, based on a variety of bus, tram and train networks, is generally good and efficient, and often easier than driving. Most cities have good metropolitan bus services, though some are curiously unaware of tourist traffic and there is many an important outlying attraction poorly served by public transport, or even missed off the bus routes completely. Some cities are compact enough for this to be a minor irritation, others are so spread out that the visitor must invest in an expensive tourist bus service or taxis. In such places staying at a hostel or B&B with free or low-cost bike hire can save a lot of money. Bear in mind that when it comes to public transport in the major centres, Australia is hardly comparable to Japan or to a lesser extent Europe or North America. In cities like Melbourne, if you ask a local to comment on their public transport system, the reply will be a few choice words and a considerable degree of frustration and anger.

Outside the cities by far the best way of seeing Australia is under your own steam, or with a tour operator with an in-depth itinerary. The further from the capitals you go, the more public transport becomes patchy. Most states have a transport service based on a combination of bus, and sometimes train, networks. Some services helpfully connect up at border towns, but it is not always so and an unwise assumption to make. If short on time and long on funds, flying can save a lot of time, both interstate and within the larger states, and in some cases is the only realistic option. Some routes pass over spectacular landscapes.

Train fares and domestic air travel can be considerably cheaper if booked in advance and on the net. For flights within Australia, try www.webjet.com.au.

AIR

Qantas, T131313, www.qantas.com.au, **Tiger Airways**, T(0)3-9999 2888, www.tiger airways.com, **Jetstar**, T131538, www.jetstar.com.au, and **Virgin Blue**, T136789, www.virgin blue.com.au, link most state capitals to each other and to many of the larger towns and main tourist destinations.

There are also several regional airways operating smaller planes on specialist routes including **Regional Express** (REX), T131713, www.regionalexpress.com.au, in east Australia. **Skywest** ① *T1300 660088 or T08-9477 8301 (outside Australia), www.skywest.com.au*, is the principal state airline with flights from Perth to all the major towns. NT's **Air North** ① *T1800 627 474, www.airnorth.com.au*, has connections between Broome, Kununurra and Darwin.

Domestic fares have dropped dramatically in recent years. Expect to pay around AU$80-$100 for a one-way ticket between Melbourne and Sydney and about for Sydney to Cairns for $175. But bear in mind with budget airlines this does not take into account cargo baggage, for which you will pay significantly more. For up-to-date information on whether a destination is served by scheduled or charter flights, contact your destination's tourist office or each airline direct.

RAIL

There is no comprehensive rail network in Australia. The main interstate tracks run across the continent from Sydney to Perth, up through the centre from Melbourne to Darwin, and up the east coast from Melbourne to Sydney/Brisbane. A car is a better option if you wish to explore or get off the beaten track. However, we do mention one route in Itinerary 3, Darwin to Adelaide. *The Ghan* connects Darwin with Adelaide and takes about 47 hours, with optional onward legs to Melbourne or Sydney.

ROAD

If you live in a small and populous country, travelling by car in Australia will be an enlightening experience, as well as an enervating one. Distances are huge and travelling times between the major cities, towns and sights can seem endless, so put on some tunes and make driving part of the whole holiday experience.If hiring or buying a car always consider the option of a campervan. These can sometimes be had for little more than the cost of a standard car, the savings on accommodation can be considerable, and itineraries are even less constrained.

For maximum flexibility there is no substitute for having your own transport. Cars, campervans, motorbikes and bicycles can all be hired or bought with little difficulty. Traffic congestion is rarely an issue in Australia, and only the Sydney and Melbourne metropolitan areas have anything like the traffic problems of most nations. Congestion on country roads and highways is practically unheard of. This means that driving itineraries can be based on covering a planned distance each day, up to, say 100 km for each solid hour's driving.

The key factor in planning transport is distance. Driving or cycling outside of the main cities is relatively stress-free, but the distances can be huge. The trip from Adelaide to Perth involves a 1000-km stretch with only roadhouses for company, spaced about 100 km apart, and not a single town. Straight sections regularly exceed 20 km. The scenery for passengers can be wonderful, but the driver can get very bored – and sleepy. There are a lot of single-vehicle accidents in Australia, and many are simply a result of drivers falling asleep. Another important factor in country driving is large animals. Collisions with animals are the other major cause of single-vehicle accidents. This means that you should drive *only* in full daylight, an important consideration when planning a self-drive itinerary. On country roads you will also meet road trains. These haulage trucks can be over 50 m long including up to four separate trailers strung along behind the main cab. Overtaking them obviously entails great care – wait for a good long stretch before committing yourself. If you are on a single track bitumen road or an unsealed road you are well advised to pull right over and slow considerably when one comes the other way. Not only can dust cause visibility to hit zero, but you will also minimize the possibility of stones pinging up and damaging your windows.

The other major factor when planning is the type of roads you may need to use. Almost all the main interstate highways are now sealed. Many country roads are unsealed, usually meaning a gravel or sand surface. When recently *graded* (levelled and compacted) they can be almost as pleasant to drive on as sealed roads, but even then there are reduced levels of handling and increased stopping distances. After grading, unsealed roads deteriorate over time. Potholes form, they can become very boggy, even impassable, when wet, and corrugations usually develop. These are regular ripples in the road surface, perpendicular to the road direction, and can go on for tens of km. Small ones simply cause an irritating judder, large ones can reduce tolerable driving speeds to 10-20 kmph. Generally, the bigger the wheel size, and the longer the wheel-base, the more comfortable journeys over corrugations will be. Most designated unsealed roads can be negotiated with a 2WD, low-clearance vehicle, but the ride will be a lot more comfortable, and safer in a 4WD, high-clearance one. Note that most hire-car companies will not allow their 2WD vehicles to be driven on unsealed roads. High-clearance, 4WD cars and campervans are available from most of the major hire companies. Some unsealed roads are designated as 4WD-only or tracks, though definitions of some differ according to the map or authority you consult. In dry weather the Oodnadatta Track, for example, can be driven in well-prepared 2WD cars. At other times they cannot, without serious risk of accident, vehicle or tyre damage or getting bogged. If in any doubt whatsoever, stick to the roads you are certain are safe for your vehicle, and you are sufficiently prepared for. With careful preparation and the right vehicles (convoys are always recommended), however, traversing the major outback tracks can be an awesome experience. Note that hire-companies have strict terms on the use of their 4WD vehicles. Many can only be used on sealed or graded unsealed roads and not taken down 4WD tracks or off-road. Always check with the hire company where you can and cannot take your vehicle, and also what your liability will be in the case of an accident.

Prepare carefully before driving to remote areas. Even if there are regular roadhouses, it is wise to carry essential spares and tools such as fan belts, hoses, gaffer tape, a tyre repair kit, extra car jack, extra spare wheel and tyre, spade, decent tool kit, oil and coolant, and a fuel can with fuel. A short course in vehicle maintenance before you travel can also save much grief. Membership of a state breakdown organization is highly recommended, as is informing friends, relatives or the police of your intended itinerary. Above all carry plenty of spare water, at least 10 litres per person, 20 if possible.

To drive in Australia you must have a current driving licence. Foreign nationals also need an international driving licence, available from your national motoring organization. In Australia you drive on the left. Speed limits vary between states, with maximum urban limits of 50-60 kph and maximum country limits of 100-120 kph. Beware that speed cameras not only reduce the road toll, but provide massive revenue for the state governments. Seatbelts are compulsory for drivers and passengers. Driving under the influence of alcohol is illegal over certain (very small) limits and penalties are severe. Also be aware that Sydney and Melbourne have fairly complex motorway toll systems. Avail yourself of these before your approach or pay close attention to the relevant toll signs and colours so you do not get caught out. As a general rule green signage indicates freeway, blue tollway.

Fuel costs are approximately half that in Britain and twice that in the US, but due to the recent increase in the price of crude are following the global trend and rising rapidly. At the time of writing they were fluctuating between $1.30 and $1.40 a litre in city centres and marginally more in the outback. Diesel is marginally more expensive than unleaded at about $1.60, but it's less prone to price gouging and fluctuations. When budgeting, allow at least $15 for every estimated 100 km. Given the huge distance involved with these itineraries, picking an economical vehicle and conserving fuel can save hundreds of dollars.

Every state has a breakdown service that is affiliated to the **Australian Automobile Association** (AAA), www.aaa.asn.au, with which your home country organization may have a reciprocal link. You need to join one of the state associations. Note also that you may be covered for only about 100 km (depending on the scheme) of towing distance and that without cover towing services are very expensive. Given the sheer distances you are likely to cover by car, joining an automobile organization is highly recommended but read the fine print with regard to levels of membership in relation to coverage outside metropolitan areas and in the outback.

Car rental costs vary considerably according to where you hire from (it's cheaper in the big cities, though small local companies can have good deals), what you hire and the mileage/insurance terms. You may be better off making arrangements in your own country for a fly/drive deal. Watch out for kilometre caps: some can be as low as 100 km per day. The minimum you can expect to pay in Australia is around $250 a week for a small car. Drivers need to be over 21. At peak times it can be impossible to get a car at short notice and some companies may dispose of a booked car within as little as half an hour of you not showing up for an agreed pick-up time. If you've booked a car but are going to be late, ensure that you let them know before the pick-up time.

The real beauty in Australia, given the weather and the environment, is that travelling on a budget does not detract from the enjoyment of the trip. On the contrary, this is a place where a night under canvas in any of the national parks is an absolute delight. Booking accommodation in advance is highly recommended, especially in peak seasons. Booking online will usually secure the best rates. Check if your accommodation has air conditioning (a/c) when booking. Note that single rooms are relatively scarce.

Most 'hotels' outside of the major towns are pubs with upstairs or external accommodation. If upstairs, a room is likely to have access to shared bathroom facilities, while external rooms are usually standard en suite motel units. The quality of pub-hotel accommodation varies considerably but is usually a budget option. Motels in Australia are usually depressingly anonymous but dependably clean and safe and offer the cheapest en suite rooms. Most have dining facilities and free, secure parking.

Bed and breakfast (B&B) is in some ways quite different from the British model. They are not expensive, but are rarely a budget option. They offer very comfortable accommodation in usually upmarket, sometimes historic houses. Some B&Bs are actually self-contained cottages or cabins with breakfast provisions supplied. Larger ones may have full kitchens.

Airbnb is a rapidly growing internet portal that allows mainly city residents to rent out their spare rooms or properties and visitors more affordable options without all the service overheads. Massively popular worldwide, it is well worth looking at especially if you are alone, or a couple. See www.airbnb.com.

Some national parks and rural cattle and sheep stations have converted old settlers' or workers' homes, which are usually self-contained. They are often magical places to stay and include many old lighthouse keepers' cottages and shearers' quarters. Stations may also invite guests to watch, or even get involved in, the day's activities.

For those travelling on a tight budget there is a large network of hostels offering cheap accommodation. All hostels have kitchen and common room facilities, almost all now have Wi-Fi and some have considerably more. A few, particularly in cities, will offer freebies including breakfast and pick-ups. Standards vary considerably and it's well worth asking the opinions of other travellers. Of several hostel associations, YHA, www.yha.org.au, and NOMADS, T1800 091905, T02-9280 4110, www.nomadsworld.com, no membership fee, seem to keep the closest eye on their hostels, ensuring a consistency of quality. The YMCA, T03-9699 7655, www.ymca.org.au, and YWCA, T02-6230 5150, www.ywca.org.au, are usually a clean and quiet choice in the major cities.

Almost every town will have at least one caravan park, with unpowered and powered sites varying from $30-40 (for two) for campers, caravans and campervans, an ablutions block and usually a camp kitchen or barbecues. Some will have permanently sited caravans (onsite vans) and cabins. Some useful organizations are: Big 4, T1300-738044, T03-9811 9300, www.big4.com.au; Family Parks of Australia, T1300-855707, T07-32522644, www.familyparks.com.au; and Top Tourist Parks, T08-8363 1901, www.toptourist parks.com.au. If you intend to use motor parks, get hold of the latest editions of the tourist park guides published by the NMRA, RACV and RACQ. They are an essential resource.

Bush camping is the best way to experience the natural environment. Some national parks allow camping, mostly in designated areas only, with a few allowing limited bush camping.

PRICE CODES

WHERE TO STAY

$$$$	over $200	$$$	$110-200
$$	$50-110	$	under $50

Prices are based on a double room in the high season.

RESTAURANTS

$$$	over $35	$$	$25-35	$	under $24

Prices refer to the cost of a two-course meal, not including drinks.

All dollars quoted in this guide are Australian unless specified otherwise.

Facilities are usually minimal, with basic toilets, fireplaces and perhaps tank water; a few have barbecues and shower blocks. Payment is often by self-registration (around $6-15 per person) and barbecues often require coins, so have some ready. In many parks you need a gas stove. If there are fireplaces you must bring your own wood as collecting wood within parks is prohibited. Even if water is supposedly available it is not guaranteed so take a supply, as well as your own toilet paper. Camping in the national parks is strictly regulated.

A popular choice for many visitors is to hire or buy a vehicle that can be slept in, combining the costs of accommodation and transport. Ranging from the popular VW Kombi to enormous vans with integral bathrooms, they can be hired from as little as $80 per day to $800. High-clearance, 4WD campervans increase travel possibilities yet further.

→FOOD AND DRINK IN AUSTRALIA

FOOD

The quintessential image of Australian cooking may be of throwing some meat on the barbie but Australia has a dynamic and vibrant cuisine all its own. Freed from the bland English 'meat and two veg' straitjacket in the 1980s by the cuisines of Chinese, Thai, Vietnamese, Italian, Greek, Lebanese and other immigrants, Australia has developed a fusion cuisine.

Asian ingredients are easily found in major cities because of the country's large Asian population. Australia makes its own dairy products so cheese or cream may come from Tasmania's King Island, Western Australia's Margaret River or the Atherton Tablelands in Far North Queensland. There is plenty of seafood, including some unfamiliar creatures such as the delicious Moreton bugs (crabs), yabbies and crayfish. Mussels, oysters and abalone are all also harvested locally. Fish is a treat too: snapper, dhufish, coral trout and red emperor or the dense, flavoursome flesh of freshwater fish such as barramundi and Murray cod. Freshness is a major feature of modern Australian cuisine, using local produce and cooking it simply. Native animals are used, such as kangaroo, emu and crocodile, and native plants that Aboriginal people have been eating for thousands of years such as quandong, wattle seed or lemon myrtle leaf. A word of warning, however: this gourmet experience is mostly restricted to cities and large towns. There are pockets of foodie heaven in the country but these are usually associated with wine regions and are the exception rather than the rule.

The barbecue on the beach or in the back garden is an Aussie classic but you will find that most eating out during daylight hours takes place outdoors. Weekend brunch is hugely popular, especially in the cities, and often takes up the whole morning. Sydney and Melbourne are the undisputed gourmet capitals, with the very best of modern Australian cuisine as well as everything from Mexican to Mongolian, Jamaican to Japanese. Brisbane also has some fine eateries. Restaurants are common even in the smallest towns, but the smaller the town the lower the quality, though not usually the price. Chinese and Thai restaurants are very common, with most other cuisines appearing only in the larger towns and cities. Most restaurants are licensed, others BYO only. Despite the corkage fee this still makes for a better deal than paying the huge mark-up on alcohol.

DRINKS

Australian wine will need no introduction to most readers. Many of the best-known labels, including **Penfolds** and **Jacob's Creek**, are produced in South Australia but there are dozens of recognized wine regions right across the southern third of Australia, where the climate is favourable for grape growing and the soil sufficient to produce high-standard grapes. The industry has a creditable history in such a young country, with several wineries boasting a tradition of a century or more, but it is only in the last 25 years that Australia has become one of the major players on the international scene, due in part to its variety and quality. There are no restrictions, as there are in parts of Europe, on what grape varieties are grown where, when they are harvested and how they are blended.

Visiting a winery is an essential part of any visit to the country, and a day or two's tasting expedition is a scenic and cultural as well as an epicurean delight. Cellar doors range from modern marble and glass temples to venerable, century-old former barns of stone and wood, often boasting some of the best restaurants in the country. In New South Wales the Hunter Valley provides one of the best vineyard experiences in the world with more than a 100 wineries, world-class B&Bs and tours ranging from cycling to horse-drawn carriage.

Australians drink more and more wine and less beer. The average rate of consumption is now 20 litres per person per year, compared to eight litres in 1970. Beer has dropped from an annual 135 litres per person in 1980 to less than 100 litres now. The price of wine, however, is unexpectedly high given the relatively low cost of food and non-tap beer. Visitors from Britain will find Australian wines hardly any cheaper here than back home in the supermarket.

The vast majority of beer drunk by Australians is lager, despite often being called 'ale' or 'bitter'. The big brands are fairly homogenous but refreshing on a hot day. If your palate is just a touch more refined, hunt out some of the imported beers on tap that are predominantly found in the pseudo-Irish pubs in almost all the main coastal towns. Beer tends to be around 4-5% alcohol, with the popular and surprisingly pleasant-tasting 'mid' varieties about 3.5%, and 'light' beers about 2-2.5%. Drink driving laws are strict and the best bet is to not drink alcohol at all if you are driving. Draught beer is expensive at up to $10 a pint for European or boutique brands. Bottleshops (bottle-o's) sell beer in cases (slabs) of 24-36 cans (tinnies or tubes) or bottles (stubbies) of 375 ml each. This is by far the cheapest way of buying beer (often under $4 per can or bottle).

ESSENTIALS A-Z

Accident and emergency

Dial 000 for the emergency services. The 3 main professional emergency services are supported by several others, including the **State Emergency Service** (**SES**) and **Country Fire Service** (**CFS**). The SES helps coordinate search and rescue operations. The CFS provides invaluable support in fighting and controlling bush fires. These services, though professionally trained, are mostly provided by volunteers.

Electricity

The current in Australia is 240/250v AC. Plugs have 2- or 3-blade pins and adaptors are widely available.

Embassies and consulates

For embassies and consulates of Australia, see www.embassiesabroad.com.

Health

Ideally, you should see your GP or travel clinic at least 6 weeks before your departure for general advice on travel risks, malaria and vaccinations. No vaccinations are required or recommended for travel to Australia unless travelling from a yellow fever-infected country in Africa or South America. Check with your local Australian Embassy. A tetanus booster is advisable if you have one due. Make sure you have travel insurance, get a dental check, know your own blood group and, if you suffer a long-term condition such as diabetes, make sure someone knows or that you have a Medic Alert bracelet/necklace with this information on it.

Health risks There are three main threats to health in Australia: the powerful sun, dengue fever and poisonous snakes and spiders.

For sun protection, a decent wide-brimmed hat and factor 30 sun cream (cheap in Australian supermarkets) are essential. Follow the Australians with their Slip, Slap, Slop campaign: slip on a shirt, slap on a hat and slop on the sunscreen.

Dengue can be contracted throughout Australia. In travellers this can cause a severe flu-like illness, which includes symptoms of fever, lethargy, enlarged lymph glands and muscle pains. The mosquitoes that carry the dengue virus bite during the day, unlike the malaria mosquitoes, which sadly means that repellent application and covered limbs are a 24-hr issue. Check your accommodation for flowerpots and shallow pools of water since dengue-carrying mosquitoes breed here.

Check loo seats, boots and the area around you for snakes and spiders if you're visiting the bush. A bite itself does not mean that anything has been injected into you. However, a commonsense approach is to clean the area of the bite (never have it sutured early on) and get someone to take you to a medical facility fast. The most common poisonous spider is the tiny, shy redback, which has a shiny black body with distinct red markings. It regularly hides under rocks or in garden sheds and garages. Outside toilets are also a favourite. Far more dangerous, though restricted to the Sydney area only, is the Sydney funnel-web, often found in outdoor loos. There are dozens of venomous snake species in Australia. Few are actively aggressive and even those only during certain key times of year, such as mating seasons, but all are easily provoked and for many an untreated bite can be fatal.

Australia has reciprocal arrangements with a few countries allowing citizens of those countries to receive free emergency treatment under the **Medicare** scheme. Citizens of New Zealand and the Republic of Ireland are entitled to free care as public patients in public hospitals and to subsidized medicines under the Pharmaceutical Benefits Scheme. Visitors from Finland, Italy, Malta, the Netherlands, Sweden and the UK also enjoy subsidized out-of-hospital treatment (ie visiting a doctor). If you qualify, check what documents you need in Australia to claim **Medicare**. You are, however, strongly advised to take out medical insurance.

Money
→ *£1 = A$1.53; €1 = A$1.24; US$1 = A$$0.95 (Dec 2012).*
All dollars quoted in this guide are Australian unless specified otherwise.
The Australian dollar is currently at a record high, around parity with a dollar US and, sadly for Britons, at a 29-year high against the pound.

The 'Big Four' major banks (as they are known), are the **ANZ**, **Westpac**, **Commonwealth** and **NAB** (**National Australia Bank**) are usually the best places to change money and traveller's cheques, though bureaux de change tend to have slightly longer opening hours and often open at weekends. You can withdraw cash from ATMs with a cash card or credit card issued by most international banks and they can also be used at banks, post offices and bureaux de change. Most hotels, shops, tourist operators and restaurants in Australia accept the major credit cards, though some may charge for using them. It's worth considering a pre-paid Cash Passport card (www.cashpassport.com) for extra security when travelling. It works in a similar way to traveller's cheques, but is easier to use. Bank opening hours are Mon-Fri 0930 to 1630.

Accommodation, particularly outside the main centres, is good value, though prices can rise uncomfortably in peak seasons. Eating out can be cheap. Around $175 is enough to cover dinner for 2 at the very best restaurants in the major cities and the bill at many still excellent establishments can be half that. Transport varies considerably in price and can be a major factor in your travelling budget. Beer is about $5-8 a throw in pubs and bars, as is a neat spirit or glass of wine. Wine will generally be around 1½ times to double the price in restaurants as it would be from a bottleshop. The general cost of living in Australia is reckoned to be equivalent to the USA and UK.

The minimum budget required, if staying in hostels or campsites, cooking for yourself, not drinking much and travelling relatively slowly is about $90 per person per day, but this isn't going to be a lot of fun. Going on the odd tour, travelling faster and eating out occasionally will raise this to a more realistic $110-140. Those staying in modest B&Bs, hotels and motels as couples, eating out most nights and taking a few tours will need to reckon on about $200-300 per person per day. Non-hostelling single travellers should budget on spending around 60-70% of what a couple would spend.

Opening hours
Generally Mon-Fri 0830-1700. Many convenience stores and supermarkets are open daily. Late-night shopping is generally Thu or Fri. See also under Money above.

Safety
In major cities, as in almost any city in the world, there is always the possibility of muggings, alcohol-induced harassment or worse. The usual simple precautions apply, like keeping a careful eye and hand on belongings, not venturing out alone at night and avoiding dark, lonely areas. For more information on road safety, see page 274.

Tax
There are currently a number of **departure taxes** levied by individual airports (such as noise tax) and the government. All departure taxes are included in the cost of a ticket, but may not be included in a quote

when you first enquire about the cost of a ticket. Almost all goods in Australia are subject to a **Goods and Services Tax** (GST) of 10%. Visitors from outside Australia will find certain shops can deduct the GST if you have a departure ticket.

Telephone

→ *Country code: +61. Australian numbers consist of a 2-digit STD area code (see below), followed by an 8-digit number.*

Most public payphones are operated by Telstra, www.telstra.com.au. Some take phonecards, available from newsagents and post offices, and credit cards. A payphone call within Australia requires $0.50. If you are calling locally (within approximately 50 km) this lasts indefinitely. **STD** calls outside this area will use up your 50c in less than a minute and cost about 1c a second thereafter.

State code numbers are 02 for central east Australia (NSW, ACT); 03 for southeast Asutralia (VIC, TAS); 04 for mobiles; 07 for QLD; and 08 for the central and west region (WA, SA and NT).

By far the cheapest way of calling overseas is to use an international pre-paid phonecard (which can't be used from a mobile phone, or some of the blue and orange public phones), unless you can find somewhere offering Skype.

Worth considering if you are in Australia for any length of time is a **pre-paid mobile phone**. Telstra and Vodaphone give the best coverage and widely available for less than $100. Calls are more expensive, of course.

Telephone numbers starting with 1300 and 1800 are toll-free within Australia.

Time

Australia covers 3 time zones: Queensland and NSW are in Eastern Standard GMT + 10 hrs. Western Standard Time is GMT+8 hrs. 1½ hrs behind SA and the NT. Daylight Saving from Apr-Oct is GMT + 9 hrs.

Tourist information

Tourist offices, or **Visitor Information Centres** (**VICs**), can be found in all but the smallest Western Australian towns. They are open daily 0900-1700 (except Christmas Day). Smaller offices may close at weekends, but given that many are run entirely by volunteers something to bear in mind when someone struggles to find an obscure piece of information the level of commitment to the visitor is impressive. All offices will provide information on accommodation, and local sights, attractions, and tours. Many will also have information on eating, local history and the environment, and sell souvenirs, guides and maps. Most will provide a free town map.

Visas and immigration

Visas are subject to change, so check first with your local Australian Embassy or High Commission. All travellers to Australia, except New Zealand citizens, must have a valid visa to enter Australia. These must be arranged prior to travel (allow 2 months) and cannot be organized at Australian airports. **Tourist visas** are free and are available from your local Australian Embassy or High Commission, or in some countries, in electronic format (an Electronic Travel Authority or ETA) from their websites, and from selected travel agents and airlines. Passport holders eligible to apply for an ETA include those from Austria, Belgium, Canada, Denmark, Finland, France, Germany, Greece, Hong Kong, the Irish Republic, Italy, Japan, Netherlands, Norway, Spain, Sweden, Switzerland, the UK and the USA. Tourist visas allow visits of up to 3 months within the year after the visa is issued. 6-month, multiple-entry tourist visas are also available to visitors from certain countries. Tourist visas do not allow the holder to work in Australia. See also www.immi.gov.au.

Weights and measures

Metric.

INDEX

PHOTOGRAPHY CREDITS

Front cover: Doug Pearson/AWL Images
Back cover: Horizon International Images Limited/Alamy; Phillip Gray/Dreamstime.com; Ingvars Birznieks/Shutterstock.com
Front cover flap: Jiri Foltyn/Shutterstock.com; jlarrumbe/Shutterstock.com; hddigital/Shutterstock.com; Ashley Whitworth/Shutterstock.com
Colour pages: Neale Cousland/Shutterstock.com p1; attem/Shutterstock.com, BMCL/Shutterstock.com p2; kwest/Shutterstock.com, Robyn Mackenzie/Shutterstock.com, hddigital/Shutterstock.com p3; kwest/Shutterstock.com p4; CoolR/Shutterstock.com p6; robert paul van beets/Shutterstock.com, John Carnemolla/Shutterstock.com p7; gravity imaging/Shutterstock.com p8; col/Shutterstock.com, Joern/Shutterstock.com, Janelle Lugge/Shutterstock.com, Steven Bostock/Shutterstock.com p9; gagliardifoto/Shutterstock.com, worldswildlifewonders/Shutterstock.com, Pete Niesen/Shutterstock.com p10; Ralph Loesche/Shutterstock.com p11; col/Shutterstock.com p12; Tanya Knight, David PETIT/Shutterstock.com p13; Carl K/Shutterstock.com p14; Janelle Lugge/Shutterstock.com, John Warburton-Lee Photograph/Alamy p15; marc m/Shutterstock.com, Mogens Trolle/Shutterstock.com, Chris Roe/Shutterstock.com p16; Janelle Lugge/Shutterstock.com, Robyn Mackenzie/Shutterstock.com, Jim Hawthorne/Alamy p17; Inc/Shutterstock.com, Liquid Productions, LLC/Shutterstock.com p19; Sebastien Burel/ Shutterstock.com p20; Peter Schickert/Alamy, Hugh Lansdown/Shutterstock.com, LOOK Die Bildagentur der Fotografen GmbH/Alamy, EcoPrint/Shutterstock.com p21; Neale Cousland/Shutterstock.com, Janelle Lugge/Shutterstock.com p22; hddigital/Shutterstock.com, KWL/Shutterstock.com, NCG/Shutterstock.com, Joern/Shutterstock.com p23; Phillipgray/Dreamstime.com p24; Creativa/Shutterstock.com p25; deb22/Shutterstock.com, Neale Cousland/Shutterstock.com, kwest/Shutterstock.com p26; kwest/Shutterstock.com p27; John Carnemolla/Shutterstock.com, David Coleman / Alamy p28; Phillip Minnis/Shutterstock.com, nicolas poizot/Shutterstock.com p29; Janelle Lugge/Shutterstock.com, Neale Cousland/Shutterstock.com, Marina C. Dannenberg/Shutterstock.com p30; Christopher Meder/Shutterstock.com p31; melissaf84/Shutterstock.com p32

CREDITS

Footprint credits

Editor: Jo Williams
Cover: Pepi Bluck
Colour section: Pepi Bluck
Maps: Kevin Feeney

Publisher: Patrick Dawson
Advertising: Elizabeth Taylor

Publishing information

Footprint **DREAM TRIP Australia**
1st edition
© Footprint Handbooks Ltd
February 2013

ISBN: 978 1 907263 651

CIP DATA: A catalogue record for this book
is available from the British Library

® Footprint Handbooks and the Footprint
mark are a registered trademark of Footprint
Handbooks Ltd

Published by Footprint
6 Riverside Court
Lower Bristol Road
Bath BA2 3DZ, UK
T +44 (0)1225 469141
F +44 (0)1225 469461
footprinttravelguides.com

Printed in Spain by GraphyCems

Distributed in the USA by Globe Pequot Press,
Guilford, Connecticut

Every effort has been made to ensure that
the facts in this guidebook are accurate.
However, travellers should still obtain
advice from consulates, airlines etc about
travel and visa requirements before travelling.
The authors and publishers cannot accept
responsibility for any loss, injury or
inconvenience however caused.